Sustainability Accounting and Accountability

The sustainability agenda poses crucial and urgent questions and problems for the future of humanity. Techniques of sustainability accounting and accountability have the potential to be powerful tools in the management, planning, control and accountability of organizations for their social and environmental sustainability. The use of such sustainability accounting techniques has been increasing rapidly in recent years. Forms of accounting and reporting affect our ability to pursue sustainable development. Furthermore, the sustainable development agenda is likely to impact on how accounts are created and the ends to which they are used.

This important new text sketches the terrain on which these interrelationships are and will be played out. It sets out to provide an explanation of the key issues involved in sustainability accounting and accountability and provides a basis from which readers will be equipped to help both develop and critique these increasingly important practices. It is essential reading for anyone studying or with an interest in this crucial and fast-changing area.

Jeffrey Unerman is Professor of Accounting and Corporate Accountability in the School of Management at Royal Holloway, University of London.

Jan Bebbington is Professor of Accounting and Sustainable Development in the School of Management at the University of St. Andrews, Director of the St. Andrews Sustainability Institute and an Associate Director of the Centre for Social and Environmental Accounting Research.

Brendan O'Dwyer is Professor of Accounting at the Amsterdam Business School at the University of Amsterdam.

Sustainability Accounting and Accountability

Edited by

Jeffrey Unerman,
Jan Bebbington and
Brendan O'Dwyer

LONDON AND NEW YORK

First published 2007
by Routledge
2 Park Square, Milton Park, Abingdon, Oxon OX14 4RN

Simultaneously published in the USA and Canada
by Routledge
270 Madison Ave, New York, NY 10016

Transferred to Digital Printing 2008

Routledge is an imprint of the Taylor & Francis Group, an informa business

Typeset in Perpetua and Bell Gothic by
RefineCatch Limited, Bungay, Suffolk
Printed and bound in Great Britain by
Antony Rowe Ltd, Chippenham, Wiltshire

British Library Cataloguing in Publication Data
A catalogue record for this book is available from the British Library

Library of Congress Cataloging in Publication Data
   Sustainability accounting and accountability / edited by Jeffrey
Unerman, Jan Bebbington and Brendan O'Dwyer.
      p. cm.
   Includes bibliographical references and index.
   1. Sustainable development reporting.   2. Social accounting.
   I. Unerman, Jeffrey.   II. Bebbington, Jan.   III. O'Dwyer, Brendan.
   HD60.3.U64 2007
   657—dc22   2006036703

ISBN 10: 0–415–38488–5 (hbk)
ISBN 10: 0–415–38489–3 (pbk)

ISBN 13: 978–0–415–38488–9 (hbk)
ISBN 13: 978–0–415–38489–6 (pbk)

Dedications

From Brendan to Kim, Tim, Seán and my father Michael
From Jan to Ben, Tim and Joshua
From Jeffrey to Franco

Contents

CONTENTS

Figures

Tables

Contributors

Carol Adams is a Professor at La Trobe University, Melbourne, Australia. Her research focuses on aspects of sustainability reporting, corporate social responsibility and links to other aspects of organizations' operations. She has over 80 publications including articles in academic journals of international standing such as *Accounting, Organizations and Society*, *Accounting Auditing and Accountability Journal*, *Abacus* and *Accounting and Business Research*. Carol serves on a number of editorial boards. She is a judge for the ACCA Australia and New Zealand Sustainability Reporting. She is a former Director and Council Member of the Institute of Social and Ethical AccountAbility.

Nicolas Antheaume is a Senior Lecturer at the University of Nantes in France and is currently detached at the French University in Egypt. He holds a Ph.D. in management with a major in accounting. His research focuses on environmental accounting; both on the tools and on motivation of companies to use these tools. He has designed and taught courses in environmental accounting in both business and engineering schools in France.

Amanda Ball is Professor of Accounting at the University of Canterbury, Christchurch, New Zealand. Her research focuses on accounting in public sector organizations and institutions, and issues of how to promote sustainability reporting in the public sector. Amanda is a member of the Chartered Institute of Public Finance and Accountancy (CIPFA) (UK) and has recently worked closely with CIPFA to promote an agenda for sustainability reporting in the public sector.

Jan Bebbington is Professor of Accounting and Sustainable Development in the School of Management at the University of St Andrews, Director of the St Andrews Sustainability Institute and an Associate Director of the Centre for Social and Environmental Accounting Research. Her research interests focus around the dual themes of corporate social reporting on sustainable development and full cost accounting and modelling. She is also an external adviser to the Scottish Cabinet Sub-committee on Sustainable Scotland and Vice-chair (Scotland) of the UK's Sustainable Development Commission.

Nola Buhr is an Associate Professor of Accounting at the College of Commerce, University of Saskatchewan, located in Saskatoon, Saskatchewan, Canada. Broadly speaking, her research is focused on accounting and reporting practice in the absence of standards. Nola has published widely in the areas of accountability and environmental and sustainability reporting. She also looks at accounting from a historical perspective. Nola is a Chartered Accountant and currently a member of the Public Sector Accounting Board of the Canadian Institute of Chartered Accountants.

David Collison is a Senior Lecturer in the School of Accountancy and Finance at the University of Dundee and an Associate Director of the Centre for Social and Environmental Accounting Research. His areas of research include: the social and environmental consequences of accounting, sustainable development and accounting/accountability, and the role of vested interests to subvert accountability. He is a Fellow of the Association of Chartered Certified Accountants and serves on its Social and Environmental Committee. He represents the Institute of Chartered Accountants of Scotland on the Sustainability Working Party of the European Federation of Accountants (FEE).

Andrea B. Coulson is a Lecturer at the University of Strathclyde and holds a doctorate in environmental accounting. For the past ten years she has conducted research and consulting focused on the assessment of environmental risk in the financial sector. Her recent research includes projects for the ISIS Asset Management, the Scottish Executive, UK Economic and Social Research Council, the UNCTAD and the UNEP Financial Institutions Initiatives. Andrea's teaching interests lie in the areas of accounting for sustainability and risk and accounting research methodologies underpinned by her research activities.

Craig Deegan is Professor of Accounting and Director of Research in the School of Accounting & Law, RMIT University, Melbourne, Australia. Craig's research focuses on social and environmental accountability and financial accounting issues, and he has published in a number of leading international accounting journals, including *Accounting Organizations and Society*; *Accounting and Business Research*; *Accounting, Auditing and Accountability Journal*; *Accounting and Finance*; *British Accounting Review*; and the *International Journal of Accounting*. He is also a judge for the ACCA Australia and New Zealand Sustainability Reporting Awards.

Colin Dey is a Lecturer in the School of Accountancy and Finance at the University of Dundee. Colin has a Ph.D. in social accounting and during his doctoral studies worked closely with the fair trade organization Traidcraft plc. Since then Colin's research interests have focused on the practical, theoretical and political aspects of external 'shadow' and 'counter' accounting, particularly as a possible antidote to the managerialism of current sustainability reporting regimes.

Jesse F. Dillard currently holds the Retzlaff Chair in Accounting and is Director of the Center for Professional Integrity and Accountability in the School of Business at Portland State University. He currently serves as editor of *Accounting and the Public Interest*. Jesse has published widely in the accounting and business literature. His current interests relate to the ethical and public interest applications of administrative and information technology particularly as they affect social and environmental accountability.

John Ferguson is a Lecturer in the School of Accountancy and Finance at the University of Dundee, Scotland. His current research interests are primarily in the area of critical accounting, in particular, the sociology of accounting knowledge. As part of this research, John is currently studying for a Ph.D. at the University of Dundee in which he is investigating the role of the textbook and other teaching materials in accounting education.

Rob Gray is Professor of Social and Environmental Accounting and Director of the Centre for Social and Environmental Accounting Research at the University of St Andrews. He is also editor of *Social and Environmental Accounting Journal* and the author of over 250 books, monographs, chapters and articles on social and environmental accounting, sustainability, social responsibility and education. His books include *Accounting for the environment* and *Accounting and accountability: Changes and challenges in corporate social and environmental reporting*. In 2001 he was elected the British Accounting Association Distinguished Academic Fellow and in 2004 became one of the 14 founding members of the British Accounting Association Hall of Fame.

Suzana Grubnic is a Lecturer in Accounting and Finance at Nottingham University Business School. Her research is focused on understanding the nature, processes and consequences of government and local management initiatives in public sector organizations and especially in the context of health care organizations. Current projects include the examination of PFI projects in housing and the development of partnerships in local authority e-government pathfinder schemes. She is a committee member of the British Accounting Association Public Services Accounting Special Interest Group.

Carlos Larrinaga-González is Associate Professor of Accounting in the Universidad de Burgos and International Associate of the Centre for Social and Environmental Accounting Research, University of St Andrews. His research interests focus on the interplay between corporate social reporting and corporate and institutional dynamics and he has publications in *Accounting, Auditing and Accountability Journal*, *Critical Perspectives on Accounting Journal* and *European Accounting Review* on these topics. Carlos is also a member of AECA's Corporate Social Responsibility Committee and leads a Spanish research project on sustainability reporting involving eight universities and is an associate editor of the *Spanish Accounting Review*.

Markus J. Milne is Professor of Accounting in the College of Business and Economics, University of Canterbury, New Zealand. His research focuses on corporate social and environmental reporting, student-centred learning, triple bottom line reporting and, recently, on critiquing corporate attempts to address (un)sustainability through a multi-year research programme supported by the Royal Society of New Zealand's Marsden Fund. Markus is a Fellow of CPA Australia, and serves as Associate Editor for the *British Accounting Review*. He sits on six editorial boards including *Accounting, Auditing and Accountability Journal*, *Accounting Forum*, and *Accounting Education: An International Journal*.

Venkat Narayanan is an Associate Lecturer at Macquarie University, Sydney. His research interests include management control in inter-firm relationships, social and environmental accounting and applications of cooperative learning approaches in tertiary education. He is currently working on developing a Ph.D. on the topic of how management control systems influence social and environmental decision-making in organizations that publicize their social and environmental awareness. He also has an interest in the use of cooperative learning techniques in management accounting education.

Brendan O'Dwyer is Professor of Accounting at the Amsterdam Business School at the University of Amsterdam. Brendan's research interests include: sustainability assurance practice; corporate and non-governmental organization (NGO) accounting and accountability; social and ethical accounting and reporting; stakeholder engagement, corporate governance; qualitative research methods; and professional accounting ethics and disciplinary procedures. His academic work has been published in *Accounting, Organizations and Society*, *Accounting, Auditing & Accountability Journal*, *Critical Perspectives on Accounting*, the *European Accounting Review* and the *British Accounting Review*.

David Owen is Professor of Social and Environmental Accounting at the International Centre for Corporate Social Responsibility at Nottingham University and an Associate Director of the Centre for Social and Environmental Accounting Research. David's main research interests lie in the field of social and environmental accounting, auditing and reporting. He is an associate editor of the *British Accounting Review* and on the editorial boards of *Accounting, Auditing and Accountability Journal*, *Accounting and Business Research*, and *Accounting, Organizations and Society*. David is a member of the judging panel for the Association of Chartered Certified Accountants Environmental and Sustainability Reporting Awards Scheme.

Lorna Stevenson is a Senior Lecturer in the School of Accountancy and Finance at the University of Dundee. Lorna's areas of research include: the social, environmental and economic consequences of accounting, and the implications of these both for wider forms of accountability and accountants' education. She qualified as a Chartered Accountant with the Institute of Chartered Accountants of Scotland and currently serves on the Institute of Chartered Accountants of Scotland Student Education Committee.

Ian Thomson is a Senior Lecturer at University of Strathclyde teaching and researching in most areas of accounting and sustainability. He has been actively researching the impact of the sustainability agenda on organizations and accounting since 1990 on topics including cleaner technology implementation, industrial ecology, salmon farming, stakeholder engagements, government policy, strategies, sustainability performance measurement and organizational decision-making. He has designed a number of courses on accounting and sustainability and taught this subject in a number of UK universities. His other main research interest is accounting education.

Carol Ann Tilt is an Associate Professor of Accounting at Flinders University. She has a Ph.D. in environmental reporting and her research interests include social and environmental reporting, accounting theory and NGOs. She has a number of publications in international journals including *Accounting, Auditing and Accountability Journal*, *Critical Perspectives on Accounting*, *Accounting Forum* and the *British Accounting Review*. Carol has also supervised a number of Ph.D. projects in areas of philanthropy, business ethics and social reporting.

Jeffrey Unerman is Professor of Accounting and Corporate Accountability in the School of Management at Royal Holloway, University of London. The main focus of his research, which has been published in a range of international academic journals including *Accounting, Organizations and Society*; *Accounting, Auditing and Accountability Journal*; *Critical Perspectives on Accounting*; the *European Accounting Review* and *Accounting Forum* – addresses issues of social and environmental accountability, with a particular emphasis on aspects of stakeholder engagement, NGO accountability and the role of differential power relations in the discharge of corporate accountability. He is also a member of the Research Committee of the ACCA.

Foreword

Sustainable development is the central public policy goal of our times. It is the only 'big idea' that provides the moral basis for grappling with the twin challenges of achieving ecological and social sustainability.

The United Kingdom recognizes two overarching priorities for sustainable development: living within environmental limits, and ensuring a strong, healthy and just society. It is self-evident that global society today is achieving neither ecological nor social sustainability. Indeed, the ecosystems are facing increasing pressures from our collective desire to consume goods and services.

The most pressing of these issues is the rising concentration of greenhouse gas emissions in the atmosphere, but this is by no means the only huge environmental problem facing us. At the same time, there is enduring poverty and inequity across much of the world, with millions of people worldwide facing bleak living conditions now and in the future. The UN's Millennium Development Goals remind us just how pressing these issues are.

Whilst it might appear on the surface to be a stretch from mega-challenges of this sort to the practice of accountancy, those connections do exist. If we're ever going to get a truly sustainable economy, then detailed information about the sustainability of organizations (or lack of it!) that make up that economy is essential. As is the creation of systems and methodologies by which 'governance for sustainability' can be achieved.

And that's where this extremely helpful book comes in, exploring as it does how accounting for and reporting on organizational sustainable development impacts may be achieved. Only with this information to hand is it possible to understand properly the distance to travel before organizations operate in accordance with the principles of sustainable development. Accounting and reporting can only move us some of the way to a sustainable economy – there are many other layers of activity that also need to be undertaken in terms of legal, market and fiscal frameworks. But without a focus on accounting and reporting that crucial task will be much harder.

Jonathon Porritt
Chair, Sustainable Development Commission, UK

Acknowledgements

We are very grateful to the editorial team at Routledge for their help and encouragement in the writing and compilation of this book. In particular we would like to thank Francesca Heslop, Jacqueline Curthoys, Emma Joyes, Lyn Richards and Graeme Leonard.

We are also deeply indebted to the authors of all the chapters in this book for the timely and high-quality completion of their chapters.

Special thanks go to Linda Lewis, Professor Stewart Lawrence and Kumba Jallow for their help in reviewing the development of this book.

Introduction to sustainability accounting and accountability

Jeffrey Unerman, Jan Bebbington and Brendan O'Dwyer

In what kind of world do you want your children, grandchildren and great-grandchildren to live? Do you want them to live in a world characterized by social harmony and social justice? Or would you be happy for them to live in a world riven by social conflict, where 'justice' is only available to a few powerful and privileged members of society – with no guarantees that your descendants would be among this privileged elite? Do you want them to live in a world which has an ecological balance capable of sustaining the lives of all its inhabitants at reasonable levels of comfort? Or would you be satisfied for them to live in a world where the ecosphere had been damaged to the extent that life for all but a small privileged elite is lived at the margins of existence, where weather patterns have become so extreme that severe storms regularly kill many people, the supply of food and water is highly erratic, and many species of plants, animals and insects have become extinct? Do you want them to live in an economically prosperous world? Or would you be satisfied for them to live in a world where the economy had failed and they were therefore unable to enjoy the material benefits of economic success?

Some of these scenarios might be considered unrealistically extreme by many, and in practice our descendants may experience a society, ecosphere and economy at any point on a continuum between these positions. In other words, like many scenarios which are presented to us in stark 'black or white' terms, these scenarios may be false dichotomies because the actual positions which can be achieved may be at any point between these extremes. But the fact that future social, ecological and economic scenarios are often portrayed in a headline-grabbing manner characterized by stark images of 'doom and gloom' should not prevent us from acknowledging that current human activities will almost inevitably have a future impact on the shape of society, the ecosphere and the economy. Some may argue that one or more of these future impacts will be beneficial, while others may argue that one, or possibly all, of these impacts will be negative. Perhaps, some may argue, the negative impacts will not be as detrimental as suggested by the scenarios of social collapse, an ecosphere unable to sustain life, and/or an economy in long-term deep recession. It seems incontrovertible, however, that the negative consequences of our current way of life will cause a situation where social relations and social justice, the state of nature, and the economy are all in a worse state than at present.

In other words, human activities taking place today are regarded by some people as having a detrimental impact on the society, ecology and economy which future generations will experience. Indeed, this is a position which is becoming ever more widely accepted by growing numbers of people throughout the world. For example, only a very small proportion of scientists currently argue that human activity is not a major contributory factor to the global warming which is causing widescale environmental damage – and which is likely to cause even more damage to the ecosphere unless substantive action is taken to reduce levels of many pollutants. Some people go further, and point to evidence that the 'doom-laden' scenarios set out in the opening paragraph of this chapter are a reality today for many people in the world – those living in extreme poverty in developing nations, who experience a growing number of natural disasters arising from extreme climatic conditions, and who are denied many aspects of social justice because their day-to-day fight for survival makes social justice more of a luxury than a reality in practice. Those living in poverty in the developed world alongside affluence are also impossible to ignore.

Many people argue that the growing social injustice experienced by ever larger numbers of people, and the growing damage to the ecosphere, are a result of a dominant – and almost unquestioned – objective of maximizing economic growth. In these terms (and several arguments supporting this linkage are discussed in a number of chapters in this book), economic growth (characterized by energy and material-intensive production and exploitative social relations) is socially and environmentally unsustainable.

It is these issues of sustainability which form the focus of this book. One way to look at these issues is in terms of the long-term need to ensure that economic activity is socially and environmentally sustainable. In the short term it might be possible to have economic growth, while damaging society and the environment. In the long term this is impossible. For example, businesses need a stable society in which to operate profitably (although some businesses might generate profits from addressing the outcomes of social conflicts, such as businesses offering security services). Therefore, if business as a whole operates in a manner which causes damage to society and thereby causes a breakdown in the social harmony necessary to provide a stable context for operations, then such business activities are neither economically nor socially sustainable. In the longer term, if business activities cause a level of damage to the ecosphere such that it cannot sustain human life on the scale we currently enjoy, then this is clearly neither socially nor economically sustainable as there can be no economic activities – let alone economic growth – without human life to sustain it. Thus, if the quest for economic growth causes significant damage to both society and the environment, such economic growth is not economically, socially or environmentally sustainable in the longer term.

These may seem like obvious points. But what might be less immediately obvious is how these points relate to issues of accounting and accountability. Accounting is a powerful tool (or range of tools) which has conventionally been used in optimizing the economic performance of organizations. A range of management accounting techniques have helped managers plan and control their activities in a manner, for commercial organizations, designed to maximize their profits. A range of financial accounting techniques have helped communicate aspects of the economic performance of the organization to a range of stakeholders (primarily the shareholders) who are not involved in the day-to-day running of the business. As such, these financial accounting techniques have provided the mechanisms through which managers have been able to discharge duties of accountability to non-managerial stakeholders.

Just as conventional management and financial accounting has been a powerful tool in the management, planning, control and accountability of the economic aspects of an organization, broader techniques of sustainability accounting and accountability have the potential to be powerful tools in the management, planning, control and accountability of organizations for their social and environmental impacts. Or, in other words, for the social and environmental in addition to the more conventional economic sustainability of the organization.

In practice, attempts to account for social, environmental and economic impacts have become more common among many organizations – particularly large multinational businesses (albeit that such practices are not always widespread and at times attract negative comment). More broadly, the concept of sustainable development has become a central organizing theme within contemporary society, which in many ways is an astonishing achievement for an idea that is usually thought to have arrived on the public policy scene in 1987 with the publication of the *Brundtland Report*. Sustainability development concerns tend to focus on how to organize and manage human activities in such a way that they meet physical and psychological needs without compromising the ecological, social or economic base which enables these needs to be met. The role of organizations in this process is significant in most countries around the globe, and especially so in the industrialized West: the epicentre of the choices which drive the majority of the environmental threats to human survival.

In public statements on their sustainable development policies and practices, many organizations claim that they recognize their social and environmental, in addition to their economic, responsibilities, and are seeking to manage and account for these activities in an appropriate manner. Some of their critics, however, argue that many businesses are simply using sustainability accounting techniques as a public relations tool to win (or maintain) the approval of those stakeholders whose continued support is crucial for the survival and profitability of the business. In this latter case, the social and environmental reporting practices adopted will have little to do with genuine sustainability, and will merely be addressing the interests of the most powerful stakeholders in any particular organization, while leaving the interests and needs of the less powerful stakeholders marginalized.

Whichever is the case, or if the truth lies somewhere between these two positions, the use of sustainability accounting techniques has been increasing rapidly in recent years. An understanding of the basis of these techniques, and the ability to critically evaluate them, is therefore important because, given the central role of accounting in the management and accountability of organizations, forms of accounting and reporting will affect our ability, at a societal level, to pursue sustainable development. Furthermore, the sustainable development agenda is likely to impact on how accounts are created and the ends to which they are used. This book attempts to sketch the terrain on which these interrelationships are and will be played out. It sets out to provide an explanation of the key issues involved in sustainability accounting and accountability, and thereby to provide a basis from which readers will be equipped to help both develop and critique these increasingly important practices. To help in realizing these aims, each chapter in this book has been written by an academic who is one of the leading thinkers in the topic area considered.

The book is divided into four parts. The first part provides a context to the issues examined in the rest of the book and contains two chapters – the first maps the terrain of sustainability accounting while the second explores some of the philosophical underpinnings of sustainability accounting and accountability. The second part then examines a number of issues related to how and why organizations report on their sustainability policies and practices to those outside the management of the organization (such as employees, customers, suppliers, regulators and a range of other stakeholders). The third part addresses a number of issues involved in the role of sustainability accounting in internal management and finance in both the private and public sectors. The final part explores a variety of other key issues – such as the applicability of some sustainability accounting practices to the growing numbers of non-governmental organizations, the role of 'shadow' and 'silent' accounting in sustainability, and issues related to sustainability accounting in the education process.

SUMMARIES OF EACH CHAPTER

Part I: Setting the context for sustainability accounting and accountability

Part I comprises two chapters which help set the context for the material in the remainder of the book. In *Chapter 1*, Ian Thomson provides a diagrammatic explanation of the areas and issues which have been examined in sustainability accounting and accountability research. The diagrammatical techniques he uses and develops help show both the interrelationships between different aspects of sustainability accounting and accountability, and the popularity of research in each of these areas. He identifies a total of 197 different themes which have been addressed within this broad area of research, and groups these into nine key themes: Ian's novel mapping of the terrain of sustainability accounting and accountability research in this manner is invaluable in helping both to identify the key issues covered within academic research in this area, and to help locate how any particular study fits into the existing literature. It also helps identify the areas which are relatively under-researched, and should therefore be of assistance in planning future research projects which will be able to make a significant contribution to developing the growing area of sustainability accounting and accountability both conceptually and empirically – rather than simply adding marginal insights to the existing literature (a factor which Ian notes is far too prevalent in many recent studies).

In *Chapter 2*, Jesse Dillard continues the context building theme of the introductory part by offering a perspective on some of the philosophical foundations underlying sustainability accounting theory and practice. He argues that while the 'social accounting project' has emerged and developed largely as a pragmatic response to concerns with issues of sustainable development, because this pragmatic response has been driven predominantly by a desire to use (social) accounting to serve the public interest it is largely consistent with the philosophical propositions of Critical Theory. These propositions encompass 'values such as justice, equity and solidarity' and aim for 'enlightenment, empowerment and emancipation'. Jesse then explains key characteristics of Critical Theory and of an 'ethic of accountability'. He relates these to social and environmental accounting practices, and to the potential manner in which these practices might be developed and empowered to further serve the public interest 'through harmonizing the relationships between human beings and the natural systems and among those who inhabit the social systems they create'. While recognizing limitations to the full realization of the philosophical conditions proposed by Critical Theory and the 'ethic of accountability', Jesse argues forcefully that Critical Theory, and an ethic of accountability grounded in Critical Theory, can still be of great value in realizing the enlightening, empowering and emancipatory potential of social and environmental accounting practices.

Part II: External reporting of sustainability policies and practices

Part II comprises eight chapters. In the first of these, *Chapter 3*, Nola Buhr examines the histories of, and rationales for, sustainability reporting. In contrast to conventional thought, which often views concerns with environmental impacts as having developed only in the last few decades, she explains that such concerns have been expressed for many centuries, with some forms of sustainability reporting developing over a century ago – following the spread of the modern corporation. Nola then reviews some of the key studies into the historical development of social and environmental reporting practices, from the earliest practices of employee reporting, through shifts towards social reporting and environmental reporting, to triple bottom line reporting. Foreshadowing the views of many authors of other chapters in this book, she argues that the final step towards actual sustainability reporting remains an as-yet-unrealized ideal. In explaining the rationales underlying these developments in social and environmental reporting, Nola sets out some of the theoretical perspectives explored in more depth in later chapters in this part. She argues that in practice, rather than providing accountability to meet the information needs of a broad range of stakeholders, social and environmental reporting has been 'driven by who the corporation thinks it is accountable to and what it is accountable for. Accordingly, corporations report with motivation, a calculated purpose and a message in mind.' Nola also addresses the debate on whether sustainability reporting should be a voluntary or mandatory practice, or a combination of both.

Carol Adams and Venkat Narayanan develop this voluntary versus mandatory theme in *Chapter 4*, when they explore various regulatory and quasi-regulatory initiatives towards the standardization of sustainability reporting. They argue that, given the importance to society and the ecosphere of sustainable business practices, it is no longer adequate for the accounting for these practices (to those outside the organization) to remain a voluntary activity whereby different organizations are free to be selective regarding those aspects of their organization's social and environmental impacts upon which they report. Carol and Venkat explain and contrast five key standardization initiatives in sustainability accounting, namely: the *Global Reporting Initiative (GRI)*; *International Standards Organization (ISO) 14000 series of standards*; the *World Business Council for Sustainable Development (WBCSD)*; the *Institute of Social and Ethical AccountAbility AA1000 standard*; and the *Sustainability Integrated Guidelines for Management (SIGMA) Project*. They also briefly discuss a number of other sustainability reporting initiatives. In contrasting the five key initiatives above, Carol and Venkat make clear that some of the bodies are acting on behalf of business, and therefore seek to promote sustainability reporting standards which will operate in a manner designed to enhance the profitability of business. Others, however, seek to develop standards which require business to take into account the views and needs of a broad range of stakeholders through processes of widespread stakeholder dialogue. They explain that without 'a robust stakeholder dialogue and reporting process . . . reporting guidelines may be used as a legitimating exercise by organizations that report the minimum required in such guidelines but omit material impacts not specifically covered by them'.

In *Chapter 5*, Jeffrey Unerman addresses issues related to these processes of identifying stakeholders' views, expectations and information needs through a variety of stakeholder engagement and dialogue processes. By locating stakeholder engagement and dialogue processes as a crucial stage within a 'hierarchical model' of the sustainability reporting process, he explains why processes of engagement and dialogue with a broad range of stakeholders are an essential prerequisite to effective sustainability reporting. He then explores some of the problems and barriers organizations are likely to face when they seek to implement processes of widespread stakeholder engagement and dialogue in practice – although he believes that in practice most organizations are not seeking to engage in genuine dialogue with a broad range of stakeholders aimed at moving the organization towards sustainability accounting. Rather, he argues that where an organization is using social and environmental reporting (rather than sustainability reporting) as a form of public relations tool to win and maintain the support of its most powerful stakeholders, this organization will only be interested in engaging with these powerful stakeholders – rather than all the stakeholders upon whom its operations may impact. He then examines some theoretical perspectives on how organizations that seek 'true' sustainability reporting can identify an acceptable consensus of stakeholder views and expectations regarding acceptable standards of organizational behaviour when they are faced with incompatible views between different stakeholders. He concludes the chapter by surveying some evidence of stakeholder engagement and dialogue mechanisms which have been employed by organizations in practice.

Carol Ann Tilt continues the theme of stakeholder involvement with social and environmental reporting in *Chapter 6*, where she examines the perspectives of a variety of stakeholders towards sustainability reporting practices. While recognizing the centrality of a range of stakeholders (and the views of these stakeholders) in sustainability reporting, Carol notes that there have been surprisingly few studies of stakeholder attitudes towards current sustainability, or social and environmental, reporting practices, or the way these should be developed in the future. In analysing some of the research studies that have been carried out in this area, Carol distinguishes between the views of: shareholders and financial investors; insurers and banks; consumers and suppliers; employees and trade unions; non-governmental organizations; the news media; and the general public. She notes that while the studies show that 'sustainability reporting is increasing in importance for most types of stakeholder . . . it is secondary stakeholders that place the greatest importance upon it'. Shareholders and other financial investors, while being interested in 'poor social and environmental performance' (presumably because this might pose a financial risk to the business), are predominantly interested in issues more directly related to financial performance 'and require only information about things that have direct financial impact'. Carol also notes that despite the secondary stakeholders placing the greatest importance upon sustainability reporting, they also tend to be rather sceptical towards the information reported. For example, many believe that 'most reporting is still "greenwash" and [is] undertaken to improve reputation without substantially changing practices, to placate and manipulate stakeholders, and to gain competitive advantage, rather than out of any real concern for society and the environment'.

Motives of this nature underlying corporate social and environmental practices are consistent with some of the predictions of *legitimacy theory*, which has been one of the most widely used theoretical frameworks in sustainability reporting research, and is the theory Craig Deegan explores in *Chapter 7*. He explains that organizational legitimacy is a resource needed by organizations, because if an organization is perceived by sufficient members of society to lack legitimacy in its operations then these stakeholders will no longer support the organization. If sufficient stakeholders upon whom the organization depends for its survival and prosperity withdraw their support, the organization will suffer economically. Therefore, to maximize their benefits from legitimacy, all organizations need to undertake a variety of strategies to '*gain, maintain* or *repair*' their legitimacy. However, Craig notes that 'it is not the *actual* conduct of the organization that is important, it is what society collectively knows or *perceives* about the organization's conduct that shapes legitimacy'. Where an organization is perceived to have deviated from the social, environmental and economic expectations which members of society have in respect of that organization (often termed the organization's social contract), then the organization will lose legitimacy. Craig explores a variety of roles which legitimacy theory assumes that social and environmental reporting has to play in bringing perceptions of organizational performance into line with these social expectations, in some cases irrespective of actual organizational performance. He argues that where organizations are using social and environmental reporting to legitimize themselves by portraying social and environmental performance that is at variance with their actual performance, these organizations 'are not really likely to be embracing a broader sustainability ethos'.

Overlapping in several respects with legitimacy theory, a further theory which seeks to understand organizational motives underlying social and environmental reporting is *institutional theory*, and this is the topic examined by Carlos Larrinaga-González in *Chapter 8*. Although it has not yet been extensively used as a theoretical framework in social and environmental accounting studies, institutional theory has the potential to become a powerful explanatory framework when exploring reasons for organizations to engage in these practices. A key underlying assumption of institutional theory is that most organizations share certain characteristics with some other organizations. These shared characteristics, for example the shared political, geographical and/or regulatory environment in which two or more organizations operate, form what are known as *organizational fields* and these organizational fields foster homogeneity (otherwise known as *isomorphism*) in practices among the organizations which are members of a particular organizational field. Carlos argues that there are several organizational fields in sustainability reporting, such as shared participation in sustainability management and reporting schemes

8

and/or shared regulatory requirements, which result in several organizations sharing similar pressures and commitments to engage in sustainability reporting. However, he argues that there is not a global organizational field in sustainability reporting, as this would result in global convergence of sustainability reporting – a factor which empirical evidence shows is not occurring. Carlos then discusses the three key mechanisms which are regarded as producing homogeneity or iso-morphism among the practices of organizations which share a particular organiza-tional field. These are coercive forces, where organizations adopt similar practices because of outside coercion, normative pressure, where organizations adopt similar practices because they share certain values and professionals norms, and mimetic forces, where an organization in a field will adopt the practices developed by other organizations in that field because they will be concerned that they may be damaged in some way if they are seen to not be adopting these 'best practices'.

One social and environmental reporting practice which is becoming insti-tutionalized among an increasing number of organizations is the practice of obtaining assurance from an external body regarding some of the contents of a social and environmental report, and attaching the assurance statement to the report. These sustainability assurance practices are examined by David Owen in *Chapter 9*, in which he explains that as users of sustainability reports are becoming ever more astute, organizations which do not provide some level of external verifi-cation or assurance for their sustainability reports will face problems over the credibility with which many stakeholders regard these sustainability reports. David traces trends in the growth of sustainability assurance practices as well as the development of a number of guidelines which have sought to standardize these practices. He explains that some of these guidelines follow a similar approach to guidelines for the audit of financial accounting reports. These exhibit a predominant concern to attest 'to the accuracy of published data, rather than the relevance of such data for external stakeholder groups' and a tendency towards providing 'low assurance levels'. Conversely, other guidelines foster a more holistic approach to assurance 'imparting a far fuller appreciation of the strengths and weaknesses of the sustainability performance of the reporting organization' – although the latter type of reports are often the result of a more in-depth consultancy-type engagement which may compromise the perceived or actual independence of the assurance provider. Despite the development of these various assurance guidelines, David notes that assurance practice 'is bedevilled by inconsistencies in approach, and certainly offers little in terms of promoting greater levels of corporate account-ability to external stakeholders'. He then makes a number of suggestions regarding how these assurance practices could be developed to help provide this greater level of accountability.

In *Chapter 10*, Markus Milne and Rob Gray conclude Part II of this book by critically evaluating current trends in corporate sustainability reporting, and assessing their potential to move corporations towards sustainable development.

Although they note a substantial proportionate rise in the numbers of companies engaging in some form of social and environmental reporting, they also highlight that the actual numbers of companies reporting is tiny compared to the numbers of multinational (let alone national) companies operating in the world. The number of companies reporting to the standard required by key sustainability reporting guidelines is even smaller, giving even less cause for optimism regarding the impact that social and environmental reporting is having on the sustainability debate within business. They suggest that there is a need for a significant increase in corporate engagement with sustainability reporting before reporting can then make a signifi-cant impact on the social and environmental sustainability of the world – although 'if reporting developments occurred among those of the largest [corporations] and those with the greatest impacts, there could be room for optimism, perhaps'. Markus and Rob then put forward an argument that rather than helping move us towards social and ecological sustainability, social and environmental reporting practices, especially where such practices are voluntary and therefore under the control of the reporting organizations, may have been counterproductive by helping businesses mask their socially and ecologically unsustainable practices 'to legitimate ongoing exploitation of people and the environment'. Furthermore, Markus and Rob argue that as sustainability is something which needs to be achieved at the level of the whole (social and ecological) system, it is questionable how relevant organiza-tional-level social and environmental reporting is. Furthermore, they argue that it would require a significant shift in the aims of corporations and western society (away from an overriding objective of economic prosperity realized through economic growth) to realize sustainability. Nevertheless, Markus and Rob note that developments in social and environmental reporting practices have had several benefits in practice.

Part III: Accounting for sustainable development within organizations

In Part III the focus of the chapters moves from examining externally orientated sustainability accounting activities to exploring internally focused sustainability accounting activities. The first focus on this exploration is consideration of the practice of full cost accounting undertaken in *Chapter 11* by Nicolas Antheaume. Full cost accounting focuses on identifying and monetizing externalities arising from corporate activities, with externalities being defined as 'a phenomenon which occurs outside the market system . . . or which shows up in the market system remotely from its source'. Negative externalities have been the most usual focus of full cost accounting experiments because costs imposed on society by corporate activity naturally attract more attention. Nicolas acknowledges at the outset of the chapter that creating full cost accounts is not without significant problems. For example, some argue that externalities should be dealt with via regulation (negating the need or usefulness of accountants producing estimates of externalities). Others are concerned that monetising externalities makes all elements of the natural world (for example) part of the economic world and thus negates the argument that the environment should be valued for moral and aesthetic reasons not solely for economic reasons. While acknowledging these reservations, the chapter goes on to describe the main attempts at full cost accounting and to draw out some of the lessons learned by organizations from these experiments. While it is acknowledged that there are considerable practical and conceptual difficulties in developing full cost accounting, the potential of this form of accounting to lead organizations to new understandings of their impacts is considerable.

In *Chapter 12* Jan Bebbington addresses the question of the extent to which sustainability accounting approaches (including internally and externally focused activities) may lead to organizational change. The rationale behind this exploration is that unless sustainability accounting leads to substantive reductions in negative social and environmental impacts then it fails to address the key challenge of sustainable development. Accounting techniques, by extension, need to lead to changes in organizations' impacts if they are to have any 'pragmatic' value (as outlined in Chapter 1). In order to understand if accounting leads to change, Jan commences the chapter with an exploration of how organizations and organizational change is theorized in the management and accounting literature. Extant literature in social and environmental accounting is then explored and implicit assumptions of how change comes about within these papers are extracted. The notion that assemblages of disturbances (compared to a single disturbance) are more likely to lead to change is developed and the nature of disturbances is considered. This chapter also explores what various writers consider change to be. This ranges from 'changes in organizational social and environmental impacts; to change in corporate rationales, routines and practices; and alterations in beliefs/attitudes or organization participants'. Evidence for changes of these various types is offered, drawing on a range of sustainability accounting work. In brief, the evidence is mixed as to whether or not sustainability accounting leads to changes of the sort outlined above. Changes in impacts can be observed in many instances while changes in the underlying rationales and culture of organizations is much less evident. The chapter closes with a plea for more, and more theoretically nuanced, explorations of change in real organizational settings.

Chapter 13 focuses on sustainability accounting and accountability in the public sector, noting that in large part sustainability accounting and practice has focused on the private sector. Amanda Ball and Suzana Grubnic convincingly argue that the public sector has much to offer society as it is often these organizations that are called upon and used by government to translate, among other things, 'the heroic demands of the environmental agenda into tangible policies and programmes'. This chapter commences with an exploration of what constitutes the public sector (itself a very diverse set of organizations and activities) and develops the distinctive characteristics that these organizations share. The contributions to sustainable development that public sector organizations can make are then developed. In the first instance, public sector organizations are argued to contribute to sustainable development through their conduct (termed housekeeping measures). More importantly, however, these organizations play a crucial role in delivery of sustainable development objectives that governments commit to via international public policy processes, on the basis of their own strategic objectives or through constitutional requirements (for example, the Government of Wales Act (1998, section 121) requires that the Welsh Assembly prepare a scheme for how its actions will enable further progress on sustainable development). Having set the context within which the public sector operates, the chapter moves on to examine what accounting and accountability mechanisms are desirable. While reporting on achievements with regard to sustainability performance is noted as an important theme (as specified by governments and supported by the Global Reporting Initiative sector supplement for public agencies), Amanda and Suzana stress that accounting techniques that reduce the public sector's environmental footprint (such as environmental management and audit systems) are also important. In addition, given that many public sector organizations are charged with delivering public goods, it is in this role that they may be seen to be contributing towards sustainable development (albeit that unless governments are also seeking to reduce their total ecological footprint and ensure social justice for all, the ability to achieve these public service objectives will be severely curtailed). This chapter closes by noting that accounting for sustainable development in the public sector is a relatively undeveloped area of research, but one where there is much potential for future work.

The final chapter in this part, *Chapter 14*, focuses on sustainable finance. Andrea Coulson opens her chapter by noting that raising finance invariably requires some form of social and environmental assessment, regardless of whether it is loan, project or equity finance being raised. In each of these areas, however, slightly different considerations exist. Screening of loan finance is most usually undertaken to prevent the risk of default arising from social and environmental factors. This approach has a long history and is the norm within the banking industry. Such screening does not challenge the rationale of bank lending decisions but Andrea notes that social, environmental and sustainable development reports are used by banks in coming to their risk assessment. Arguably of more interest is the way in which lenders are coming under pressure in the area of project finance. Andrea notes that the screening of project finance, especially of development projects in the developing world, is being influenced by the adoption by many banks of the Equator principles (these require environmental risk assessments for projects with high or medium risk levels and that total in excess of $50 million, and also take into consideration aspects of socio-economic values). Given that project finance is often being raised in the context of large development projects in the developing world, such screening is more likely to consider sustainable development principles than more straightforward risk assessment approaches. It is in the area of equity finance, however, that sustainable development considerations (at least in rhetoric) have the most traction. Building on the back of the ethical investment movement, Andrea documents the rise of stock exchange indexes (notably the FTSE4Good and the Down Jones Sustainability Indexes) which purport to track the performance of companies that operate according to sustainable development principles.

Part IV: Other issues

The chapters in Part IV examine three additional key areas of sustainability accounting and accountability that cut across the themes of the previous two parts. In *Chapter 15*, Brendan O'Dwyer focuses on non-governmental organizations (NGOs), in particular advocacy-oriented NGOs, by examining their accountability for their social sustainability impacts. Brendan suggests that recent calls for greater NGO accountability, in particular those questioning NGOs' legitimacy and representativeness, have arisen primarily due to widespread perceptions of NGOs' increasing power and influence in political and business circles. Demonstrating accountability is deemed especially complex for NGOs as they have multiple, oft competing, constituencies, and few agreed measures of organizational performance. This complexity has led to some resistance among NGOs to calls for enhanced accountability, with some claiming that they lack resources to implement robust accountability mechanisms. A lack of understanding among some NGOs regarding what NGO accountability entails, allied to concerns that it may cause NGOs to lose focus, have further fuelled this resistance. Added NGO unease has arisen due to widespread suspicions that it is mainly powerful stakeholders (such as financial donors) who are demanding increased accountability, often for impacts which have little relevance to NGOs' core goals. Brendan proceeds to outline a variety of NGO accountability mechanisms currently in use worldwide. He focuses on emerging mechanisms revolving around forms of stakeholder engagement aimed at privileging downward accountability to NGO beneficiaries. In this context, the Global Accountability Project (GAP) is discussed and its dimensions of NGO accountability are outlined. Successful examples of NGOs pioneering downward accountability are then examined. The chapter concludes by considering recent research assessing the quality of NGO reporting on their social and environmental impacts. This paints a poor picture of disclosure among many large international NGOs. Brendan argues that enhanced NGO accountability should be embraced as it can act to protect those NGOs advocating for social sustainability when they are faced with legitimacy threats from sources seeking to derail the sustainability agenda.

In *Chapter 16*, Colin Dey echoes many other authors' concerns about the credibility, reliability and nature of stakeholder dialogue underpinning current social, environmental and sustainability reporting (SER). He, however, offers specific ways of countering these accountability deficiencies by examining the accountability potential of two emerging forms of external reports, termed 'shadow' and 'silent' accounts. Silent accounts refer to disclosures of accounts of corporate SER compiled from all other formal corporate reporting channels outside of company SER mediums such as annual reports and press releases. Shadow accounts consist of other relevant accountability information easily available in the public domain but, unlike the silent accounts, they use information produced independently of the subject organization and published externally from it. Colin proceeds to critically assess recent academic and NGO experiments in silent and shadow accounting using the criteria of reliability, credibility and the nature of stakeholder dialogue. Academic experiments are largely praised for their rigour and systematic coverage, although Colin argues that some reports need to be more critical of their information sources. His analysis of NGO reports specifically focuses on shadow reports produced by Friends of the Earth (FOE) (on Shell) and Action on Smoking and Health (ASH) (on British American Tobacco (BAT)). FOE's report is criticized for being arguably as selective and unreliable as the Shell report they challenge. However, the ASH report is praised for being more systematic through its use of extant social reporting standards and frameworks and its closer alignment with the aforementioned academic experiments. Colin proceeds to make a number of suggestions regarding the future of silent and shadow reporting. For example, he proposes that academics could become more involved in encouraging and offering guidance to NGOs on the production of more consistent and complete shadow accounts. He also suggests applying the principles currently used to guide organization-centred SER, such as the AA1000 and GRI guidelines and standards, to these accounts. Colin is conscious that both forms of account need clear and explicit frameworks if they are to provide complete and transparent pictures of organizational accountability. To this end, the chapter concludes with a suggested structure to guide this more systematic production of future silent and shadow accounts.

In *Chapter 17*, David Collison, John Ferguson and Lorna Stevenson concentrate on the role of sustainability accounting in the educational curriculum. They firstly highlight the role of education, in particular the nature of the accounting curriculum, in reproducing and sustaining power relations. The accounting curriculum tends, they argue, to privilege certain assumptions such as the 'ideology of shareholder capitalism' which not only sustains relations of power but also presents as unproblematic the notion that the wider society and the natural environment should be treated as 'externalities'. This dismisses the perceived relevance of areas such as sustainability accounting. The authors proceed to outline debates regarding how social and environmental accounting (SEA) teaching might challenge this existing 'hegemonic' discourse. They review research tracking the evolution of SEA education in British and Australian universities. While trends in Britain have changed little, with SEA education still remaining somewhat isolated, greater potential is unveiled in Australia where research suggests a potentially increased adoption of stand-alone SEA courses. The role of the accounting profession in encouraging greater adoption of SEA education forms the final part of the chapter. Here, the authors reveal the power that 'career relevance' has on students' adoption of optional courses, and the need for professional accounting bodies to systematically shift the way they educate future leaders by asserting the primacy of the wider public interest over clients' commercial interests. The results of recent research seeking to determine the importance of SEA among the education departments of European professional accounting bodies in the training of accountants are then presented. These suggest that these departments see SEA education as important but underestimated by professional bodies. The SEA emphasis in current curricula in these bodies is, however, found to be minimal. The authors clearly articulate the challenges facing educators and interested students in exposing and being exposed to elements, such as SEA, currently 'hidden' by most conventional accounting curricula.

USE OF THIS BOOK

This book is intended to be of use to a variety of readers. In addition to providing a broadly based view of current issues in sustainability accounting and accountability to anyone with an interest in the subject, it should also provide a good starting point for anyone wanting to conduct research in this area by enabling them to identify relevant prior studies in the specific area they wish to research, and to locate this area within the broader context of sustainability accounting and accountability research. It is also intended to support the growing number of courses in this area, both where such courses are stand-alone sustainability accounting and accountability courses, and where material on sustainability accounting and accountability is incorporated as part of broader accounting courses.

In respect of the latter, there is increasing recognition in many universities that as more and more organizations adopt and develop sustainability accounting and accountability practices, the study of accounting solely focusing on its financial aspects without the social and environmental dimensions does not adequately equip students with the accounting knowledge and understanding they will require once they have graduated. Therefore a growing number of more broadly based financial and management accounting courses are now incorporating elements of sustainability accounting and accountability, and chapters from this book can be used, either individually or in combination, to support the teaching and learning of these elements.

There are also a growing number of universities that are developing whole courses in sustainability accounting and accountability – both at undergraduate and post-graduate levels. This book provides the ideal text for such courses, as the chapters can be combined to support the typical 10 to 12 week single term (or semester) course. One example of how this could be done for a 10 week course is shown in Table I.1:

Table I.1 *An example of a semester course*

Week	Topic	Chapters from this book
1	Introduction and setting the scene	1 and 2
2	Development and standardization of sustainability reporting	3 and 4
3	Role of stakeholders in sustainability reporting	5 and 6
4	Motives underlying sustainability reporting	7 and 8
5	Sustainability assurance and future directions	9 and 10
6	Full impact accounting and organizational change	11 and 12
7	Sustainability accounting and accountability in the public sector and in NGOs	13 and 15
8	Role of sustainability accounting and accountability in ethical investment	14
9	Developing silent and shadow accounts	16
10	Sustainability accounting and education	17

We hope that readers will find the material presented in this book both useful and informative. As it has been written to inform a variety of readers about the current and potential role of accounting in the crucially important area of sustainable development, we also hope that it helps contribute towards both practical and theoretical developments in accounting practices, such that accounting can contribute towards more sustainable, or less unsustainable, business, public sector and third sector (NGO) operations.

Any comments that readers may have on the structure and contents of this book are most welcome.

Part I

Setting the context for sustainability accounting and accountability

Chapter 1

Mapping the terrain of sustainability accounting

Ian Thomson

INTRODUCTION

Since its emergence in the 1970s, the literature on sustainability accounting has grown enormously. This chapter is based on a review of around 700 articles based on studies in over 22 countries that use 19 research methods, develop 31 research themes and utilize 34 different theoretical frameworks, and this sample of literature is far from complete. Any scholar entering into the field would find it difficult to quickly grasp the intellectual terrain and see the full diversity of work labelled sustainability accounting. As the body of literature grows so does the difficulty of remembering and appreciating past contributions to knowledge, as well as locating oneself in the field. Many academics have been involved in this area for a considerable period of time and are aware (and contribute to) the evolving literature, yet others may not have had the opportunity of watching this field grow.

The purpose of this chapter is not to provide a true and fair account of sustainability accounting, but is one person's codification of the literature. The review is designed to stimulate and structure the development of a collaborative knowledge modelling process. These maps are an invitation for others to contribute their expertise in mapping the field. The diagrams in this chapter provide an alternative visual representation of the literature associated with sustainability accounting. They are intended to complement the existing literature reviews (e.g. Mathews, 1997; Bebbington, 2001; Gray *et al.*, 1999; Gray, 2002; Gray and Tinker, 2003). This style of visual representation has been successfully used in many different areas, largely because it creates a different form of visibility to the written word.

The mapping of concepts, attributes and things creates opportunities for visualizing the relationship between concepts, stimulating idea generation, organizing ideas, communicating complex ideas and evaluating any particular contribution to the field (see Buzan and Buzan, 2003; Benking, 2001; Laszlo, 1994). It is also suggested that visual mapping can contribute to epistemology and ontology building. As will be discussed later the evidence presented identifies the need for a focused discourse on the epistemologies and ontologies of sustainability accounting.

The mapping techniques used in this chapter are stylized representations of issues involving images, words and lines, arranged intuitively according to spatial arrangement of concepts organized into groups, branches or areas. These techniques can help contextualize, simplify and make sense of large volumes of material and/or complex issues. There are a number of ways of constructing these maps: mindmaps, sketchmaps, spider diagrams or many other spatial representations (Buzan and Buzan, 2003; Benking, 2001; Laszlo, 1994). The choice of how to present the information is a personal one and in this chapter the diagrams used are a composite of different techniques, integrated to reflect the particular features of the subject area.

In this chapter, the use of mapping is intended to represent knowledge, yet in doing so it constructs knowledge. There is a danger that these maps may capture knowledge and thus restrain knowledge development. As such, readers must not interpret them uncritically or reify them in any way. They are a personal codification of a selection of articles representing sustainability accounting. These maps are intended as learning devices to aid institutional knowledge preservation and help determine the shared understanding of the sustainable accounting community.

DESIGNING THE MAPS

Selecting the sample

Subjective judgement played a major part in the selection of articles, particularly given the limited number of articles published in accounting journals with the words 'sustainability' or 'sustainable development' in the title. Therefore a choice was made to include papers that dealt with key attributes of sustainability, i.e. eco-efficiency, eco-justice and eco-effectiveness. This requires the inclusion of accounting articles on social and ethical issues as well as environmental issues and articles that challenged unsustainable systems of governance, control and markets.

A decision then had to be made on the parameters of accounting research. Did it include academic accountants who also published in non-accounting journals or non-accounting academics who publish on accounting issues in non-accounting journals? Or should it include material from the sustainability discourse that clearly has implications for sustainability accounting and has been influential in constructing the sustainability accounting discourse?

Drawing the parameters for this review was problematic and a pragmatic decision was taken to use articles from two sources. The first source was the bibliography from *Accounting for the Environment* (A4E hereafter) (Gray and Bebbington, 2001) which comprised of around 500 articles. The second source was the 230 articles reviewed in *Social and Environmental Accounting Journal* 1998–2004[1]

(SEAJ hereafter). These articles have been used by others to inform the sustainability accounting debate either by utilizing them in a highly influential book or by reviewing them and legitimating them as part of the academic discourse.

One objection to both of these sources is the influence of the Centre for Social and Environmental Accounting Research (CSEAR), presently located at St Andrews University. This influence is recognized, but given that CSEAR was established in 1991 as a networking institution to gather and disseminate information about the practice and theory of social and environmental accounting and reporting, I would suggest that it is a both a legitimate limitation and a reasonable compromise.

These two sources allowed two analytical possibilities. Firstly, A4E provided a historic review of the literature going back to 1960 (e.g. Ackoff, 1960; Carson, 1962), drawing upon a wide range of publication media and giving some insights into the genealogy of the field. The review of academic articles from SEAJ provided an insight into recent publications on sustainability accounting and accountability and included 63 publications from non-accounting journals.

The SEAJ sample did not change the structure of the concept map (Figures 1.1–1.4), other than some additions in terms of sub-topics, evaluatory frameworks, organizations studied and geographic locations. The SEAJ review allowed a confirmation of the usefulness of the concept map in understanding the literature. Only SEAJ was used to construct the topology maps (Figures 1.5–1.11). The topology map is based on the underlying concept map with an additional dimension.

Visualizing sustainability accounting literature

In trying to visualize the literature in a way that made sense to me, it became clear that two-dimensional mapping was inadequate. Whilst more conventional approaches to mapping were informative in determining the scope of sustainable accounting literature, they did not reflect the differential volume of activities observed on each of the key attributes or their interrelationships. To describe the field there was a need to construct a conceptual topography (Benking, 2001), a form of superstructure that defines topics as logical places in order to display relationships and connections within these topics or issues. A useful analogy is the difference between ordinance survey maps (in particular the use of contour lines) and schematic maps of city centres on tourist leaflets. The concept map is the equivalent of the tourist map and the topology maps represent the beginnings of a process to construct these contour lines.

The concept map emerged during the literature review and was subject to continual revision until arriving at its present form. The basic structure consists of nine main branches each representing a key emergent theme to codify and make sense of the literature. Figure 1.1 provides an overview of the whole subject area whilst being able to observe individual details. This should enable researchers to position themselves and their work within the field. It is recognized that Figure 1.1

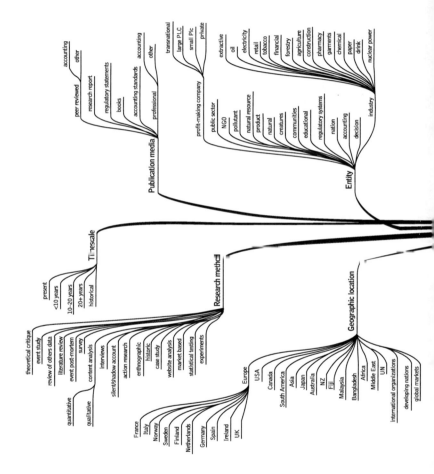

Publication media
- peer reviewed
  - accounting
  - other
- research report
- regulatory statements
- books
- accounting standards
- professional
  - accounting
  - other

Entity
- profit-making company
  - transnational
  - large PLC
  - small Plc
  - private
- public sector
- NGO
- pollutant
- natural resource
- product
- natural
- creatures
- communities
- educational
- regulatory systems
- nation
- accounting
- decision
- industry
  - extractive
  - oil
  - electricity
  - retail
  - tobacco
  - financial
  - forestry
  - agriculture
  - construction
  - pharmacy
  - garments
  - chemical
  - paper
  - drink
  - nuclear power

Timescale
- present
- <10 years
- 10–20 years
- 20+ years
- historical

Research method
- theoretical critique
- event study
- review of others data
- literature review
- event post-mortem
- survey
- content analysis
- quantitative
- qualitative
- interviews
- silent/shadow account
- action research
- ethnographic
- historic
- case study
- website analysis
- market based
- statistical testing
- experiments

Geographic location
- Europe
  - France
  - Italy
  - Norway
  - Sweden
  - Finland
  - Netherlands
  - Germany
  - Spain
  - Ireland
  - UK
- USA
- Canada
- South America
- Asia
- Japan
- Australia
- NZ
- Fiji
- Malaysia
- Bangladesh
- Africa
- Middle East
- UN
- International organizations
- developing nations
- global markets

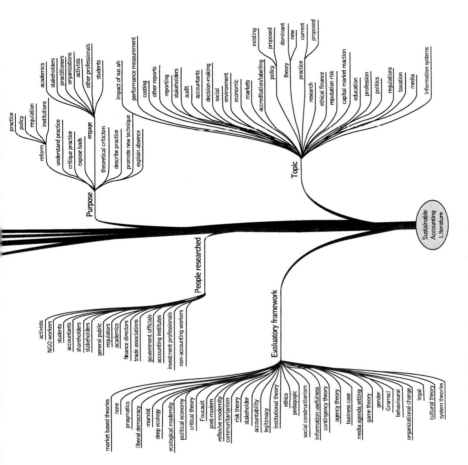

Figure 1.1 *Overall conceptual map of sustainability accounting literature.*

is difficult to view as displayed in this book, but is included to demonstrate the thematic shape of the literature.[2] To allow readers to view this concept map, it has been split into three sub-maps.

Figure 1.2 presents the 9 main themes: evaluatory frameworks, article topic, research method, geographic location, entities researched, people researched, time-scale of the study, article type and its underlying purpose. Each of these themes is split into detailed sub-themes or attributes as displayed in Figures 1.3 and 1.4. The current version of this map comprises 197 attributes or sub-themes arranged around 9 key themes.

The concept map was derived from the review of both the A4E and SEAJ samples, but it can also be used to classify individual articles. To avoid the problem of infinite regression, a level of topic or thematic deconstruction was used. For example, an article on *'The impact of proposed accounting regulations on environmental disclosures in annual reports'* would be classified in the topic theme as: *'environmental'*, *'reporting'*, *'policy-proposed'*, *'regulations'*. Similarly, articles can be classified using multiple research methods, multiple purposes, multiple entities, multiple geographic locations, multiple people researched. In many ways it is an extension of the 'key-words' used to classify journal articles.

To illustrate this process examples of the classifications of two articles are shown in Table 1.1. These two articles demonstrate two different styles of contributing to

Table 1.1 *Examples of conceptual classification of two journal articles*

	Thomson and Bebbington (2005)	Campbell *et al.* (2003)
Evaluatory framework	Pedagogic, reflexive modernity	Legitimacy, ethics, contingency theory
Timescale	Not specified	20+ years
Geographic location	UK	UK
Research method	Theoretical critique, case study	Content analysis – quantitative
Publication media	Peer reviewed accounting	Peer reviewed accounting
Entity	Large PLC, not specified	Large PLC, tobacco, drink, retail
Purpose	Reform and critique practice, promote new techniques, engage stakeholders	Understand practice, engage academics
Topic	Impact of sus a/c, stakeholders, social, environment, current practice, proposed practice	Stakeholders, performance measurement, reporting, social, environment, current practice, media, ethical
Participants	Stakeholders	

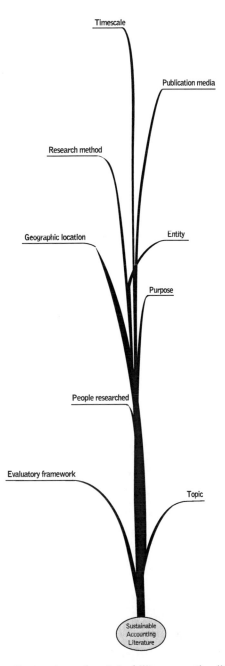

Timescale

Publication media

Research method

Geographic location

Entity

Purpose

People researched

Evaluatory framework

Topic

Sustainable
Accounting
Literature

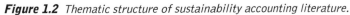

Figure 1.2 *Thematic structure of sustainability accounting literature.*

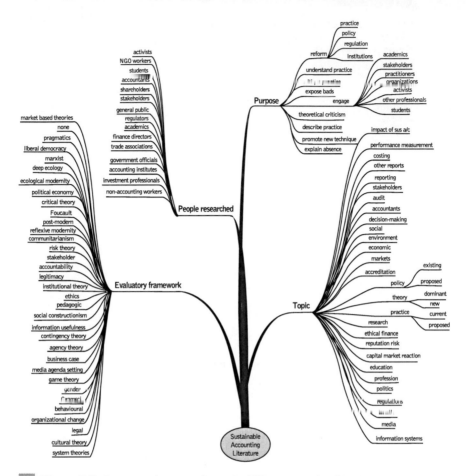

Figure 1.3 *Conceptual map 1 of sustainability accounting literature.*

the academic sustainable accounting literature. They are *Social and environmental reporting in the UK: A pedagogic evaluation* by Thomson and Bebbington (2005) and *Voluntary Reporting in Three FTSE sectors: A comment on perception and legitimacy* by Campbell *et al*. (2003).

It is argued that the maps portrayed in Figures 1.1–1.4 are based on important attributes of the sustainable accounting literature. Table 1.1 demonstrates how they can be used to identify articles' similarities, strengths and weaknesses and suggest how they fit with different families of research. Figures 1.1–1.4 collectively represent a way to make sense of the sustainable accounting literature and contribute to the discourse on 'sustainable accounting'. They achieve this by providing a schematic 'tourist-map' of the ontology, epistemology, methodology, teology, research methods and empirical sites of published sustainable accounting literature.

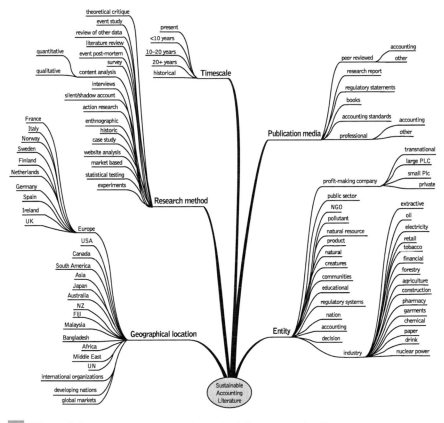

Figure 1.4 *Conceptual map 2 of sustainability accounting literature.*

Viewing the terrain

The concept map represents the scope of the literature, but it does not illustrate differential patterns of the application of these attributes. To address this an attempt was made to construct a partial topology of sustainability accounting's conceptual panorama (Benking, 2001; Laszlo, 1994). Constructing a conceptual topology allows the possibility to map the unfolding of the scope and activity levels of different attributes. The process of building this dynamic topology is at an early stage and Figures 1.5–1.11 are static representations of the academic articles reviewed in SEAJ in the period 1998–2004.

These topographies are produced according to a constant scale with the vertical height of the triangle representing their frequency of use. To help with their interpretation Table 1.2 provides some indicative figures. These diagrams are designed to produce a qualitative impression of the field, by juxtapositioning different elements rather than to provide a quantitative analysis. Each of the groupings are linked to the key branches of the concept map; however, they were repositioned slightly

Table 1.2 *Values to assist in interpreting Figures 1.5–1.11*

Figure		Frequency
1.5	Legitimacy theory	49
1.6	Content analysis – quantitative	67
1.7	UK	57
1.8	Understand practice	78
1.9	Large plcs	99
1.10	Environment	144
1.11	Non-accounting workers	41

according to similarity of themes and by volume of activities. For example, in Figure 1.5 the evaluatory frameworks were clustered by similarities in their ontological and epistemological dimensions. Similarly in Figure 1.6 the research methods were clustered according to methodological similarities. Another factor in the positioning relates to the need to avoid certain aspects obscuring others due to the volume of publications in certain areas.

Once the concept map was established, each article was classified according to its specific assemblage of concepts (see Table 1.1). Each article's assemblage was layered on top of each other to provide the beginnings of a conceptual topography and an alternative visibility of sustainable accounting literature. The topology maps do not cover all of the 197 attributes, but concentrate on 7 themes. Publication media is not used as almost all of the articles sampled are peer reviewed journal articles. The empirical timescale is not used due to limitations in the data and more work needs done to clarify the timescale of empirical studies in individual articles.

The introduction of this vertical dimension to the concept map provides a different and arguably a more informative representation of the field. Attempts to produce a whole topography of the 9 themes on a single diagram have proved too difficult to produce in a format that is intelligible in a book format, but poster size graphics are available from the author on request.

In the spirit of conceptual mapping and a dialogical approach to learning (Thomson and Bebbington, 2004), I will provide my interpretations of the diagrams used in this chapter *after* the presentation of the conceptual topology maps, rather than providing a detailed critique of each individual image.

PERSONAL OBSERVATIONS AND CONCLUDING COMMENTS

The sustainable accounting literature has developed over time, drawing on most theories and research methods used in the academic accounting and finance literature. The literature has flourished from a trickle of articles in the 1970s and 1980s into a rich and diverse field.

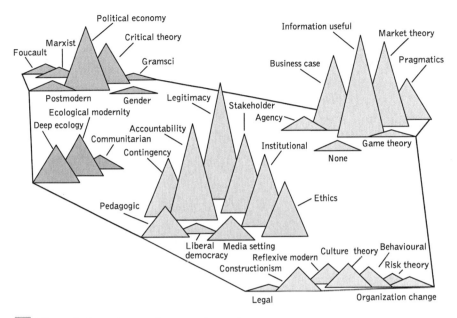

Figure 1.5 *Evaluatory frameworks used.*

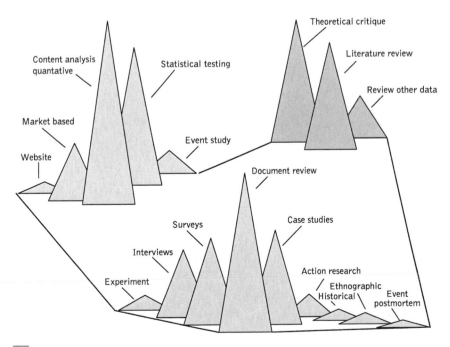

Figure 1.6 *Research methods.*

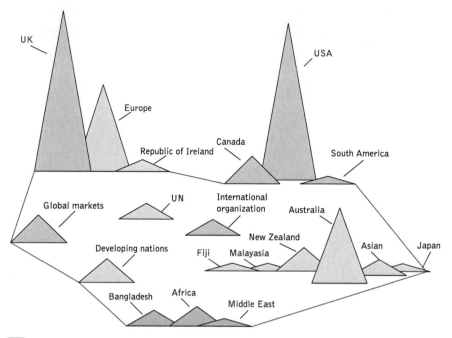

Figure 1.7 *Geographic location.*

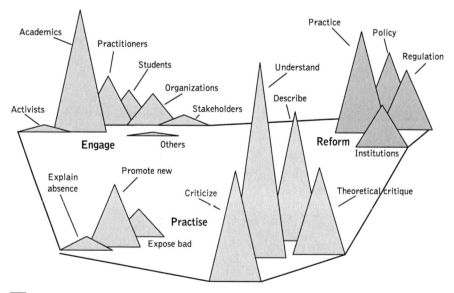

Figure 1.8 *Purpose of article.*

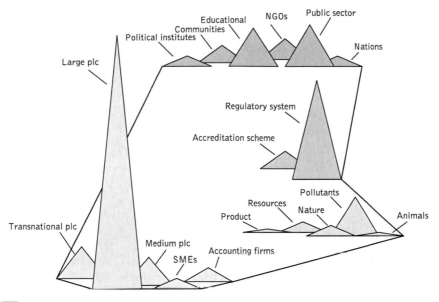

Figure 1.9 *Empirical sites.*

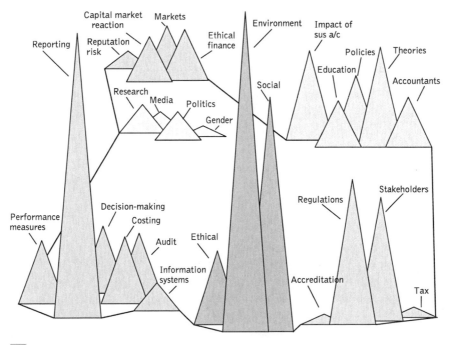

Figure 1.10 *Research topics.*

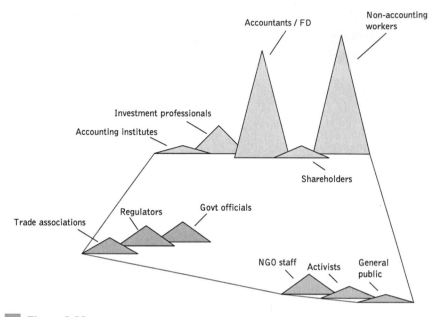

Figure 1.11 Research participants.

Certain key fashions can be observed to dominate sustainability accounting publications. Very crudely, the early literature up to the mid 1980s concentrated on social issues. There was a lull in publications until the early 1990s when the main focus was on environmental issues. From the late 1990s the focus changed to social and ethical issues. In the most recent articles it is difficult to discern a trend, but concerns over sustainability, governance and accountability seem to be appearing in the literature.

Research publications seem to be numerically dominated by content analysis of social and environmental disclosures of annual reports, most commonly explained by some variant of legitimacy theory. However, in many cases what is referred to as legitimacy theory should more correctly be labelled contingency theory. Another trend is the number of publications that do not have an explicit theoretical framework, relying on implicit references to *the business case*, market theories, informational usefulness or pragmatics. These descriptive works are still evident in recent publications despite significant developments in the wider field. The topological analysis also identifies a predominance of empirical concern with profit-oriented organizations traded on some stock exchange in developed Anglo-Saxon, English-speaking countries.

The literature published exhibits a clear geographic and ideological bias, and is under-developed in a number of topics, geographic locations and entities studied. The list of these areas would be extremely long and is self-evident from Figures 1.7, 1.9, 1.10 and 1.11. Encouragingly many of these areas are the subject of chapters in this book and recent conference papers (see for example papers presented: the Asia Pacific Interdisciplinary Research in Accounting Conference 2004; the Centre for Social and Environmental Research Conference 2004 and 2005).

From my perspective what was the least encouraging feature of the SEAJ conceptual topology related to their teology. Many papers seem to limit their contributions to describing practice or atheoretical attempts at understanding practice within a managerialist framework, without any engagement with prior research. I would argue that given the volume of publications and research activity, as a community we should be moving on from this stage. This is not a new observation as many others have made this point in the past (for example Gray, 2002; Gray and Tinker, 2003; Mathews, 1997; Gray et al., 1999; Lehman, 2001, 2002; Neu et al., 2001).

The sustainability accounting literature does not appear to have been subject to strong epistemological discipline from a single point. Quality control appears to have been exerted via the editorial policies of individual journals.[3] Having said that, sustainability accounting has cut across all prior notions of accounting and finance academic sub-disciplines, disrupting previous clusters of research topics, research methodologies and methods. Sustainable accounting literature has infected almost every area of accounting and finance research. Whilst this is an indication of the importance of sustainability as an accounting research topic, it has meant that sustainability accounting literature has not had a common ontological or epistemological conceptual core. Perhaps one reason for the dissipative and fragmented literature is the privileging of journal publication criteria over subject area coherence.

Given the unfolding of sustainability concepts since the 1970s and the novelty of researching accounting's sustainability impacts, it is difficult to imagine how else the research field could have evolved. It has co-evolved with changes in sustainability concepts, policies and practice and changes in accounting and finance research. However, I feel that there is an absence of any strong self-organizing dynamic in the literature. This is creating a major tension within the literature and the strong possibility of a bifurcation point emerging between a normative engagement critical trajectory and quantitative empirical studies.

Personally, I was surprised at the volume and persistence of descriptive empirical studies based on content analysis of annual financial reports. Much of the growth in the literature has been due to transferring disclosure studies into other geographic areas or into different organizations, but not necessarily engaging with a core theoretical debate. Recent qualitative studies have introduced 'new' evaluatory frameworks, theories and concepts to explain, critique and/or transform sustainability accounting. This is potentially encouraging as it enriches the theoretical discourse surrounding sustainability accounting. However, many of these papers could be criticized for introducing new theories that do not add much to what was already there nor do they engage with prior research findings. Perhaps this could be explained by the current system of publications in accounting academia which over-emphasizes 'deliberate difference' in contribution, rather than persistent rigorous discourse. The shape of the map and the topological reviews suggest that this dissipative process is accelerating rather than diminishing or self-organizing around particular paradigms.

There is also evidence of a potential corrective force in what can only be described as periodic 'academic rows' (e.g. Gray et al., 1999; Gray, 2002; Gray and Tinker, 2003; Lehman, 2001, 2002; Neu et al., 2001; Newton and Harte, 1997). These rows are where influential researchers have published well informed critiques of the field, introducing alternative theoretical concepts and suggesting different directions for future research agendas. To date there is little evidence of this having any substantive impact on the overall research field or its direction.

Now it is important to recognize this study's reliance on academic journal articles, in particular the potential irrelevance of this communication channel to those researchers involved in engagement action programmes. There are a number of difficulties in translating these studies into journal articles and the limited nature of the readership of academic journals. Alternative media and communication channels are perhaps more relevant to those driving change in policy making and actions. Research monographs, books, press articles, policy consultations, policy engagements, speaking at political, NGO and/or business conferences, contributing to NGO shadow accounts or even direct action are all channels for researchers to use to engage with a wider group of people rather than other academics. These discourses/publications are at present 'off-radar' from this chapter. However, it is intended that this study will be extended to incorporate a number of these 'alternative' publications.

Echoing the words of those who have been party to rows in the past, it is now time to enter into a meaningful discourse on whether sustainability accounting is a coherent cognate field of study in its own right. Or is it simply another manifestation of accounting and therefore subject to the discipline of management accounting, market-based accounting research, international reporting, financial reporting and auditing, public sector accounting, critical accounting or accountability studies? In other words, is sustainability accounting simply an interesting empirical site for accounting and finance researchers to focus their empirical and theoretical microscopes on?

Prior to completing these maps, I felt sustainability accounting and accountability was a coherent cognate field and that the literature supported this perception. Having undertaken the research for this chapter, I have realized that this perception was due to my limited reading. My overall impression now is of an energetic diffusion of literature, based on 'deliberative difference', without a rigorous problematization and reflection of the key thematic issues surrounding sustainability and accounting. There is an absence of a reflexive discourse on the overall field in the academic literature. There are pockets of researchers engaging in this type of discourse but they tend to be disconnected from other sustainability accounting discourses.

The intention of these alternative representations of the sustainability accounting field is to challenge and problematize others' preconceptions of the literature and inform the ongoing development of sustainability accounting.

NOTES

1   Articles reviewed in SEAJ before 1998 were largely incorporated into A4E.

2   A3 version of this map is available from the website associated with this publication.

3   However, it is worth noting the contribution of sustainability-related special issues of journals in providing critical focus points in the development of the field. For example, *Accounting, Auditing and Accountability Journal, Critical Perspectives on Accounting, Accounting Forum, European Accounting Review* and *Accounting Education: An International Journal.*

REFERENCES

Ackoff, R. L. (1960) Systems, organizations and interdisciplinary research. *General Systems Theory Handbook,* 5(1): 1–8.

Bebbington, J. (1997) Engagement, education and sustainability: A review essay on environmental accounting. *Accounting, Auditing and Accountability Journal,* 10(3): 365–81.

Bebbington, J. (2001) Sustainable development: A review of the international development, business and accounting literature. *Accounting Forum,* 25(2): 128–57.

Benking, H. (2001) Setting common frames of reference. *Knowledge Management, Auditing and Mapping Journal,* 1(5), http://www.knowmap.com/0105/benking_spacial_spatiali.html.

Buzan, T. and Buzan, B. (2003) *The mind map book: Radiant thinking – major evolution in human thought.* London: BBC Books.

Campbell, D., Craven, B. and Shrives, P. (2003) Voluntary reporting in three FTSE sectors: A comment on perception and legitimacy. *Accounting, Auditing and Accountability Journal,* 16(4): 558–81.

Carson, R. (1962) *Silent spring.* Boston: Houghton Mifflin.

Everett, J. and Neu, D. (2000) Ecological modernisation and the limits of environmental accounting. *Accounting Forum,* 24(1): 5–29.

Gray, R. (2002) The social accounting programme and accounting, organization and society, privileging engagement, imaginings, new accounting and pragmatics over critique. *Accounting Organizations and Society,* 27(7): 687–707.

Gray, R. and Bebbington, J. (2001) *Accounting for the environment,* 2nd edn. London: Sage.

Gray, R. and Tinker, T. (2003) Beyond a critique of pure reason: From policy to polity to praxis in environmental and social research. *Accounting, Auditing and Accountability Journal,* 16(5): 727–61.

Gray, R., Bebbington, J. and Owen, D. (1999) Seeing the wood for the trees: Taking the pulse of social and environmental accounting. *Accounting, Auditing and Accountability Journal,* 12(1): 47–51.

Laszlo, S. (1994) *Changing vision: Human cognitive maps – past, present and future.* London: Adamantine Press.

Lehman, G. (2001) Reclaiming the public sphere: Problems and prospects for corporate social and environmental accounting. *Critical Perspectives on Accounting,* 12: 713–33.

Lehman, G. (2002) Global accountability and sustainability: Research prospects. *Accounting Forum,* 26(3/4): 219–32.

Mathews, M. R. (1997) Twenty-five years of social and environmental accounting research: Is there a silver jubilee to celebrate? *Accounting, Auditing and Accountability Journal,* 10(4): 481–531.

Neu, D., Cooper, D. and Everett, J. (2001) Critical accounting interventions. *Critical Perspectives on Accounting,* 12. 735–62.

Newton, T. and Harte, G. (1997) Green business: Technist kitsch? *Journal of Management Studies,* 34(1): 75–98.

Thomson, I. and Bebbington, J. (2004) It doesn't matter what you teach? *Critical Perspectives on Accounting,* 15: 609–28.

Thomson, I. and Bebbington, J. (2005) Social and environmental reporting in the UK: A pedagogic evaluation. *Critical Perspectives on Accounting,* 16: 507–33.

Chapter 2

Legitimating the social accounting project

An ethic of accountability

Jesse F. Dillard[1]

INTRODUCTION

Philosophically, the social accounting project[2] is, at least on the surface, pragmatic (Gray, 2002), and quite proud of its proclivity for 'getting its hands dirty'. 'If social accounting is anything, it is the opening of new spaces, of new accountings, not simply reacting to old ones. The project seeks engagement and the changing of practice. Imagining, engagement, and changing practice are not easy activities to undertake' (Gray, 2002, p. 698). Those pursuing the project recognize the need to change current accounting techniques and practices to include new descriptions, an expanded set of events seen as a relevant, and a more inclusive user group. Environmental accounting provides an example of these themes. The new descriptions should include the effects of organizational action on the natural system. This would require expanding the relevant set of events recognized by the accounting system to include descriptions of such events as greenhouse gas emissions. The primary user set expands beyond the shareholders to include a broader set of affected stakeholders, including future generations.

The practitioners of social accounting seem more intent on action than theorizing, and given the current rate of deterioration in both the natural and social systems, such a position seems imminently logical. However, there appears to be a growing affinity with social theory, especially that typically characterized as alternative/critical.[3] The social accounting project is enhancing, and reaffirming, a growing awareness that the objectives of a sustainable natural and social world are probably not attainable within the current context of global market capitalism. The unfettered demand of capital markets for growth and wealth accumulation subordinate all other objectives. The social accounting project, therefore, has experienced frustrations with creating and implementing a more complete accounting for organizations that recognize and report on their rights and responsibilities to various constituencies. Alternative/critical accounting studies provide support for this desire. However, there is an obvious tension between the practicalities of a new accounting and the ideological purity of the philosophical basis upon which one might be constructed.[4]

With this in mind, I wish to consider the philosophical frame for the social accounting project, including accounting for sustainable development. This includes considering the pragmatic philosophical perspective as well as elaborating on its critical energy. The next major section identifies acting in the public interest as the fundamental legitimating criteria for the social accounting project and proposes an ethic of accountability as a philosophical basis upon which the project might move forward. A discussion of the rights and responsibilities of the accounting profession and the accounting academy related to the social accounting project comprise the concluding section.

A PHILOSOPHICAL FRAMEWORK FOR THE SOCIAL ACCOUNTING PROJECT

Gray (2002) states that the social accounting project is a response to Medawar (1976), empowered by Bronner (1994). From an implementation perspective, Medawar, taking a pointedly pragmatic and practical perspective, argues that precise measurement and objectivity in reporting should not be allowed to impede the implementation of social accounting, while independence is critical. As discussed in Bronner, critical theory holds that through critique people can come to understand and live in more enlightened ways. The process and possibilities associated with this critique and the necessary engagement provide the energizing dimensions of the social accounting project.[5] Thus, from a philosophical perspective, it seems appropriate to consider the pragmatic groundings of the project and then to explore sustainability, accounting, and accountability through a critical theory lens. The following discussion attempts to provide a more complete articulation of these connections.

A pragmatic perspective

Pragmatism[6] is 'a philosophy that stresses the relation of theory to praxis and takes the continuity of experience and nature as revealed through the outcome of directed action as the starting point for reflection' (Audi, 1995, p. 638). Subject and object are constituted, and reconstituted, within, and because of, the flow of lived experience. Truth can only be determined by the outcome of inquiry and cannot be derived apart from the contextually defined goals and values. Knowledge is an instrumental tool that constitutes the basis for discerning truth. Thus, truth claims are validated through experience, and, as such, truth is subject to revision.

Generally following the Burrell and Morgan (1979)[7] philosophy of science typology, ontology[8] can be positioned along a continuum from subjective to objective. Epistemology[9] is specified along a continuum from positivist to anti-positivist. Human nature is viewed as ranging from determinist to voluntarist,[10] and applicable methodologies range from ideographic to nomothesistic.[11] As a point of reference, functionalism is the predominant category of traditional accounting research[12] suggesting that, to varying degrees, it is philosophically objectivist, positivist, deterministic and nomothesist.[13] This presumes that there is an external world separate and distinct from the observer and that world can be known through empirical exploration and measurement. Although a majority of the empirical-based social accounting studies, especially the work evaluating the information content and economic effects of social and environmental reporting, fall into this category, the social accounting literature has spanned the spectrum of alternative approaches and theories (see Deegan, 2002; Gray, 2002; Mathews, 1997). There is a growing recognition that reality may be, at least at some level, socially constructed, and interpretivist type methodology such as case studies and in-depth interviews are being more extensively employed.[14] This expanding horizon naturally follows with the centrality of critique to the project's energy and direction.

Consistent with its pragmatic nature, the current body of social accounting research appears to be somewhat inconsistent with respect to the philosophy of science underpinnings discussed above. Take, for example, the environment. There is little doubt that it exists separate from the human beings who are destroying it at an unprecedented rate. How could such a world be socially constructed? However, human beings understand this world through their shared perceptions and as such construct and reconstruct it in their own image – an objective world, subjectively reconstructed.[15] In this way the environment becomes a socially constructed domain.

Critical theory provides the theoretical context for the social accounting project and is predicated on metaphysical values such as justice, equity and solidarity. These values are realized through a process of enlightenment, empowerment, and emancipation. The philosophical dimensions of critical theory are a mirror image of the functionalist perspective. A comparison of the alternative perspectives provides insights and a synthesis whereby the social accounting project can continue to move in a direction of enhancing the human condition through harmonizing the relationships between human beings and the natural systems and among those who inhabit the social systems they create.

The social accounting project as a critical undertaking

Following Gray (2002), critical theory is argued as providing the empowering theoretic of the social accounting project. In a previous essay (Dillard, 1991), I concluded that, given the capture of conventional accounting by financial capital, it seemed impossible to consider accounting to be an instrumental means for emancipatory action. This raises the following question: can accounting, as currently practised, assist members of society in gaining enlightenment, empowerment and emancipation?[16] However, if conventional accounting represents a subset of what is here termed social accounting, and if the social accounting project can accurately be described as being on the 'frontiers of environmental and social justice' with its principal justification being 'in its emancipatory and radical possibilities' (Gray, 2002, p. 689), then such a conclusion may warrant review.

Critical theory sees understanding as a means for facilitating a society so configured as to foster the realization of its human potential, whereas the traditional functionalist perspective sees understanding as an end in itself. Critical theory ontology is a subjective one where the social world is created and recreated by the social actors. The epistemology is anti-positivist. It makes the voluntaristic assumption that individuals possess agency and, thus, can act otherwise if they so choose. Following the ontological and epistemological positions, the preferred methodological approach focuses on subjective and historical accounts of actions and events by the individuals carrying out the actions and living through the events.

Applying critical theory as an empowering philosophy for social accounting provides insights into its idealized objectives, a basis for designing research and application programmes as well as a set of criteria by which progress can be measured. Human agency is central, and self-understanding provides the motivating factor as well as the guiding force for change. Human beings are presumed to be estranged from their natural and intended state of existence. Under the capitalist mode of production, human beings, just as are all other resources, are means to the ends of economic growth and wealth accumulation. An individual's worth is only that which is reflected in the market value of the person's commodified labour. Thus, the individual is estranged from his or herself, from their fellow human beings, and the natural system within which they live. The natural and intended state is that human beings live in harmony with themselves, with the other members of society, and with the natural system. This is accomplished through self-reflection motivated by the insights gained from a more realistic understanding of one's current physical and social existence as well as an appreciation of future possibilities. Individuals gain emancipation through empowerment that is motivated by enlightenment. Each step results in a change within the actor as well as within their social context. While traditionally critical theory has been concerned with the revolutionary praxis at a societal level, Laughlin (1987, 1988) has applied these ideas to the study of accounting and accountability systems. Following Habermas (1984, 1987), recognized as the current leading critical theorist (e.g., see Held, 1980; White, 1988), Laughlin's analysis focuses on the emancipatory potential of language.

Following Fay (1987), critical theory can be described using four related components that concern the interrelationships between individual self-perceptions and social practices and institutions. These form the context within, as well as means by, which change is brought about. The four primary categories are characterized as:

false consciousness, crisis, education and transformative action. If social accounting is to be empowered by these ideas, they must be understood and addressed in research and applications projects.

False consciousness

Critical theory is based on the assumption of self-estrangement. Self-estrangement presumes that human existence is comprised of two spheres. One is that manifested in one's conscious understanding of the everyday activities, and the other is embedded within ideologically prescribed social structures and hidden from view within the unconscious. Self-estrangement concerns the way self-understandings are artificial and, at times, incoherent. As a result, the lived experience is needlessly frustrating and opaque, leading to unsatisfying, and in some situations detrimental, modes of existence. Through critique (enlightenment), these illusions must be recognized in order to overcome the false consciousness that is impeding growth and fulfilment. Critical theory presumes that the ideological critique will reveal alternatives superior to the prevailing social context. As the enlightened under-standing of the social context expands, the individual recognizes preferable alternatives are possible and conceives of means for attaining them. As a result, one's existence becomes more satisfying, increasing the likelihood of realizing one's full potential.

Crisis

Crises that spur change are presumed to be inherent within the extant social system. These perturbations provide a stimulus for self-reflection and inquiry that reveal the nature and causes inherent within the prevailing social systems. An understanding of the genesis of crisis includes a historical appreciation of how the interaction between social structures and false consciousness results in crisis. Under the current social order, alienation and social instability cannot be overcome because of individual false consciousness coupled with the basic organization of society. The current environmental crisis is an example.

Education

Education makes people aware of the possibility for change. This awareness arises out of the self-awareness and the recognition of crises, revealing shared beliefs and possible means for changing the beliefs. Initial conditions as well as the mechanisms for emancipatory enlightenment are specified. Within the context and limitations of rational reflection, necessary and sufficient conditions for emancipatory change are specified, and the likelihood of realizing these conditions through critical analysis increases.

41

Transformative action

The preceding categories are primarily concerned with informing and motivating transformative action by revealing the alienating aspects of life and what must be changed if reconciliation is to be achieved. Transformative action requires a programme indicating how, and by whom, emancipatory change can be brought about. In order to appropriately resolve crises, the conditions for the requisite changes in self-perception and in social organizations must be specified followed by a plan of action including a programme for its implementation. The resulting social transformations bring about emancipatory change. This would precipitate and characterize the social accounting project.

Limitations

As we contemplate the application of critical theory in facilitating the social accounting project, we must be cognizant of, and attentive to, the theory's limitations. The efficacy of human reason in initiating change is central to critical theory, ideas represent the sole determinant of behaviour, and clarity of vision leads to emancipatory action. If these assumptions do not hold, the means for overcoming oppression and alienation are not operative. These assumptions have their limitations, which are relevant to the theory's constructive application to social accounting. There appear to be limits on the extent to which human beings are, or can be, activists within given institutional contexts, thus limiting the effect of enlightenment. Due to the inherent indeterminacy of human existence and the historicity and physicality of human situatedness, human beings cannot achieve the level of self-clarity necessary for the rational analysis presumed as the basis for enlightened understanding leading to emancipatory action. Humans are always already active participants and perpetuators of the emerging existence and as such cannot overcome this situatedness by stepping outside of their circumstances as required for rational analysis. Internally, somatically acquired traits and dispositions are not necessarily accessible or modifiable through mental processes. Externally applied force can also be a significant impediment to individual emancipation, with death being the ultimate impediment of a satisfying and fulfilled existence. Further, there are severe limitations in the, at least implicit, assumption that freedom equates with happiness or that freedom necessarily leads to consensus of opinion or action following from collective autonomy.

In summary, the energetic and pragmatic approach taken by the social accounting project is compatible with, and a consequence of, its acquaintance with critical theory. While there are significant limitations, they do not negate the value of critical theory as a useful theoretic. What it does suggest is the need to incorporate a theoretical formulation that explicitly considers the interaction of the agent with the social structures that enable and constrain the realization of enlightenment, empowerment and emancipation. The dispersion and diversity of the current offerings seem to suggest a need at this point to become more attentive to the project's moral groundings and how they might be useful in legitimating and organizing social accounting, providing a framework for developing, focusing, and evaluating this ongoing research programme. Thus, one might conclude that Gray's empowering philosophical basis, while reflecting the passion and critique of 'critical theory and its theorists', could do with just a bit more development.

THE LEGITIMATING CRITERIA OF SOCIAL ACCOUNTING

Acting in the public interest is acting so as to enhance the well-being of society within the context of sustainable natural, social, and economic systems. The moral legitimacy of the social accounting project rests on acting in the public interest. Not only does acting in the public interest provide the moral context wherein an action or activity is contemplated and legitimized, it also represents a central tenet of social integration.[17] Acting in the public interest represents a central component of an individual or a profession's social and professional responsibility and legitimizes the distinguishing characteristic of the social contract by granting rights, privileges and status.

The focus of the social accounting project has been primarily business or work organizations.[18] Within this context, the purpose of social accounting is to assist these organizations in fulfilling their public interest responsibility. Business organizations represent one of the primary institutions within human societies and play a central role in ensuring the long-term viability of a democratically governed society grounded in justice, equality, and trust and supported by sustainable natural, social, and economic systems. Organizational management is specifically granted fiduciary responsibility over society's economic resources.[19] By exercising these rights, an *ethic of accountability* is established whereby the actor agrees to being held accountable by those who grant these rights, and those who grant the rights accept the responsibility for holding the recipients accountable for the related outcomes. Providing relevant and understandable information is a necessary condition for being held accountable. In addition, accountability requires that actual outcomes be evaluated relative to a set of relevant criteria. The grantors of the rights are also responsible for establishing evaluation criteria used in holding the organizations accountable. Care must be taken so that the evaluation criteria reflect the norms and values of the society, not those of special interests or those in power.

An ethic of accountability[20]

An ethic of accountability situates the actor as a member of an ongoing community and consists of four primary elements: solidarity, interpreted actions, the contemplated action, and accountability. Solidarity refers to the ongoing, situated, purposeful interrelatedness of human agents as they act as members of social and natural systems. Social solidarity recognizes that action takes place within the context of an ongoing community. Natural solidarity recognizes that action of human agents[21] also takes place within, and has an effect on, natural systems. Interpreted action refers to the recognition that moral behaviour requires the actor to be aware of the historic and physical interrelatedness of events as evidenced by observed outcomes from previous acts with respect to their effect on both social and natural systems. Contemplated action refers to actors' deliberations with respect to the act to be carried out. As a member of an ongoing community, the actor is obliged to consider the anticipated act and its propriety in light of the projected effect as judged by the effect of past actions and the anticipated implications for members of the community. An ethic of accountability requires a moral act to be preceded by a serious and conscious consideration of the physical and historical context within which an act is to be carried out. The actor acts within, and as a responsible member of, an ongoing community, accepting the right of the community to require an account of both process and outcome. In turn, the community accepts its responsibility to hold the actor accountable. A part of this process includes establishing and implementing, through enlightened democratic processes, evaluation criteria, as well as effective monitoring mechanisms and reporting requirements.[22]

Conceptually, an ethic of accountability is not a one-time, isolated event, but an ongoing conversation between that actor and all affected parties carried out within a sustaining, and sustainable, community. An ethic of accountability does not seek 'the good' in a utilitarian sense or 'the right' in a deontological sense, though both are consistent with the ideal. The good and the right are delineated as part of the process of determining the appropriate action within the ongoing community. An ongoing community presumes sustainable natural and social systems.

Fitting action as well as the act of holding accountable depends upon open and trustworthy discourse between the actor and the community members as well as among the community members themselves. A preliminary condition in implementing an ethic of accountability requires the stipulation of what constitutes legitimate communal dialogue whereby the rights and responsibilities of all community members are recognized. The level of trustworthiness among the actors is developed as a result of ongoing interactions and is central to establishing a sense of loyalty and responsibility. If the communal discourse is controlled by powerful, self-interested agents who exploit the social and physical resources to achieve self-serving objectives, an ethic of accountability becomes impossible, and its pretence becomes a means for manipulation and exploitation with any possibility of solidarity destroyed.

Following Habermas (1984, pp. 92–104), legitimate communication provides the basis for ethical action. Communication is legitimate if it satisfies the following three validity claims:

1 *Propositional validity (physical)*: concerns the correspondence between the claim and the external or objective evidence. This relates to the extent a claim is true and requires the speaker to provide the grounds upon which the claim is being made.

2 *Normative validity (social)*: concerns the correspondence between the claim and the extant social norms and relates to the degree to which the claim is consistent with the prevailing social norms. The speaker is required to provide justification.

3 *Subjective authenticity (personal)*: concerns the correspondence between perceived and actual intent of the speaker. This relates to the extent that a claim is genuine, as opposed to strategic/manipulative and requires that the speaker prove her or his trustworthiness.

These claims define the conditions under which an ethic of accountability can be successfully pursued.

Clearly, these conditions are restrictive and difficult to obtain. Nonetheless, they represent criteria for initiating and sustaining meaningful and ongoing dialogue among members of an ongoing community seeking to identify and carry out moral courses of action. The inability to satisfy these validity claims calls into question the veracity of the communal discourse; thus, imposing limiting conditions on the operationalization of an ethic of accountability. Alternatively, actors (e.g., work organizations) committed to acting sustainably can use these criteria as guidelines for facilitating open discussion and community dialogue. For example, emerging issues arise from, and relate to, unique contextual circumstances. Legitimate communal dialogue provides the means for selecting and prioritizing interests and outcomes, with alternatives chosen based on the strength of the better argument.

Seriously implementing an ethic of accountability results in an expanded scope of behaviour alternatives, a framework for setting priorities, a more widely understood and accepted set of evaluation criteria, and a higher likelihood of successful applications. The process does not prescribe a set of generally applicable rules but emphasizes the importance of context and accountability in issues associated with sustainability and thus related to the social accounting project.

The action space

A social accounting project based on an ethic of accountability as discussed above presumes that to act in the public interest requires the explicit consideration of natural, social and economic systems. Natural systems provide the context and the sustenance for social systems and social systems provide the context and objectives for economic systems. All three systems must be respected, nurtured, and sustained, and an ethic of accountability requires that accountability systems address all three. The social accounting project sees the accounting profession's responsibility as facilitating and monitoring organizational management in carrying out their fiduciary responsibility with respect to the natural, social and economic systems. As such, accountants are concerned with the integrity and accountability of reporting and administrative systems and those who design, implement and use them.

The social accounting project presumes that the academic accounting community has a responsibility to facilitate, and engage in, dialogue among members of the community regarding accounting's (the profession, the professionals, the systems) and organizational management's public interest responsibilities. Accountants, the business community, members of academy and representatives of the civil community have a responsibility to engage in and sustain this discourse. Applying the tenets of critical theory, the action space of the accounting academic related to the social accounting project includes scholarly activities leading to enlightenment, educational innovation leading to empowerment, and community action/ interaction facilitating emancipation.

Enlightenment

In developing and implementing an ethic of accountability, the expertise of faculty, students, and the business and civil communities can be brought together to identify and consider the critical public interest issues associated with sustainability and accountability. At a general level, the quest for enlightenment deems it important to identify critical sustainability issues and responsibilities facing accounting and organizational management. Such an undertaking requires an appreciation of both the historical and current role of organization management, accounting, the accounting profession and accounting systems. This entails studying these within the current and historical economic, political, social, ecological and organizational context utilizing a broad range of methodologies, addressing a wide variety of research topics.

Much of the extant research contributes to a more complete understanding with respect to the availability, use, and implications of social and environmental information.[23] For example, a significant portion of the empirical work addresses publicly reported information and the associated market and stakeholder reactions (for a review see Deegan, 2002). Internally, the related research considers the social and environmental implications of the interplay between autonomy and control within work organizations and the related technological (scientific as well as administrative) applications such as material conversion processes as well as budget and management control systems (see Deegan, 2002 and Mathews, 1997, for a review of the work in these areas).

The research agenda must continue to enlighten our understanding of issues surrounding the social accounting project. Sustainability issues should become an integral part of corporate governance, especially as these issues relate to legislation and regulation, and the scope of disclosure should include any affected constituency, past, present and future.[24] Management information systems, of which social and environmental accounting systems are a part, must provide information relevant for effectively managing a sustainable organization. Also, in designing these systems, issues such as the social consequences of information access, implications for creating human capabilities, as well as the moral implications of technological applications must be considered.

Empowerment

Empowerment follows from enlightenment as the deeper understanding is conveyed to members of the ongoing community. The social accounting project is concerned with applying appropriate tools for constructing the sustainability-related issues facing accounting and organizational management.[25] Community members gain an appreciation of current and historical context within which their life situation is enacted as well as the associated rights and responsibilities. The educational process also provides the means for identifying and developing new opportunities for responsible and responsive development especially as they relate to sustainability and accountability. This requires innovative thinking in terms of pedagogy, course, programme and curriculum development, as well as the accompanying teaching materials, case studies and related research.[26]

The key to empowerment is critique. A realization of possibilities comes from critique of the current state of affairs. Critique must be embedded within educational undertakings that facilitate an appreciation of the complexities associated with the interface between organizations and social and natural systems. Relative to the social accounting project, this implies a much broader range of knowledge, transcending the understanding of rules and traditional practices. A social accounting approach integrates technical competence with a deep understanding of the complex responsibilities of accounting to organizations, society and the environment. For example, empowerment integrates an appreciation of the source and situatedness of professional roles, implicit and explicit multiple associated constituencies and responsibilities, and their interrelatedness with natural and social systems.

Emancipation

Emancipation is brought about through action carried out by enlightened members of the ongoing community that follows from their expanded appreciation of the possibilities and necessities arising from the new understandings. Within the context of this discussion, action facilitating sustainability through accountability follows from, and facilitates, enlightened and sustained discourse within the ongoing community.[27] Action is directed towards creating, identifying and acting on opportunities for advancing the cause of sustainability, both environmental and social. All members of the community share these responsibilities. Emancipation is the result of an enabling and ongoing dialogue among all relevant constituents and becomes evident in actions to bring the anticipated world order to fruition through active engagement.

CLOSING REMARKS

Social accounting includes all other accountings, both manifest and imagined. The legitimacy of the social accounting project is grounded in a responsibility to act in the public interest. Acting in the public interest recognizes the critical inter-relationship among the natural, social and economic systems. An ethic of account-ability provides the legitimating justification for the social accounting project, and pragmatism provides the operational framework whereby the social accounting project is to be realized. Upon these tenets accountants' and accountings' moral obligations for a sustainable society are based, and a general plan for action can be formulated. The following are means consistent with these tenets whereby the social accounting project may be facilitated.

In light of the heightening awareness of the accelerating degradation of both social and natural systems, a larger segment of society appears to recognize the criticality of social and environmental sustainability. As one of the primary societal institutions, organizations are situated within, and dependent upon, both natural and social systems. If those responsible for managing these organizations are not keenly aware and held accountable for both, they cannot adequately address the risks, opportunities, and responsibilities associated with their actions. Given the constraints of global market capitalism and business's historical stance and traditional intransigence, we must seriously question organizational management's ability, motivation and commitment to act in the public interest working towards a more sustainable society. While laws and regulations have begun to codify society's expectations, they cannot substitute for a genuine ethic of accountability accepted by all parties and supported by a comprehensive system of accountability.

Those associated with external auditing and related activities have a direct and unambiguous responsibility for rendering the actions of organizations transparent by facilitating the provision of relevant, reliable and understandable information by the reporting entity to external and internal constituencies. Those associated with accounting in its organizationally related applications serve the ethic of account-ability by providing the information necessary for others to understand the entities' actions and to hold those responsible for the outcomes. For example, the accounting function prepares communications used by creditors, owners, sponsors, contri-butors, employees, unions, managers, politicians, regulators and society. All have the right to expect objective, understandable and honest reporting by the entity and the responsible business professional.

The controllership function is a primary administrative component charged with ensuring that the organization fulfils its fiduciary responsibilities to society, responsibilities that extend substantially beyond the legal requirements stated in a corporate charter or codified in laws and regulations. To adequately fulfil the societal responsibilities, processes and associated reporting and administrative systems must be designed and implemented that safeguard social and environmental systems as well as economic ones. The social accounting project presumes that the controllership function will take a leading role in developing and implementing these information systems.

Relatedly, internal auditing and management accounting activities involve recognizing risks associated with legal, financial, social and environmental implications of an organization's activities. Those associated with the collection and conveyance of organizational information enjoy a unique opportunity, and responsibility, to identify and communicate activities and behaviours that jeopardize or enhance the organization's ability to carry out its responsibilities. Social and environmental accounting issues should be at the forefront of these efforts.

Members of the accounting academy must recognize and embrace the scope of the social accounting project, ensuring that it is represented in the accounting curriculum and in their research programmes. As scholars, we must accept our responsibility as the thought leaders of society, recognizing that it is critique that energizes the social accounting project, and where appropriate, helps to more fully and clearly articulate the rights and responsibilities implicated in an ethic of accountability. If these responsibilities are embraced by those who teach and practise accounting, there is a modicum of hope that a social accounting can transcend the current constraints of its neoclassical economic proclivities and respond with an enabling and sustaining accounting grounded in an ethic of accountability.

NOTES

1   I wish to acknowledge the helpful comments of Darrel Brown and support received from the Center for Professional Integrity and Accountability, School of Business Administration, Portland State University.

2   Within this project, I include sustainability, accounting and accountability.

3   Roslender and Dillard (2003) suggest that the alternative/critical project is far from a coherent project and care should be given in appropriating the label. Here, I reserve the term critical theory in referring to a particular branch of neomarxist social theory originally associated with the Frankfurt School (see Held, 1980; White, 1998; Bronner, 1994). Critical accounting studies include those studies that are motivated by the recognized need for radical politically motivated change. Alternative accounting studies are those providing a critique of the status quo without a specific political programme.

4 For example, see Tinker and Gray (2003), Tinker *et al.* (1991), Lehman (1995, 1996, 1999, 2001).

5 However, Bronner (1994) notes a general reluctance on the part of its advocates to participate in actual engagements.

6 This discussion follows from Audi (1995, pp. 638–9).

7 See Chua (1986), Hopper and Powell (1985), Laughlin and Lowe (1989), Roberts and Scapens (1985) for a discussion of associated limitations.

8 By ontology I am referring to what there is to know. For example, is there an objective world to be discovered or is there only a subjectively created artifact?

9 By epistemology I am referring to how I come to know what there is to know. Can I come to know the world through precise measurement and observation, or do I come to know the world through abstract mental reasoning?

10 That is, individuals are assumed to either be, respectively, entirely shaped by the circumstances they find themselves in or have the ability to shape their own futures.

11 This distinction dictates how data could be gathered in order to shed light on 'reality'. The basic choice is between large-scale standard surveys (which, given an assumption that everyone reacts in the same way to events, is a sound way to generate knowledge) and more narrow but in-depth examinations.

12 A casual review of what some consider the traditional research journals (e.g., *Accounting Review, Accounting Horizons*, etc.) in accounting will confirm this observation.

13 Aspects of ontology, epistemology and methodology (along with assumptions about human nature) combine together along logically consistent lines.

14 See Gray (2002), Bebbington (1997), Bebbington *et al.* (1999), Gray (1992), Gray *et al.* (1997), Gray and Milne (2004), Everett (2004), Everett and Neu (2000), Lehman (1995, 1996, 1999, 2001), Power (1991) and Tinker *et al.* (1991).

15 See Searle (1995) for a philosophical discussion of these permutations and combinations.

16 These attributes are relevant for enhancing the human condition with respect to both social and natural systems.

17 By social integration I mean facilitating individuals coming together and working together to accomplish common goals.

18 See Deegan (2002) and Mathews (1997).

19 These natural, human, financial, and technological resources

20 These ideas follow from Niebuhr's (1963) responsibility ethic as developed in Dillard and Yuthas (2001).

21 The focus is on the human agent as the only purposeful actor.

22 These ideas are not inconsistent with various forms of stakeholder theory such as normative stakeholder theory (Donaldson and Preston, 1995) and provide a moral grounding for them.

50

23 A complete review of the areas considered in the extant literature as well as the important areas in need of consideration is beyond the scope of this discussion. See, for example, Deegan (2002), Gray (2002), Gray and Bebbington (2001), and Mathews (1997).

24 For example, see the work by Owen *et al.*, 2000, 2001, concerning stakeholder involvement.

25 For example, see Bebbington and Gray (2001) and Gray *et al.* (1997).

26 For work directly applying the ideas included in critical theory to education and educational processes see particularly Bebbington (1997) and Thomson and Bebbington (2004, 2005)

27 Gray and Bebbington (2001) provide an illustration of the current social and environmental accounting practices as well as the substantial opportunities with respect to implementing the social accounting project.

REFERENCES

Audi, R. (ed.) (1995) *The Cambridge dictionary of philosophy*. Cambridge: Cambridge University Press.

Bebbington, J. (1997) Engagement, education and sustainability: A review essay on environment accounting. *Accounting, Auditing and Accountability Journal*, 10: 365–81.

Bebbington, J. and Gray, R. (2001) An account of sustainability: Failure, success and a reconceptualization. *Critical Perspectives on Accounting*, 12(5): 557–87.

Bebbington, K. J., Gray, R. H. and Owen, D. L. (1999) Seeing the wood for the trees: Taking the pulse of social and environmental accounting. *Accounting, Auditing and Accountability Journal*, 12(1): 47–51.

Bronner, S. (1994) *Of critical theory and its theorists*. Oxford: Blackwell.

Burrell, G. and Morgan, G. (1979) *Social paradigms and organizational analysis*. London: Heinemann.

Chua, W. (1986) Radical developments in accounting thought. *Accounting Review*, 61(4): 601–32.

Deegan, C. (2002) The legitimating effect of social and environmental disclosures: A theoretical foundation. *Accounting, Auditing and Accountability Journal*, 15(3): 281–311.

Dillard, J. (1991) Accounting as a critical social science. *Accounting, Auditing and Accountability Journal*, 4(1): 8–28.

Dillard, J. and Yuthas, K. (2001) A responsibility ethic of audit expert systems. *Journal of Business Ethics*, 30: 337–59.

Donaldson, T. and Preston, L. (1995) The stakeholder theory of the corporation: Concepts, evidence and implications. *Academy of Management Journal*, 20: 65–91.

Everett, J. (2004) Exploring (false) dualisms for environmental accounting praxis. *Critical Perspectives on Accounting,* 15: 1061–84.

Everett, J. and Neu, D. (2000) Ecological modernization and the limits of environmental accounting. *Accounting Forum,* 24(1): 5–30.

Fay, B. (1987) *Critical social science.* Ithaca: Cornell University Press.

Gray, R. (1992) Accounting and environmentalism: An exploration of the challenge of gently accounting for accountability, transparency, and sustainability. *Accounting Organizations and Society,* 17(5): 399–425.

Gray, R. (2002) The social accounting project and *Accounting, Organizations and Society*: Privileging engagement, imaginings, new accountings and pragmatism over critique? *Accounting, Organizations and Society,* 27: 687–709.

Gray, R. and Bebbington, J. (2001) *Accounting for the environment,* 2nd edn. London: Sage.

Gray, R. and Milne, M. J. (2004) Towards reporting on the triple bottom line: Mirages, methods and myths. In A. Henriques and J. Richardson (eds) *The triple bottom line: Does it all add up?* London: Earthscan.

Gray, R., Dey, C., Owen, D., Evans, R. and Zadek, S. (1997) Struggling with the praxis of social accounting: Stakeholders, accountability, audits and procedures. *Accounting, Auditing and Accountability Journal,* 10(3): 325–64.

Habermas, J. (1984) *The theory of communicative action,* vol. 1. Trans. T. McCarthy. Boston: Beacon Press.

Habermas, J. (1987) *The theory of communicative action,* vol. 2. Trans. T. McCarthy. Boston: Beacon Press.

Held, D. (1980) *Introduction to critical theory: Horkheimer to Habermas.* Berkeley: University of California Press.

Hopper, T. and Powell, A. (1985) Making sense of research into the organizational and social aspects of management accounting: A review of its underlying assumptions. *Journal of Management Studies,* 22(5): 429–65.

Laughlin, R. (1987) Accounting systems in organizational contexts: A case for critical theory. *Accounting, Organizations and Society,* 12(4): 479–502.

Laughlin, R. (1988) Accounting in its social context: Analysis of the accounting systems of the Church of England. *Accounting, Auditing and Accountability Journal,* 1(2): 19–42.

Laughlin, R. and Lowe, A. (1989) A critical analysis of accounting thought: Prognosis and prospects for understanding and changing accounting systems. In D. Cooper and T. Hopper (eds) *Critical accounting.* New York: Macmillian.

Lehman, G. (1995) A legitimate concern for environmental accounting. *Critical Perspectives on Accounting,* 6(6): 393–412.

Lehman, G. (1996) Environmental accounting: Pollution permits or selling the environment. *Critical Perspectives on Accounting,* 7: 667–76.

Lehman, G. (1999) Disclosing new worlds: A role for social and environmental accounting and auditing. *Accounting, Organizations and Society,* 24(3): 217–42.

Lehman, G. (2001) Reclaiming the public sphere: problems and prospects for corporate social and environmental accounting. *Critical Perspectives on Accounting*, 12: 713–33.

Mathews, R. (1997) Twenty-five years of social and environmental accounting research. *Accounting, Auditing and Accountability Journal*, 10(4): 481–531.

Medawar, C. (1976) The social audit: A political view. *Accounting, Organizations and Society*, 1(4): 389–94.

Niebuhr, R. (1963) *The responsible self.* San Francisco: Harper Press.

Owen, D., Swift, T. and Hunt, K. (2001) Questioning the role of stakeholder engagement in social and ethical accounting. *Accounting Forum*, 25(3): 264–82.

Owen, D., Swift, T., Humphrey, C. and Bowerman, M. (2000) The new social audits: Accountability, managerial capture or the agenda of social champions? *European Accounting Review*, 9(1): 81–98.

Power, M. (1991) Auditing and environmental expertise: Between protest and professionalization. *Accounting, Auditing and Accountability Journal*, 4(3): 30–42.

Power, M. (1997) Expertise and the construction of relevance: Accountants and the environmental audit. *Accounting, Organizations and Society*, 22(2): 123–46.

Roberts, J. and Scapens, R. (1985) Accounting systems and systems of accountability: Understanding accounting practices in their organizational context. *Accounting, Organizations and Society*, 10(4): 443–56.

Roslender, R. and Dillard, J. (2003) Reflections on the interdisciplinary perspectives on accounting project. *Critical Perspectives on Accounting*, 14(3): 325–52.

Searle, J. (1995) *The construction of social reality.* New York: Free Press.

Thomson, I. and Bebbington, J. (2004) It doesn't matter what you teach? *Critical Perspectives on Accounting*, 15(4–5): 609–28.

Thomson, I. and Bebbington, J. (2005) Social and environmental reporting in the UK: A pedagogic evaluation. *Critical Perspectives on Accounting*, 16(5): 507–33.

Tinker, T. and Gray, R. (2003) Beyond critique of pure reason: From policy to policies to praxis in environmental and social accounting. *Accounting, Auditing and Accountability Journal*, 16(5): 727–61.

Tinker, T, Lehman, C. and Neimark, M. (1991) Falling down the hole in the middle of the road: Political quietism in corporate social accounting. *Accounting, Auditing and Accountability Journal*, 4(2): 28–54.

White, S. (1988) *The recent works of Jürgen Habermas.* New York: Cambridge University Press.

Part II

External reporting of sustainability policies and practices

Chapter 3

Histories of and rationales for sustainability reporting

Nola Buhr

INTRODUCTION

I am not convinced that such a thing as sustainability reporting exists. So it would seem this is a chapter on the history of and rationales for something that is yet to be and, quite possibly, may never be. Certainly, sustainability reporting is an admirable target to work towards, even though the pathway thus far has been unclear, disputed and much longer than many would like. This chapter looks at that pathway beginning with some very quick thoughts on sustainability and the scope of reporting. Then, a brief history of sustainability reporting, a few comments on accountability and various rationales for reporting are provided. As the rationales pertain to the voluntary nature of sustainability reporting and the role of regulation, a discussion follows as to what is meant by voluntary and mandatory. Finally, if we are to think about the history of the future, it is helpful to consider what we need to do to find our way forward.

SUSTAINABILITY

There is not much disagreement on the definition of sustainability as 'meeting the needs of the present without compromising the ability of future generations to meet their own needs' (United Nations World Commission on Environment and Development, 1987, p. 8). However, understanding how this gets put into practice is a tricky bit of work. Does it come down to carrying your own mug and using both sides of every piece of paper? Hardly. I don't believe that we understand what sustainability means. Yes, it includes the environmental, the social and the economy. But, what does it say about timeframe, justice, geography, values and use of capital (natural, social and economic)? Bebbington and Thomson (1996) interviewed 45 individuals who were environmental managers and accountants and asked them to detail the implications that arise from the pursuit of sustainability. They found that there was 'No coherent picture of what a sustainable society or a sustainable business would look like' (pp. i–ii).

Gray and Milne (2004) question whether corporations can even be in the sustainability business for notions of social responsibility run counter to the fundamental self-interest of business. We would like companies to be socially responsible, care for the planet and pursue sustainability or at the very least provide lots of jobs so that we can live in a robust community. For the most part though, capitalism punishes non-economic behaviour. Gray and Milne indicate that the fundamental nature of capitalism is such that there is a conflict between moral and financial criteria and the best that can be done is to get companies to comply with the law. Accordingly, they say what we need to do is work at making laws to enforce the behaviour we want, conscious of the role corporations play in the law-making process.

I do not believe that we (citizens, shareholders, governments and NGOs) have yet sorted out the corporation's role in society. Therefore, if we do not know or agree on what the corporation is, how can we know or agree on what the corporation should do vis-à-vis reporting? Even if we could agree, I believe that we are still left with the question as to how one part (i.e. a single corporation) in a social ecosystem can fully understand and report on the role it plays and the impact it has on the rest of the social ecosystem. Hence, sustainability reporting may remain an unattainable ideal.

REPORTING

Nevertheless, I will press on here and look back at how we got to where we are now with sustainability reporting. To my mind, the reporting part of sustainability reporting encompasses a wide range of activities, not all of which are found in print. These activities include: advertising (print, radio, billboard and TV); public relations (press releases); securities filings (press releases, annual reports, in the US a 10K and in Canada an Annual Information Form); voluntary environmental or sustainability reports; and glossy brochures for employees or the curious public. What all of these activities have in common is that they are opportunities for the corporation to represent itself and communicate with various stakeholders. Zéghal and Ahmed (1990) and Unerman (2000), among others, have pointed out the need to examine a broad range of communication outputs in order to understand the full nature of a company's reporting.

For the most part, the literature and therefore this chapter focus on sustainability reporting by corporations. It is corporations who are the most involved in this area even though only a small percentage of them engage in environmental or sustainability reporting in a meaningful way. If we held all parts of our social ecosystem to account, we might expect sustainability reporting by governments, NGOs, not-for-profits and perhaps even households. There have been some forays into sustainability reporting, or at least into developing indicators for reporting, by various governments. For example, in Canada, the National Round Table on the Environment and the Economy, as mandated by the federal government, has developed a set of national indicators of environment and sustainable development (National Round Table on the Environment and the Economy, 2003). However, the possibility of a broad spectrum of non-corporate sustainability reporting is much further down the road from where we are now.

(A BRIEF) HISTORY OF SUSTAINABILITY REPORTING

Contrary to popular belief, environmental awareness did not begin with Rachel Carson's 1962 book *Silent Spring*. Rather, environmental and social controversies have been troubling the public for centuries. Looking at a history of environmental issues, Neuzil and Kovarik (1996) provide an interesting timeline and show us that we have had a long legacy of environmental problems, many of which relate to human health. They note that in 1306 Edward I of England forbade coal burning when Parliament was in session. In 1739 Benjamin Franklin and others petitioned the Pennsylvania Assembly to stop waste dumping in the Delaware River. In 1775 English scientist Percival Pott found that coal was causing an unusually high incidence of cancer among chimney sweeps. In 1804 the first health inspector in the United States was appointed in New York. The list goes on.

Despite centuries of concern over environmental and social issues, the beginnings of social, environmental and sustainability reporting are largely linked with the dawn of the modern corporation. The maturation of accounting, reporting and standardization is a slow process. For thousands of years accountants have worked on capturing the economic world by developing different forms of financial and managerial accounting. Yet, it is only within the last century or so, with the need for corporate financing, that accountants started establishing accounting standards for external financial reporting. Similarly, sustainability accounting, reporting and standardization is following a slow process that is not much over a hundred years old. The process begins with employee reporting and then moves on to social reporting, environmental reporting, triple bottom line reporting and eventually, and ideally, sustainability reporting.

Employee reporting

The academic literature started to take a hard look at social reporting in the 1970s but this does not mean that such reporting did not exist before then. Hogner (1982) and Guthrie and Parker (1989) provide examples of long histories of corporate social reporting. Hogner looked at eight decades of reporting by US Steel for the period 1901 to 1980 and found that the initial decades included such information as: dwellings built for workers; community development; worker safety; and mortgage assistance for employees. Guthrie and Parker looked at the annual reports of BHP for the 100-year period from 1885 onwards. Similar to US Steel, the early decades of BHP reporting cover employee and community issues.

The early reports reviewed by Hogner and Guthrie *et al.* tend to emphasize reporting on employee issues over other issues. This type of employee reporting is what I consider to be the first developments of sustainability reporting. Employee reporting also includes the practice of reporting directly to employees as documented by Lewis *et al.* (1984) for the 1919 to 1979 period that they studied.

Social reporting

In the report, *Good News & Bad: The Media, Corporate Social Responsibility and Sustainable Development*, SustainAbility *et al.* (2002, p. 7) chart the rise and fall of the CSR (Corporate Social Responsibility) and the SD (Sustainable Development) agenda in the OECD region from 1961 to 2001. There is no constant increase in interest in these topics but rather a waxing and waning depending on various societal factors. Conservative politics (Reagan and Thatcher) and tough economic times are linked with a diminishing interest in social and environmental issues whereas UN initiatives and disasters like Bhopal and the *Exxon Valdez* are associated with an increasing interest. This changing interest results in changing levels of disclosure. See, for example, Patten (1992) who notes a significant increase in environmental disclosure provided by oil and gas companies after the *Exxon Valdez* disaster. Gray *et al.* (1996, p. 97) reinforce this changing emphasis on social and environmental issues and describe the changes with reference to the UK:

> the early 1970s focused on social responsibility; by the mid–late 1970s this had shifted to employees and unions; the 1980s saw explicit pursuit of economic goals with a thin veneer of community concern and a redefinition of employee rights as the major theme; while in the 1990s attention shifted to environmental concern.

These fluctuations are similar to what transpired in North America and it would therefore be apt to label the 1970s as the social reporting decade. This does not mean that there was no mention of pollution or environmental issues but that the social took precedence. In 1971, Ernst & Ernst (the pre-cursor of the accounting firm Ernst & Young) began publishing an annual survey of social responsibility disclosure found in annual reports of Fortune 500 Industrials. Their 1978 survey covered the following categories: environment; energy; fair business practices (including employment and advancement of minorities and women); human resources (including employee health and safety); community involvement; products; and other. At the time, 1 per cent of the Fortune 500 companies provided a separate social responsibility booklet to shareholders along with the annual report. This translates into 7 companies in 1976 and 6 companies in 1977.

Environmental reporting

By the end of the 1970s social reporting was fading out and it took until the late 1980s and into the early 1990s for the next stage, environmental reporting, to emerge. Because of the hiatus of the early 1980s, environmental reporting hit the scene fresh and new, even though it was really a recycled phenomenon arising from its earlier associations with social reporting. Interestingly, the focus remained on things environmental for about ten years despite the 1987 Brundtland report (United Nations World Commission on Environment and Development), *Our Common Future*, which moved past the environment and established the notion of sustainable development.

In 1993, at a time when a few adventuresome companies had just begun producing environmental reports, *Coming Clean* (Deloitte Touche Tohmatsu International and SustainAbility) laid out a route for getting all the way to sustainability reporting. The report outlined five stages. The first stage was green glossy newsletters and a short statement in the annual report. Stage 2 was a one-off environmental report. Stage 3 was annual reporting linked to environmental management systems. Stage 4 was provision of a Toxic Release Inventory (TRI) report to the public (at the time, TRI reporting to government was mandatory in the US). Finally, stage 5 saw the company providing sustainable development reporting by linking environmental, economic and social aspects of corporate performance.

Triple bottom line reporting

As laudable as the *Coming Clean* stage 5 may be, it is not sustainable development reporting. Instead, it is what has come to be known as triple bottom line reporting. Connecting the environmental, the economic and the social only gets us part way to sustainability. Other aspects, like justice, equity and timeframe, will need to be incorporated before we get all the way there. Elkington, who indicates he is to be credited with introducing the term 'Triple Bottom Line' in 1994 (Elkington, 2004), readily admits that the triple bottom line is not the same thing as sustainability.

Sustainability reporting

I believe that our history of sustainability reporting has only reached as far as triple bottom line reporting (and is just barely there). Whether we can ever achieve a state where meaningful sustainability reporting can be produced remains to be seen.

Regardless though, there are many firms attaching this label to their reports. Many of the adventuresome companies who began producing environmental reports in the early 1990s have now shifted perspective and are producing what they are calling sustainability reports.

Shifting perspective

By looking at a leading Canadian mining company, Noranda, we can see a good example of this shifting perspective. Noranda has long been the darling of the Canadian Institute of Chartered Accountants (CICA) reporting awards for both its regular annual reports as well as its environmental/sustainability reports. Noranda produced its first stand-alone environmental report in 1991, reporting on environmental performance for 1990. For the reporting years 1990 to 1994 Noranda's report was titled an 'Environmental' report. In 1995 the report was titled 'Environment, Health and Safety' and the three components, environment, health and safety, were part of the report title until 1999 when the report was titled a 'Sustainable Development' report, a title that it has retained up to and including the 2004 report.

ACCOUNTABILITY

Employee, social, environmental, triple bottom line and sustainability reporting all serve as mechanisms to fulfil accountability requirements. Regardless of which variety of reporting is undertaken the rationales and the voluntary versus mandatory issues are common. Such reporting is driven by who the corporation thinks it is accountable to and what it is accountable for. Accordingly, corporations report with motivation, a calculated purpose and a message in mind. What is produced is provided in response to various pressures, expectations and social change. What corporations choose to address is their reaction to public opinion as well as a reflection of what they interpret public opinion to be. With the act of reporting, corporations, in turn, contribute to public discourse and serve to shape the public opinion that they are responding to. Governments, NGOs, individuals and the media (Neuzil and Kovarik, 1996; SustainAbility et al., 2002) also play a role in this public discourse by their presence in the debate as well as their absence. It is this malleable public discourse that leads to shaping expectations that leads to shaping laws.

RATIONALES FOR SUSTAINABILITY REPORTING

If one were to take a theoretical approach, there are several theories that could be employed to explain the motivation for sustainability reporting. The most popular of these includes: accountability, legitimacy, political economy and stakeholder theory. Rather than provide a review of these theories, the various rationales for sustainability reporting (or not) are outlined in Table 3.1 using common vernacular. The rationales have been drawn from the literature, including the following sources: Buhr (2002); Deloitte Touche Tohmatsu International and SustainAbility (1993); Freedman and Stagliano (1995); Gray and Bebbington (2000); Neu *et al.* (1998); Newton and Harte (1997); O'Dwyer (2002); Oliver (1991); Patten (1992); Suchman (1995); SustainAbility and United Nations Environment Programme (1994); *The Economist* (2002); and Ullmann (1985).

These rationales do not operate in isolation. Many of them are employed together as a way for an organization to understand its reporting situation. These rationales are cast in Table 3.1 in a proactive–reactive dichotomy for ease of illustration. However, there is a range of attitudes within each rationale and only the more extreme ends of the range have been presented. Some of the cells in the table do capture more than one attitude to illustrate the complexity of this range. It should be noted that many of these rationales are associated with the voluntary and mandatory aspects of reporting.

VOLUNTARY VERSUS MANDATORY

Discussion on voluntary versus mandatory disclosure plays prominently in the literature on corporate reporting. But, something that has not been well explored is the idea of voluntary and mandatory being different shades of a rainbow instead of black or white possibilities. Voluntary and mandatory are a spectrum, not an on–off switch.

Activities that are thought of as voluntary can exert a subtle (or not so subtle) peer pressure (and this may be no bad thing if one believes in the merits of sustainability reporting). For example, reporting awards such as the CICA annual awards for environmental reporting have been in place since 1993. Yes, they are voluntary awards. Yet, what happens if one is a largish company that never appears in the rankings or even the honourable mentions? Is there any danger to the company's reputation and industry standing? Similarly, as there is (hopefully) more and more take-up of voluntary standards such as the Global Reporting Initiative (GRI), established in 2002, one has to ask the question: What happens to the public perception of those companies that ignore the GRI?

Unfortunately, waiting for voluntary reporting standards or the merits of peer pressure to raise the bar for everyone is overly optimistic and naïve. As a result,

Table 3.1 Rationales for sustainability reporting

Rationale	Proactive	Reactive
Moral and ethical reasons, duty	We see this sort of reporting as our ethical duty. This reporting is part of the accountability equation and we have a champion in the upper ranks of management who want us to do this.	What we must do is comply with the law. If the law does not require this reporting we see no moral duty to engage in it.
Competitive advantage	We would like to be seen as a leader in this area. This is the vision that we have of ourselves.	We do not see any competitive advantage in being a leader in this area. We view it as too costly to be on the leading edge.
Party to setting of voluntary standards – GRI	We would like to work with others setting voluntary international standards. We might believe that voluntary standards are the way to go to stave off (costly) regulation.	We are not interested in or able to participate in such voluntary activity.
Party to setting of mandatory standards – government, accounting or securities based	We should do this so our views can be heard and represented in the process. This might include a conscious desire to 'capture' the agenda and ensure the results are compatible with what we are willing to do.	We do not want mandatory standards therefore we will not participate in the process except perhaps to resist.
Peer and industry pressure	We believe that it is important for our industry association to endorse this reporting. We want our industry to have a better image. We want to bring others in our industry up to our level of reporting.	Too many of our competitors are engaging in this reporting. We must provide some sort of reporting and not lag too far behind unless we are willing to tolerate some form of competitive disadvantage.

Corporate performance	We are really doing better than people think we are and we need to let them know.	Our corporate performance is not so hot and 'least said soonest mended'.
Image management, public relations, corporate reporting awards	This sort of reporting is a great way to beef up our image. Let's get our spin-doctors on it right away. This is a symbolic way for us to show how progressive we are.	There is a reaction to a disaster 'X' in our industry. We must do collateral damage control and report on how we have safeguards in place so that we are not like disaster 'X'.
Social pressures, social licence to operate	We believe in enlightened self-interest and win–win situations. Let's use this as one way to get the local community to understand what we are doing.	Why do we need to communicate with anyone other than shareholders? But, maybe if we do we can avoid the attacks by those NGOs and rabid interest groups.
Financial benefits from investor reactions	We believe that we can attract investors with this sort of reporting. We feel that we can lower our cost of capital because this sort of reporting indicates how we have solid systems, top-notch strategic thinking and corporate transparency.	We do not see any financial benefit from engaging in this reporting and in fact we see these reports as costing too much money, time, trouble and effort to produce.
Existing regulation – government, accounting or securities based	We have regulations in this area and we want to do a good job of providing full and fair disclosure, complying with both the form and the spirit of the regulation.	Sure there is regulation in this area but we do not think that it is well enforced and we are not afraid of the penalties if we are caught. Let's just ignore this and keep a low profile and see what happens. Maybe we will have to do something if our auditors or the securities regulators raise the issue.

there are numerous authors that call for regulated reporting to set things right (see, for example, Gallhofer and Haslam, 1997). The general idea is that better disclosure equals more transparency which equals more accountability which equals better sustainability performance. Therefore, the call goes out that we need to mandate more disclosure.

However, mandatory disclosure is a more elastic phenomenon than people might think. It takes a variety of forms and arises from a variety of institutional bodies. Disclosure can be mandated by accounting standards, government legislation or securities regulation. Just because disclosure is mandated does not necessarily mean that it will be provided. Adams *et al.* (1995) make this case with regard to the failure to provide mandated corporate equal opportunities disclosure. Also, even when disclosure is provided, there is room within the confines of 'mandatory' for selective and subjective disclosure.

Bebbington *et al.* (2003, p. 15) provide a legal perspective on the ramifications of making something 'mandatory':

> [l]awyers, in contrast, regard regulation as a continuum with traditional 'command and control' type regulation at one end and voluntary regulation through industry codes of conduct or agreements/non-enforceable contracts with regulators at the other.

Regulation without consensus, buy-in and co-operation is not regulation at all. Regulation assumes that breaches do not happen often, that if they do they are uncovered and that there is a sanction that serves as a deterrent. These are all pretty big ifs that make the benefit of command and control regulation questionable. In addition, such regulation is not only costly but it can serve to stifle innovation. Because of rules and expectations and sanctions there is the potential for a race to the bottom that provides little room for experimentation or creativity.

On the other hand, companies that choose to be creative can use regulation perversely as a legitimating device. This possibility can best be illustrated by looking at the Management Discussion and Analysis (MD&A) section of the annual report. Although securities regulators require the MD&A, it is doubtful that they make significant efforts to ensure that the information is credible and reliable. The external auditor has little to do with the MD&A, save for ensuring that it is not in blatant disagreement with the financial statements. Thus, it may be that companies wishing to gain more credibility choose to put some of their public relations information inside the MD&A instead of outside of it. Because the MD&A is mandatory it legitimizes and increases the believability of any information it contains.

CONCLUSION: A WAY FORWARD?

In reading the last few pages, it must seem that the prospects for sustainability reporting are pretty bleak. We do not seem to have been able to maintain our focus or build sufficient momentum in this area. Issues have waxed and waned over the decades like men's moustaches and women's hemlines. Voluntary reporting is not enough and mandatory reporting is not the panacea some would think.

Furthermore, we are deluding ourselves if we think that we can save the planet by sustainability reporting (flawed or not). Reporting will not save the planet. Instead, we need to think of our pathway to sustainability reporting as a reflection of how we are changing (or not) as a society and what our capacity is for working together and what role each of us adopts. Tongue in cheek, Newton and Harte (1997, p. 81) say 'in sum, business leaders have the ultimate duty to save the planet, since seemingly no one else will'.

Total reliance on business to save the planet is misplaced. Accountability is a two-way street that involves not only the giving of accounts but also the receiving of accounts. Accountability requires the engagement of a civil society that seeks to change, thoughtfully and democratically, the way we exist within our social eco-system (Buhr, 2001). It is this engagement that propels social change and it is this engagement that is crucial in the bid to seek sustainability and the sustainability reporting that follows.

On a final (more positive I hope) note, there is something to be said for pushing on with the sustainability reporting agenda. The very act of providing accounts has the potential to change behaviour. The process of reporting should serve to change management strategies and information systems and in turn lead to changes in management philosophies and practices (Dierkes and Antal, 1985). *The Economist* (2002, p. 56) notes:

> [s]plashing out on a big report may keep activists off a company's back. But although sucking up to politically correct lobbyists might seem a small price to pay to keep them quiet, in reality it can reinforce the feeling that companies have a case to answer.

It remains for us to continue to work to make that case loud and clear.

REFERENCES

Adams, C. A., Coutts, A. and Harte, G. (1995) Corporate equal opportunities (non-) disclosure. *British Accounting Review*, 27: 87–108.

Bebbington, J. and Thomson, I. (1996) *Business conceptions of sustainability and the implications for accountancy*, ACCA Research Report 48. London: Certified Accountants Educational Trust.

Bebbington, J., Kirk, E. and Larrinaga, C. (2003) A regime theory perspective on regulating environmental reporting. *AccountAbility Quarterly*, September: 15–19.

Buhr, N. (2001) Corporate silence: Environmental disclosure and the North American Free Trade Agreement. *Critical Perspectives on Accounting*, 12: 405–21.

Buhr, N. (2002) A structuration view on the initiation of environmental reports. *Critical Perspectives on Accounting*, 13: 17–38.

Carson, R. (1962) *Silent spring*. New York: Houghton Mifflin.

Deloitte Touche Tohmatsu International, International Institute for Sustainable Development and SustainAbility (1993) *Coming clean: Corporate environmental reporting*. London: Deloitte Touche Tohmatsu International.

Dierkes, M. and Antal, B. (1985) The usefulness and use of social reporting information. *Accounting, Organizations and Society*, 10(1): 29–34.

Economist, The (2002) Irresponsible: The dangers of corporate social responsibility, 23 November p. 56.

Elkington, J. (2004) Enter the triple bottom line. In A. Henriques and J. Richardson (eds) *The triple bottom line: Does it all add up?* London: Earthscan, pp. 1–16.

Ernst & Ernst (1978) *Social responsibility disclosure: 1978 survey*. Cleveland, OH.

Freedman, M. and Stagliano, A. J. (1995) Disclosure of environmental cleanup costs: The impact of the Superfund Act. *Advances in Public Interest Accounting*, 6: 163–76.

Gallhofer, S. and Haslam, J. (1997) The direction of green accounting policy: Critical reflections. *Accounting, Auditing and Accountability Journal*, 10(2): 148–74.

Gray, R. and Bebbington, J. (2000) Environmental accounting, managerialism and sustainability: Is the planet safe in the hands of business and accounting? *Advances in Environmental Accounting & Management*, 1: 1–44.

Gray, R. and Milne, M. (2004) Towards reporting on the triple bottom line: Mirages, methods and myths. In A. Henriques and J. Richardson (eds) *The triple bottom line: Does it all add up?* London: Earthscan, pp. 70–80.

Gray, R., Owen, D. and Adams, C. (1996) *Accounting & accountability: Changes and challenges in corporate social and environmental reporting*. London: Prentice-Hall.

Guthrie, J. and Parker, L. D. (1989) Corporate social reporting: A rebuttal of legitimacy theory. *Accounting and Business Research*, 19(76): 343–52.

Hogner, R. H. (1982) Corporate social reporting: Eight decades of development at US Steel. *Research in Corporate Social Performance and Policy*, 4: 243–50.

Lewis, N. R., Parker, L. D. and Sutcliffe, P. (1984) Financial reporting to employees: The pattern of development 1919 to 1979. *Accounting, Organizations and Society*, 9(3–4): 275–89.

National Round Table on the Environment and the Economy (2003) *The state of the debate on the environment and the economy: Environment and sustainable development indicators for Canada.* Ottawa: Renouf Publishing.

Neu, D., Warsame, H. and Pedwell, K. (1998) Managing public impressions: Environmental disclosures in annual reports. *Accounting, Organizations and Society,* 23(3): 265–82.

Neuzil, M. and Kovarik, W. (1996) *Mass media & environmental conflict: America's green crusades.* Thousand Oaks, CA: Sage.

Newton, T. and Harte, G. (1997) Green business: Technicist kitsch? *Journal of Management Studies,* 34(1): 75–98.

O'Dwyer, B. (2002) Managerial perceptions of corporate social disclosure: An Irish story. *Accounting, Auditing and Accountability Journal,* 15(3): 406–36.

Oliver, C. (1991) Strategic responses to institutional processes. *Academy of Management Review,* 16(1): 145–79.

Patten, D. M. (1992) Intra-industry environmental disclosures in response to the Alaskan oil spill: A note on legitimacy theory. *Accounting, Organizations and Society,* 15(5): 471–75.

Suchman, M. (1995) Managing legitimacy: Strategic and institutional approaches. *Academy of Management Review,* 20(3): 571–610.

SustainAbility and United Nations Environment Programme (1994) *Company environmental reporting: A measure of the progress of business & industry towards sustainable development.* Paris: UNEP IE.

SustainAbility, Ketchum and the United Nations Environment Programme (2002) *Good news & bad: The media, corporate social responsibility and sustainable development.* London: SustainAbility, Ltd.

Ullmann, A. A. (1985) Data in search of a theory: A critical examination of the relationships among social performance, social disclosure, and economic performance in US firms. *Academy of Management Review,* 10(3): 540–57.

Unerman, J. (2000) Methodological issues: Reflections on quantification in corporate social reporting content analysis. *Accounting, Auditing and Accountability Journal,* 13(5): 667–80.

United Nations World Commission on Environment and Development (1987) *Our common future.* The Brundtland Report. Oxford: Oxford University Press.

Zéghal, D. and Ahmed, S. A. (1990) Comparison of social responsibility information disclosure media used by Canadian firms. *Accounting, Auditing and Accountability Journal,* 3(1): 38–53.

Chapter 4

The 'standardization' of sustainability reporting [1]

Carol Adams and Venkat Narayanan

INTRODUCTION

The issue of sustainability is one that is becoming increasingly important for organizations around the world. Sustainability is no longer a fad that can be dealt with on a surface level through voluntary disclosures in corporate annual reports. The meaning of sustainability itself is often contentious and has drawn much debate in the accounting literature (Bebbington, 1997, 2001). The 'Brundtland Report' defines sustainable development as development which 'meets the needs of the present without compromising the ability of future generations to meet their own needs' (UNWCED, 1987, p. 8). The issue of sustainability is gaining prominence in the agenda of governmental and non-governmental organizations which are increasingly putting pressure on companies to incorporate sustainable practices into their business operations. For instance, the European Union commissioned a project which involved academic institutions, businesses and governmental organizations in the development of a conceptual framework for sustainability and sustainable development. This resulted in the European Corporate Sustainability Framework (for a detailed description of this framework see Hardjono and de Klein, 2004). Similar initiatives have been undertaken in Australia and Canada (the Australian and Canadian initiatives are covered later in this chapter).

The business case for sustainable business practice is also a strong one and this has been the major motivating factor for many organizations that report on their sustainability activities (Adams and Zutshi, 2004; Simms, 2002; World Business Council for Sustainable Development: Annual Review, 2004). A recent survey by KPMG of over 1,600 companies worldwide confirms this as it shows that 74 per cent of respondent organizations considered 'economic reasons' an important driver for their sustainability practices (KPMG, 2005). Some of the resistance to sustainability reporting comes from those who do not see the link between positive social and environmental performance and financial performance. Barry Stickings,

President of the Chemical Industries Association and Chairman of BASF, in finishing his lecture to the Royal Society of Edinburgh on 'Sustainable Development and Innovation' in 2001, said: 'I see the continuing debate over sustainable development as an opportunity for responsible industries such as ours to rehabilitate the word, "profit" and bring the positive role of profits back to the centre-stage of public debate' (2001, p. 27).

The reporting of sustainability issues by organizations is an important part of the sustainability agenda and in recent times there have been several initiatives by independent and governmental organizations to assist organizations with sustainability reporting. In this chapter we discuss the initiatives taken by some of the major bodies that promote sustainability reporting. This is followed by a critical evaluation of the impact of these initiatives on business practice. We conclude with some implications for the future direction of sustainability reporting.

THE BODIES THAT PROMOTE SUSTAINABILITY REPORTING

There are several national and international bodies that promote sustainability reporting and provide guidance through reporting standards concerned with indicators to be reported, reporting processes and/or reporting principles. In this section, we briefly introduce some of these bodies and provide summaries of their initiatives and contributions to sustainability reporting. The bodies that will be discussed are the Global Reporting Initiative (GRI), the International Standards Organization (ISO), the World Business Council for Sustainable Development (WBCSD), AccountAbility, and the Sustainability Integrated Guidelines for Management project (SIGMA). Additionally, we present some of the other bodies at both national and international levels that contribute to sustainability issues in general as opposed to sustainability reporting specifically. The majority of the bodies discussed in this chapter were chosen following the 'Race to the Top' (The World Bank Group, 2003) survey which asked executives about the standards, guidelines or policies that influenced their corporate social responsibility practices. The respondents in this survey were senior executives from 107 multinational organizations from across the globe. The results of this survey reveal that respondents viewed the ISO 14000 standard on Environmental Management (47 per cent), the GRI guidelines (38 per cent), the World Business Council for Sustainable Development (37 per cent), International Labour Organization (ILO hereafter) Core Conventions (37 per cent) and the Global Compact (32 per cent) as being influential on their business operations. It is important to note that not all of the above-mentioned standards, policies and forums provide guidance on sustainability reporting, thus, in this chapter, we focus our attention on the bodies that provide guidance specifically on this issue. In addition to those noted above we include a discussion of AccountAbility's AA1000 standard, the SIGMA guidelines and some national initiatives specifically concerned with aspects of sustainability reporting. We begin our discussion with the Global Reporting Initiative (GRI) guidelines.

THE GLOBAL REPORTING INITIATIVE (GRI)

Overview

GRI is an independent institution 'whose mission is to develop and disseminate globally applicable sustainability reporting guidelines' (GRI Guidelines, 2002, p. 1). The GRI was initiated by CERES (www.ceres.org) and the United Nations Environment Programme, in 1997, and it became an independent body in 2002. The GRI is a multi-stakeholder organization which includes members from the broader business and public sectors (organizational stakeholders) that elect a stakeholder council which in turn elects the Board of Directors. The other components that form part of the organizational structure of the GRI are the technical advisory committee and the secretariat. The board is ultimately responsible for the development and publication of the GRI guidelines, and receives support and advice from the other organizational units.

The 2002 guidelines were developed subsequent to the GRI symposium in 2000 following the provision of extensive feedback by companies that had adopted the 2000 guidelines. A Revisions Working group was also established to revise and refine the 2000 guidelines. At the time of writing this chapter, the GRI is in the process of developing an enhanced version of the guidelines which it has coined 'G3'; these guidelines are to be released in October 2006. The main improvements include: improved indicators, a complete set of technical protocols, a relevance test, report registration, tiered reporting levels, harmonization with other prominent guidelines, a special section for the financial sector, and a digital interface for communication of reports (GRI G3, 2005).

The GRI guidelines

The GRI guidelines are broadly aimed to assist organizations (regardless of size or industry, etc.) in reporting on the economic, social and environmental perspectives of their operations. The GRI guidelines are made up of three key components as shown in Table 4.1.

The GRI guidelines for reporting on sustainability are based on reporting principles of transparency, inclusiveness, auditability, completeness, relevance, sustainability context, accuracy, neutrality, comparability, clarity and timeliness. The contents of a typical report should address the areas of: vision and strategy, organizational profile, governance structure and management systems, GRI content index, and performance indicators (on the economic, social and environmental

Table 4.1 *Key components of the GRI guidelines*

The reporting guidelines	Technical protocols	Sector supplements
Applicable to all organizations and represent the core component of the GRI guidelines	Assist organizations in measuring their performance on sustainability-related issues, for instance, measuring water or energy usage	These are specific supplements available for certain sectors/industries

dimensions). It is important to note that like many other standards and guidelines on sustainability the GRI guidelines have no legal power and are voluntary. As a result the take-up rate of these guidelines is still very slow. For instance, there are a mere 74 organizations in the USA and 79 organizations in the UK that report using the GRI standards.[2]

Recently, the GRI has been invited by the International Standards Organization to collaborate in the process of developing a series of international standards on social responsibility, the 26000 series. The project commenced in 2004 and the standards are due to be released in 2008.

INTERNATIONAL STANDARDS ORGANIZATION (ISO)

Overview

The ISO is a non-governmental organization which comprises the national standards organizations, mainly private sector organizations, of 149 countries from both developing and developed countries. In the field of environmental management the ISO has been developing standards since 1996 when ISO 14001 – 'Environmental management systems: specification with guidelines for use' was released. At present, there are 15 ISO standards that have been released in the area of environmental management (ISO, 2002).

The 14000 series of standards

The 14000 series of ISO standards were identified as the most influential on business practice by executives from 107 multinational organizations in the 'Race to the top survey' conducted by the World Bank (World Bank Group, 2003). It is important to note that the ISO standards are procedural in their approach to environmental management and do not make in-principle statements on sustainability and sustainability reporting issues. Other tools such as the UN's Global Compact and the ILO core conventions could be used in conjunction with the procedural ISO standards in order for the reporting organization to view sustainability and sustainability reporting from a broader perspective considering the ideology behind sustainability and the key sustainability impacts of their business.

The ISO 14000 range of standards cover various aspects of environmental management. These are:

■ environmental management systems: ISO 14001, 14004;
■ environmental management: ISO 14015, 14031, 14050;
■ environmental management – lifecycle assessment: 14040–14043;
■ guidelines for environmental auditing: ISO 19011 (previously covered by ISO 14010, 14011, 14012);
■ environmental labels and declarations: ISO 14020, 14021, 14024, 14025 (ISO: Environmental Management, 2002).

In addition to these standards, the 'Technical Reports' provide guidance on: environmental performance evaluation (ISO/TR 14032), lifecycle assessment (ISO/TR 14047 and 14049), information that assists forestry organizations in using ISO 14001 and 14004, and product design/development and environmental management (ISO/TR 14062).

ISO's progress on sustainability reporting

At present there are no standards in relation to sustainability reporting in the ISO series of standards. However, ISO/WD 14063 is a working draft on environmental communication and deals with how organizations can communicate their performance in relation to environmental management. The ISO has also set up a working group to develop their 26000 series of standards on social responsibility.[3] The ISO's decision to develop a series of standards on social responsibility stems directly from the issues that emerged from the ISO conference on social responsibility held in Sweden in 2004. Despite there being a lack of standards on sustainability reporting at present, the environmental management standards do provide a platform from which sustainability issues can be further developed by organizations. For instance, the implementation of the ISO standards on environmental management might better facilitate the implementation of the GRI guidelines (or other such guidelines), and would provide a comprehensive framework for sustainable practice for organizations.

It is interesting to note that the three pillars of sustainable development: economic, social and environmental are mentioned prominently in the ISO's 'ISO in Brief' document. This document claims that the ISO standards 'make up a complete offering for all three dimensions of sustainable development – economic, environmental and social' (ISO in Brief, 2005, p. 2). This indicates that the issue of sustainability is clearly on the ISO's agenda, however much progress needs to be made in this area.

THE WORLD BUSINESS COUNCIL FOR SUSTAINABLE DEVELOPMENT (WBCSD)

Overview

Prior to the Rio Earth Summit of 1992, a team of CEOs from about 50 companies formed a fledgeling Business Council for Sustainable Development. The Council participated at Rio to provide a voice for business. This initial council had 50 members who were CEOs from many countries across the globe. This council decided to continue playing a role in the sustainability agenda and in 1995 merged with the World Industry Council for the Environment, to form the WBCSD. At present the WBCSD comprises 175 international companies from 35 countries. Their stated purpose is 'to provide business leadership as a catalyst for change toward sustainable development, and to promote the role of eco-efficiency, innovation and corporate social responsibility' (WBCSD *Annual Review*, 2004, p. 1).

The guidance provided by the council falls into the following categories: (1) accountability and reporting, (2) advocacy and communication, (3) capacity building, (4) energy and climate, (5) sustainable health systems, (6) sustainable livelihoods, and (7) water.

WBCSD guidelines

As part of their efforts to promote sustainability reporting, the WBCSD has published a document titled 'Sustainable development reporting: striking the balance' (WBCSD, 2002). This document deals with why sustainable development reporting is important to business and goes on to provide some guidance as to how these reports should be prepared. The document provides guidance on the following key areas as shown in Table 4.2.

As part of their WWW service, the WBCSD also provides a portal where organizations can display their sustainability reports for use as examples by other member organizations.[4] The WBCSD views sustainability reporting predominantly as a business tool for enhanced competitive position and as a risk-mitigating device. It does however urge businesses to 'walk the talk' (WBCSD, 2002, p. 1), nevertheless the WBCSD is a business-oriented organization and is primarily concerned with the bottom line effect of sustainability reporting to businesses.

Table 4.2 *Key areas of WBCSD guidance*

The importance and benefits of sustainability reporting	The WBCSD argues that the business case for sustainable development is a strong one, and that keeping ahead of sustainability reporting practice can be part of the organization's value-creation process for shareholders and stakeholders. Additionally, sustainability reporting, whilst still voluntary in most parts of the world, is a step forward for business and may form part of mandatory Corporations law in the near future, and it therefore encourages businesses to report on their sustainability activities.[a]
How to address stakeholder groups in a sustainability report	The WBCSD takes the view that not every stakeholder group can be addressed in one report. They urge the business to make choices about their target audience: 'Choosing the "right" audience brings clarity and focus to a report. It is thus up to each company to decide who is, or are, its primary target audience(s)' (WBCSD, 2002, p. 16).
How to address the financial community	In addressing the financial community, businesses need to show through their reports how their sustainability activities/initiatives lead to an improved bottom line. The document also discusses the need for greater standardization in the way that rating agencies assess businesses on their sustainability reporting.
Developing a framework for sustainability reporting	The ideal properties of a framework for sustainability reporting are discussed in this section along with dilemmas that businesses face when developing a sustainability report. These dilemmas range from the meaning of sustainability to the subjectivity of information presented in sustainability reports. These dilemmas present challenges for policy makers as well as businesses that report on their sustainability activities.
Specific guidance on sustainability reporting includes	Defining the reporting objectives, Planning the report, Constructing the report, Distributing the report, Collecting and analysing feedback.

Note: [a] This seems to suggest that the WBCSD is in favour of self-regulation rather than legislation. Furthermore, it appears that the WBCSD is suggesting that by reporting on sustainability issues, organizations can perhaps forestall legislation on sustainability reporting.

ACCOUNTABILITY: INSTITUTE OF SOCIAL AND ETHICAL ACCOUNTABILITY (AA1000)

Overview

The AA1000 standard was developed by AccountAbility in the UK in 1999 in response to the need for greater clarity on issues of social and ethical accountability and reporting. The AA1000 framework was designed to (1) link together other specialized standards covering aspects of sustainability reporting such as the GRI guidelines, Social Accountability International (SA 8000) standards and the ISO standards through a 'common currency of principles and processes' (AA1000, 1999, p. 1), and (2) to serve as a stand-alone framework for dealing with accountability-related issues. The framework itself consists of the standard, supporting guidelines and professional qualification guidelines.

The basic premise of AA1000 is that through the process of social and ethical accounting, auditing and reporting, an organization should be able to improve its long-term financial prospects and viability (AA1000, 1999). The AA1000 standard encourages adopting organizations to build social and ethical accounting, auditing and reporting into their strategic planning process and ultimately their operations. The AA1000 standard can be used to improve accountability and performance on dimensions such as measurement of key performance indicators, quality management, improved employee loyalty, external stakeholder engagement, improved supply chain relationships, risk management, investor relations, governance, and relations with regulators.

The AA1000 principles and process standard

The AA1000 standard is comprised of a set of principles as well as process standards. Each will be examined below.

Principles of the AA1000 framework: The AA1000 principle has been influenced by the principles of financial accounting. The principle of accountability is the overarching principle which an organization must incorporate into its social and ethical accounting, auditing and reporting processes. Accountability includes transparency, responsiveness and compliance with legal requirements and policies. A key addition to financial accounting principles is the principle of inclusivity, the requirement to reflect the needs and concerns of stakeholders, including 'voiceless' stakeholders in all stages of the social and ethical accounting, auditing and reporting process. The other principles of the AA1000 standard that flow from inclusivity are:

1   *Completeness, materiality, regularity and timeliness*: these assist in evaluating the nature and scope of an organization's social and ethical accounting, auditing and reporting.
2   *Quality assurance, accessibility and information quality*: these principles assist in assessing the meaningfulness of information reported by an organization.
3   *The principles of embeddedness and continuous improvement*: these principles assist in evaluating the management of process on an ongoing basis.

Process standards: the process of social and ethical accounting, auditing, and reporting is based on five processes or stages in the AA1000 model (see Table 4.3).

It is important to note that 'AA1000 is a process standard, not a substantive performance standard. That is, it specifies the processes that an organisation should

Table 4.3 *The five stages in the AA1000 model*

Planning	Where an organization commits to the process and sets the scene by defining objectives.
Accounting	The scope of the process is defined and refined, performance targets are developed and set.
Auditing and reporting	A report on the organization's accountability performance is developed, externally audited and made available to stakeholder groups.
Embedding	Throughout this process systems and structures of accountability are created within the organization and are incorporated into its operations.

Underlying all of the above processes is stakeholder engagement; it drives the decisions made during the course of the four processes shown above.

follow to account for its performance, and not the levels of performance the organisation should achieve' (AA1000, 1999, p. 11). This focus is based on the premise that unless, for example, corporate values are embedded, and unless governance systems, data-collection systems, stakeholder-engagement methods and audit processes are sound, reporting is unlikely to be representative of performance or reflect stakeholder information needs. AA1000 provides little guidance on *what* should be reported, contrasting the approach taken in the GRI guidelines which focus more on report content than reporting processes.

SUSTAINABILITY INTEGRATED GUIDELINES FOR MANAGEMENT (SIGMA) PROJECT

Overview

The SIGMA project was developed to provide practical guidelines to businesses on sustainability issues. It was formed in 1999 by the British Standards Organization, Forum for the Future and AccountAbility, with the support of the UK Department of Trade and Industry (SIGMA Guidelines, 1999). This project had the objective of developing guidelines for business which were practical, flexible and able to be integrated with existing frameworks such as the ISO standards and AA1000, etc. The main purpose of the SIGMA project is to help businesses 'effectively meet challenges posed by social, environmental and economic dilemmas, threats and opportunities, and become architects of a more sustainable future' (SIGMA Guidelines, 1999, p. 8).

The three elements of the SIGMA guidelines

SIGMA guidelines are made up of three elements, the guiding principles, the management framework and the SIGMA toolkit. The guiding principles are built around two dimensions: (1) the holistic management of the five types of capital: human, manufactured, financial, social and natural, and (2) the inclusion of accountability into the organization's mentality, especially in dealing with stakeholders. To elaborate, natural capital is seen as sustaining the other four types of capital, as life itself is sustained by the natural environment and ecosystems. Human, social, financial and manufactured capital must all be effectively managed bearing in mind the impact they have on the natural environment, and the interdependencies between them. No one form of capital may be compromised in favour of another. Overarching these types of capital is the notion of accountability, that is, in managing these five types of capital, organizations must be transparent and should engage with their stakeholders and deal with their views and concerns.

The management framework consists of four distinct phases which are designed to help an organization implement sustainability-related issues into the organization's operations. The four phases are shown in Table 4.4.

Finally, the SIGMA toolkit provides useful information on how to implement the four management framework phases: for instance, it includes a business case tool, performance review tool, etc. The SIGMA guidelines therefore provide a comprehensive framework for dealing with sustainability issues in general, not just sustainability reporting.

Table 4.4 *The four phases of the SIGMA management framework*

Leadership and vision	The actions needed in this stage include, building a business case for implementing sustainable practices, gaining top management's commitment, developing a vision, mission and operating principles, communicating the importance of sustainability issues to organizational members and building a receptive organizational culture.
Planning	The actions needed in this stage include, determining the current sustainability status of the organization, identifying key sustainability issues, developing strategic plans in line with the visions, mission and key issues that are identified, consultation with stakeholders and formulation of short-term action plans with clear objectives and targets for performance.
Delivery	Issues to consider here include, change management and setting up systems of internal control to ensure that the plans in the first two phases are being implemented.
Monitor, review and report	Actions that need to be taken include, reviewing performance against standards, providing assurance in relation to the sustainability processes of the organization and communicating the performance on sustainability issues to stakeholders via sustainability reports.

COMPARISON OF THE FIVE BODIES PROMOTING SUSTAINABILITY REPORTING

Table 4.5 summarizes the differences between the five bodies that have been discussed above. Whilst these organizations are all independent, their guidelines/ standards are designed to meet the needs of different stakeholder groups, and this is driven predominantly by their governance structure. For instance, the WBCSD is a conglomerate of businesses and thus its guidelines are aimed at assisting businesses stay out of the public eye and to influence potential legislation. Not surprisingly, the WBCSD dedicates an entire section of its guidelines to assist organizations in catering for the needs of the financial sector. Furthermore, the WBCSD guidelines clearly state that all stakeholder needs cannot be dealt with in a report and that choices should be made by the reporting organization in relation to which stakeholder groups its report will address. Thus, one could argue that the WBCSD guidelines are designed by business for businesses. Some would argue that the AccountAbility and SIGMA standards also fall into the category of business-oriented standards, although they are multi-stakeholder organizations with NGO as well as business involvement.

The GRI and ISO standards do not appear to advocate the use of sustainability reporting by businesses solely for their own benefit. Whilst the business case for sustainability is a necessary precursor to the broad adoption of sustainability reporting, it should not dominate the sustainability agenda to the extent where it serves to benefit some sections of society at the expense of other less influential sections. However, whilst the standards/guidelines presented above assist organizations in setting up systems to collect and report on sustainability issues, organizations can use their discretion to decide what gets reported.

OTHER BODIES

Thus far the bodies discussed have been international bodies that have developed specific guidelines in relation to sustainability reporting. In addition to these, there are a number of other initiatives, some of which provide general guidance on sustainability issues and others which provide specific guidance, but on a national level. Given the important role of collecting and reporting data in the identification of issues on which sustainability performance needs to be improved and in monitoring performance on these issues, some of these important initiatives are discussed here.

United Nations: Global Compact

The Global Compact, for instance, is part of the United Nations Environment Programme (UNEP), which provides general guidance on sustainability issues

Table 4.5 *Comparing the guidance provided by various bodies*

Organization/ body	Governance	Voluntary/legal requirement	Main focus of guidance
GRI	Independent body, controlled by the board of directors elected through a stakeholder council.	Voluntary	The primary focus is on providing guidance on content of sustainability reports. Also provides principles that assist in preparing sustainability reports.
ISO	Independent body, comprising of national standards organizations.	Voluntary	Procedural standards. Main focus is on processes of environmental management. Do not currently provide guidance on what to report or how to report.
WBCSD	Coalition of 175 international companies.	Voluntary	Provides guidance on how sustainability reporting and development could be used to improve economic, social and environmental performance of organizations.
AccountAbility	The council is comprised of members from business, non-profit organizations, consultancies, and the research community.	Voluntary	Focuses on the process of social and ethical accountability, auditing and reporting. The inclusion of stakeholders in that process is central to AA1000.
SIGMA	Steering committee members come from business, government, professional bodies and civil organizations.	Voluntary	Provides guidance on incorporating accountability into organizations via their management framework.

Sources: GRI Guidelines (2002); ISO: Environmental Management (2002); WBCSD (2002); SIGMA Project (1999); AA1000 (1999)

through its ten principles model. The principles of the Global Compact broadly address the issues of; human rights, labour standards, the environment and anti-corruption. Organizations that commit to the Global Compact are expected to report their progress on an annual basis.

Business in the Community (UK)

Business in the Community (BITC) is a UK-based organization which provides advisory services to organizations that wish to incorporate social and environmental responsibility into their operations. BITC's purpose is to assist 'businesses improve their positive impact on society' (www.bitc.org.uk). BITC also rates organizations on their social and environmental activities and publishes a corporate responsibility index annually. Whilst this organization does not provide specific guidance on sustainability reporting, it does provide advice to organizations in relation to sustainability issues which may be subsequently used in preparing sustainability reports. BITC's advisory services include advice on incorporating responsible business practices into business operations, and advice on specific areas of corporate responsibility such as: community, environment, workplace and marketplace issues.

Canadian and Australian initiatives

Other initiatives worthy of note on a national level include the two Canadian sustainability reporting initiatives, the Sustainability Report, and the Sustainability Reporting Toolkit and the Australian government's Corporate Sustainability Reporting Toolkit. The Sustainability Report (a Canadian, non-partisan, not-for-profit organization) reports on the progress of the Canadian sustainability agenda, by publishing the reports of Canadian corporations on their website (www.sustreport.org). This programme therefore provides a channel through which the sustainability reports of organizations can be disseminated. The Sustainability Reporting Toolkit provides Canadian organizations with specific guidance on producing sustainability reports. The toolkit was developed in response to the need of businesses to have specific guidance in developing reports; this initiative was undertaken by the Canadian Federal government and Stratos Incorporated. The Australian government has also provided similar tools for sustainability reporting. These general guidelines were developed by the Australian Department of the Environment and Heritage, and encourage corporations to report on the impact of their operations on the environment and society.

SUMMARY

It is evident that there are a number of guidelines and initiatives that are available for businesses to choose from. The various guidelines differ in:

■   the extent to which they are concerned with the sustainability of communities and the environment and the sustainability of individual businesses;

■ the extent to which they focus on reporting principles versus organizational processes versus report content; and

■ the particular aspects of sustainability reporting that they address.

Where guidelines focus on the needs of business and the benefits to business of reporting, the result may be reports which don't demonstrate accountability for material social and environmental impacts of concern to key stakeholder groups. This would undermine trust between the organization and its stakeholders which ultimately may be detrimental to reporting organizations.

A concern with guidelines which prescribe report content at the expense of concern with a process which includes stakeholders, is that there is no guarantee that reports will be complete. It is possible that a key sustainability issue for a particular company or industry is not addressed in a general guideline specifying report content (see Adams, 2004). A robust stakeholder dialogue and reporting process would identify such omissions, but without them reporting guidelines may be used as a legitimating exercise by organizations that report the minimum required in such guidelines but omit material impacts not specifically covered by them.

Until it is widely accepted that corporations should be accountable for their sustainability impacts and that they have a role in minimizing negative and achieving positive impacts, and until this is reflected in and facilitated by corporate govern-ance structures, it is unlikely that there will be convergence between sustainability reporting guidelines. Whilst there has already been some convergence in terms of incorporating both reporting process and outcome elements, as evidenced by developments in the GRI guidelines, tensions between serving the short-term financial interests of shareholders and longer-term interests of other stakeholder groups will remain.

It is unlikely that any of the guidelines mentioned will address all of an organiza-tion's perceived needs. Organizations will consider the needs of their own indi-vidual business and its stakeholders and turn to other sources to guide them in developing their reporting. These will include: the criteria for sustainability report-ing awards schemes and corporate social responsibility indices; the reports of competitors and 'best practice' reporters; and industry association guidelines developed for their particular industry. Despite evidence that corporate social responsibility pays off in bottom line benefits (see Margolis and Walsh, 2004; Orlitzky *et al.*, 2003), without mandatory reporting guidelines focusing on processes of reporting and governance structures, some companies will continue to produce reports which leave out impacts which are material to key stakeholder groups (see Adams, 2004).

NOTES

1   The area of standardization of sustainability reporting is rapidly evolving. This chapter was completed in August 2006 and its contents, therefore, describe the situation at this point in time. In addition, all website references were correct as of that date.

2   Refer to the GRI website for details on reporting organizations in other countries at http://www.globalreporting.org/workgroup/regional.asp.

3   The process of developing the 26000 series of standards is a collaborative effort involving several organizations with expertise in social responsibility. As previously mentioned the GRI is part of this working group. For details on the progress of the 26000 series of standards visit http://www.iso.org/iso/en/info/Conferences/SRConference/communique.htm.

4   The WBCSD's website is www.wbcsd.ch.

REFERENCES

AccountAbility (AA1000) (1999) *AccountAbility 1000: The foundation standard – an overview.* London.

Adams, C. A. (2004) The ethical, social and environmental reporting-performance portrayal gap. *Accounting, Auditing and Accountability Journal,* 17(5): 731–57.

Adams, C. A. and Zutshi, A. (2004) Corporate social responsibility: Why business should act responsibly and be accountable. *Australian Accounting Review,* 14(3): 31–9.

Bebbington, J. (1997) Engagement, education and sustainability: A review essay on environmental accounting. *Accounting, Auditing and Accountability Journal,* 10(3): 365–81.

Bebbington, J. (2001) Sustainable development: A review of the international development, business and accounting literature. *Accounting Forum,* 25(2): 128–57.

Global Reporting Initiative (GRI) (2002) *Sustainability reporting guidelines.* Amsterdam.

Global Reporting Initiative (GRI) (2005) *GRI G3 development work in progress, edition 1.* Amsterdam.

Hardjono, T. and de Klein, P. (2004) Introduction on the European Corporate Sustainability Framework (ECSF). *Journal of Business Ethics,* 55: 99–113.

ISO in Brief (2005) *International standards for a sustainable world.* Geneva.

ISO (2002) *Environmental management: The ISO 14000 family of international standards.* Geneva.

KPMG (2005) *International survey of corporate responsibility reporting*. Amsterdam: KPMG Global Sustainability Services.

Margolis, J. D. and Walsh, J. P. (2004) Misery loves companies: Rethinking social initiatives by business. *Administrative Science Quarterly*, 48: 268–305.

Orlitzky, M., Schmidt, F. L. and Rynes, S. L. (2003) Corporate social and financial performance: A meta-analysis. *Organizational Studies*, 24: 403–41.

SIGMA Project (1999) *The SIGMA guidelines: Putting sustainable development into practice – a guide for organizations*. London.

Simms, J. (2002) Business: corporate social responsibility: You know it makes sense. *Accountancy*, 130(1311): 48–50.

Stickings, B. (2001) 'Sustainable development and innovation', Clinical Industries Association, lecture at the Royal Society of Edinburgh, 13 September.

United Nations World Commission on Environment and Development (UNWCED) (1987) *Our common future, the Brundtland Report*. Oxford: Oxford University Press.

World Bank Group (2003) *Race to the top: Attracting and enabling global sustainability business: Business survey report*. Corporate Social Responsibility Practice.

World Business Council for Sustainable Development (2002) *Sustainable development reporting: Striking the balance*. Geneva.

World Business Council for Sustainable Development (2004) *Annual Review: A decade of action and learning*. Geneva.

Websites

AccountAbility: http://www.accountability.org.uk

Australian Department of the Environment and Heritage: http://www.deh.gov.au

Business in the Community:http://www.bitc.org.uk

Ceres: http://www.ceres.org

GRI: http://www.globalreporting.org

ISO's series on environmental management: http://www.iso.org/iso/en/prods-services/otherpubs/iso14000/index.html

Sustainability Reporting Toolkit (Canadian Initiative): http://www.sustainabilityreporting.ca

The Sustainability Report (Canadian Initiative): http://www.sustreport.org

United Nations – Global Compact: http://www.unglobalcompact.org

WBCSD: http://www.wbcsd.ch

Chapter 5

Stakeholder engagement and dialogue

Jeffrey Unerman

A key point identified by the judges for the 2003 *ACCA UK* [Sustainability Reporting] Awards was the poor quality of stakeholder identification and involvement in the submitted reports. Beyond this, stakeholder engagement as an overall activity and more specifically as part of the reporting process is becoming increasingly high on the agenda in both the public and private sectors. It is therefore more important than ever before for such processes to demonstrate a clear rationale, transparency, and impact.

(ACCA, 2005)

The above quotation encapsulates the key issues which are addressed in this chapter. It indicates that engagement and dialogue with stakeholders are increasingly recognized as crucial elements of sustainability reporting, while conceding that there is a shortage of evidence within social and environmental reports that such engagement and dialogue is actually taking place. In addressing these important issues, the aims of this chapter are to:

- explain why engagement and dialogue with a range of stakeholders are crucial elements of sustainability reporting;
- examine various theoretical perspectives regarding the prioritization of different stakeholders' needs and expectations, as identified through stakeholder dialogue, in the social and environmental reporting process;
- evaluate some of the key difficulties faced when an organization seeks to engage a broad range of stakeholders in the determination and discharge of the organization's social and environmental responsibilities, and the duties of accountability allied to these responsibilities;
- identify some of the stakeholder engagement and dialogue processes employed in practice by organizations.

But before addressing these issues, it will be helpful to define what is meant by the terms *stakeholder engagement and dialogue*. Thomson and Bebbington (2005, p. 517) provide a useful definition when they state that:

> [s]takeholders are involved [in the social and environmental reporting process] in a number of different ways including, identifying what issues are important to report on, how well the company has performed on specific issues and how to communicate this performance . . . Stakeholder engagement describes a range of practices where organisations take a structured approach to consulting with potential stakeholders. There are a number of possible practices which achieve this aim including: internet bulletin boards, questionnaire surveys mailed to stakeholders, phone surveys, and community based and/or open meetings designed to bring stakeholders and organisational representatives together.

A further perspective on the role of stakeholder engagement and dialogue is provided through the Institute of Social and Ethical AccountAbility's framework, AA1000. Within this framework, dialogue between a company and its stakeholders is one of the central principles of 'good' accountability practices:

> [l]aunched in 1999, the AA1000 framework is designed to improve accountability and performance by **learning through stakeholder engagement**.
>
> It was developed to address the need for organisations to integrate their stakeholder engagement processes into daily activities. It has been used worldwide by leading businesses, non-profit organisations and public bodies.
>
> The Framework helps users to establish a systematic stakeholder engagement process that generates the **indicators, targets, and reporting systems** needed to ensure its effectiveness in overall organisational performance.
>
> (ISEA, 2005, emphasis in original)

This importance of stakeholder engagement was further emphasized by the Institute of Social and Ethical Accountability when it published a draft standard on stakeholder engagement in September 2005 (AccountAbility, 2005). This draft (p. 9) states that:

> [T]he overall purpose of stakeholder engagement is to drive strategic direction and operational excellence for organisations, and to contribute to the kind of sustainable development from which organisations, their stakeholders and wider society can benefit by:

Learning:

- Identifying and understanding
  - the needs, expectations and perceptions of internal and external stakeholders;
  - the challenges and opportunities identified by those stakeholders; and,
  - the material issues of internal and external stakeholders.

Innovating:

- Drawing on stakeholder knowledge and insights to inform strategic direction and drive operational excellence.
- Aligning operations with the needs of sustainable development and with societal expectations.

Performing:

- Enhancing performance.
- Developing and implementing performance indicators that enable internal and external stakeholders to assess the organisation's performance.

Having provided a broad overview of the meaning and importance of stakeholder engagement and dialogue, this chapter will now proceed to examine why these processes are central to social and environmental reporting.

THE CORE ROLE OF STAKEHOLDER ENGAGEMENT AND DIALOGUE

To understand why stakeholder engagement and dialogue are crucial elements of social and environmental reporting, it is necessary to place these elements within the context of the overall social and environmental reporting process. Several commentators have characterized social and environmental reporting as a hierarchical staged process, whereby the decisions taken at each stage in the hierarchy determine the issues to be considered and decided in the subsequent stages.

For example, Deegan and Unerman (2006, Chapter 9) and O'Dwyer *et al.* (2005b) argue that there are four broad hierarchical stages involved in the social and environmental reporting process. Deegan and Unerman (2006, pp. 311–13) label these as the *'why – who – for what – how'* stages, which are shown in Figure 5.1. The *why* stage involves determining an organization's philosophical motivations, or objectives, for engaging in social and environmental reporting – which are likely to be closely aligned to that organization's motives for adopting (or refusing to adopt) corporate social responsibility (CSR) policies and practices. The *who* stage identifies the stakeholders to whom an organization considers itself responsible and account-

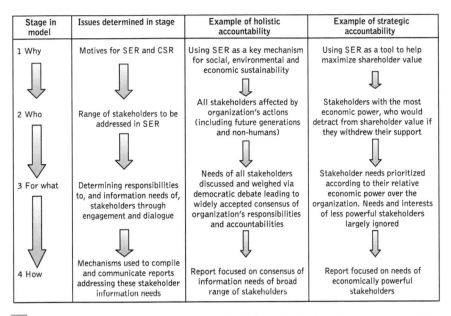

Stage in model	Issues determined in stage	Example of holistic accountability	Example of strategic accountability
1 Why	Motives for SER and CSR	Using SER as a key mechanism for social, environmental and economic sustainability	Using SER as a tool to help maximize shareholder value
2 Who	Range of stakeholders to be addressed in SER	All stakeholders affected by organization's actions (including future generations and non-humans)	Stakeholders with the most economic power, who would detract from shareholder value if they withdrew their support
3 For what	Determining responsibilities to, and information needs of, stakeholders through engagement and dialogue	Needs of all stakeholders discussed and weighed via democratic debate leading to widely accepted consensus of organization's responsibilities and accountabilities	Stakeholder needs prioritized according to their relative economic power over the organization. Needs and interests of less powerful stakeholders largely ignored
4 How	Mechanisms used to compile and communicate reports addressing these stakeholder information needs	Report focused on consensus of information needs of broad range of stakeholders	Report focused on needs of economically powerful stakeholders

Figure 5.1 *A staged hierarchical model of the social and environmental reporting (SER) process.*

able if it is to achieve its philosophical objectives for engaging in social and environmental reporting. The *for what* stage is the stakeholder engagement and dialogue stage (and the main focus of this chapter), where the social, environmental, ethical and economic expectations of these stakeholders are identified and prioritized. The *how* stage comprises the mechanisms and reports which the organization employs to address these stakeholder expectations.

Although the focus of this chapter is stage 3 from this model, decisions taken at stages 1 and 2 will clearly shape the stakeholder dialogue and engagement processes employed by any organization. The relevant aspects of these stages are explored in a little more depth below, before focusing on stage 3.

Stage 1: understanding organizational motives for stakeholder engagement and dialogue

While there may be a combination of different motives driving any organization's social and environmental reporting and CSR in practice, the academic literature examining these motives can be very broadly divided into two perspectives (which may be viewed as two opposite ends of a continuum). One of these perspectives regards social and environmental reporting and CSR as processes which should be aimed at transforming business practices so they become socially and environmentally sustainable. Proponents of this holistic perspective often argue that a continual drive for short-term economic sustainability (in the form of maintenance or growth in financial profits) is incompatible in practice with social and environmental sustainability, as the generation of financial profits is almost always accompanied by direct and/or indirect negative social and environmental impacts (Bebbington, 2001; Gray, 2006; Gray and Bebbington, 2000; Meadows *et al.*, 2004). From this perspective, therefore, *social and environmental reporting* can only be regarded as *sustainability reporting* if it is structured in such a manner as to help in holding the organization (or its managers) truly responsible and accountable for all of their social and environmental impacts on all stakeholders – not just for those impacts or activities prioritized by the organization's managers (Bebbington, 2001; Bebbington and Gray, 2001).

The other broad perspective regards social and environmental reporting as a tool used by managers to win or retain the support of those stakeholders who have power to influence the achievement of an organization's goals (usually maximization of profit). Various theoretical perspectives (discussed in other chapters of this book) highlight how social and environmental reports can be used strategically almost as a marketing tool, aimed at aligning perceptions of an organization's social and environmental policies and practices with the ethical values of its economically powerful stakeholders (see, for example, Bailey *et al.*, 2000; Deegan, 2002; Neu *et al.*, 1998; O'Dwyer, 2002, 2003). In this context CSR is often portrayed in terms of a 'win–win' practice, whereby organizational actions which apparently reduce the negative (or increase the positive) impacts of an organization's activities on society and/or the environment also help to increase that organization's profits (Norris and O'Dwyer, 2004; O'Dwyer, 2002, 2003; Thomson and Bebbington, 2005). However, the rarely declared corollary to this argument is that any reductions in negative social and/or environmental impacts on some stakeholders which would also result in a negative economic impact (for example reduced overall short- or medium-term profits) will not be undertaken. Thus, increased profit may be regarded as the prime motive underlying CSR and social and environmental reporting within this 'win–win' perspective, which has little to do with moving the organization towards a position where it is socially, environmentally and economically sustainable (if such a position could ever exist in practice) and accountable to a broad range of stakeholders. Spence (2005) argues that the 'win–win' business case has achieved such a dominant position in business thinking and in discourse about CSR, that it effectively suppresses many arguments which may highlight the social and environmental damage caused by many business activities, thus facilitating the continued unsustainability of business. For these reasons, social and environmental reporting strategically driven by a profit-oriented, economic, motive will not be referred to as *sustainability reporting* in this chapter, but will be simply referred to as *social and environmental reporting*.

Stage 2: linking stakeholder identification to motives for reporting

Having determined the broad philosophical motives or objectives underpinning why an organization wishes to produce a sustainability report, the next stage in the social and environmental reporting process involves identifying *to whom* the organization needs to report if it is to achieve these philosophical objectives. This identification of stakeholders has to take place after the philosophical motives for engaging in CSR and social and environmental reporting have been determined, because the range of stakeholders to be taken into consideration by any organization will be directly dependent upon its motives for engaging in CSR and social and environmental reporting. For example, an organization whose managers undertake CSR and social and environmental reporting because they believe it will maximize shareholder value will tend to focus only on those stakeholders who are able to exert the greatest economic influence on the organization's operations (Bailey *et al.*, 2000; Freeman, 1984; Freidman and Miles, 2002; Neu *et al.*, 1998; O'Dwyer, 2005b; Unerman and Bennett, 2004). Conversely, managers whose motives for engaging in CSR and sustainability reporting are grounded in a broader moral philosophy, of being responsible, responsive and accountable to all those upon whom their organization's activities might impact, are likely to be concerned with the whole of this broader range of stakeholders – rather than a narrower group of stakeholders whose needs are prioritized simply because the stakeholders' actions can impact upon the organization (Deegan and Unerman, 2006; Gray *et al.*, 1997; O'Dwyer, 2005b; Unerman and O'Dwyer, 2006).

Moving from stakeholder identification to stakeholder engagement and dialogue

Once the stakeholders who are the audience for an organization's social and environmental reporting have been identified, the third broad stage in the social and environmental reporting process is, according to Deegan and Unerman (2006), to identify the social, environmental and economic expectations of these stakeholders. This stage is crucial because these expectations will indicate both what behaviour these stakeholders require and consider acceptable from the organization, and the information needed by these stakeholders to enable them to judge the organization's performance in relation to these expectations.

Only once an organization knows *for what* issues its identified stakeholders regard it as being responsible and accountable can it then begin to produce a social and environmental report which addresses these specific issues. In other words, an organization cannot determine *how* to compile an effective social and environmental report – for example, to decide upon which issues to address in the report – until it has identified its stakeholders' information needs and expectations, because without this identification of stakeholders' information needs and expectations any resultant social and environmental report will be providing information which is not targeted at any particular purpose. Without appropriate targeting of the information, its purpose and impact is questionable (AccountAbility, 2005).

In such circumstances, only by luck will a social and environmental report be effective in addressing the information needs of, or discharging any duties of accountability which the organization has to, its identified stakeholders. Consequently it will be an ineffective mechanism for systematically holding the organization, and its managers, accountable for the social, environmental and economic impacts which the organization's actions may have upon its identified stakeholders. This is why stakeholder engagement and dialogue is a crucial element of social and environmental reporting (O'Dwyer, 2005b; Owen *et al.*, 2001; Owen *et al.*, 2000; Thomson and Bebbington, 2005).

Having established the importance of stakeholder engagement and dialogue to social and environmental reporting, we can now address some of the key issues and difficulties involved in the implementation of stakeholder engagement and dialogue processes.

KEY ISSUES AND DIFFICULTIES IN STAKEHOLDER ENGAGEMENT AND DIALOGUE

Identifying the range of stakeholders to be considered

The first key issue which needs to be addressed in the implementation of any stakeholder engagement and dialogue process is the identification of stakeholders with whom the organization seeks to communicate. As indicated in the previous section, the range of stakeholders whose views are considered in any organization's stakeholder engagement and dialogue processes will be dependent upon the organization's (or its managers') motives for engaging in CSR and social and environmental reporting.

For an organization using social and environmental reporting strategically to help maximize shareholder value, those stakeholders with the most economic power will usually be significant in the organization's day-to-day operations. They will consequently be readily identifiable by the organization and may also be readily accessible through communication media prevalent in the areas where the organization operates. For example, a multinational corporation with a head office in a Western nation and whose products are sold primarily in Western nations may find that most of its economically powerful stakeholders are also based in Western nations. A multinational such as this can use a range of interactive communication media prevalent in Western nations (such as the internet, focus groups, opinion research) to engage in dialogue with, and to help identify, its economically powerful Western stakeholders' social, environmental and economic expectations (Swift *et al.*, 2001).

Conversely, where the motives of an organization's managers for engaging in CSR and sustainability reporting are based on a more holistic concern to be responsible and accountable for their impact on all those upon whom they have an impact, the process of identifying and engaging in dialogue with this broad range of stakeholders is likely to be much more problematic for several reasons.

Impossibility of direct dialogue and engagement with some stakeholders

Firstly, as organizational actions which take place today can, in many instances, have long-term impacts on nature and society, stakeholders affected by an organization's operations are likely to include future generations (World Commission on Environment and Development, 1987). It is difficult to conceive how an organization can engage stakeholders from future generations in dialogue today regarding current organizational responsibilities and accountabilities. Certain groups of contemporary stakeholders (such as some non-governmental organizations) might position themselves as guardians of specific interests of future generations, but engaging in dialogue with such 'proxy' stakeholder groups involves a vicarious representation of the interests of future generations which may be different from the actual interests yet to be judged by the future generations themselves (Unerman and O'Dwyer, 2006).[1]

Similar issues arise when recognizing that an organization's actions might impact on a range of non-human stakeholders today such as fauna other than humans (Singer, 1993) or, more broadly, the ecosystem (Gray, 2006; Meadows *et al.*, 2004), and/or on some human stakeholders who are less able to articulate their own concerns and interests (for example, infants or the mentally impaired).

Addressing heterogeneous stakeholder views and expectations

Secondly, even if all stakeholders who are affected (or likely to be affected) by an organization's actions were in a position to articulate their own interests, the needs and expectations of different stakeholders are often likely to be mutually exclusive (Lehman, 1995; Neu *et al.*, 1998; Unerman and Bennett, 2004). Faced with a range of mutually exclusive demands from different stakeholders, managers need a mechanism to determine which social, environmental and economic needs and expectations they will seek to address in their CSR and social and environmental reporting.

For managers of organizations strategically motivated to engage in CSR and social and environmental reporting by a belief that these processes will enhance shareholder value, choosing between mutually exclusive stakeholder demands is likely to be fairly straightforward – as they will simply prioritize the demands of those stakeholders with the most economic power over the organization (Adams,

2002; Bailey *et al.*, 2000; Boyce, 2000; Buhr, 2002; Mouck, 1995; O'Dwyer, 2003). Furthermore, in situations where many of the economically powerful stakeholders of a multinational corporation are likely to share a broadly similar cultural background (because for example they are mostly from the more wealthy sections of Western nations), it may be expected that these stakeholders' broad social, environmental and economic expectations will often be similar if, as argued by some, these expectations are largely dependent upon shared cultural and social backgrounds (Lewis and Unerman, 1999). In such situations, it may be expected that multinationals whose managers regard themselves as responsible and account-able solely to those stakeholders with the most economic power over their organization will face a largely homogenous set of broad social, environmental and economic expectations and demands from their selected (often relatively wealthy, predominantly Western) stakeholders.

However, managers who are motivated to engage in CSR and sustainability reporting by a desire to minimize the negative social, environmental and economic impacts of their organization's operations on all those stakeholders who are affected by these operations will face greater problems in identifying a single set of stake-holder expectations from a wide range of often mutually exclusive expectations (Thomson and Bebbington, 2005; Unerman and Bennett, 2004).

Prioritizing stakeholder needs on the basis of maximum negative consequences

One way to identify a single set of expectations would be to prioritize the needs and expectations of those stakeholders upon whose lives the organization's operations have (or are likely to have) the greatest negative impact. But there are several problems with this method of prioritizing stakeholder needs. Firstly, it risks ignor-ing the views of some stakeholders upon whose lives the organization's operations cause a substantial negative impact in situations where there are other stakeholders whose lives are impacted to a much greater negative extent by the organization's operations. Secondly, it assumes that the negative impacts caused by an organiza-tion's operations on each stakeholder can be assessed with a reasonable degree of certainty. And thirdly, it presupposes that it is possible to objectively rank the negative impacts suffered by different stakeholders in order to determine which stakeholder suffers the most from the organization's operations. In practice, any ranking of this nature is likely to be based (at least in part) on the subjective perceptions of the person observing the outcome of the organization's actions, and two observers with slight differences between their respective value systems may place different weightings on different outcomes, thereby resulting in different rankings of the significance of perceived negative outcomes suffered by different stakeholders.[2]

Negotiating a consensus among mutually exclusive stakeholder views through discourse ethics

An alternative method of seeking to arrive at a single set of stakeholder expectations from among mutually exclusive competing stakeholder claims and expectations, while still prioritizing the needs of those who are the most negatively affected by an organization's operations, has been advocated by Unerman and Bennett (2004). This method is based on the discourse ethics of Jürgen Habermas (1992), which provide a theoretical model for arriving at a consensus view of moral standards and values within a society through the use of discourse mechanisms (see, also, Alexy, 1978).

In summary, these discourse ethics mechanisms rely upon two key philosophical propositions. The first of these is derived from Immanuel Kant's (1949) eighteenth-century philosophical proposition of the Categorical Imperative (which has influenced numerous philosophers since Kant), and judges the validity of any moral proposition by the willingness of the person proposing this moral value to accept its validity in all possible situations. In other words, a judgement on the morality of a particular act can only be considered to have force if the person proposing this moral value would make the same moral judgement no matter in what position they found themselves in relation to the act whose morality was being evaluated. Thus, for example, if a wealthy member of a society who owned shares in many companies but was not reliant on paid work maintained that voluntary corporate initiatives to protect the health and safety of employees were immoral, this moral position would only be considered valid if this person would hold the same view if they found themselves stripped of their wealth (and investment income) and were then in the position of an impoverished worker who relied upon income from employment – and had no choice regarding whether to accept unsafe working conditions. Put another way, actions which are considered acceptable to someone with power, wealth and privilege would only be considered morally acceptable if that person would consider these actions to be equally morally acceptable if they lost their power and wealth, and were looking at (and experiencing) the outcomes of these actions from the position of the least privileged members of society (Lehman, 1995; Rawls, 1971).

The second key mechanism within Habermas' framework required to arrive at a universally acceptable and accepted consensus regarding the morality of behaviour is that each person's moral values and arguments should be tested and evaluated through debate with others who may hold alternative views. Habermas argues that the process in the first key stage (of judging the moral acceptability of actions by putting oneself in the position of others affected by the actions) is insufficient alone to arrive at a universally accepted consensus, because each person is likely to have a different conception of the possible outcomes of particular actions on a range of different stakeholders, and is likely to weight the significance of these outcomes

95

differently. Only through the process of a democratic debate, where each person is free to articulate their own views regarding how particular acts are likely to impact upon them, and are free to challenge the views and arguments proposed by others, does Habermas believe that a universally (intersubjectively) accepted and acceptable moral consensus will be arrived at. But for this process to work, it is important that specific protocols of debate are observed so that the force of the better argument is recognized and accepted by all. The rules of debate proposed by Habermas to ensure that the debate produces and recognizes the 'best' arguments are termed an *ideal speech situation* and, in addition to requiring each participant to engage in the debate openly, honestly, and with willingness to recognize and accept the force of the better argument, they require that:

1   Every subject with the competence to speak and act is allowed to take part in a discourse.
2   a) Everyone is allowed to question any assertion whatever.
    b) Everyone is allowed to introduce any assertion whatever into the discourse.
    c) Everyone is allowed to express [their own] attitudes, desires and needs.
3   No speaker may be prevented, by internal or external coercion, from exercising [their own] rights as laid down in (1) and (2).

(Alexy, 1978, p. 40, as quoted in Habermas, 1992, p. 89)

However, Unerman and Bennett (2004) and Lewis and Unerman (1999) argue that, in practice, the theoretical ideal of an *ideal speech situation* is unlikely to ever be (or have been) realized in practice in the determination of organizational social, environmental and economic responsibilities and accountabilities. Among the reasons for this are that:

■ many stakeholders who are potentially affected positively or negatively by an organization's actions are not able to participate in the debate and represent their own interests because, as indicated earlier in this chapter, they may not yet have been born (future generations), may be non-human species of fauna or flora, or may not have the mental ability to articulate their own interests;

■ among those who are able to articulate their own interests, some may be better at articulating their interests than others, thus giving the more articulate a debating advantage over the less articulate in the process of discursively testing the arguments aired in the debate;

■ in practice, many people may participate in the debate strategically, aiming to further their own interests irrespective of the impacts these may have on others – rather than being open and honest regarding these impacts and rather than being willing to recognize the strength of the more compelling moral arguments.

Nevertheless, Unerman and Bennett (2004) argue that although the requirements of an *ideal speech situation* debate are unlikely to ever be realized in practice, they have the potential to inform stakeholder dialogue processes. In other words, these ideal speech procedures should not be regarded as an 'all-or-nothing', but should be regarded as one end of a continuum ranging from no democratically informed procedures to a full ideal speech situation debate (see, also, Power and Laughlin, 1996). Unerman and Bennett argue that any movement along this continuum away from managers simply taking into account the information needs of only those stakeholders with the greatest economic power over achievement of the organization's objectives, and towards a democratic debate among all stakeholders who are affected by the organization's actions, is desirable and should not be sacrificed simply because the full 'ideal speech situation' is unachievable in practice. In the context of the distinction made at the beginning of this chapter between sustainability reporting (aimed at helping realize social, environmental *and* economic sustainability) and social and environmental reporting (motivated by an imperative to increase profits irrespective of negative social and environmental impacts which may arise), any movement towards a democratic consensus in the determination of organizational social, environmental and economic responsibilities and accountability should help move us away from profit-oriented strategic social and environmental reporting and towards more holistic sustainability reporting.

An important aspect of such an 'emancipatory' debate among stakeholders regarding the social, environmental and economic responsibilities of a business is that the debate should not be controlled by the business itself (Thomson and Bebbington, 2005). Such control limits the scope of the debate, and may result in important stakeholder concerns being marginalized (Gray *et al.*, 1997). Thomson and Bebbington (2005) indicate that one possible outcome of a process of stakeholder engagement where the organization itself invites selected stakeholders to participate and determines both the agenda and the channels of communication to be used (ensuring 'difficult' issues are not adequately aired), can be the production of accounts which support and reinforce a falsely objectified 'win–win' image of organizational social and environmental impacts, whose role is 'to tell a more or less passive audience that "everything" is fine and to discourage further questioning of the organizations' (p. 521). Thomson and Bebbington (2005, p. 520) further argue that stakeholder engagement and dialogue mechanisms which would support sustainability accounting and accountability would require that:

- measures be taken to equalize power between the organization and its stakeholders (and, presumably, between different stakeholders);
- the difficulties (or impossibility) of achieving business social and environmental sustainability are explicitly recognized in the stakeholder dialogue; and

97

■ the views of stakeholders regarding all of the impacts which the organization has on them and on the environment are accorded a central place in any social and environmental report resulting from the dialogue process.

The next section of this chapter examines evidence of stakeholder engagement and dialogue practices to see how well they measure up to the principles discussed above.

EVIDENCE OF STAKEHOLDER ENGAGEMENT IN PRACTICE

So far this chapter has explored a variety of issues related to stakeholder engagement and dialogue from a largely theoretical perspective, explaining: why stakeholder engagement is a crucial element of the sustainability reporting or social and environmental reporting process; how the range of stakeholders that any organization's managers will seek to engage is related to their philosophical objectives for engaging in CSR; and some of the difficulties involved in seeking to identify, from amongst mutually exclusive competing stakeholder social, environmental and economic expectations, a consensus set of expectations which the organization can then address in its sustainability reporting. This section moves away from these rather abstract (but nevertheless important) theoretical considerations to examine evidence of stakeholder engagement and dialogue practices.

A broad view on the general attitude in practice among large UK corporations towards stakeholder definition and prioritization is offered by Owen et al. (2005). In a survey of managerial attitudes, they found that managers considered shareholders to be the most important group of stakeholders in social and environmental reporting. After shareholders, the ranking among managers for the importance of different stakeholder groups in sustainability reporting was: employees, environmental pressure groups, government/regulators, local communities, customers, long-term lenders and suppliers. However, this ranking cannot be regarded as applicable universally as, for example, Adams (2002) found differences between the stakeholders who were considered the most important by a sample of German managers and those considered the most important by managers in the UK.

Among the academic studies which have commented upon aspects of stakeholder dialogue mechanisms in practice are Thomson and Bebbington (2005), Swift et al. (2001), Unerman and Bennett (2004), Owen et al. (2001), O'Dwyer (2005a) and O'Dwyer et al. (2005a, 2005c).

The dialogue mechanisms mentioned by Thomson and Bebbington (2005) covered: 'internet bulletin boards, questionnaire surveys mailed to stakeholders, phone surveys, and community based and/or open meetings designed to bring stakeholders and organisational representatives together' (p. 517) in addition to focus groups and tear-off comment cards included in social and environmental reports. In commenting on the (lack of) use of the latter, Thomson and Bebbington (2005, p. 523) state:

> [t]hese forms are usually fairly small, they cover a very small set of questions or solicit feedback of a very general nature. All the evidence which exists . . . suggests that very few individuals provide feedback on these preprinted, enclosed feedback forms.

In addition to the dialogue mechanisms outlined by Thomson and Bebbington (2005), Swift *et al.* (2001) found evidence for the use of interviews and company newsletters.

Unerman and Bennett (2004) conducted an in-depth analysis of the use of one stakeholder dialogue mechanism employed by Shell – an internet web-forum in the form of a bulletin board of social and environmental issues hosted on Shell's website. This web-forum, which is a mechanism also used by other companies, allowed anyone with internet access and an email address to post comments on any of the topics covered by the web-forum (which included a catch-all 'other' category). Shell officials replied to many, but not all, of the comments posted by external stakeholders, but Unerman and Bennett found little evidence of external stakeholders commenting on each others' comments. They therefore concluded that the web-forum was not being used by external stakeholders as a mechanism to debate their views, but rather appeared to be used to state views with little evidence of a willingness to engage in debate which might challenge (and possibly lead to a change in) these views. Furthermore, Unerman and Bennett commented that as many stakeholders potentially affected by Shell's operations may not have access to the internet (for example those in less developed nations), and as there were no translation facilities provided for non-English language users, the web-forum could not be used in practice to engage in dialogue with all possible stakeholders. Thus, while the facilities of this web-forum had the potential to move a little way towards the realization of an 'ideal speech situation' democratic debate among stakeholders with divergent views on the social and environmental responsibilities and accountabilities of Shell, in practice it was not used by either Shell or many of its external stakeholders to conduct such a debate.

Rather than commenting upon specific stakeholder dialogue mechanisms, Owen *et al.* (2001) examined managerial attitudes towards the overall process of stakeholder dialogue and engagement. They found that while there was recognition of the importance of stakeholder dialogue and engagement in social and environmental reporting:

> [t]he views of many of the corporate respondents . . . give rise to some suspicion that their commitment to stakeholder engagement is largely confined to a desire to manage expectations and balance competing

interests, whilst leaving much scope for the exercise of managerial discretion.

(Owen *et al.*, 2001, p. 270)

Broadly similar insights are provided by some of the findings of O'Dwyer (2005a). Furthermore, in an interview-based study examining the perceptions of one form of stakeholder (non-government organizations) in Ireland towards corporate stakeholder engagement, O'Dwyer *et al.* (2005a) found that these stakeholders believed there was active resistance by many corporations to meaningful engagement and dialogue with some stakeholders (to the extent that some viewed the relationship between corporations and stakeholders as antagonistic).

The above attitudes by corporations towards stakeholder engagement and dialogue in practice would indicate that these measures are used strategically as part of a business case, 'win–win' oriented social and environmental reporting process which has more to do with improving economic performance than it has to do with moving us towards sustainability. However, in a further study, O'Dwyer *et al.* (2005c) found that most of the Irish NGOs who responded to a questionnaire survey considered their relationships with corporations to be amicable, indicating that antagonism between corporations and stakeholders might not be a significant impediment to meaningful stakeholder engagement and dialogue – although a majority of the respondents did not actually take the opportunities which they perceived as being available for engagement and dialogue in helping to determine corporate social and environmental responsibilities and duties of accountability.

SUMMARY AND CONCLUSIONS

This chapter has explored a variety of issues related to the role of stakeholder engagement and dialogue in the process of social and environmental reporting. It located these practices in the context of the motives for organizations engaging in social and environmental reporting, with these motives only being regarded as leading to sustainability accounting if they aimed at making the organization responsible, responsive and accountable to all those stakeholders upon whom their operations may have an impact. It further discussed the problems in operationalizing stakeholder dialogue and engagement mechanisms where these are motivated by concerns to address the expectations of this very broad range of stakeholders. It outlined theoretical procedures for arriving at a consensus among competing, mutually exclusive stakeholder needs and expectations, but indicated that in practice such procedures were not evident. If we are to achieve an improvement in the sustainability of business, then stakeholder dialogue mechanisms which give greater empowerment to a broad range of stakeholders will need to be developed and employed. Otherwise, stakeholder dialogue may continue to be used to provide a fig-leaf for strategically motivated social and environmental reporting which has little to do with making business more holistically sustainable in practice.

NOTES

1 It may also be considered problematic for an individual to identify today their own interests in any more than a few years into the future.

2 Nevertheless, there have been some attempts in the academic literature to rank the significance of perceived negative social and environmental consequences of organizational activities – for example in developing full cost accounting models designed to account for externalities (see, for example, Bebbington *et al.*, 2001).

REFERENCES

ACCA (2005) Improving stakeholder engagement reporting: An ACCA and the Environment Council workshop – March 2005, London: Certified Accountants Educational Trust.

AccountAbility (2005) *Stakeholder engagement standard: Exposure draft.* London: AccountAbility.

Adams, C. A. (2002) Internal organizational factors influencing corporate social and ethical reporting. *Accounting, Auditing and Accountability Journal*, 15(2): 223–50.

Alexy, R. (1978) Eine theorie des praktischen ciskurses. In W. Oelmüller (ed.) *Normenbegründung, Normendurchsetzung.* As cited in J. Habermas (1992), *Moral consciousness and communicative action.* Trans. C. Lenhardt and S. W. Nicholsen. Cambridge: Polity Press.

Bailey, D., Harte, G. and Sugden, R. (2000) Corporate disclosure and the deregulation of international investment. *Accounting, Auditing and Accountability Journal*, 13(2): 197–218.

Bebbington, J. (2001) Sustainable development: A review of the international development, business and accounting literature. *Accounting Forum*, 25(2): 128–57.

Bebbington, J. and Gray, R. (2001) An account of sustainability: Failure, success and a reconceptualization. *Critical Perspectives on Accounting*, 12(5): 557–88.

Bebbington, J., Gray, R., Hibbitt, C. and Kirk, E. (2001) *Full cost accounting: An agenda for action.* London: Association of Chartered Certified Accountants.

Boyce, G. (2000) Public discourse and decision-making: Exploring possibilities for financial, social and environmental accounting. *Accounting, Auditing and Accountability Journal*, 13(1): 27–64.

Buhr, N. (2002) A structuration view on the initiation of environmental reports. *Critical Perspectives on Accounting*, 13(1): 17–38.

Deegan, C. (2002) Introduction: The legitimising effect of social and environmental disclosures a theoretical foundation *Accounting, Auditing and Accountability Journal*, 15(3): 282–311.

Deegan, C. and Unerman, J. (2006) *Financial accounting theory: European edition*. Maidenhead: McGraw-Hill.

Freeman, R. E. (1984) *Strategic management: A stakeholder approach*. Boston: Pitman.

Freidman, A. L. and Miles, S. (2002) Developing stakeholder theory. *Journal of Management Studies*, 31(1): 1–21.

Gray, R. (2006) Social, environmental and sustainability reporting and organisational value creation? Whose value? Whose creation? *Accounting, Auditing and Accountability Journal*, 19: 793.

Gray, R. H. and Bebbington, J. (2000) Environmental accounting, managerialism and sustainability. *Advances in Environmental Accounting and Management*, 1(1–44).

Gray, R., Dey, C., Owen, D., Evans, R. and Zadek, S. (1997) Struggling with the praxis of social accounting: Stakeholders, accountability, audits and procedures. *Accounting, Auditing and Accountability Journal*, 10(3): 325–64.

Habermas, J. (1992) *Moral consciousness and communicative action*. Trans. C. Lenhardt and S. W. Nicholsen. Cambridge: Polity Press.

ISEA (2005) 'Accountability: AA1000 Series', http://www.accountability.org.uk/aa1000/default.asp, accessed 8 June 2005.

Kant, I. (1949) *The foundation of the metaphysics of morals in the philosophy of Immanuel Kant*. Trans. L. W. Beck (first published in 1785 edn). Chicago: University of Chicago Press.

Lehman, G. (1995) A legitimate concern for environmental accounting. *Critical Perspectives on Accounting*, 6(5): 393–412.

Lewis, L. and Unerman, J. (1999) Ethical relativism: A reason for differences in corporate social reporting? *Critical Perspectives on Accounting*, 10(4): 521–47.

Meadows, D. H., Randers, J. and Meadows, D. L. (2004) *Limits to growth: The 30 year update*. London: Earthscan Publications.

Mouck, T. (1995) Financial reporting, democracy and environmentalism: A critique of the commodification of information. *Critical Perspectives on Accounting*, 6: 535–53.

Neu, D., Warsame, H. and Pedwell, K. (1998) Managing public impressions: Environmental disclosures in annual reports. *Accounting, Organizations and Society*, 23(3): 265–82.

Norris, G. and O'Dwyer, B. (2004) Motivating socially responsive decision-making: The operation of management controls in a socially responsive organisation. *British Accounting Review*, 36(2): 173–96.

O'Dwyer, B. (2002) Managerial perceptions of corporate social disclosure: An Irish story. *Accounting, Auditing and Accountability Journal*, 15(3): 406–36.

O'Dwyer, B. (2003) Conceptions of corporate social responsibility: The nature of managerial capture. *Accounting, Auditing and Accountability Journal*, 16(4): 523–57.

O'Dwyer, B. (2005a) The construction of a social account: A case study in an overseas aid agency. *Accounting, Organizations and Society*, 30(3): 279–96.

O'Dwyer, B. (2005b) Stakeholder democracy: Challenges and contributions from social accounting. *Business Ethics: A European Review*, 14(1): 24–41.

O'Dwyer, B., Unerman, J. and Bradley, J. (2005a) Perceptions on the emergence and future development of corporate social disclosure in Ireland: Engaging the voices of non-governmental organisations. *Accounting, Auditing and Accountability Journal*, 18(1): 14–43.

O'Dwyer, B., Unerman, J. and Brocklebank, C. (2005b) Non-government organisational accountability: The case of Amnesty Ireland. Paper presented at the 17th International Congress on Social and Environmental Accounting Research, University of St Andrews, St Andrews.

O'Dwyer, B., Unerman, J. and Hession, E. (2005c) User needs in sustainability reporting: Perspectives of stakeholders in Ireland. *European Accounting Review*, 14(4): 759–87.

Owen, D. L., Swift, T. and Hunt, K. (2001) Questioning the role of stakeholder engagement in social and ethical accounting, auditing and reporting. *Accounting Forum*, 25(3): 264–82.

Owen, D., Shaw, K. and Cooper, S. (2005) *The operating and financial review: A catalyst for improved corporate social and environmental disclosure?* London: ACCA.

Owen, D. L., Swift, T. A., Humphrey, C. and Bowerman, M. (2000) The new social audits: accountability, managerial capture or the agenda of social champions? *European Accounting Review*, 9(1): 81–98.

Power, M. and Laughlin, R. (1996) Habermas, law and accounting. *Accounting, Organizations and Society*, 21(5): 441–65.

Rawls, J. (1971) *A theory of justice*. Oxford: Oxford University Press.

Singer, P. (1993) *Practical ethics*, 2nd edn. Cambridge: Cambridge University Press.

Spence, C. (2005) Social and environmental reporting in the UK: A neo-Gramscian perspective, unpublished doctoral thesis, University of St Andrews, St Andrews.

Swift, T., Owen, D. L. and Humphrey, C. (2001) *The management information systems dimensions of social accounting and accountability*, CIMA Research Report. London: Chartered Institute of Management Accountants.

Thomson, I. and Bebbington, J. (2005) Social and environmental reporting in the UK: A pedagogic evaluation. *Critical Perspectives on Accounting*, 16: 507–33.

Unerman, J. and Bennett, M. (2004) Increased stakeholder dialogue and the internet: Towards greater corporate accountability or reinforcing capitalist hegemony? *Accounting, Organizations and Society*, 29(7): 685–707.

Unerman, J. and O'Dwyer, B. (2006) Theorising accountability for NGO advocacy. *Accounting, Auditing and Accountability Journal*, 19(3): 349–76.

World Commission on Environment and Development (1987) *Our common future, the Brundtland Report*. Oxford: Oxford University Press.

Chapter 6

External stakeholders' perspectives on sustainability reporting

Carol Ann Tilt

INTRODUCTION

Corporate Social Disclosure (CSD), more recently termed Triple Bottom Line or Sustainability Reporting, has long been considered to have as its primary focus the ability to make a firm more transparent, and thus, more accountable to its stakeholders. Many researchers in the area consider that less powerful stakeholders, in particular, need to be given a greater voice if there is to be true accountability (O'Dwyer et al., 2003). Thus, sustainability reporting should be part of a process of engagement, reporting and organizational change if it is to be successful. This is only likely to come about through a mix of stakeholder dialogue, standardized reporting and independent verification (Gray et al., 1987; Gray et al., 1996), but the involvement of non-financial stakeholders is an important first step towards permanent change.

This chapter considers the perceptions that various stakeholders have about current and future social, environmental and sustainability disclosure made by corporations, and outlines some examples of stakeholder views and corporate–stakeholder relationships. It also identifies some best practice examples of reporting to stakeholders, and finally notes where further research would be helpful.

STAKEHOLDERS

Broadly defined, a stakeholder is 'an individual or group having a legitimate claim on the firm – someone who can affect or is affected by the firm's activities' (Freeman, 1984; Mattingly and Greening, 2002, p. 268). The major stakeholders of a company have been variously categorized, and include shareholders, employees, creditors, suppliers, customers, banks, government, community, public interest groups and the general public (Estes, 1976; Ogan and Ziebart, 1991; Tilt, 1997). Of these, research has predominantly centred around economic or *primary* stakeholders – 'without whose continuing participation the corporation cannot survive as a going concern' (Clarkson, 1995, p. 106) – such as shareholders and investment analysts, and their information needs for decision-making. Much of this research, however, has ignored social and environmental information until recently. Studies on less economic, or *secondary* stakeholders – 'those who influence or affect, or are influenced or affected by, the corporation, but . . . are not engaged in transactions with the corporation and are not essential for its survival' (Clarkson, 1995, p. 107) – have been much more limited but are the focus of a number of recent studies of CSD. These studies are reviewed and discussed in the following sections.

STAKEHOLDER PERCEPTIONS OF SOCIAL, ENVIRONMENTAL AND SUSTAINABILITY REPORTING

A comprehensive study of what stakeholders require in environmental reports was undertaken by Azzone *et al.* (1997) who outline the information requirements of eight major stakeholder groups. Although the study did not attempt to assess stakeholders' perceptions of current reporting, the authors did find a consensus on the need for certain characteristics to be included in reports, such as, regulatory compliance information and future programmes and strategies. This type of information has become the benchmark against which corporate social disclosure has been judged. Milne *et al.* (2000, 2001), for example, sent a 'mock' environment report to both stakeholders and companies in Australia and New Zealand to gauge their reactions. The framework for the report included sections on organizational profile, board level commitment, policy statement, targets and achievements, performance and compliance, management systems, site level data and independent verification. Stakeholders all found the report to be useful, rating targets and achievements, and verification statements as most important.

The ACCA Sustainability Reporting Awards criteria are similar, and emphasize the use of performance indicators, third party verification and stakeholder involvement (ACCA, 2004a). Details are provided in Table 6.1.

The importance and usefulness of CSD and sustainability reporting to specific stakeholders has been the topic of a number of studies. Others consider the influence that these stakeholders have and thus their ability to affect reporting practices.

Shareholders and investors

Shareholders have long been considered an important target group for environmental disclosure (Elkington, 1993) and have been found to exert pressure for changes to organizations' products and/or processes (Hardwick, 1991). In 1995 a

Table 6.1 *ACCA Sustainability Reporting Awards judging criteria*

Completeness (40%)
- Corporate context
- Key (direct and indirect) environmental impacts
- Environmental policy and management commitment
- Environmental targets and objectives
- Scope of the report (by entity)
- Reporting and accounting policies
- Report audience identified

Credibility (35%)
- Contingency planning and risk management
- Compliance/non-compliance record
- Environmental impact data
- Environmental financial statements and full cost accounting
- Approaches to stakeholder dialogue
- Third party statement

Communication (25%)
- Layout and appearance
- Understandability, readability, accessibility, appropriate length
- Innovative approaches
- Availability of a summary report and/or executive summary
- Use of internet
- Appropriateness of graphs, illustrations, photos

Source: ACCA Australia and New Zealand Sustainability Reporting Awards Report of Judges 2004

study by the Social Investment Forum found that shareholders influenced approximately US$450 billion of assets, and such activism was predicted to continue to increase (Gaines, 1995). Similarly, Deegan and Rankin (1997) found shareholders were among the groups of users of annual reports who classified environmental information as material to their decision-making. In contrast, a KPMG (1996) survey found that shareholders were not among the key target audiences of environmental reports.

The influence of shareholders on companies' decision-making raises the issue of how influential shareholders can actually be in relation to environmental issues. In the US in the 1980s there was a 'steady erosion of shareholder rights' while 'institutional investors (played) . . . a much more assertive role in corporate governance' (Heard, 1990, p. 253). Large shareholders have become more active since the 1980s (Heard, 1990) and have been shown to be significant as a monitor of management and Board financial activities (Lange *et al.*, 2000). However, the role of these large, particularly institutional, shareholders in Board decision-making regarding social and environmental issues has still not been adequately researched. If an institutional shareholder is avoiding undertaking environmental reporting issues itself, it may also choose to actively discourage reporting by the company in which it has invested.

The area of shareholder influence requires further investigation, but research to date suggests only limited evidence that shareholders perceive social, environmental and sustainability disclosure as important. Encouragingly, a survey of 939 adults in the UK found that 87 per cent of respondents considered that if they were a shareholder, they would expect to see a copy of a company's social report (Dawkins and Lewis, 2003). O'Rourke (2003, p. 228) presents evidence that some shareholders are becoming active in lobbying on certain issues and are therefore being 'targeted by social and environmental activists'. Activists as a stakeholder are considered later.

Coopers and Lybrand (1993, p. 3) state that 'investors are becoming wary of bad environmental practice because it can increase liabilities and risks, which diminish profits'. Interest in 'ethical investment schemes' demonstrates the desire of some people to invest only in companies that are responsible and ethical (Welford and Gouldson, 1993). These funds initially grew quite quickly, at a rate of 475 per cent between 1990 and 1996 (Fayers, 1998), but despite this they are still an, albeit significant, minority (Cowton, 2004). Australian investors invested less than AUD$5 (US$6.6) per capita in organizations promoting ethical investments during the 1990s, contrasting with the USA, where per capita investment in ethical funds was approximately US$2,200 (Deegan, 1996). In the USA, ethical investment reached US$19.2 trillion in 2003 (Social Investment Forum, 2003), while in the UK it passed the GBP10 billion mark in 2005 (Cooperative Financial Services, 2005). Deegan and Rankin (1997), however, found that Australian stockbrokers place less importance on environmental information than other users.

Investment analysts in New Zealand perceive 'bad' environmental disclosure as important to their decisions (being less likely to invest in those companies that indicate poor performance), but the provision of information about 'good' environmental performance has little impact on investors' decisions (Chan and Milne, 1999). Looking specifically at narrative disclosures, Milne and Chan (1999, p. 452) found that analysts 'largely ignore narrative social disclosures for their investment decision making'. The authors suggest that narrative presentations of the material are not 'sufficient to satisfy (their) analytical requirements' (Milne and Chan, 1999, p. 453), and indicate that these stakeholders require quantified, monetary information directly incorporated into financial statements.

More recently, Dawkins and Lewis (2003) surveyed 93 analysts and 50 investors and found that 45 per cent and 54 per cent respectively considered companies' information on environmental, social and sustainability performance to be of poor quality.

Insurers and banks

One instance where companies may feel pressure to disclose environmental activities is in their dealings with financiers. Industrial operations may be required to lodge bonds to guarantee compliance with environmental laws such as clean-up requirements. Many banks require borrowers to state their environmental liabilities, and to comply with environmental laws as a condition of loans. They also ask borrowers to report on their compliance with environmental laws as a condition of further drawings. Some banks, in relation to major projects, are required to conduct regular independent environmental audits, and to provide them to financiers (Taberner *et al.*, 1991). In 1988, the World Bank reported that over 38 per cent of all of its loans were described as having important environmental objectives, which covered at least 5 per cent of the project cost. There were also indications that 'a growing concern for the environment would be even more evident in future lending operations' (Warford and Partow, 1989, p. 6). Ten years later, environmental considerations are included in the majority of lending applications. As Deegan (1996, p. 126) states, 'organizations which show that they are environmentally aware . . . may also find that they are able to attract finance at a lower cost than would otherwise be possible'.

A notable aspect of banks' approach to environmental issues is the concentration on technical, 'eco-efficiency', methods of dealing with the environment (audits, costings, etc.). The eco-justice element is ignored; in particular, the debate regarding the third world's ability to meet environmental objectives, which may be at the expense of (for example) conditions for workers. In May 1992, five major banks signed a UN declaration to commit themselves to sustainability criteria when judging and assisting commercial, industrial and government borrowers (Stikker, 1992), indicating that the environment is on the agenda of the financial sector.

CONSUMERS AND SUPPLIERS

Polonsky *et al.* (1992, p. 25) consider the green consumer to be 'arguably . . . the most powerful force in changing business environmental policies'. While consumer buying power plays a large part in changing companies' product design and processing (Worldwatch Institute, 1992), there has been only limited investigation on consumers' perceptions of reporting. One study did find that 'preferential purchasing' campaigns was one of the major ways that NGOs acted for or against companies (Tilt, 1994) and the KPMG Environmental Reporting Survey (1996) found that companies identified customers as one of the main 'driving forces' behind environmental reporting and that they were seen as a key target audience for their environmental reports. In the UK food retailing sector, for example, consumers were found to be the most influential of all stakeholders in exerting ecological pressures (Bansal, 1993).

Tilt (1994) included consumer groups in her paper on pressure group influence on social and environmental disclosure, but did not find them to be significantly different in their perceptions from other NGOs (discussed later). All groups in her sample found the level of disclosure (including annual reports, advertising and labelling) to be insufficient and the quality (credibility) of the disclosure to be poor.

Surprisingly, a 1993 survey of managers in Europe, North America and Japan undertaken by the International Institute for Sustainable Development placed customers as one of the least influential groups when considering reasons for providing environmental disclosures in annual reports (Deegan, 1996). This suggests that, at least in the past, consumers were perhaps not considered to be an annual report user, but were communicated with in other ways, i.e. through advertising. A survey in 2003 found that only 26 per cent of customers expected to see a company's social report, but 44 per cent considered that they would like to know that one was being produced (Dawkins and Lewis, 2003).

Related to the influence of consumers is the pressure applied by trading partners. Often an organization does not sell into the 'end-consumer' market and thus does not feel direct pressure from consumers, but may feel pressure indirectly through their trading partners (Welford and Gouldson, 1993). Many organizations are selecting their suppliers based on environmental as well as other factors (Stikker, 1992), including undertaking supplier audits before engaging in trade with them. It is reasonable to assume therefore that suppliers desire accurate reporting in order to make such assessments, but again, little investigation has been undertaken on their views of current reporting.

Employees and trade unions

There is some evidence from Western countries that companies with a 'green' image find it easier to recruit and keep employees than those perceived as having poor environmental commitment (Tuininga and Groenewegen, 1993). One explanation offered for this is that most of the workforce is in the younger age group and younger people are more environmentally aware (Ford, 1992). It has also been suggested that a company demonstrating that it cares about the environment will pass on the perception that it will care about its employees and other people who depend upon the organization (Ford, 1992). Coopers and Lybrand (1993, p. 4) state that 'employees want to work for clean, safe and innovative companies. Few people wish to work for a company with a poor environmental record and, as a result, potential recruits are increasingly questioning company environmental policy.' This is supported by Owen et al. (1996) and KPMG (1996), who found that employees were identified as a target audience for environmental reporting by an increasing number of companies. In a study of the employees of six companies, 63 per cent expected to see a copy of the company's social report (Dawkins and Lewis, 2003) but no information was collected on their perceptions of the quality of reporting.

Trade unions are introducing quality of environmental management into their negotiations (Tuininga and Groenewegen, 1993), and becoming involved in the environmental agenda and debate. In Australia, for example, the Australian Council of Trade Unions (ACTU) has an *Environment and Sustainable Development Policy*. It states that 'Sustainable development is a workplace issue as well as an issue for the broader community. A strong union voice arguing for sustainable development is a voice for a fairer and just society' (ACTU, 2003, section 6). The Policy also refers to Corporate Australia 'leveraging sustainability and triple bottom line reporting for commercial gain' (ACTU, 2003, section 8) and they plan to develop social partnerships and relationships with community groups, business and the research community to promote sustainable practices.

Non-governmental organizations (NGOs)

While research on secondary stakeholders has been limited, one group that has been studied more extensively than the others is public interest groups or NGOs. This research includes interviews and surveys about NGOs' perceptions of corporate reporting, collaborations between NGOs and companies, and case studies of particular NGOs. As Bendell and Lake (2000, p. 227) state, 'a whole industry has now developed among NGOs, research institutes and consultants in analysing, comparing, benchmarking, advising and standard-setting for environment reporting'. NGOs have also been involved in the development of an international standardized framework for sustainability reporting, the Global Reporting Initiative (GRI), under the auspices of the NGO Coalition for Environmentally Responsible Economies.

NGOs are becoming much more professional, and members are often highly educated and knowledgeable in a number of areas. Corporate management must enter into communications with such groups in order to gain acceptance within the community, and to be seen as part of the social system, rather than at the centre of the social system (Müller and Koechlin, 1992). NGOs, particularly international ones such as Amnesty International, Friends of the Earth, Greenpeace and Oxfam, have had 'notable influence on developments in [CSD]' (Gray *et al.*, 1996, p. 128). Although their influence is difficult to quantify, one of the tools used by NGOs in the UK has been an 'external social audit' (Gray *et al.*, 1996, p. 141) where external organizations present assessments, and alternative views, of a company's social and environmental performance. While the practice is not as widespread as it was in the 1970s (Johnson, 2001), it is still used by some issue-specific organizations, such as the recent Action on Smoking and Health (ASH) report which was released as an alternative to British American Tobacco's *Social Report 2001–02* (ASH, 2002). At the turn of the century there are three areas in which it could be said that social audits are still being applied: through social 'screens', used for socially responsible investing; as part of social assessments by public interest groups to evaluate corporate compliance to various standards; and through internal audits initiated by companies themselves (Johnson, 2001, p. 30).

NGOs are, however, often ignored by corporations in favour of more economically powerful stakeholders, yet in many respects they are one of the most important stakeholders for CSD as they, or those they represent, are often the most affected by corporate actions (Tinker, 1985; Unerman and Bennett, 2004; O'Dwyer et al., 2005). Prior research has attempted to identify whether NGO influence on companies' reporting practices is direct (e.g. direct lobbying to change their reporting practices) or indirect (e.g. using the media to expose poor company practice, see Tilt, 1994, 2004). As reported by Tilt (1994, p. 50), 'many statements emerge [in the literature] describing pressure groups as a major influence on the production of [CSD]' and even now there exists a 'general presumption in the social and environmental accounting literature that lobby groups are a major source of pressure . . . upon the . . . disclosure policies of companies' (Deegan and Blomquist, 2006, p. 1). Evidence that NGOs try to directly influence companies' *reporting practices*, however, is limited. One example, however, is the Corporate Responsibility (CORE) Coalition which represents over 130 charities in the UK and campaigns for companies to 'report against a set of key social, environmental and economic indicators'[1] and recently provided a submission to the Accountancy Standards Board's guidance on a proposed (but not eventually implemented) mandatory Operating and Financial Review to be produced by companies in the UK. Another area where there has been engagement to improve environmental reporting practices is with development NGOs. In this area, development NGOs are providing input and expertise for the development of locally relevant, often non-quantified, performance indicators as these issues are familiar concepts to development NGOs (Bendell and Lake, 2000). There is plenty of evidence that stakeholders, including NGOs, do attempt to influence companies' *activities and behaviour*, which may in turn influence their reporting practices (King and Mackinnon, 2002).

O'Dwyer (2002) has called for more analysis of the demand for CSD, yet, since the Tilt (1994) study, only a limited number of studies have been undertaken on NGOs' influence on reporting (Tilt, 1994; Gadenne and Danastas, 2004; O'Dwyer et al., 2005). Other studies indicate that the relationship between corporations and these groups is changing. Deegan and Gordon (1996, p. 195) surveyed 41 organizations that undertook 'activities of a lobbying nature' and that dealt with environmental issues, asking them to rate the extent to which they had targeted, for its environmental activities, each of 50 industries. From this, indices of the top ten most environmentally sensitive industries were developed. The level of sensitivity was then compared to the level of environmental disclosure made by each industry and a positive relationship was discovered. In addition, Deegan and Gordon (1996) found a positive relationship between increases in membership of environmental organizations and environmental disclosure by companies. Membership of such groups increased from just under 9,000 in 1975 to 168,000 by 1991 (Deegan and Gordon, 1996). In 1996 there were approximately 250,000 members of various broad issue groups, and 320,000 if specific issue groups are included (ACF, 1996).

Deegan and Blomquist (2006) investigated the influence of one of the major environmental organizations in Australia: the World Wildlife Fund (WWF) and found that they were able to influence environmental reporting practices in some way. In 1999 and 2000 the WWF produced a *Mining Company Environmental Report Scorecard* for Australian mining companies that were signatories to the *Australian Minerals Industry Code for Environmental Management* (WWF, 1999). The Scorecard rates each company's environmental report according to a set of criteria. Deegan and Blomquist (2006) show that production of the Scorecard has resulted in changes in the reporting behaviour of individual companies, as well as revisions to the Code itself. In their first report, WWF (1999) found the greatest shortcomings of the reports analysed included a lack of verification, limited information on environmental management systems and little information on community involvement.

The Age newspaper in Australia also produces a scorecard, called the *Company Reputation Index (CRI)*, which rates the top 100 Australian companies according to six measures that include environmental, social and ethical performance (*Age*, 2000). The criteria used to produce the measures are developed by representatives from social and environmental community groups, and each company is then rated (out of 100) by these same representatives. The results are published in two major national newspapers. Interestingly, on environmental performance companies have scored very poorly and have been accused 'of rhetoric when it comes to their environmental policies' (Batt, 2000, p. 1) and on social performance companies 'differed radically across sections of the community' (O'Rourke, 2000, p. 1). Similar reputation indexes exist in the USA, such as the FORTUNE/Roper Corporate Reputation Index which classifies companies into, among other things, 'winners', 'losers', 'irrelevant' and 'falling stars' (PR Influences, 2005b).

One of the first studies to consider NGO perceptions of CSD was by Tilt (1994), a study that was replicated ten years later (Gadenne and Danastas, 2004; Tilt, 2004). The 1994 study showed that NGOs considered CSD to be insufficient and low in credibility. They also stated preference for quantified information although at the time most reporting was simply narrative. There was also support for the use of separate social reports (as opposed to providing this information in annual reports), which is a practice that seems to have become more widespread. In 2004, there did not appear to be very much change in the perceptions of NGOs with a number stating that they did not consider companies to be honest about their social and environmental impacts (Tilt, 2004), and most still ranking both credibility and sufficiency as very low (Gadenne and Danastas, 2004; Tilt, 2004).

Another, more recent, study on NGOs is O'Dwyer *et al.* (2005), who interviewed lobby groups in the Republic of Ireland about the current production of

CSD by Irish companies. The authors found that there is a demand for social disclosure information by these groups, motivated primarily by a desire for accountability, but that current CSD practice in Ireland is viewed with scepticism (O'Dwyer et al., 2005). They also found that there is predominantly an antagonistic relationship between corporations and NGOs. Irish NGOs favour 'stand alone, holistic/inclusive social and environmental reports' that are externally verified, and reject the current voluntary nature of reporting, overwhelmingly supporting some form of regulation for at least minimum levels of disclosure (O'Dwyer et al., 2005, p. 24). This mirrored the findings of Tilt (1994, 2004), who found that the majority of Australian NGOs also support mandatory reporting. The Irish NGOs emphasized the need for stakeholder engagement, but cited major obstacles such as corporate resistance and antagonism, and the current political environment in Ireland favouring the interests of corporations.

Interestingly, Tilt (1997) found that the companies themselves do not perceive NGOs as having a major influence on their behaviour. In a study of the top 500 companies in Australia, she found that legislation was considered most influential; followed by public opinion; shareholders, consumers and insurance companies; and finally lobby groups and the media. NGOs were rated by these companies for their influence on reporting activities, and received a mean rank of only 2.1 out of 5. Notwithstanding this, there are a number of examples of firms and NGOs entering into collaborations, some of which include collaborating on the production of sustainability reports. These are discussed further in later sections.

The media

The media is said to reflect the changing values of the general public, and may also influence companies' activities in that they have enormous power to project company image and influence consumer behaviour (Rappaport and Dillon, 1991). Research has shown evidence of a link between the visibility of an organization via the media, and their favourable attitudes towards it (PR Influences, 2005a). In 2001, a survey of 30 journalists found that 54 per cent of those surveyed considered the quality of companies' social, environmental and sustainability performance information to be of poor quality (Dawkins and Lewis, 2003).

O'Donovan (1997) found a significant relationship between news reports that link a company to negative environmental issues and disclosure in the annual report. He found similar findings for news reports linking the industry in which the company operates and annual report disclosure levels, concluding that company managers do respond to public pressure. Thus, while research has identified that firms do disclose more environmental information after media attention has been paid to a particular event (Deegan et al., 2000), more research on the relationship between the actions of NGOs, public opinion, and media attention would be illuminating.

113

In another study examining environmental issues reported in the popular press a paucity of reporting on environmental issues was found, and there was little evidence of any negative reporting (Thomas and Kenny, 1997). Where press reports were found, companies in the study often chose not to mirror them in their annual report, suggesting that the media is not a major influence on reporting. It may in fact be more reasonable to suggest that causality flows in the opposite direction, that the media obtains its information from the companies themselves, thus also explaining the lack of negative reports (Thomas and Kenny, 1997). Further research could also provide insight if the ownership of the press outlets were considered. In many countries, much of the print media is owned by a small number of individuals who also have interests in many large corporations. Owen *et al.* (1997) suggest that multinational companies control the media and thus have used this control in an attempt to 'capture' the social and environmental accounting agenda, to 'ensure that any radical movement in these concepts is removed' (Owen *et al.*, 1997, p. 184).

The general public

Public concern about the environment is abundant. A 1988 study of European countries showed that the majority of the public consider environmental protection favourably (McGrew, 1993). In 1994, an Australian report indicated that 71 per cent of people ranked environmental protection equal in importance to economic growth and 18 per cent considered it to be more important (Keen, 1995). Historically, public concern has led to the enactment of legislation (Rappaport and Dillon, 1991) and in most countries laws to protect the environment are increasing.

Again in the social accounting literature many references have been made to the public or society being the cause of companies' disclosure practices over the years. Gray and Perks (1982, p. 101) claim that 'society' expects more socially responsible attitudes from corporations, Wiseman (1982, p. 53) states that companies have been forced to implement pollution control as a result of 'societal demands' and Benston (1982, p. 88) considers that companies 'are seen as accountable to . . . society in general'. KPMG (1996) identified the 'local community' as a target audience for environmental reports by international companies and Coopers and Lybrand's 1995 survey found that public expectation was a major factor motivating 72 per cent of organizations to produce environmental reports (Coopers and Lybrand, 1995).

The attitudes and expectations of the general public, however, are difficult to assess, and just how influential the public is, or what their views on current reporting practices are, has not been greatly researched due to the difficulties in obtaining data. Similarly, the definition of public influence varies, thus making it difficult to assess organizations' reaction to public attitudes. For example, the influence of the media and lobby groups is often commingled with that of the general public.

Some attempts have been made, however, and a survey of 25,000 adults across 23 countries showed that society is becoming more sceptical of the profit motive. In the study, 56 per cent of respondents ranked 'responsibility' as most important in forming an impression of a company. This is compared to only 34 per cent who ranked financial performance as most important (Dawkins and Lewis, 2003, pp. 190–1). The same study found a 'clear and explicit demand for information on companies' responsibility programmes' but that the 'quality of this information is poor'. The main problems identified in the reports were a lack of quantified information and few performance indicators.

Summary of stakeholder perceptions of sustainability reporting

It appears from studies that have been undertaken, that sustainability reporting is increasing in importance for most types of stakeholder, but that it is secondary stakeholders that place the greatest importance upon it. Primary stakeholders, while recognizing that social and environmental issues are important and necessary considerations for organizations, still give precedence to financial issues and require only information about things that have direct financial impact. These stakeholders appear to be more interested in the disclosure of poor social and environmental performance than good performance. This may be because they perceive that negative information will have a negative financial impact, whereas positive information is less likely to result in increased returns.

Secondary stakeholders, on the other hand, represent those more affected by the non-financial activities of organizations. Consumers are concerned about product safety, NGOs (among other things) about environmental damage, and employees about working conditions. Therefore it is not surprising that these stakeholders place greater importance on CSD. There appears to be, however, a level of scepticism towards corporate sustainability reporting with most stakeholders indicating that the current level of reporting is insufficient and lacks credibility. There is a view that most reporting is still 'greenwash' and being undertaken to improve reputation without substantially changing practices, to placate and manipulate stakeholders, and to gain competitive advantage, rather than out of any real concern for society and the environment.

Notwithstanding such scepticism, however, there are still some examples of excellent stakeholder engagement practices, and sustainability reporting practices, being undertaken by companies in many countries. The next section therefore provides some examples of both reporting and engagement that have been recognized as providing a benchmark for excellence.

EXAMPLES OF SUSTAINABILITY REPORTING AND STAKEHOLDER ENGAGEMENT

Some examples of sustainability reporting that incorporates stakeholder engagement are provided in this section (taken from the ACCA Sustainability Reporting Awards), along with some examples of successful collaborations between NGOs and companies. These are merely illustrations and their inclusion does not imply any superiority over others.

ACCA Sustainability Reporting Awards

In the United Kingdom, the ACCA awards include a theme for each year. During 2004 'Stakeholder Engagement Reporting' was focused on and reports entered for the awards were assessed in terms of how well they reported on engagement with stakeholders. In 2004 the best reports were judged as those that used case studies and targets, those that aligned stakeholder engagement with their business priorities, and those that provided details such as stakeholder maps, feedback and contact details (ACCA, 2004d). The criteria used to judge good stakeholder engagement reporting are summarized in Table 6.2.

The 2004 ACCA UK report of the judges singled out 6 of 84 applicants for special mention for excellence in stakeholder engagement reporting. These reports fully integrated the importance of stakeholders and stakeholder issues into their reports, providing holistic and detailed information, with metrics and targets. They all included information on when and where targets or achievements were not met, and what there is still to be done.

The judges of the 2004 ACCA Sustainability Reporting Awards in Australia commented on the report from the Toyota Motor Company for being 'different, succinct, visually appealing and easy to read' (ACCA, 2004a, p. 11) and contained a separate section on 'stakeholder and community engagement' (see Figure 6.1). A similar report was produced in 2005, and all reports produced are independently verified.

There are also awards for the United States (ACCA, 2004b) and Europe (ACCA, 2004c). In 2004, Hewlett Packard won the best US sustainability report as, among

Table 6.2 ACCA Stakeholder Engagement Reporting Awards criteria

1   Stakeholder identification
2   Evidence of engagement
3   Targets and metrics
4   Integration of engagement (into company practice)
5   Use of engagement in developing the report
6   Feedback on reports

Source: *ACCA UK Awards for Sustainability Reporting: Report of the judges 2004*

10
Community & Stakeholder Engagement

Key Focus Area for 2003	Performance
• Involve dealerships in local community projects.	• Toyota Community Spirit Program expanded nationally.

Engaging with local communities and other stakeholders enables Toyota to work cooperatively, seek feedback and share the company's knowledge and expertise. Toyota's community partnerships also enable Toyota employees and dealers to participate in local community activities.

Altona Community Liaison Committee

The Altona Community Liaison Committee (CLC) provides a forum for community feedback on the environmental performance of Toyota's manufacturing operations in Altona. During 2003, the CLC met monthly and included representatives from the Environment Protection Authority (Vic), City West Water, Hobsons Bay City Council, local residents, industry neighbours and Toyota. A range of Toyota representatives were invited to attend meetings and share information with the CLC.

Environment Improvement Plan

A key activity of the CLC in 2003 was the development and launch of Toyota's first community-based Environment Improvement Plan. For more information, refer to the Manufacturing pages.

Environment Improvement Plan

National Tree Day

In July 2003, Toyota worked with Planet Ark to coordinate National Tree Day 2003. Since Toyota's involvement began in 2000, approximately six million trees have been planted at National Tree Day events. This year local schools, community groups, Toyota employees, 163 Toyota dealers, and a record breaking 247,000 volunteers planted more than 2.2 million trees and shrubs at 3,340 sites across Australia.

Planting native trees contributes to re-establishing habitats for native flora and fauna, reversing the effects of salination and sequestering CO2. National Tree Day sites and the trees and shrubs planted were selected by local environmental groups to help restore local habitats.'Your Town Tree Day' allowed communities to select a day for planting that is favourable in local environmental conditions. ⓘ

Toyota Community Spirit

Toyota Community Spirit is Toyota's corporate citizenship program. It provides financial and in-kind support for national and state partnerships and local community programs. Employee and dealer participation is a key element of Toyota Community Spirit. ⓘ

National Partnership with Conservation Volunteers Australia

During 2003, teams of Toyota dealers and employees and members of the community worked on more than 20 local environmental projects including Powerful Owl habitat revegetation in Warrandyte, Victoria and conservation of Barramundi habitat in Townsville, Queensland.

State Partnership with Phillip Island Nature Park – Coastal Ambassadors

The *Coastal Ambassadors* program is a series of camps for year 9 students held at Phillip Island. Students learn about environmental issues facing Australia's coasts and develop an action plan for marine conservation in their home, school or local community. In 2003, *Coastal Ambassadors* won the Achievement in Secondary Marine Education category at the Dolphin Research Institute Awards.

Trees planted

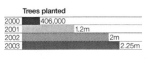

Trees planted	
2000	406,000
2001	1.2m
2002	2m
2003	2.25m

Volunteers

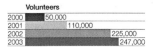

Volunteers	
2000	50,000
2001	110,000
2002	225,000
2003	247,000

Dealers involved

Dealers involved	
2000	N/A
2001	102
2002	153
2003	163

75% of Toyota dealers were involved in National Tree Day 2003.

Employee Volunteer Day – Phillip Island

In November 2003, approximately sixty Toyota employees and their families spent a day building penguin nest boxes and revegetating areas at Phillip Island Nature Park.

Community Training Workshops

In 2003, Toyota partnered with Hobsons Bay City Council to deliver a series of Community Training Workshops that address the training needs and priorities of local groups.

Altona's Bayside Festival

In 2003 a Toyota volunteer assisted the Altona Bayside Festival to develop safety and emergency management plans. This volunteer placement won the 2003 Australia Business Arts Foundation Advice Bank Award.

Involvement in government and industry forums

Toyota engages in discussions with government and industry to stay abreast of emerging issues, identify opportunities for partnerships and to work collaboratively by sharing expertise. In 2003, Toyota was recognised for its environmental leadership by being invited to participate in a range of industry forums and roundtables.

EPA Victoria secondment

During 2003 Toyota seconded an EPA Victoria employee for six months, confirming the open relationship between the two organisations. The secondee's experience and expertise was utilised in the verification of the 2002 Environmental Report, scoping and implementation of the waste audit and the development of the Waste Tender.

Key Focus areas for 2004

• Increase stakeholder communication activity.
• Expand national component of Toyota Community Spirit.
• Increase employee and dealership participation in Toyota Community Spirit.

Figure 6.1 Extract from: *This Way. Environment and Community Report 2004. Toyota Motor Company, Section 10. Community and Stakeholder Engagement*

Source: Reproduced with permission. Full report available from http://www.toyota.com.au/TWP/Upload/Media/319.pdf or www.accaglobal.com/sustainability

other things, it 'Provides stakeholder engagement tables that characterizes the type of interactions with main stakeholder groups' (ACCA, 2004b, p. 3). Also, VanCity Credit Union received a commendation for its 2002–03 Accountability Report, and it was noted that their report contains 'excellent stakeholder engagement elements, including community leader feedback on last report and elements such as stakeholder relevance guide in table of contents' (ACCA, 2004b, p. 6).[2]

In 2004 the ACCA award judges identified a number of concerns regarding stakeholder reporting. This includes the need to (ACCA, 2004a, p. 12):

1   Report credible, unedited third-party commentary which demonstrates that it is 'willing to subject itself to a critical external eye' and a 'genuine effort to engage with stakeholders'. It is suggested that such commentary could come from NGOs, governments, analysts, or customers.
2   Disclose who the key stakeholders are, how they were identified and to which stakeholder groups the report is targeted.
3   Describe and disclose how stakeholders were involved in the reporting process and how stakeholder feedback was used.
4   Provide details of how stakeholder involvement changed the reporting process and disclose the 'weighting' different stakeholder groups have to facilitate change.

In addition to reporting, other forms of stakeholder engagement include 'public meetings . . . surveys, . . . a formal dialogue on project options', actual involvement of community members in particular projects (Ebrahim, 2003, p. 818), or the use of dialogue mechanisms (Unerman and Bennett, 2004). Such participation with the community is emphasized by NGOs as an important means of ensuring their own accountability to members (Cronin and O'Regan, 2002). Unerman and Bennett (2004) found, however, that the 'web forum' of a large oil company was not really utilized for engagement or debate, but rather for posting of particular views.

An example of a company that works with a particular stakeholder is Argyle Diamonds in Australia, who reported on an agreement with the traditional owners of the land on which their diamond mine is situated. The company reported in 2002 (and won an ACCA reporting award in that year) on an agreement it was negotiating with local Aboriginal people, recognizing their shared future. The Argyle Diamonds report demonstrates one way in which organizations can collaborate with stakeholders. Collaborations and partnerships are becoming an important strategy for both firms and stakeholders, and therefore some examples, particularly with NGOs, are discussed next.

Collaborations

Many NGOs are working with organizations in order to find mutually beneficial outcomes rather than using hostile tactics (Crane, 2000; Friedman and Miles, 2002; Lawrence, 2002; Adams and Frost, 2003; LaFrance and Lehmann, 2005). In a book on the subject, Elkington and Fennell (2000) outline the various types of company–NGO relationships ranging from adversarial to strategic joint ventures. Pearce (2003, p. 41) states that 'environment groups . . . are engaged in a savage reappraisal of their philosophy' and some groups, such as WWF, have concluded that current conservation practice, including having an adversarial relationship with companies, is doing more harm than good. The groups suggest that their new outlook encompasses more than just the environment, but considers sustainability in a social, economic and environmental context (Pearce, 2003). Examples of such collaborations include the Conservation Law Foundation's collaboration with public utilities, and Royal Dutch/Shell Group's stakeholder engagement programme (Bliss, 2002). Even Greenpeace, whose reputation is for confrontation and conflict, have entered into alliances recognizing that 'both parties have something to gain from this relation' (Friedman and Miles, 2002, p. 14).

In Australia, Fiedler and Deegan (2002, p. 30) investigated some interactions between NGOs and businesses using the case study method. They considered the construction industry's collaborations with four environmental organizations and found that collaborations were motivated by stakeholder pressure, publicity, and the ability to 'set an example for other . . . projects to follow'. While recent studies indicate that the adversarial nature of the relationship has softened somewhat, the research has been concentrated mostly in the area of environment and has been limited to a few large, high profile, NGOs. In addition, while there are a number of collaboration initiatives currently in operation (Crane, 2000), most concentrate on environmental management practices, rather than on reporting.

An interesting development is that of academics collaborating with companies to improve or develop their sustainability practices and reporting. A number of organizations have welcomed academics into their midst to undertake case studies and generally become involved in their social and environmental activities. For example, Adams et al. (2005) initially observed an organization's process of developing a report and then provided feedback to assist them to improve and enhance their reporting practices. While they noted that the organization seemed committed to sustainability, and that their report was comprehensive, they suggested some changes such as seeking feedback from various stakeholder committee members and including information about this procedure and the feedback that was given in the report; getting letters from experts in various fields to comment on the report content; and undertaking external verification.

119

CONCLUDING COMMENTS AND FURTHER RESEARCH

Research into stakeholder involvement in, and perceptions of, social, environmental and sustainability reporting has not been abundant. However, those studies that have been undertaken have shown that stakeholder concerns around issues of sustainability and corporate accountability are evident. Stakeholder groups attempt to influence companies' activities and reporting through a variety of measures, including antagonism, cooperation and collaboration. Their involvement and engagement has resulted in improved reporting and transparency and an ongoing and increasing awareness of the importance of sustainability reporting.

There is, however, a need for further research into stakeholders, particularly secondary stakeholders, and how they use sustainability reporting information. A better understanding of the uses to which this information is put should lead to better and more comprehensive reporting, and thus greater transparency of organizations. It can be seen from the preceding review that we do not know very much about the views and perceptions of many stakeholders when it comes to sustainability reporting. More work on the views and influence of institutional investors, banks and trading partners should improve reporting in annual reports; determining better ways of communicating with consumers and the public might help to open up dialogue between firms and stakeholders; and a better understanding of the role played by the media and its influence on other stakeholders will help us to grasp the complexities of the reporting process.

In addition, further research into various collaborations would be illuminating, particularly to show how firms and stakeholders can work together to improve both social and environmental performance, and subsequent reporting. Similarly, case studies of stakeholder consultation and engagement practices would provide valuable exposure of the process and practices undertaken, and the resultant improvements from both a social and environmental perspective, but also from an organizational perspective. Finally, research on external verification of reports will help us determine how stakeholders can be involved in this process.

NOTES

1   http://www.corporate-responsibility.org/, p. 1.

2   The winning reports for all years can be viewed on the ACCA website at http://www.accaglobal.com/sustainability.

REFERENCES

ACCA (2004a) Australia and New Zealand awards for sustainability reporting: Report of the judges 2004, www.accaglobal.com/sustainability, accessed 28 July 2005.

ACCA (2004b) CERES–ACCA North American awards for sustainability reporting: Report of the judges 2004, www.accaglobal.com/sustainability, accessed 28 July 2005.

ACCA (2004c) ESRA European sustainability reporting awards: Report of the judges 2004, www.accaglobal.com/sustainability, accessed 28 July 2005.

ACCA (2004d) UK awards for sustainability reporting: Report of the judges 2004, the Association of Chartered Certified Accountants, www.accaglobal.com/sustainability, accessed 28 July 2005.

ACF (1996) *Green pages, directory of environment groups in Australia.* Australian Conservation Foundation.

ACTU (2003) A fair Australia environment and sustainable development policy, www.actu.asn.au/public/about/environment.html, accessed 26 July 2005.

Adams, C. and Frost, G. (2003) Stakeholder engagement strategies: Possibilities for the internet. Paper presented at the 2nd CSEAR Australasian Summer School, Bathurst, Australia, April.

Adams, C. A., McNicholas, P. and Zutshi, A. (2005) Making a difference: Journeying with an organization towards social and environmental accountability. Paper presented at the A-CSEAR Conference, Victoria, Australia, April.

Age, The (2000) Company reputation index: Methodology. *The Age*, 26 October, www.theage.com.au/news/20001030/A8982–20000ct26.html, accessed 26 March 2001.

ASH (2002) British American Tobacco: The other report to society, www.ash.org.uk/html/conduct/html/reporttosocietysum.html, accessed 16 January 2006.

Azzone, G., Brophy, M., Noci, G., Welford, R. and Young, W. (1997) A stakeholders' view of environmental reporting. *Long Range Planning*, 30(5): 699.

Bansal, P. (1993) Environmental management in the UK food retailing sector. Templeton College Management Research Paper 23/93.

Batt, C. (2000) Companies far from passing the green test. *The Age*, 26 October, www.theage.com.au/news/20001026/A8985–20000ct26.html.

Bendell, J. and Lake, R. (2000) New frontiers: Emerging NGO activities to strengthen transparency and accountability in business. In J. Bendell (ed.) *Terms for endearment: Business, NGOs and sustainable development.* Sheffield: Greenleaf Publishing.

Benston, G. J. (1982) Accounting and corporate accountability. *Accounting, Organizations and Society*, 7(2): 87–105.

Bliss, T. (2002) Citizen advocacy groups: Corporate friend or foe? In J. Andriof, S. Waddock, B. Husted and S. Sutherland Rahman (eds) *Unfolding stakeholder thinking*. Sheffield: Greenleaf Publishing.

Chan, C. C. and Milne, M. J. (1999) Investor reactions to corporate environmental saints and sinners: An experimental analysis. *Accounting and Business Research*, 29(4): 265–9.

Clarkson, M. B. E. (1995) A stakeholder framework for analyzing and evaluating corporate social performance. *Academy of Management Review*, 20(1): 92–117.

Cooperative Financial Services (2005) Ethical Investments Break Gbp10 Billion Barrier, PR Newswire Europe Ltd., www.prnewswire.co.uk/cgi/news/release?id=151206, accessed 16 January 2006.

Coopers and Lybrand (1993) *Environmental management services: Responding to the challenge*. Sydney: Coopers and Lybrand Consultants.

Coopers and Lybrand (1995) *Environmental management practices: A survey of major Australian organisations*. Sydney: Coopers and Lybrand Consultants.

Cowton, C. J. (2004) Managing financial performance at an ethical investment fund. *Accounting, Auditing and Accountability Journal*, 17(2): 249–75.

Crane, A. (2000) Culture clash and mediation: Exploring the cultural dynamics of business–NGO collaboration. In J. Bendell (ed.) *Evidence that NGOs try to directly influence companies' reporting practices is limited*. Sheffield: Greenleaf Publishing.

Cronin, D. and O'Regan, J. (2002) *Accountability in development aid: Meeting responsibilities, measuring performance*, Research Report for Comhlamh. Dublin: Comhlamh Aid Issues Group.

Dawkins, J. and Lewis, S. (2003) CSR in stakeholder expectations and their implication for company strategy. *Journal of Business Ethics*, 44(2–3): 185–93.

Deegan, C. (1996) Environmental reporting for Australian corporations: An analysis of contemporary Australian and overseas environmental reporting practices. *Environment and Planning Law Journal*, 13(2): 120–32.

Deegan, C. and Blomquist, C. (2006) Stakeholder influence on corporate reporting: An exploration of the interaction between the Worldwide Fund for Nature and the Australian minerals industry. *Accounting, Organizations and Society*, 31(4–5): 343–72.

Deegan, C. and Gordon, B. (1996) A study of the environmental disclosure practices of Australian corporations. *Accounting and Business Research*, 26(3): 187–99.

Deegan, C. and Rankin, M. (1997) The materiality of environmental information to users of annual reports. *Accounting, Auditing and Accountability Journal*, 10(4): 562–83.

Deegan, C., Rankin, M. and Voght, P. (2000) Firms' disclosure reactions to major social incidents: Australian evidence. *Accounting Forum*, 24(1): 101–30.

Ebrahim, A. (2003) Accountability in practice: Mechanisms for NGOs. *World Development*, 31(5): 813–29.

Elkington, J. (1993) Coming clean: The rise and rise of the corporate environmental report. *Business Strategy and the Environment*, 2(2): 42–4.

Elkington, J. and Fennell, S. (2000) Partners for sustainability. In J. Bendell (ed.) *Terms for endearment: Business, NGOs and sustainable development*. Sheffield: Greenleaf Publishing.

Estes, R. W. (1976) *Corporate social accounting*. New York: John Wiley and Sons.

Fayers, C. (1998) Environmental reporting and changing corporate environmental performance. *Accounting Forum*, 22(1): 74–94.

Fiedler, T. and Deegan, C. (2002) Environmental collaborations within the building and construction industry: A consideration of the motivations to collaborate. Paper presented at the Critical Perspectives on Accounting Conference (aux.zicklin.baruch-.cuny.edu/critical/html2/8036deegan.html), New York, 23 July 2003.

Ford, R. (1992) The green organization. In D. Koechlin and K. Müller (eds) *Green business opportunities: The profit potential*. London: Pitman, pp. 157–72.

Freeman, R. E. (1984) *Strategic management: A stakeholder approach*. Boston: Pitman.

Friedman, A. L. and Miles, S. (2002) Developing stakeholder theory. *Journal of Management Studies*, 39(1): 1–21.

Gadenne, D. and Danastas, L. (2004) A study of external pressure group influence on corporate social disclosure. Paper presented at the Corporate Governance and Ethics Conference, Sydney, 28–30 June.

Gaines, S. (1995) Growing pains, *Better World*, www.betterworld.com/BWZ/9604/cover2.htm, accessed 20 July 2005.

Gray, R. and Perks, B. (1982) How desirable is social accounting? *Accountancy*, April: 101–02.

Gray, R., Owen, D. and Adams, C. A. (1996) *Accounting and accountability: Changes and challenges in corporate social and environmental reporting*. London: Prentice-Hall.

Gray, R., Owen, D. and Maunders, K. (1987) *Corporate social reporting: Accounting and accountability*. London: Prentice-Hall.

Hardwick, J. (1991) Learning to live with green law. *International Financial Law Review, Special Supplement*: 3–6.

Heard, J. E. (1990) Institutional investors and corporate governance: The US perspective. In J.L. Lufkin and D. Gallagher (eds) *International corporate governance*. London: Euromoney Books.

Johnson, H. H. (2001) Corporate social audits: This time around. *Business Horizons*, 44(3): 29–36.

Keen, S. (1995) How green is my accountant? *New Accountant*, 8(20): 8.

King, D. and Mackinnon, A. (2002) Who cares? Community perceptions in the marketing of corporate citizenship. In J. Andriof, S. Waddock, B. Husted and S. Sutherland Rahman (eds) *Unfolding stakeholder thinking*. Sheffield: Greenleaf Publishing.

KPMG Peat Marwick (1996) *UK environmental reporting survey*. London: KPMG.

LaFrance, J. and Lehmann, M. (2005) Corporate awakening: Why (some) corporations embrace public–private partnerships. *Business Strategy and the Environment*, 14: 216–29.

Lange, H., Ramsay, I. and Woo, L. (2000) Corporate governance and anti-takeover defences: Evidence from Australia. *Corporate Governance: An International Review*, 8(3): 227–43.

Lawrence, A. T. (2002) The drivers of stakeholder engagement: Reflections on the case of Royal Dutch/Shell. In J. Andriof, S. Waddock, B. Husted and S. Sutherland Rahman (eds) *Unfolding stakeholder thinking*. Sheffield: Greenleaf Publishing.

Mattingly, J. E. and Greening, D. W. (2002) Chapter 14: Public-interest groups as stakeholders – a 'stakeholder salience' explanation of activism. In J. Andriof, S. Waddock, B. Husted and S. Sutherland Rahman (eds) *Unfolding stakeholder thinking*. Sheffield: Greenleaf Publishing.

McGrew, A. (1993) The political dynamics of the 'new' environmentalism. In D. Smith (ed.) *Business and the environment: Implications of the new environmentalism*. London: Paul Chapman.

Milne, M. J. and Chan, C. C. (1999) Narrative corporate social disclosures: How much of a difference do they make to investment decision-making? *British Accounting Review*, 31: 439–57.

Milne, M. J., Owen, D. and Tilt, C. A. (2000) Environmental reporting in Australia and New Zealand: corporate reactions to best practice. School of Commerce Research Paper Series, Flinders University, no. 00–21, www.ssn.flinders.edu.au/commerce/researchpapers/#00, accessed 15 September 2005.

Milne, M. J., Owen, D. L. and Tilt, C. A. (2001) Environmental reporting in Australia and New Zealand: Corporate reactions to best practice. *Auckland University Business Review*, 3(2). 24–36.

Müller, K. and Koechlin, D. (1992) Environmentally conscious management. In K. Müller and D. Koechlin (eds) *Green business opportunities: The profit potential*. London: Pitman, pp. 33–57.

O'Donovan, G. (1997) Legitimacy theory and corporate environmental disclosure: Some case study evidence. Paper presented at the Accounting Association of Australia and New Zealand Conference, Hobart, Australia, 6–9 July.

O'Dwyer, B. (2002) Managerial perceptions of corporate social disclosure: An Irish story. *Accounting, Auditing and Accountability Journal*, 15(3): 406–36.

O'Dwyer, B., Unerman, J. and Bradley, J. (2003) Stakeholder perceptions of corporate social disclosure in Ireland: A story of antagonism, powerlessness and poor practice. Paper presented at the 13th CSEAR Research Summer School, Dundee, Scotland, 1–3 September.

O'Dwyer, B., Unerman, J. and Bradley, J. (2005) Perceptions on the emergence and future development of corporate social disclosure in Ireland: Engaging the voices of non-governmental organisations. *Accounting, Auditing and Accountability Journal*, 18(1): 14–43.

Ogan, P. and Ziebart, D. A. (1991) Corporate reporting and the accounting profession: An interpretive paradigm. *Journal of Accounting, Auditing and Finance*, 6(3): 387–406.

O'Rourke, A. (2003) A new politics of engagement: Shareholder activism for corporate social responsibility. *Business Strategy and the Environment*, 12: 227–39.

O'Rourke, C. (2000) Support for arts and culture, but human rights neglected. *The Age*, 26 October, www.theage.com.au/news/20001026/A8995–2000Oct26.html, accessed 26 March 2001.

Owen, D., Gray, R. and Adams, R. (1996) Corporate environmental disclosure: Slow but steady progress. *Chartered Accountant*, 88(3): 18–22.

Owen, D., Gray, R. and Bebbington, J. (1997) Green accounting: Cosmetic irrelevance or radical agenda for change. *Asia-Pacific Journal of Accounting*, 4(2): 175–98.

Pearce, F. (2003) A greyer shade of green. *New Scientist*, 178(2400): 40–3.

Polonsky, M., Zeffane, R. and Medley, P. (1992) Corporate environmental commitment in Australia: A sectorial comparison. *Business Strategy and the Environment*, 1(2): 25–39.

PR Influences (2005a) Corporate reputation: Media still an important foundation, http://www.compad.com.au/cms/prinfluences/articles/588, accessed 16 January 2006.

PR Influences (2005b) US reputation survey tells how it is, www.compad.com.au/cms/prinfluences/articles/225, accessed 16 January 2006.

Rappaport, A. and Dillon, P. (1991) Private-sector environmental decision-making. In R. A. Chechile and S. Carlisle (eds) *Environmental decision-making: A multi-disciplinary perspective*. New York: Van Nostrand Reinhold.

Social Investment Forum (2003) 2003 report on socially responsible investing trends in the United States. *SIF Industry Research Program*, www.socialinvest.org/areas/research, accessed 16 January 2006.

Stikker, A. (1992) Foreword: Sustainability and business management. *Business Strategy and the Environment*, 1(3): 1–8.

Taberner, J., Gibb, S. and Sweeney, D. (1991) Learning to live with green law. *International Financial Law Review, Special Supplement*, February: 7–10.

Thomas, P. B. and Kenny, S. Y. (1997) Environmental reporting: A comparison of annual report disclosures and popular financial press commentary. Paper presented at the 5th International Perspectives on Accounting Conference, Manchester, 7–9 July.

Tilt, C. A. (1994) The influence of external pressure groups on corporate social disclosure: Some empirical evidence. *Accounting, Auditing and Accountability Journal*, 7(4): 47–72.

Tilt, C. A. (1997) Environmental policies of major companies: Australian evidence. *British Accounting Review*, 29(4): 367–94.

Tilt, C. A. (2004) Influences on corporate social disclosure: A look at lobby groups ten years on. *School of Commerce Research Paper Series, Flinders University*, no. 01–01, www.ssn.flinders.edu.au/commerce/researchpapers/#04, accessed 28 July 2005.

Tinker, T. (1985) *Paper prophets*. Eastbourne: Holt, Rinehart and Winston.

Tuininga, E. J. and Groenewegen, P. (1993) Sustainable development: A challenge for Dutch industry? *Business Strategy and the Environment*, 2(2): 28–41.

Unerman, J. and Bennett, M. (2004) Increased stakeholder dialogue and the internet: Towards greater corporate accountability or reinforcing capitalist hegemony? *Accounting, Organizations and Society*, 29(7): 685–707.

Warford, J. and Partow, Z. (1989) Evolution of the World Bank's environmental policy. *Finance and Development*, 26(4): 5–8.

Welford, R. and Gouldson, A. (1993) *Environmental management and business strategy*. London: Pitman.

Wiseman, J. (1982) An evaluation of environmental disclosures made in corporate annual reports. *Accounting, Organizations and Society*, 7(1): 53–63.

Worldwatch Institute (1992) *State of the world 1992: A report on progress toward a sustainable society*. New York: W. W. Norton and Company.

WWF (1999) *Mining environmental reports: Ore or overburden?* Melbourne: World Wildlife Fund, Australia.

Chapter 7

Organizational legitimacy as a motive for sustainability reporting

Craig Deegan

INTRODUCTION

This chapter provides an overview of legitimacy theory. In doing so it firstly defines *organizational legitimacy* and describes how organizational legitimacy can be considered to be a *resource* that is necessary to the survival of an organization. We then proceed to describe legitimacy theory as a *positive theory* that embraces a *systems oriented perspective* and which is derived from *political economy theory*.

Central to legitimacy theory is the theoretical construct known as the *social contract*. We will explore the meaning of the *social contract* and discuss how compliance with it is essential for establishing and maintaining *organizational legitimacy*. We will consider the implications that will flow should an organization breach its social contract and we will describe the strategies that managers of organizations might adopt should the social contract be violated.

We will briefly review a number of studies that have utilized legitimacy theory to explain corporate motivations for disclosing social and environmental information. We will also question whether organizations that appear to be behaving in accordance with legitimacy theory are actually acting in the broader interests of society. We will conclude the chapter by considering some of the limitations of legitimacy theory and some future research directions.[1]

ORGANIZATIONAL LEGITIMACY – WHAT IS IT?

From an organization's perspective, *legitimacy* has been defined by Lindblom (1994, p. 2) as:

> a condition or status which exists when an entity's value system is congruent with the value system of the larger social system of which the entity is

a part. When a disparity, actual or potential, exists between the two value systems, there is a threat to the entity's legitimacy.

Legitimacy is a relative concept – it is relative to the social system in which the entity operates and is *time* and *place* specific. As Suchman (1995, p. 574) states:

> Legitimacy is a generalised perception or assumption that the actions of an entity are desirable, proper, or appropriate *within* some socially constructed system of norms, values, beliefs, and definitions.

Legitimacy is considered to be a *resource* on which an organization is dependent for survival (Dowling and Pfeffer, 1975; O'Donovan, 2002). It is something that is conferred upon the organization by society, and it is something that is desired or sought by the organization. However, unlike many other 'resources', it is a 'resource' that the organization is considered to be able to impact or manipulate through various disclosure-related strategies. Legitimacy theory would suggest that whenever managers consider that the supply of the particular resource – *legitimacy* – is vital to organizational survival, then they will pursue strategies to ensure the continued supply of that resource. As we will see shortly, strategies aimed at gaining, maintaining or repairing legitimacy (often referred to as legitimation strategies) typically rely upon targeted disclosures.

For an organization seeking to be legitimate it is not the *actual* conduct of the organization that is important, it is what society collectively knows or *perceives* about the organization's conduct that shapes legitimacy. As Suchman (1995, p. 574) states:

> An organization may diverge dramatically from societal norms yet retain legitimacy because the divergence goes unnoticed. Legitimacy is socially constructed in that it reflects a congruence between the behaviours of the legitimated entity and the shared (or assumed shared) beliefs of some social group; thus legitimacy is dependent on a collective audience, yet independent of particular observers.

Consistent with the view that 'legitimacy' is based on *perceptions*, Nasi *et al.* (1997, p. 300) state:

> A corporation is legitimate when it is judged to be 'just and worthy of support' (Dowling and Pfeffer, 1975). Legitimacy therefore is not an abstract measure of the 'rightness' of the corporation but rather a measure of societal perceptions of the adequacy of corporate behaviour (Suchman, 1995). It is a measure of the attitude of society toward a corporation and its activities, and it is a matter of degree ranging from highly legitimate to

highly illegitimate. It is also important to point out that legitimacy is a social construct based on cultural norms for corporate behaviour. Therefore, the demands placed on corporations change over time, and different communities often have different ideas about what constitutes legitimate corporate behaviour.

WHAT 'TYPE' OF THEORY IS LEGITIMACY THEORY?

Legitimacy theory has been utilized by researchers when attempting to explain *why* corporate management undertake certain actions – such as disclosing particular items of social and environmental information. It is not a theory that is used to provide prescription about what management *ought* or *should* do. Hence, it is generally accepted that legitimacy theory is a *positive theory* (it seeks to explain or predict particular managerial activities).

Legitimacy theory has also been described as a *systems-based theory*. According to Gray *et al.* (1996, p. 45):

> a systems-oriented view of the organisation and society . . . permits us to focus on the role of information and disclosure in the relationship(s) between organisations, the State, individuals and groups.

Within a *systems-oriented perspective* (also sometimes referred to as an *open-systems perspective*), the entity is assumed to be influenced by, and in turn, to have influence upon the society in which it operates. Within a broader systems-oriented perspective, the perceptions of the organization, as held by other parties within that social system, are of importance to the survival of the organization. Commenting on the use of open-systems theorizing Suchman (1995, p. 571) states:

> Open-system theories have reconceptualised organisational boundaries as porous and problematic, and institutional theories (Powell and DiMaggio, 1991) have stressed that many dynamics in the organisational environment stem not from technological or material imperatives, but rather, from cultural norms, symbols, beliefs and rituals. Corporate disclosure policies are considered to represent one important means by which management can influence external perceptions about their organisation. At the core of this intellectual transformation lies the concept of organisational legitimacy.

Suchman (1995) also identifies that studies of legitimacy seem to fall within two distinct groups, these being the *strategic* and the *institutional* groups. In explaining the difference, Suchman (1995, p. 572) states:

129

Work in the strategic tradition (e.g., Ashforth and Gibbs, 1990; Dowling and Pfeffer, 1975; Pfeffer, 1981; Pfeffer and Salancik, 1978) adopts a managerial perspective and emphasises the ways in which organisations instrumentally manipulate and deploy evocative symbols in order to garner societal support. In contrast, work in the institutional tradition (e.g., Di Maggio and Powell, 1983; Meyer and Rowan, 1991; Meyer and Scott, 1983; Powell and Di Maggio, 1991; Zucker, 1987) adopts a more detached stance and emphasises the ways in which sector-wide structuration dynamics generate cultural pressures that transcend any single organisation's purposive control.

The vast majority of research that has utilised legitimacy theory, and which has focused on social and environmental or sustainability reporting, has been informed by the strategic (or managerial) perspective of legitimacy theory – and this will be the focus of this chapter.

Legitimacy theory (which we have so far described as a positive, systems-based theory which can either have a managerial or an institutional focus) originates from another theory – political economy theory. According to Deegan and Unerman (2006, p. 269):

> The 'political economy' itself has been defined by Gray et al. (1996, p. 47) as 'the social, political and economic framework within which human life takes place'. Political economy theory explicitly recognises the power conflicts that exist within society and the various struggles that occur between various groups within society. The perspective embraced in political economy theory, and also legitimacy theory, is that *society*, politics and *economics* are inseparable and economic issues cannot meaningfully be investigated in the absence of considerations about the political, social and institutional framework in which the economic activity takes place. It is argued that by considering the *political economy* a researcher is better able to consider broader (societal) issues which impact how an organisation operates, and what information it elects to disclose.

Following on from the above point, Guthrie and Parker explain the relevance of accounting within a political economy perspective. They state (1990, p. 166):

> The political economy perspective perceives accounting reports as social, political, and economic documents. They serve as a tool for constructing, sustaining, and legitimising economic and political arrangements, institutions, and ideological themes which contribute to the corporation's private interests.

Consistent with the view that organizations are part of a broader social system, the perspectives provided by legitimacy theory (which, as stated, build on foundations provided by political economy theory) indicate that organizations are not considered to have any inherent right to resources. Organizations exist to the extent that the particular society considers that they are *legitimate*, and if this is the case, the society 'confers' upon the organization the 'state' of *legitimacy*. If 'society' considers that organizations are not legitimate then this will have implications for the ongoing support and survival of the organization.

Whilst legitimacy theory is considered to derive from political economy theory, as we have indicated above, political economy theory itself has two broad branches. Legitimacy theory is derived from one of these branches. As Deegan (2006, p. 274) states:

> Political Economy Theory has been divided (perhaps somewhat simplistic-ally, but nevertheless usefully) into two broad streams which Gray, Owen and Adams (1996, p. 47) have labelled 'classical' and 'bourgeois' political economy. Classical political economy is related to the works of philo-sophers such as Karl Marx, and explicitly places 'sectional (class) interests, structural conflict, inequity, and the role of the State at the heart of the analysis' (Gray *et al.*, 1996, p. 47). This can be contrasted with 'bourgeois' political economy theory which, according to Gray, Kouhy and Lavers (1995, p. 53), largely ignores these elements and, as a result, is content to perceive the world as essentially pluralistic.

Classical political economy would tend to explain corporate disclosures as being a tool which powerful individuals (perhaps those in control of capital) use to maintain their own positions to the detriment of those individuals without power. Classical political economy focuses on the structural conflicts within society.[2]

By contrast, legitimacy theory – which is embedded in the 'bourgeois' branch of political economy theory – does not consider or question structural or class-based conflicts within society. It assumes that the views of a reasonably unified and pluralistic society shape the activities of organizations.[3] It is the failure to consider class struggles that has fuelled criticisms of legitimacy theory from many researchers working within the critical perspective of accounting.

Hence, to this point we can summarize the above discussion by noting that:

- within legitimacy theory, the resource of importance is *organizational legitimacy*;
- legitimacy theory is a *positive* theory;
- legitimacy theory is a *systems-oriented* (or open-system) theory;
- legitimacy theory has a *managerial branch* and an *institutional branch*, with most of the research within accounting being informed by the managerial branch;

131

■ legitimacy theory derives from the *bourgeois branch* of political economy theory, and as a result assumes a *pluralistic society*.

It should also be stressed that legitimacy theory has many similarities with another theory frequently used within the social and environmental accounting literature — this being stakeholder theory — which in itself is considered to have a managerial and ethical branch. Stakeholder theory (from the managerial branch) provides a view that organizations will react to the demands of those stakeholder groups that control resources necessary to the organization's operations (deemed to be 'powerful stakeholders') and will tend to disregard the concerns of those groups without power.[4] As Ullmann (1985, p 2) states:

> Our position is that organisations survive to the extent that they are effective. Their effectiveness derives from the management of demands, particularly the demands of interest groups upon which the organisation depends.

According to stakeholder theory, the disclosure of particular types of information can be used to gain or maintain the support of particular groups. That is, corporate disclosure is a strategy for managing, or perhaps *manipulating*, the demands of particular groups (Gray *et al.*, 1996).

Because of the many similarities between stakeholder theory and legitimacy theory, any attempt to treat them as sharply discrete theories would be wrong. As Deegan and Blomquist (2006) state:

> Both theories [legitimacy theory and stakeholder theory] conceptualise the organisation as part of a broader social system wherein the organisation impacts, and is impacted by, other groups within society. Whilst legitimacy theory discusses the expectations of society in general (as encapsulated within the 'social contract'), stakeholder theory provides a more refined resolution by referring to particular groups within society (stakeholder groups). Essentially, stakeholder theory accepts that because different stakeholder groups will have different views about how an organisation should conduct its operation, there will be various social contracts 'negotiated' with different stakeholder groups, rather than one contract with society in general. Whilst implied within legitimacy theory, stakeholder theory explicitly refers to issues of stakeholder power, and how a stakeholder's relative power impacts their ability to 'coerce' the organisation into complying with the stakeholder's expectations.

Legitimacy theory also has many similarities with another theory known as institutional theory. Indeed, Deegan (2006) argues that institutional theory provides a useful complement to both legitimacy theory and stakeholder theory. Specifically, Deegan (2006, p. 305) states:

> A key reason why institutional theory is relevant to researchers who investigate voluntary corporate reporting practices is that it provides a complementary perspective, to both Stakeholder Theory and Legitimacy Theory, in understanding how organisations understand and respond to changing social and institutional pressures and expectations. Among other factors, it links organisational practices (such as accounting and corporate reporting) to the values of the society in which an organisation operates, and to a need to maintain organisational legitimacy. There is a view that organisational form and practices might tend towards some form of homogeneity – that is, the structure of the organisation (including the structure of its reporting systems) and the practices adopted by different organisations tend to become similar to conform with what society, or particular powerful groups, consider to be 'normal'. Organisations that deviate from being of a form that has become 'normal' or expected will potentially have problems in gaining or retaining legitimacy.

Whilst we will not pursue further discussion of stakeholder theory or institutional theory – those individuals interested in applying legitimacy theory should make the effort to consider the many similarities legitimacy theory has with both stakeholder and with institutional theory.

Returning to legitimacy theory, one theoretical construct that is very important to the utilization of legitimacy theory is the 'social contract' which we will now discuss.

THE SOCIAL CONTRACT AND ITS RELEVANCE TO LEGITIMACY THEORY

A central premise of legitimacy theory is that organizations can maintain their operations only to the extent that they have the support of the community. Such support is earned as a result of the organization being *perceived* by society as complying with the expectations of the society with which they interact. The expectations that society has with regards to how an entity shall act are considered to constitute the *social contract* between the organization and society. Specifically, it is considered that an organization's survival will be threatened if society perceives that the organization has breached its social contract. As Deegan (2006, p. 280) states:

> Where society is not satisfied that the organisation is operating in an acceptable, or *legitimate* manner, then society will effectively revoke the

organisation's 'contract' to continue its operations. This might be evidenced through, for example, consumers reducing or eliminating the demand for the products of the business, factor suppliers eliminating the supply of labour and financial capital to the business, or constituents lobbying government for increased taxes, fines or laws to prohibit those actions which do not conform with the expectations of the community.

It is emphasized that the social contract is a theoretical construct, and hence an individual cannot simply go and find a copy of the contract. Different managers will have different perceptions about how society expects the organization to behave across the various attributes of its activities – and this in itself can explain, at least in part, why some managers will elect to do things differently to other managers. If a manager undertakes certain actions that are subsequently found to be unacceptable to the community (for example, sourcing clothing from Asian 'sweatshops' – an issue that recently outraged many people within the community) then legitimacy theory would explain this in terms of the manager misinterpreting the terms of the social contract. Consider the implications for Nike, GAP and other clothing and footwear manufacturers when the media ran campaigns about their association with various abusive 'sweatshops'.

The social contract is considered to be made up of numerous terms (or clauses) – some explicit and some implicit. As Deegan (2006, p. 278) states:

> Gray, Owen and Adams (1996) suggest that legal requirements provide the *explicit terms* of the contract, while other non-legislated societal expectations embody the *implicit terms* of the contract. That is, there is an imperfect correlation between the law and societal norms and according to Dowling and Pfeffer (1975), there are three broad reasons for the difference. Firstly, even though laws are reflective of societal norms and values, legal systems are slow to adapt to changes in the norms and values in society. Secondly, legal systems often strive for consistency whereas societal norms and expectation can be contradictory. Thirdly, it is suggested that whilst society may not be accepting of certain behaviours, it may not be willing or structured enough to have those behavioural restrictions codified within law. It is in relation to the composition of the implicit terms of the 'contract' that we can expect managers' perceptions to vary greatly.[5]

IMPLICATIONS OF CORPORATE NON-COMPLIANCE WITH THE SOCIAL CONTRACT

According to Deegan (2006), the term 'legitimacy gap' has been utilized to describe the situation where there appears to be a lack of correspondence between how society believes an organization *should* act and how it is *perceived* that the organization has acted. In relation to how legitimacy gaps arise, Sethi (1977) describes two major sources of the gaps. Firstly, societal expectations might change, and this will lead to a gap arising even though the organization is operating in the same manner as it always had. As an example of this source of a legitimacy gap, Nasi *et al.* (1997, p. 301) state:

> For American tobacco companies in the 1970s, for example, the increasing awareness of the health consequences of smoking resulted in a significant and widening legitimacy gap (Miles and Cameron, 1982). The tobacco companies had not changed their activities, and their image was much the same as it had been, yet they suddenly faced a significantly different evaluation of their role in society; they faced a significant and widening legitimacy gap.

As we have already emphasized, community expectations are not considered static, but rather, change across time, thereby necessitating the organization to be responsive to current and future changes to the environment in which they operate. Whilst organizations might modify their behaviour to conform with community expectations, if the momentum of their change is slower than the changing expectations of society, then legitimacy gaps will arise.

Legitimacy itself can be threatened even when an organization's performance is not deviating from society's expectations of appropriate performance. This might be because the organization has failed to make disclosures that show it is complying with society's expectations, which in themselves, might be changing across time. That is, legitimacy is assumed to be influenced by disclosures of information, and not simply by (undisclosed) changes in corporate actions. If society's expectations about performance change, then arguably an organization will need to show that what it is doing is also changing (or perhaps it will need to explicitly communicate and justify why its operations have *not* changed). In relation to the dynamics associated with changing expectations, Lindblom (1994, p. 3) states:

> Legitimacy is dynamic in that the relevant publics continuously evaluate corporate output, methods, and goals against an ever evolving expectation. The legitimacy gap will fluctuate without any changes in action on the part of the corporation. Indeed, as expectations of the relevant publics change the corporation must make changes or the legitimacy gap will grow as the

level of conflict increases and the levels of positive and passive support decreases.

The second major source of a legitimacy gap, according to Sethi (1977), occurs when previously unknown information becomes known about the organization — perhaps through disclosure being made within the news media. In relation to this possibility, Nasi *et al.* (1997, p. 301) make an interesting reference to 'organisational shadows'. They state:

> The potential body of information about the corporation that is unavailable to the public – the corporate shadow (Bowles, 1991) – stands as a constant potential threat to a corporation's legitimacy. When part of the organisational shadow is revealed, either accidentally or through the activities of an activist group or a journalist, a legitimacy gap may be created.

In relation to the above source of a legitimacy gap, we can consider how society reacted to media revelations made about certain sportswear companies' alleged sourcing of products from sweatshops in Asia (for example, Nike); revelations about the pollution being caused by mining companies' tailings dams in remote environments (for example, BHP Billiton's operations in Papua New Guinea); or, revelations about how the products of particular companies impact consumer health (for example, the reaction to the McDonald's investigation as told within the movie *Supersize me*). All these revelations arguably had significant cost implications for the respective companies involved – and to solve the legitimacy problems the organizations typically relied upon various disclosure strategies.

HOW WILL AN ORGANIZATION RESPOND WHEN A LEGITIMACY GAP IS PERCEIVED TO EXIST?

Much of the work that has been undertaken within the social and environmental accounting area, and which has embraced legitimacy theory, has typically addressed actions undertaken by organizations to *regain* their legitimacy after some form of legitimacy-threatening event occurs. But as authors such as Suchman (1995) and O'Donovan (2002) indicate, legitimation strategies might be used to either *gain*, maintain, or *repair* legitimacy. According to O'Donovan (2002, p. 349):

> Legitimation techniques/tactics chosen will differ depending upon whether the organisation is trying to gain or extend legitimacy, to maintain its current level of legitimacy, or to repair or to defend its lost or threatened legitimacy.

136

Whilst researchers have proposed that legitimation tactics might differ depending upon whether the entity is trying to *gain*, *maintain*, or *repair* legitimacy, the theoretical development in this area remains weak. Although the literature provides some general commentary, there is a lack of guidance about the relative effectiveness of legitimation strategies with regard to either gaining, maintaining, or regaining legitimacy. In terms of the general commentary provided within the literature, gaining legitimacy occurs when an organization moves into a new area of operations in which it has no past reputation. In such a situation the organization suffers from the 'liability of newness' (Ashforth and Gibbs, 1990) and it needs to proactively engage in activities to win acceptance.

The task of *maintaining* legitimacy is typically considered easier than *gaining* or *repairing* legitimacy (O'Donovan, 2002; Ashforth and Gibbs, 1990). One of the 'tricks' in maintaining legitimacy is to be able to anticipate changing community perceptions. According to Suchman (1995, p. 594), strategies for maintaining legitimacy fall into two groups — forecasting future changes and protecting past accomplishments. In relation to monitoring or forecasting changing community perceptions, Suchman (1995, p. 595) states:

> Managers must guard against becoming so enamored with their own legitimating myths that they lose sight of external developments that might bring those myths into question. With advanced warning, managers can engage in pre-emptive conformity, selection, or manipulation, keeping the organization and its environment in close alignment; without such warning, managers will find themselves constantly struggling to regain lost ground. In general, perceptual strategies involve monitoring the cultural environment and assimilating elements of that environment into organizational decision processes, usually by employing boundary-spanning personnel as bridges across which the organization can learn audience values, beliefs, and reaction.

In relation to protecting past (legitimacy-enhancing) accomplishments, Suchman (1995, p. 595) states:

> In addition to guarding against unforeseen challenges, organizations may seek to buttress the legitimacy they have already acquired. In particular, organizations can enhance their security by converting legitimacy from episodic to continual forms. To a large extent this boils down to (a) policing internal operations to prevent miscues, (b) curtailing highly visible legitimation efforts in favour of more subtle techniques, and (c) developing a defensive stockpile of supportive beliefs, attitudes and accounts.

In relation to *maintaining* legitimacy, the greater the extent to which the organization trades on its level of legitimacy the more crucial will it be for that organization to ensure that it does not deviate from the high standards that it has established. For example, compare an armaments manufacturer with, say, The Body Shop. The products of armaments manufacturers are designed to kill – such an organization arguably has less to worry about in terms of its legitimacy than The Body Shop. The Body Shop trades on its reputation for caring about the environment, society, and the welfare of animals. If, perhaps, an organization within the supply chain of The Body Shop – and without the knowledge of The Body Shop – undertook activities that were somehow related to animal testing or with particular environmental damage and such facts were found out by the media, for example, then this could be extremely costly to the organization. It has a lot of *investment in legitimacy* to lose.

In considering *repairing* legitimacy, Suchman (1995, p. 597) suggests that related legitimation techniques tend to be reactive responses to often unforeseen crises. In many respects, *repairing* and *gaining* legitimacy are similar. As O'Donovan (2002, p. 350) states:

> Repairing legitimacy has been related to different levels of crisis management (Davidson, 1991; Elsbach and Sutton, 1992). The task of repairing legitimacy is, in some ways, similar to gaining legitimacy. If a crisis is evolving proactive strategies may need to be adopted, as has been the case for the tobacco industry during the past two decades (Pava and Krausz, 1997). Generally, however, the main difference is that strategies for repairing legitimacy are reactive, usually to an unforseen and immediate crisis, whereas techniques to gain legitimacy are usually *ex ante*, proactive and not normally related to crisis.

In the discussion that follows we will consider the strategies that can be used by corporate management in an effort to *gain*, *maintain* or *regain* legitimacy. As we have already indicated, our theoretical development has not developed sufficiently to link specific legitimation techniques with efforts to either gain, maintain or regain legitimacy. Most of the proposed legitimation techniques appear to relate to regaining legitimacy in the light of particular crises – something that has tended to be the focus of many researchers working within the social and environmental accounting area (and who embrace legitimacy theory). Nevertheless, all legitimation strategies rely upon disclosure.

In considering organizational strategies for maintaining or creating congruence between the social values implied by an organization's operations, and the values embraced by society, we can usefully apply the insights provided by Dowling and Pfeffer (1975). Dowling and Pfeffer outline the means by which an organization, when faced with legitimacy threats, may legitimate its activities (p. 127). Tactics might include the following:

- The organization can adapt its output, goals and methods of operation to conform to prevailing definitions of legitimacy.
- The organization can attempt, through communication, to alter the definition of social legitimacy so that it conforms to the organization's present practices, output and values.
- The organization can attempt through communication to become identified with symbols, values or institutions which have a strong base of legitimacy.

Consistent with Dowling and Pfeffer's strategy of 'communication', Lindblom (1994) proposes that an organization can adopt a number of strategies where it perceives that its legitimacy is in question because its actions (or operations) are perceived to be at variance with society's expectations and values. Lindblom (1994) identifies four courses of action (there is some overlap with Dowling and Pfeffer) that an organization can take to obtain, or maintain, legitimacy in these circumstances. The organization can:

1   seek to educate and inform its 'relevant publics' about (actual) changes in the organization's performance and activities which bring the activities and performance more into line with society's values and expectations;
2   seek to change the perceptions that 'relevant publics' have of the organization's performance and activities – but not change the organization's actual behaviour (while using disclosures in corporate reports to falsely indicate that the performance and activities have changed);
3   seek to manipulate perception by deflecting attention from the issue of concern onto other related issues through an appeal to, for example, emotive symbols, thus seeking to demonstrate how the organization has fulfilled social expectations in other areas of its activities; or
4   seek to change external expectations of its performance, possibly by demonstrating that specific societal expectations are unreasonable.

In all cases, the disclosure of information to 'relevant publics' is essential for influencing legitimacy. A corporation may use a variety of legitimating techniques to execute its chosen strategy. Consistent with the above discussion, Ashforth and Gibbs (1990) provide two general categories of legitimating techniques that a corporation may adopt – substantive and symbolic management techniques. The use of *substantive* management techniques 'involves real, material change in organizational goals, structures, and processes or socially institutionalised practices' (Ashforth and Gibbs, 1990, p. 178). Alternatively, the corporation may change its relevant publics, or the level of degree to which it is dependent on those publics' resources. At the other end of the spectrum the corporation may adopt techniques to actively align the values of society to those of the corporation (Ashforth and

Gibbs, 1990). Regardless of the approach adopted, substantive management techniques involve a *real* change in the behaviour of the corporation.

In contrast, *symbolic* management techniques of legitimation involve the *portrayal* of corporate behaviour in a manner to '*appear* consistent with social values and expectations' (Ashforth and Gibbs, 1990, p. 180). Companies may publish policies on various issues including the environment, but may not enforce or set in place mechanisms for the full adoption of such policies. According to Ashforth and Gibbs (1990), it is not necessary to use either substantive or symbolic management techniques exclusively. Corporations may adopt a mix of substantive and/or symbolic legitimating techniques and may apply these with varying levels of intensity.

Whichever one of the above legitimizing strategies is adopted, we again emphasize that they will rely upon disclosure if they are to be successful. In providing an illustration of the first strategy proposed by Dowling and Pfeffer we can refer to the leading sportswear company, Nike. As Deegan (2005, p. 1141) explains, Nike had been heavily criticized because people manufacturing its products were paid extremely low (and perceived unfair) wages, and were subject to various types of abuse. This impacted the sales of Nike's products. In reaction to the community concern Nike ultimately undertook reviews (or social audits) of the various factories supplying its goods. The background to the reviews, the results of the reviews, and the organizational changes brought about as a result of the reviews were publicized by Nike in its publicly available social report, as well as providing detailed commentary on its website. Legitimacy theory would suggest that Nike took the action it did because the revelations about sweatshop abuses (heavily publicized in the media) had created a significant *legitimacy gap* which in turn was undermining the entity's performance. The gap needed to be reduced and the disclosure of information about various activities would be expected to help reduce the gap.

In relation to the second approach to legitimation described by Dowling and Pfeffer we might consider tobacco companies. In recent years tobacco companies have been heavily criticized because of their impacts on addicted consumers. A number of the major producers have responded by releasing social reports, which, among other things, emphasize that consumers make the choice to smoke cigarettes and that the companies are simply satisfying a legal demand. The reports also tend to emphasize the work of tobacco companies within the community – for example, supporting sporting events and putting in place mechanisms to discourage young smokers.

As an example of the third legitimating tactic identified by Dowling and Pfeffer we could consider the example of where industry bodies develop social and environmental codes of conduct. Deegan and Blomquist (2006) provide an Australian example wherein the Australian Mineral Council developed a Code of Environmental Management to be followed by its members. The Code was considered to be a symbol of legitimacy. Hence, legitimizing strategies can also occur at an industry level. Having a code of environmental management could arguably be seen as a symbolic commitment to improved environmental performance by the industry body that developed the code, and by those companies who commit to it.

USE OF LEGITIMACY THEORY IN STUDIES OF SOCIAL AND ENVIRONMENTAL REPORTING

There have been numerous studies in the social and environmental accounting literature that have embraced legitimacy theory.[6] Whilst the following discussion is far from comprehensive, it does provide reference to some of the main research papers in the area.

One of the early studies to embrace legitimacy theory was Hogner (1982). Hogner examined corporate social reporting in the annual reports of US Steel Corporation over a period of eighty years, commencing in 1901, the data being analysed for year-to-year variation. Hogner showed that the extent of social disclosures varied from year to year and he speculated that the variation could represent a response to society's changing expectations of corporate behaviour.

Another influential paper was Guthrie and Parker (1989). Guthrie and Parker sought to match the disclosure practices of BHP Ltd (BHP Ltd is a large Australian company and has subsequently become BHP Billiton) across the period from 1885 to 1985 with a historical account of major events relating to BHP Ltd. The argument was that if corporate disclosure policies are reactive to major social and environmental events, then there should be correspondence between peaks of disclosure, and events which are significant in BHP Ltd's history. Whilst this paper did not provide evidence supportive of legitimacy theory (perhaps due to data limitations, as Deegan *et al.*, 2002, explain) a large number of subsequent research studies have used and refined their arguments.

Another important paper was Patten (1992) which focused on the change in the extent of environmental disclosures made by North American oil companies, other than just Exxon Oil Company, both before and after the *Exxon Valdez* incident in Alaska in 1989. Patten argued that if the Alaskan oil spill resulted in a threat to the legitimacy of the petroleum industry, and not just to Exxon, then Legitimacy Theory would suggest that companies operating within that industry would respond by increasing the amount of environmental disclosures in their annual reports. Patten's results indicate that there were increased environmental disclosures by the petroleum companies for the post-1989 period, consistent with a legitimation perspective. This disclosure reaction took place across the industry, even though the incident itself was directly related to one oil company.

Gray *et al.* (1995) performed a longitudinal review of UK corporate social and environmental disclosures for the period 1979 to 1991. After considering the extent and types of corporate disclosures, they stated (p. 65):

Increasingly, companies are being required to demonstrate a satisfactory performance within the environmental domain. Corporate social reporting would appear to be one on the mechanisms by which the organisations satisfy (and manipulate) that requirement.

In relation to trends found in regard to health and safety disclosures Gray *et al.* (p. 65) stated:

> We are persuaded that companies were increasingly under pressure from various 'relevant publics' to improve their performance in the area of health and safety and employed corporate social reporting to manage this 'legitimacy gap'. That is, while the disclosure did not, as such, demonstrate improved health and safety records (lack of previous information makes such assessment impossible), it did paint a picture of increasing concern being given by companies to the matter of protecting and training their workforce. This disclosure then helped add to the image of a competent and concerned organisation which took its responsibilities in this field seriously.

Brown and Deegan (1998) extended the legitimacy theory literature by incorporating media agenda-setting theory. Media agenda-setting theory is explained by Ader (1995, p. 300):

> The agenda-setting hypothesis . . . posits a relationship between the relative emphasis given by the media to various topics and the degree of salience these topics have for the general public. Individuals note the amount of and distribution of media coverage among issues, and this determines the salience of each issue for the individuals. According to the agenda-setting hypothesis, the media do not mirror public priorities as much as they influence them.[7]

Brown and Deegan used the extent of media coverage given to a particular environmental issue as a measure (or proxy) of community concern. In terms of causality, increased media attention is believed to lead to increased community concern for a particular issue. The results in Brown and Deegan (1998) indicate that for the majority of the industries studied, higher levels of media attention given to specific social and environmental issues (as determined by a review of a number of print media newspapers and journals) are significantly associated with higher levels of annual report environmental disclosures in relation to such issues. In concluding their study, Brown and Deegan stated:

> This study has contributed to the literature because it has shown, unlike any other known study, that the environmental disclosure strategies of

management within some industries is associated with the extent of media attention. More specifically, variations in media attention appear to be associated with variations in corporate disclosures. It has further contributed to the literature by showing that not all industries react in the same manner to variation in the level of media attention. Taken together, the results provide a further resource for those individuals/organisations attempting to explain or understand what drives particular entities to voluntarily disclose environmental information in their annual report.

Deegan and Rankin (1996) utilized Legitimacy Theory to try to explain systematic changes in corporate annual report environmental disclosure policies around the time of proven environmental prosecutions. Deegan and Rankin found that prosecuted firms disclosed significantly more environmental information (of a favourable nature) in the year of prosecution than any other year in the sample period. Consistent with the view that companies increase disclosure to offset any effects of environmental prosecutions, the prosecuted firms also disclosed more positive environmental information, relative to non-prosecuted firms.

In another study, Deegan and Gordon (1996) reviewed annual report environmental disclosures made by a sample of companies from 1980 to 1991. They investigated the objectivity of corporate environmental disclosure practices and trends in environmental disclosures over time. They also sought to determine if environmental disclosures were related to concerns held by environmental groups about particular industries' environmental performance. The results derived by the Deegan and Gordon (1996) study indicated, among other findings, that during the period covered by the study: (1) increases in corporate environmental disclosures over time were positively associated with increases in the levels of environmental group membership; (2) corporate environmental disclosures were overwhelmingly self-laudatory; and (3) there was a positive correlation between the environmental sensitivity of the industry to which the corporation belonged and the level of corporate environmental disclosure.[8]

ARE LEGITIMATING STRATEGIES IN THE INTERESTS OF SOCIETY?

In this chapter we have provided evidence to suggest that, consistent with legitimacy theory, corporate social and environmental disclosures appear to react to community expectations – but we can briefly reflect upon whether this is actually a 'good thing'. Further, are such corporate disclosures really reflective of an acceptance that an organization has an accountability for its social and environmental performance, *or* are they merely a mechanism to support the existence of the organization? As Deegan *et al.* (2002) state:

143

Legitimising disclosures mean that the organisation is responding to particular concerns that have arisen in relation to their operations. The implication is that unless concerns are aroused (and importantly, the managers *perceive* the existence of such concerns) then **unregulated** disclosures could be quite minimal. Disclosure decisions driven by the desire to be legitimate are not the same as disclosure policies driven by a management view that the community has a *right-to-know* about certain aspects of an organisation's operations. One motivation relates to survival, whereas the other motivation relates to responsibility. Arguably, companies that simply react to community concerns are not truly embracing a notion of accountability. Studies providing results consistent with Legitimacy Theory (and there are many of them) leave us with a view that unless specific concerns are raised then no *accountability* appears to be due. Unless community concern happens to be raised (perhaps as a result of a major social or environmental incident which attracts media attention), there will be little or no corporate disclosure.

Further, and utilizing the work of Cooper and Sherer (1984), Deegan *et al.* argue that legitimizing disclosures simply act to sustain corporate operations which are of concern to some individuals within society. To the extent that the corporate social and environmental disclosures reflect or portray management concern as well as corporate moves towards actual change, the corporate disclosures may be merely forestalling any *real* changes in corporate activities. Taking this position even further, Puxty (1991, p. 39) states:

> I do not accept that I see legitimation as innocuous. It seems to me that the legitimation can be very harmful indeed, insofar as it acts as a barrier to enlightenment and hence progress.

From the above discussion we can argue that organizations that are shown to be embracing legitimizing strategies – and evidence indicates that there are many of them – are not really likely to be embracing a broader sustainability ethos. 'True' sustainability would require management to accept that they have a responsibility and an accountability to the environment and to current and future generations which would not simply be reactive to community concerns. The evidence provided in numerous social and environmental accounting research studies suggests that higher levels of social and environmental disclosure will only occur when community concerns are aroused. Globally, there is a general lack of regulatory requirements for corporations to make sustainability-related disclosures meaning that corporate management is typically in charge of determining the extent of disclosure. In this regard, Deegan *et al.* (2002) emphasize that if corporate legitimizing activities are successful then public pressure for government to introduce disclosure legislation will be low and managers will retain control of their social and environmental reporting practices. Accountability will be 'captured' and progress towards sustainability will be hindered.

LIMITATIONS OF LEGITIMACY THEORY AND FUTURE 'WAYS FORWARD'?

Whilst legitimacy theory is widely used in social and environmental accounting research, it nevertheless is not without its critics. Some of the criticisms include the following.

■ There is a lack of research that demonstrates that legitimizing disclosures *actually* work in reducing *legitimacy gaps*.

■ There is a lack of research that explores which specific types of disclosures are relatively more effective in changing community expectations.

■ There are problems of resolution – legitimacy theory tends to focus on society at large and does not explore whether particular groups within society might be relatively more influenced by corporate disclosures.

■ Research utilizing legitimacy theory fails to provide insights about the attributes of managers that influence how they respond to legitimacy threats – or indeed, how they perceive the existence of *legitimacy threats*.

■ There is little research undertaken on how managers become aware of the terms of the *social contract*.

■ Proponents of legitimacy theory often talk about 'society', and compliance with the expectations of society (as embodied within the *social contract*). However, this provides poor resolution given that *society* is clearly made up of various groups having unequal power or ability to influence the activities of other groups. Stakeholder theory provides some assistance.

■ Whilst researchers have proposed that legitimation tactics might differ depending upon whether the entity is trying to *gain*, *maintain*, or *repair* legitimacy, the theoretical development in this area remains weak.

Legitimacy theory, whilst providing some useful insights into corporate disclosure practices, is therefore not without its limitations. Nevertheless, its popularity amongst researchers appears to be far from waning. At present legitimacy theory requires greater development and it is expected that researchers seeking to publish in the area will be required to refine the theory so as to address such points as those identified above.

NOTES

1   The material in this chapter is largely based on material that appears in Deegan (2002), Deegan and Unerman (2006) and Deegan (2006).

2   As we will see later in this chapter, authors such as Puxty (1991) have indicated that legitimizing disclosures made by corporations tend to allow businesses to continue in a 'business-as-usual' way even when the corporations are creating harm to other less powerful sectors of society.

3   A pluralistic perspective assumes (typically implicitly) that many classes of stakeholders have the power to influence various decisions by corporations, government and other entities. Within this perspective, accounting is not considered to be put in place to favour specific interests (sometimes referred to as 'elites'). By using 'society' as the topic of focus rather than *subgroups* within society, theories such as Legitimacy Theory ignore 'struggles and inequities within society' (Puxty, 1991).

4   It should be appreciated however that 'stakeholder theory' is a broad 'umbrella' term for a number of theoretical perspectives. As discussed in Deegan and Unerman (2006) there is a normative branch of stakeholder theory which prescribes how organizations *should* interact with their stakeholders (for example, see Freeman and Reed, 1983; Hasnas, 1998). There is also a managerial branch of stakeholder theory that explains how organizations do interact with their stakeholders (for example, Ullman, 1985; Roberts, 1992; Nasi *et al.*, 1997).

5   As Deegan and Unerman (2006) indicate, the theoretical construct of the social contract is not new, having been discussed by philosophers such as Thomas Hobbes (1588–1679), John Locke (1632–1704), and Jean-Jacques Rousseau (1712–1778).

6   A number of journals have run special editions that have addressed social and environmental accounting issues, and which have utilized legitimacy theory. For example, see *Accounting, Auditing and Accountability Journal* (vol. 10, no. 4, 1997, and vol. 15, no. 3, 2002), *Accounting Forum* (vol. 19, no. 2/3, 1995 and vol. 24, no. 1, 2000, vol. 28, no. 1, 2004), *European Accounting Review* (vol. 9, no. 1, 2000) and *Asia Pacific Journal of Accounting* (vol. 4, no. 2, 1997). Also, the Centre for Social and Environmental Accounting Research (CSEAR) provides, on its website, reference to various papers that have embraced legitimacy theory – see the reading lists provided at www.st-andrews.ac.uk/management/csear/.

7   For an explanation of Media Agenda Setting Theory see McCombs and Shaw (1972); Zucker (1978); Eyal *et al.* (1981); Blood (1981); Mayer (1980); McCombs (1981); Ader (1995).

8   Environmental sensitivity was determined by use of a questionnaire to environmental lobby groups in which office bearers were required to rate industries (on a 0 to 5 scale) on the basis of whether the industry had been made the focus of action as a result of its environmental performance/implications.

REFERENCES

Ader, C. (1995) A longitudinal study of agenda setting for the issue of environmental pollution. *Journalism & Mass Communication Quarterly*, 72(3): 300–11.

Ashforth, B. and Gibbs, B. (1990) The double edge of legitimization. *Organization Science*, 1: 177–94.

Blood, R. W. (1981) Unobtrusive issues and the agenda-setting role of the press, unpublished doctoral dissertation, Syracuse University, New York.

Brown, N. and Deegan, C. (1998) The public disclosure of environmental performance information: A dual test of media agenda setting theory and legitimacy theory. *Accounting and Business Research*, 29(1): 21–41.

Cooper, D. J. and Sherer, M. J. (1984) The value of corporate accounting reports: Arguments for a political economy of accounting. *Accounting, Organizations and Society*, 9(3–4): 207–32.

Deegan, C (2002) The legitimising effect of social and environmental disclosures: A theoretical foundation. *Accounting, Auditing and Accountability Journal*, 15(3): 282–311.

Deegan, C. (2005) *Australian financial accounting*, 4th edn. Sydney: McGraw-Hill.

Deegan, C. (2006) *Financial accounting theory*, 2nd edn. Sydney: McGraw-Hill.

Deegan, C. and Blomquist, C. (2006) Stakeholder influence on corporate reporting: An exploration of the interaction between WWF–Australia and the Australian Minerals Industry. *Accounting, Organizations and Society*, 31(4–5): 343–72.

Deegan, C. and Gordon, B. (1996) A study of the environmental disclosure practices of Australian corporations. *Accounting and Business Research*, 26(3): 187–99.

Deegan, C. and Rankin, M. (1996) Do Australian companies report environmental news objectively? An analysis of environmental disclosures by firms prosecuted successfully by the environmental protection authority. *Accounting, Auditing and Accountability Journal*, 9(2): 52–69.

Deegan, C. and Unerman, J. (2006) *Financial accounting theory*, European edn. London: McGraw-Hill UK.

Deegan, C., Rankin, M. and Tobin, J. (2002) An examination of the corporate social and environmental disclosures of BHP from 1983–1997. *Accounting, Auditing and Accountability Journal*, 15(3): 312–43.

DiMaggio, P. J. and Powell, W. W. (1983) The iron cage revisited: Institutional isomorphism and collective rationality in organizational fields. *American Sociological Review*, 48: 146–60.

Dowling, J. and Pfeffer, J. (1975) Organisational legitimacy: Social values and organisational behavior. *Pacific Sociological Review*, 18(1): 122–36.

Eyal, C. H., Winter, J. P. and DeGeorge, W. F. (1981) The concept of time frame in agenda setting. In G. C. Wilhoit (ed.) *Mass communication yearbook*, Beverly Hills, CA: Sage.

147

Freeman, R. and Reed, D. (1983) Stockholders and stakeholders: A new perspective on corporate governance. *Californian Management Review*, 25(2): 88–106.

Gray, R., Kouhy, R. and Lavers, S. (1995) Corporate social and environmental reporting: A review of the literature and a longitudinal study of UK disclosure. *Accounting, Auditing and Accountability Journal*, 8(2): 47–77.

Gray, R., Owen, D. and Adams, C. (1996) *Accounting and accountability: Changes and challenges in corporate social and environmental reporting*. London: Prentice-Hall.

Guthrie, J. and Parker, L. D. (1989) Corporate social reporting: A rebuttal of legitimacy theory. *Accounting and Business Research*, 19(76): 343–52.

Guthrie, J. and Parker, L. (1990) Corporate social disclosure practice: A comparative international analysis. *Advances in Public Interest Accounting*, 3: 159–75.

Hasnas, J. (1998) The normative theories of business ethics: A guide for the perplexed. *Business Ethics Quarterly*, 8(1): 19–42.

Hogner, R. H. (1982) Corporate social reporting: Eight decades of development at US Steel. *Research in Corporate Performance and Policy*, 4: 243–50.

Lindblom, C. K. (1994) The implications of organisational legitimacy for corporate social performance and disclosure. Critical Perspectives on Accounting Conference, New York.

Mayer, H. (1980) Power and the press. *Murdoch University News*, 7(8).

McCombs, M. (1981) The agenda-setting approach. In D. Nimmo and K. Sanders (eds) *Handbook of political communication*. Beverly Hills, CA: Sage.

McCombs, M. and Shaw, D. (1972) The agenda setting function of mass media. *Public Opinion Quarterly* 36: 176–87.

Meyer, J. W. and Rowan, B. (1977) Institutionalized organizations: Formal structure as myth and ceremony. *American Journal of Sociology*, 83: 340–63.

Miles, R. and Cameron, K. (1982) *Coffin nails and corporate strategies*. Englewood Cliffs, NJ: Prentice-Hall.

Nasi, J., Nasi, S., Phillips, N. and Zyglidopoulos, S. (1997) The evolution of corporate social responsiveness: An exploratory study of Finnish and Canadian forestry companies. *Business & Society*, 38(3): 296–321.

O'Donovan, G. (2002) Environmental disclosures in the annual report: Extending the applicability and predictive power of legitimacy theory. *Accounting, Auditing and Accountability Journal*, 15(3): 344–71.

Patton, D. M. (1992) Intra-industry environmental disclosures in response to the Alaskan oil spill: A note on legitimacy theory. *Accounting, Organizations and Society*, 15(5): 471–75.

Pfeffer, J. and Salancik, G. (1978) *The external control of organizations: A resource dependence perspective*. New York: Harper & Row.

Powell, W. W. and DiMaggio, P. J. (eds) (1991) *The new institutionalism in organizational analysis*. Chicago, IL: University of Chicago Press.

Puxty, A. (1991) Social accountability and universal pragmatics. *Advances in Public Interest Accounting*, 4: 35–46.

Roberts, R. (1992) Determinants of corporate social responsibility disclosure: An application of stakeholder theory. *Accounting, Organizations and Society*, 17(6): 595–612.

Ronen, J. (1979) The dual role of accounting: A financial economic perspective. In J. L. Bicksler (ed.) *Handbook of financial economics*. Amsterdam: North Holland.

Sethi, S. P. (1977) Dimensions of corporate social performance: An analytical framework. In A.B. Carroll (ed.) *Managing corporate social responsibility*. Boston, MA: Little, Brown.

Suchman, M. C. (1995) Managing legitimacy: Strategic and institutional approaches. *Academy of Management Review*, 20(3): 571–610.

Ullmann, A. (1985) Data in search of a theory: A critical examination of the relationships among social performance, social disclosure, and economic performance of US firms. *Academy of Management Review*, 10(3): 540–57.

Zucker, H. G. (1978) The variable nature of news media influence. In B. D. Rubin (ed.) *Communication yearbook no. 2*. New Jersey: Transaction Books, pp. 225–45.

Zucker, L. G. (1987) Institutional theories of organizations. *Annual Review of Sociology*, 13: 443–64.

Chapter 8

Sustainability reporting

Insights from neoinstitutional theory

Carlos Larrinaga-González

INTRODUCTION

The results of KPMG surveys of corporate social reporting reveal that while, in 1993, 13 per cent of the top 100 companies in 10 countries published a separate report about their environmental and social impacts, this figure almost tripled to 33 per cent (for 16 countries) in the 2005 survey. At the same time casual observation leads to the conclusion that in the 1990s 'environmental' and/or 'health and safety' reports dominated the reporting scene. More recently, however, most companies publish an 'environmental and social' or a 'sustainability' report. In particular, from the 2002 survey to the 2005 survey, the percentage of separate reports (for the global top 250 companies) that correspond to the label 'sustainability' and 'social and environmental' have increased from 24 per cent to 85 per cent, with a corresponding decline (from 73 per cent to 13 per cent) for environmental, health and safety reports. These trends are explored in this chapter using the lens of institutional theory to assist our understanding of these large-scale shifts in both report production and reporting nomenclature. Questions that arise in this context include: what mechanics underlie the process of the largest corporations moving in the same direction? Why do so many reports evolve in a similar way over such an array of countries, in such different contexts?

In order to make sense of the dynamics involved in corporate practices, neoinstitutional theory has been extensively used in organizational analysis. This theoretical perspective allows understanding the actions of groups of organizations, as well as individual companies. Even though the explicit use of institutional theory for the analysis of sustainability reporting (hereafter SR) is low (but see Kolk, 2005), this theoretical approach warrants examination because it overlaps with some of the established research themes in social and environmental accounting (such as legitimacy theory). This chapter uses institutional theory to (1) build an explanation of the development of SR and (2) ascertain the consequences of the institutionalization of SR. Accordingly the chapter will outline the prior research that has been conducted in sustainability management and reporting using a neoinstitutional lens. The next sections will explore how different notions such as organizational fields or mechanisms of institutionalization apply to SR. Then, the chapter will discuss the relationship between institutionalization and change and how this affects SR. The next section will sketch the relationship between institutional theory and the often used (in accounting research) concept of legitimacy theory. Finally, given the lack of previous research on institutional explanations of SR, this chapter presents some conclusions that are necessarily speculative and exploratory in nature.

Consistent with the theme of the book, the rest of the chapter will use the term SR to refer to reporting which is labelled 'social and environmental reporting' as well as 'SD reporting', while recognizing that such labels present some challenges.

PRIOR RESEARCH IN NEOINSTITUTIONAL THEORY

Organizational structures and processes have been studied from the theoretical perspective adopted in this chapter: new institutionalism (Powell and DiMaggio, 1991) or contemporary institutional theory (Scott, 1995). Circumscribed to the purpose of this chapter, a neoinstitutional theory perspective has been adopted by Hoffman (1999) and Christmann (2004) in their studies of corporate environmentalism, as well as by Jennings and Zandbergen (1995) and Bansal (2005) in their studies of 'sustainable' organizations.

Hoffman (1999), for example, studied the evolution of environmentalism in the US chemical industry from 1962 until 1993 and found four distinctive periods in terms of the institutionalization of environmental concerns. Institutionalization is usually conceived as both the process and the outcome of a process, by which a social practice/behaviour becomes usual, desirable and/or taken for granted in organizations. Hoffman argues that the last period identified was characterized by the adoption of organizational and strategic innovations and the production of environmental reports, among other things. Thus, SR was identified as an element of institutionalization. Indeed, as previously observed SR has become a common practice for many large firms which is powerful evidence of institutionalization. Further, and more focused on reporting, Kolk (2005) analysed the convergence/divergence of multinational corporations regarding environmental reporting. Kolk (2005) studied the prevalence of environmental reporting by the Global Fortune 250 companies, considering whether they are based in Europe, Japan or the US, and found that the region in which the MNC is based is significantly more important over time and that the differences in environmental reporting between US and European/Japanese companies have increased over time. Crucial in both of these studies, and institutional theory generally, is the notion of an organizational field.

ORGANIZATIONAL FIELDS

Neoinstitutional theory 'asks questions about how social choices are shaped, mediated, and channeled by the institutional environment' (Hoffman, 1999, p. 351). The institutional environment is commonly thought to be composed of organizations and organizational fields. This section considers the latter concept, which is central in institutional analysis. An organizational field is formed by those organizations that collectively constitute a recognized area of institutional life (DiMaggio and Powell, 1983) 'that partake of a common meaning system and whose participants interact more frequently and fatefully with one another than with actors outside the field' (Scott, 1995, p. 56)). The institutional analysis literature has identified fields around common technologies or common regulation, such as the electricity industry or the public hospitals in a given geographical area. Those fields would include 'key suppliers, resource and product consumers, regulatory agencies, and other organizations that produce similar services or products' (DiMaggio and Powell, 1983, p. 145).

When investigating the institutionalization of environmental concerns in the US chemical industry, Hoffman (1999) deduced the existence of one changing field that was formed around issues that became important to the interests and objectives of the organizations in the field. Its varying composition included, at different moments in the four periods that Hoffman found between 1962 and 1993, the Environmental Protection Agency, the organizations and the industry, NGOs and insurance companies.

Drawing on Hoffman's (1999) propositions about issue-based fields, it is interesting to discuss whether there is one or various organizational fields based on the issue of SR. Organizational fields 'should be analytically detected . . . through observing (1) an increase in the extent to which certain organizations interact, (2) an increase in the information load that they share, and (3) the development of a mutual awareness that they are involved in a common debate' (Hoffman, 1999, p. 352, quoting DiMaggio, 1983).

It could be argued that around the issue of SR there has been a growing number of interactions between companies, governmental agencies, international bodies and NGOs. Increasingly, companies submit their reports to reporting awards schemes; there have been meetings and conferences on the issue; there is collaboration and discussion between companies, NGOs and academics; and the companies participate in the Environmental Management and Audit Scheme (EMAS) or the Global Reporting Initiative (GRI). Progressively, new guidelines are issued, there are new prized reports to benchmark (see Table 8.2). Additionally, the field of SR is being

152

defined with, for example, sustainability services being offered by leading consulting firms. Thus, this empirical setting fits in the three aforementioned conditions for the existence of fields.

Assuming the existence of organizational fields around the issue of SR (Kolk, 2005), the question that emerges is whether there is a unique global organizational field or whether there are different local organizational fields. One basic proposition of institutional theory is that different pressures in one organizational field lead to convergence in organizational forms and practices (see next section in this chapter). Thus, if the former holds true the frequency and quality of reporting would converge worldwide. This contrasts with Kolk (2005) where differences in environmental reporting between US and European/Japanese companies were increasing.

These results suggest that currently there is no convergence in SR internationally and hence global reporting could not be seen as being part of the same organizational field. One possible explanation is that there are several organizational fields for SR, with Japan and Europe having some element of convergence (Kolk, 2005, would favour this conclusion). It should, however, be noted that reporting in Japan is different, relying to a lesser extent on external verification (Kolk, 2005). In addition, Kolk also notes considerable differences in reporting between different European countries, a finding that chimes with Adams and Kuasirikun (2000 – a comparative study, where it was found that the proportion of companies reporting environmental information and the volume of such reporting was consistently higher in Germany than in the UK). Further, Jennings and Zandbergen (1995) propose that, for a sustainable value or practice, organizational fields tend to be local rather than non-local. This conclusion supports the different patterns of SR described above.

Thus, in order to cover the variance of SR practice, the existence of the following locally based SR fields could be speculatively proposed:

■ Environmental Management and Audit Scheme (hereafter EMAS, European Commission, 2001). The first SR field would be operating in those countries (Austria, Denmark, Germany, Italy and Spain) in which EMAS gained acceptance and organizations are disseminating environmental reports as a response to EMAS' requirements. Organizations in some of these countries have a long experience in mass balance reporting. As a result, environmental reporting is still dominant in this SR field. In these five countries there were 2,751 organizations registered in EMAS as of September 2005. All these organizations have to publish an environmental report.

■ Triple bottom line. This SR field can be found in those countries, with a long experience in social reporting, where social and environmental reporting has merged into SR. This field is dominated by UK companies. The development of the Global Reporting Initiative (hereafter GRI) itself could be viewed as the outcome of academic leadership and corporate experimentation in the UK.

153

- Japan is the first country worldwide in terms of companies issuing sustainability reports and companies certified to ISO 14001. There are industry guidelines and governmental encouragement for SR (Kolk, 2005). However, most sustainability reports are not externally verified.

- US companies led environmental reporting in the 1990s. However, the litigious tradition in this country seems to have prevented many organizations from producing SR. On the contrary, a compliance-oriented approach can be observed in this country, consistent with a general trend not to externally verify the reports (Kolk, 2005).

- The *Bilan Social* disclosure obligation in the annual reports of French companies was strengthened in 2001 (2001–420 Law), making environmental disclosure in the management report compulsory (Mikol, 2003). Possibly, as a result of this the number of French companies that published a separate SR doubled from 2001 to 2004 (KPMG, 2005). These characteristics would indicate the existence of a differentiated SR field in France.

- Norway and Sweden made some environmental disclosure compulsory in their financial statements. These two countries, together with Finland, have experienced a decline in SR from 2001 to 2004 (KPMG, 2005).

To close these speculative propositions about the existence of SR fields, it should be noted that SR is confined to the rich and western countries. For example, as of May 2006, only 17 Brazilian, 8 Indian and 6 Chinese organizations had produced a sustainability report, according to the GRI databases, with these three countries amounting to less than 4 per cent of sustainability reports (www.globalreporting.org), but to 40 per cent of world population.

MECHANISMS OF INSTITUTIONALIZATION

The previous section provided an outline of the concept of organizational fields, which refers to those organizations that collectively constitute a recognized area of institutional life. This section moves on to consider other central elements of institutional theory as they are evidenced by individual organizational responses.

Organizations find themselves immersed in a certain cultural and historical context, which is portrayed by the existence of systems of shared beliefs, symbols and regulation requirements (Scott and Meyer, 1985). Arguably, the basis of neoinstitutional thinking is its 'skepticism towards atomistic accounts of social processes and a common conviction that institutional arrangements and social processes matter' (DiMaggio and Powell, 1991, p. 2). Instead of viewing institutions – as institutional economists do – as social arrangements intended to minimize transaction costs or as 'provisional, temporary resting places on the way to an efficient equilibrium solution' (DiMaggio and Powell, 1991, p. 10), institutional theorists think that institutions are less likely to change than other structures (Zucker, 1977).

Thus, the interest of a great part of the institutional literature focuses on institutional stability and inertia. Further, DiMaggio and Powell (1983) contend that institutionalization brings about a homogenization of organizations (a process they call isomorphism). This process of homogenization of organizational structures is viewed as arising from the need for organizations to respond to environmental expectations, guarantee their survival and increase their success possibilities in a particular environment. In a similar vein, Scott (1995) develops the notion of legitimacy: 'from an institutional perspective, legitimacy is not a commodity to be possessed or exchanged but a condition reflecting cultural alignment, normative support, or consonance with relevant rules or laws' (p. 45).

Isomorphism emerges through three different mechanisms: coercive, normative and mimetic (DiMaggio and Powell, 1983). Scott (1995) phrases this differently, arguing that legitimacy is based on three pillars (regulative, normative and cognitive). In this visualization, institutions 'consist of cognitive, normative, and regulative structures and activities that provide stability and meaning to social behaviour. Institutions are transported by various carriers – cultures, structures and routines – and they operate at multiple levels of jurisdiction' (Scott, 1995, p. 33). Which view is utilized varies in the different approaches to institutional theory. Neoinstitutionalists, for example, tend to favour the normative and, especially, the cognitive elements of legitimacy. Table 8.1 summarizes these elements.

In the context of SR, these ideas suggest that reporting need not be the outcome of a rational process of decision-making by organizations acting independently. Rather, reporting could become institutionalized, determining to some extent the choice of organizations in terms of whether or not to publish a sustainability report and how to publish it. As an institution, SR would consist of regulative, normative and cognitive structures and activities which would describe what type of reporting is produced, for who, by whom and with what assumed purpose. Each element is further delineated below.

Regulative structures

First, the regulative pillar of institutions in Scott is based on rule setting, monitoring, recompense and punishment. It corresponds with the coercive isomorphic mechanism of DiMaggio and Powell. In this case, the environment (in this instance, environment does not refer to the natural environment) acts over the organizational structure through the imposition of structures (DiMaggio and Powell, 1983; Scott, 1987). Examples of coercive mechanisms are the enforcement of regulation, the discipline of markets or the exercise of power. Those coercive mechanisms lead the organization, in order to gain legitimacy and survive, to comply and align its structures with the dominant rules (see Table 8.1). For example, manufacturers

Table 8.1 *Elements of institutionalization*

DiMaggio and Powell	Scott	Examples
Coercive mechanisms, such as the law or the market, lead organizations to comply and to align with the norms in such a way that behaviour becomes very similar in all of them.	Regulative structures, such as the law or the market, involve the capacity to establish rules, inspect conformity and manage sanctions in order to influence future behaviour.	Consumer boycotts (against child labour or environmental accidents) lead companies to change structures and practices. Environmental regulation makes companies to adopt new technologies.
Normative mechanisms, propelled through professionalization, formal education and professional networks, lead individuals to act according to values and norms.	Normative structures are based on social values and norms, leading individuals to act according to societal expectations.	Deontological codes shape practice in many professions, such as doctors or accountants.
Mimetic mechanisms. Organizations imitate those peer organizations that seem to be more successful and legitimate.	Cognitive structures are taken for granted symbols, meanings and roles that support the legitimacy of organizations.	It is argued that the waves in the use of some concepts and techniques by organization are associated with vogues (imitation) rather than with rationality.

adopt health and safety procedures in order to comply with regulation. The underlying logic followed is based on the interests of the organization (or that of the leading actors in the organization), in terms of acquiring or maintaining organizational resources. Thus, public agencies could decide to close or fine a company that is not complying with environmental regulations. Along the same lines, consumers and environmentalists campaigning against some organizational practices, such as child labour or poor environmental practices, may lead companies to change their practices. For example, in 1995 Greenpeace and other organizations started a campaign against Shell's intentions of disposing the Brent Spar oil installation through deep-water disposal. While Shell tried to defend its decision, resistance within public opinion and among consumers meant that Shell finally decided to reverse it.

In the context of SR, regulative structures and activities would include reporting regulations and their enforcement, as well as the threat of regulation of reporting. Several examples of these can be found:

■ In 2001 the European Commission issued a Recommendation to member countries on the inclusion of environmental issues in corporate financial statements. As a result, different European countries (Bebbington *et al.*, 2005) enacted regulations, making compulsory environmental disclosures in the financial statements. Thus, many organizations are reporting on environmental issues in their financial statements, the rationale being based on self-interest and the need to comply with regulations.

■ In April 1998, at an ACCA awards ceremony, Michael Meacher MP (the then UK Minister of the Environment) named and shamed some non-reporters and stated that if reporting did not develop voluntarily then legislation would be enacted (Bebbington *et al.*, 2005). It could be argued that part of the leadership of UK companies in environmental and SR could be explained as an attempt to avoid regulation in light of Government members indicating that it would come unless firms voluntarily developed reporting norms.

Normative structures

Secondly, the normative pillar of institutional theory (see Table 8.1) focuses on values and norms that could be applicable to all members of the collective or to specific actors (in which case those values and norms are termed 'roles' (Scott, 1995)). To understand the difference between the regulative and the normative pillars, the logic of each, instrumentalism and appropriateness (March and Olsen, 1989), respectively, should be distinguished. While self-interest is compatible with a regulative conception of institutions, a normative conception leads to the belief that individuals act routinely following coded expectations rooted in their roles in organizations. For example, there is controversy over whether corporate social responsibility makes good economic sense (from the organizational viewpoint). But it could be simply argued, from a neoinstitutional standpoint, that organizations engage in socially responsible practices, regardless of their financial impact, because they have emerged as shared social values that organizations have to adapt to be legitimate. DiMaggio and Powell (1983) argue that normative isomorphism is reached through professionalization, formal education and professional networks: those are the networks in which values and norms are acquired. However, it is important to stress that the normative structures are not acquired by coercion or imposition, but through a legitimate authority of norms and values (Scott, 1987): organizations adopt those structures because they genuinely think that given their role in society, it follows that they have to acquire some structures or engage in some practices. For example, arguably some companies think that they have to sign the Global Compact[1] (despite the United Nations' lack of power to enforce it) simply because this commitment has been accepted by society, and especially within the organizational field in which the company operates, as a norm. This does not mean that organizations act unintentionally as slaves to social conventions, but that they are attentive and adapt to societal and organizational rules.

In the context of SR, normative structures refer to rules that are followed on moral/ethical grounds or in order to conform to norms established by referential bodies. Some examples follow:

■ EMAS requires all the organizations that voluntarily implement an environmental management system to prepare and disseminate an environmental report. EMAS has obtained some success in Continental Europe. Though not strictly compulsory, EMAS has created a structure in some countries, particularly Germany, where the norm for some industries has become to register in EMAS and, subsequently, publish an environmental report (Wenk, 2004).

■ Since the 1990s, different European institutions started to give awards for best environmental and sustainability reports. In 1991 the ACCA established the UK Environmental Reporting Awards, which in 2001 transformed into the Awards for Sustainability Reporting. Likewise, the European Environmental Reporting Awards (EERA), launched in 1996, was re-named the European Sustainability Reporting Awards (ESRA) scheme in 2001. Each participant in the latter is an accountancy body from a European country. Some of the reports awarded in these two schemes are displayed in Table 8.2. These awards have been

Table 8.2 Award winners in the ACCA and ESRA Awards, 1997–2005

		Categories	
	Year	Environmental report	Sustainability report
European environmental reporting awards – EERA (1996–9) and European sustainability reporting awards (2000 onwards)	1997	BT Plc and Novo Nordisk	—
	1998	Novo Nordisk A/S (Denmark)	—
	1999	Neste Fortum Group (Finland)	—
	2000	Shell International (UK)	Novo Nordisk A/S (Denmark)
	2001	—	—
	2002	SCA (Sweden)	The Co-operative Bank plc (UK)
	2003	Aalborg Portland A/S (Denmark)	Novo Nordisk A/S (Denmark)
	2004	—	Co-operative Financial Services (UK)
	2005	Memo Group	Rabobank Group
ACCA UK Environmental reporting awards (1991–2000) and awards for sustainability reporting (2001 onwards)	1997	British Telecom	—
	1998	Eastern Group plc	—
	1999	United Utilities	—
	2000	Shell International and the Co-operative Bank plc	—
	2001	ScottishPower	BT Group plc
	2002	Unilever	Co-operative Bank plc
	2003	GlaxoSmithKline	Co-operative Bank plc
	2004	Thames Water Utilities Ltd	Co-operative Financial Services
	2005	Unilever plc	Anglo-American plc and BT Group plc

instrumental in codifying values and norms of SR. For example, one of the key qualities of environmental reporting that emerged through the years was external verification. Therefore, it became a norm that a proper sustainability report should be externally verified, beyond the calculus of the consequences for the organization.

■ The GRI was initiated in 1997 as a multi-stakeholder institution that develops and spreads guidelines for SR. The GRI has played a similar (but more potent) role than the awards. It has codified the norms and rules of SR. For example, before 1997 SR was confined to the theme of the environmental impact of the organization. The GRI established the norm that SR should address the triple bottom line and, thus, it became appropriate to report not only on environmental issues, but also on social aspects of sustainable development, such as poverty or human rights.

Cognitive structures

Third and finally, institutions are also considered to be founded on a cognitive dimension. Sociology has long acknowledged the importance of symbols and meanings in social action, but (according to Scott, 1995) the change introduced in neoinstitutional theory is the treatment of symbolic systems and cultural rules as objective and external to individuals. That is, symbols, meanings and rules are social constructions that are created, sustained and changed by social interaction (Berger and Luckmann, 1967). Thus, the social construction of roles and organizations varies over time and space and contributes to stability through compliance because other types of behaviour are inconceivable (Scott, 1995). Cognitive structures 'form a culturally supported and conceptually correct support of legitimacy that becomes unquestioned' (Hoffman, 1999). For example, '[i]nstitutional rules in the West have accorded greater individual autonomy and independence to social actors – both persons and firms – than have related rules in Eastern societies . . . Relations among persons or firms that the West views as collusion, the East sees as normal, inevitable and beneficial' (Scott, 1995, pp. 43–4).

The isomorphic mechanisms in organizations that, according to DiMaggio and Powell (1991), better capture the cognitive dimension is imitation (mimetic processes). Organizations imitate those peer organizations that seem to be more successful and legitimate (Tolbert and Zucker, 1983), the underlying logic being that of 'orthodoxy': we prefer to act in conventional ways, to act according to routines (DiMaggio and Powell, 1991).

The existence of cognitive structures is very difficult to prove empirically. However, their existence could be induced indirectly from the fact that in some countries and/or industries, it is taken for granted that a company will publish a sustainability report. Additionally, there is some evidence of a mimetic process in SR that is connected with the convergence hypothesis (isomorphism) of neoinstitutional

159

theory. Organizations imitate the peers that are perceived to have obtained success with respect to their reporting practices. Arguably, convergence is taking place in some organizational fields (see last section), where reports are evolving rapidly from environmental reports to corporate social responsibility reports (and sustainability reports in some instances), making these reports progressively alike through a process of benchmarking that is not unrelated to the normative structures.

INSTITUTIONALIZATION AND CHANGE

As one of the principal interests of institutional theory is the explanation of stability and inertia, it has been charged for its failure to address change (Greenwood and Hinings, 1996; Hoffman, 1999). Hoffman, however, has studied how organizations and fields evolve as regards environmental concerns and demonstrated how coercive, normative and cognitive pressures have different importance over time and how the organizational fields are changing. Thus, while coercive, normative and cognitive structures (Scott, 1995; DiMaggio and Powell, 1983) or interpretive schemes[2] (Greenwood and Hinings, 1996) are thought to lead to inertia and stability, for some reason organizational evolution takes place unexpectedly and produces discontinuities. As regards change and the institutionalization of SR, four themes deserve closer inspection: (1) the initiating event that may alter the institutional arrangements; (2) whether or not, and if so how, may fields evolve; (3) what elements play a part in changes to coercive, normative and cognitive structures; and (4) what relationships exist between competitive forces and institutional structures in the process of institutionalization.

Firstly, the initiating event of institutional change is viewed as potentially taking different forms, including: milestones, catastrophes and legal/administrative happenings (Hoffman, 1999). The uncertainty created by those events leads organizations to experiment and to go beyond established practice, which may eventually lead to new institutional arrangements. If we consider the institutional evolution of SR, it is not difficult to think of events that shaped changes. Given the nature of sustainability, this often takes the the form of catastrophes.[3] However, consistent with our proposition on the diversity of SR fields, the initiating events are likely to be highly dependent on context. In his analysis of the institutionalization of environmentalism in the US chemical industry, Hoffman (1999) suggests that from 1989, reaction to the Bophal accident, the *Exxon Valdez* oil spill, but also the Superfund regulation as well as the Montreal Protocol, led to environmental reporting being adopted by a number of US firms (in addition to other organizational and strategic innovations). Conversely, in the European context it seems that catastrophes have played a less significant role, and European organizations have been more attentive to governmental (EU's Environmental Action Programmes and EMAS) and private initiatives (GRI) encouraging SR (Kolk, 2005).

160

Secondly, according to Hoffman (1999) fields should be conceived as evolving, allowing changes in the composition and in the balance of power of participants. Additionally, changes bring about a redefinition of institutions that reflect the interests of the newly formed field. When environmental reporting emerged in the late 1980s and early 1990s, it could hardly be said that there was a SR field. Instead, SR seemed a monologue by reporting organizations. However, a few years later a number of institutions became interested in SR, initiated a dialogue with the reporting entities, thus entering the field and modifying it. Professional bodies (in particular ACCA), governments (as has been explained in the previous section), as well as other stakeholders (international agencies, NGOs, unions, industry associations and socially responsible investors), entered into the field in the 1990s, changing the balance of power in the field and redefining SR. While previously environmental reporting dominated the scene, in the new field it became evident that sustainability also involved social and ethical aspects, for example human rights and working conditions emerged as legitimate aspects of SR, as evidenced by the evolution of the GRI guidelines.

Thirdly, regarding the role of different structures on institutional change, Scott (1995) contends that coercive, normative and cognitive structures are a matter of emphasis and underlying assumptions, i.e. one has to choose between perspectives because they are not logically consistent, as one should be either a social constructionist (preferring cognitive structures) or a social realist (endorsing coercive structures), but not both at the same time. However, Hoffman (1999) proposes that those structures are not analytically and operationally distinct, and that regulative, normative and cognitive pillars are connected. In particular, in his study Hoffman found that change followed a sequence that started through a questioning of prior institutional beliefs and evolved through regulative and normative institutions, to finish as a cognitive institution. This pattern of change parallels what Greenwood and Hinings (1996) call colonization, a change that is imposed from above. Hoffman (1999) suggested four periods of response from the US chemical industry from 1962 to 1993. Rebuttal of environmental criticism was prevalent in the 1960s with this paving the way to an attitude in the 1970s of complying with regulation. The 1980s began with a more co-operative attitude, finishing in the late 1980s and early 1990s with a more proactive strategy, including environmental reporting. Thus, Hoffman argues that in response to an imposed change a pathway of institutionalization leads eventually to changing normative and (possibly) cognitive structures.

However, the pattern of change identified by Hoffman (1999) may be less helpful in explaining SR. There are three reasons for this: first, Hoffman studied environmentalism; sustainability is even more difficult to evaluate and more subtle than the environmental protection against chemicals. Second, the regulation on SR is very limited. Finally, given the lack of regulation, the attitude of organizations vis-à-vis SR has not been as negative as Hoffman (1999) identified in the first phases of environmentalism in the US chemical industry. These points, however, are

161

speculative because (apart from Kolk, 2005) there is a relative lack of literature concerning the institutionalization of SR.[4]

Finally, a further aspect of institutional evolution is that DiMaggio and Powell (1991) contend that in processes of institutionalization, early adoption tends to be related to competitive isomorphism (economic or technical explanations) and is supplanted later by institutional explanations (coercive, normative and cognitive structures). Following this hypothesis, Bansal (2005) argues for the evolution of the sustainability agenda, that in early years some firms will benefit 'generating rents from resources and capabilities because of imperfectly competitive strategic factor markets . . . created by the ambiguity of the meaning and impact of sustainable development' (p. 203). Following this hypothesis, the firms that do not act early will imitate other firms, facilitating the institutionalization of sustainability in later years.

As regards to the particular case of the adoption of sustainability strategies, however, Bansal (2005) found that institutional pressures could be important for early adoption. Media attention (a surrogate he used for normative structures) and mimicry (related to cognitive structures) were positively associated in Bansal's study with sustainability strategy adoption. He also found that for later adopters of sustainability strategies the importance of media attention diminishes while mimicry remains equally important. As these findings contradict Bansal's propositions, he explains that in this particular case, institutional pressures could be important because of the ambiguity associated with the meaning, measurement and impact of sustainable development (Bansal, 2005). Even though there is no comparable study on SR to Bansal (2005) it seems possible that the story of SR could be very similar.

However, Bansal's (2005) explanation provokes several caveats. First, the approach in the research to 'corporate sustainable development' is, at least, contentious. The author himself warns about the ambiguity of corporate sustainability; but in measuring sustainable development the research adopts an end-of-pipe, business-as-usual perspective. This is most apparent in the issues considered for, and the approach to, social equity (with social equity being addressed through stakeholder management (Bansal, 2005, p. 199)). Second, the very attempt to measure corporate sustainability makes the conclusions somehow unreliable. Third, Bansal goes on (pp. 213–14) speculating about the possibility that resource-based arguments could be more important at later stages. This is contradictory with the results of the research: Bansal found negative correlations between return on equity and sustainability strategy adoption. In conclusion, this research reveals the limited version of sustainable development that is used not only in corporate practice but also in academic research.

NEOINSTITUTIONALISM AND LEGITIMACY THEORY

This penultimate section seeks to explore the overlap between institutional theory and theories more frequently used to explore SR: specifically legitimacy theory. There is an apparent overlap between institutional arguments about SR and the overwhelming amount of legitimacy theory literature in social and environmental accounting. Legitimacy is an element of institutions: Scott (1995) contends that legitimacy explains organizational stability, by giving a normative dignity to its practical imperatives (Berger and Luckmann, 1967). However, the usual approach to legitimacy in social and environmental accounting is not always consistent with its use in institutional theory. A more resource-based view of legitimacy is common: it is conceived in accounting literature as a resource, or it enables organizations to attract resources that are employed in pursuit of organizational goals (Tilling, 2004).

While there is overlap between institutional theory and legitimacy theory (Deegan, 2002), it could be said that the former is richer than the latter. Legitimacy in the social and environmental accounting literature assumes a manipulative logic, based on self-interest, which could correspond with coercive structures. Deegan (2002), for example, explains that 'legitimacy is considered to be a resource on which an organization is dependent for survival . . . that the organization also can impact or manipulate' (p. 293). Likewise, Patten (1992) argues that 'social disclosures represent one of the methods that firms can use to influence the public policy process . . . The desired effect . . . is to reduce . . . the "exposure" of the company to the social and political environment' (p. 472).

Institutional theory, however, also permits different motives to be explored: primarily based on the logics of appropriateness and on the social construction of reality. In particular, the theory does not privilege any of the three explanations (coercive, normative or cognitive), but argues that they operate at different levels and moments through the institutionalization process. Additionally, this theoretical framework encourages the examination of organizations in their context as well as the notion of organizational fields which helps to explain behaviour inside firms. Finally, institutional theory is above all a theory of institutionalization: its main interest is the longitudinal study of institutional change and how organizations became institutionalized. Thus, it could be argued that while legitimacy theory could be more useful for determining in the short term why a given organization is making particular sustainability disclosures, institutional theory could be more helpful in the explanation of why given SR practices become common in a particular context.

CONCLUDING COMMENTS

This chapter commenced questioning why we are observing waves in SR practice and proposed that neoinstitutional theory has some explanatory power. Along these lines, the chapter has presented the main elements of neoinstitutional theory and has discussed their relevance for SR.

We observed that the empirical studies of sustainability management (and SR) provide some evidence of the institutionalization of such practices. Using the notion of organizational fields, and Hoffman's (1999) proposition of the existence of issue-based fields in this area, we questioned whether there are SR fields. The answer is that there appears to be multiple fields, with convergence arising at the local, rather than at the global, level. Then we moved on to explain the coercive, normative and mimetic mechanisms of institutionalization, and illustrated how they can explain different processes of institutionalization in SR. Coercion can account for SR as a response to regulation or consumer pressure. Normative mechanisms would explain SR as a response to voluntary initiatives on the grounds of social responsibility. Finally, mimicry could explain how SR could be the consequence of some trend. Although there is a lack of research in these aspects, it is likely that SR is the result of a mixture of these three mechanisms, taking different weights in different contexts.

The discussion over the relationship between institutionalization and change also revealed some patterns that could be observed in the case of SR. In this respect, we illustrated how different events served to initiate SR in different contexts, and how the evolving composition of organizational fields allowed the redefinition of the institution, with the emergence in recent years of SR aspects of the social and ethical aspects of sustainability. However, other propositions made in the strategic management literature cannot be confirmed and reveal the use of disputed notions of sustainability.

As regards the commonalities and differences between neoinstitutionalism and the often used legitimacy theory, it seems that the latter is a particular case of the former, related to the regulative pillar. The precision of legitimacy theory makes it testable, but at the same time opens it to question, as legitimacy being a concept drawn from neoinstitutional theory has a wider meaning than is often recognized in the literature.

NOTES

1   www.globalcompact.org.

2   The term 'interpretive schemes' can be read as synonymous to normative/cognitive structures and refers to the core values of the organization that makes sense of the rest of its structures.

3   For example oil and gas industry disclosures subsequent to the *Exxon Valdez* spill
     (Patten, 1992) or Shell's change in reporting alter the twin blows of the Brent Spar
     controversy and the execution of Ken Saro Wira and others in Nigeria.

4   Gray and Bebbington (2001) have a different interpretation about corporate
     attitude vis-à-vis SD. They suggest that while at the surface companies did not react
     against SD, their active practice of capturing the sustainability agenda would be
     indicative of hostility towards SR.

REFERENCES

Adams, C. and Kuasirikun, N. (2000) A comparative analysis of corporate reporting
    on ethical issues by UK and German chemical and pharmaceutical companies.
    European Accounting Review, 9(1): 53–79.

Bansal, P. (2005) Evolving sustainability: A longitudinal study of corporate sustainable
    development. *Strategic Management Journal*, 26: 197–218.

Bebbington, J., Kirk, E. and Larrinaga-González, C. (2005) Building regimes for effective
    regulation: The example of environmental reporting in the electricity sector in Spain
    and the United Kingdom. Working paper.

Berger, P. and Luckmann, T. (1967) *The social construction of reality*. New York:
    Doubleday, Anchor Books.

Christmann, P. (2004) Multinational companies and the natural environment: Determin-
    ants of global environmental policy standardization. *Academy of Management
    Journal*, 47(5): 747–60.

Dacin, M. T. (1997) Isomorphism in context: The power and prescription of institutional
    norms. *Academy of Management Journal*, 40(1): 46–81.

Deegan, C. (2002) Introduction: The legitimising effect of social and environmental
    disclosure: A theoretical foundation. *Accounting, Auditing and Accountability
    Journal*, 15(3): 282–311.

DiMaggio, P. J. (1983) 'State expansion and organizational fields'. In R. H. Hall and
    R. E. Quinn (eds) *Organization theory and public policy*. Beverly Hills: Sage.

DiMaggio, P. J. and Powell, W. W. (1983) The iron cage revisited: Institutional iso-
    morphism and collective rationality in organizational fields. *American Sociological
    Review*, 48: 147–60. Reprinted in *Advances in Strategic Management*, 17: 143–66.

DiMaggio, P. J. and Powell, W. W. (1991) Introduction. In W. W. Powell and
    P. J. DiMaggio (eds) *The new institutionalism in organizational analysis*. Chicago,
    IL: University of Chicago Press, pp. 1–38.

European Commission (2001) Regulation (EC) no. 761/2001 of the European parlia-
    ment and of the council of 19 March 2001 allowing voluntary participation by
    organisations in a Community eco-management and audit scheme (EMAS). *Official
    Journal* L 114, 24/04/2001, pp. 0001–0029

Gray, R. and Bebbington, J. (2000) Environmental accounting, managerialism and sustainability. *Advances in Environmental Accounting and Management,* 1: 1–44.

Gray, R. and Bebbington, J. (2001) *Accounting for the environment.* London: Sage.

Greenwood, R. and Hinings, C. (1996) Understanding radical organizational change: Bringing together the old and the new institutionalism. *Academy of Management Review,* 21(4): 1022–54.

Hoffman, A. J. (1999) Institutional evolution and change: Environmentalism and the U.S. chemical industry. *Academy of Management Journal,* 42(4): 351–71.

Jennings, P. D. and Zandbergen, P. A. (1995) Ecologically sustainable organizations: An institutional approach. *Academy of Management Review,* 20(4): 1015–52.

Kolk, A. (2003) Trends in sustainability reporting by the Fortune Global 250. *Business Strategy and the Environment,* 12(5): 279–91.

Kolk, A. (2005) Environmental reporting by multinationals from the triad: Convergence or divergence? *Management International Review,* 45: 145–66.

KPMG (2005) *KPMG International survey of corporate sustainability reporting.* Amsterdam.

March, J. G. and Olsen, J. P. (1989) *Rediscovering institutions.* New York: Free Press.

Meyer, J. W. and Rowan, B. (1977) Institutionalized organizations: Formal structure as myth and ceremony. *American Journal of Sociology,* 83(2): 340–63.

Meyer, J. W. and Scott, W. R. (1985) *Organizational environments: Ritual and rationality,* 3rd edn. 1st edn 1983. Beverly Hills, CA: Sage.

Mikol, A. (2003) Les organisations face au renforcement du contrôle *Revue Française de Gestion,* 29: 147–59.

Miller, P. (1994) Accounting as social and institutional practice: An introduction. In A. G. Hopwood and P. Miller (eds) *Accounting as a Social and Institutional Practice.* Cambridge: Cambridge University Press.

Patten, D. (1992) Intra-industry environmental disclosures in response to the Alaskan oil spill: A note on legitimacy theory. *Accounting, Organizations and Society,* 17(5): 471–5.

Powell, W. W. (1991) Expanding the scope of institutional analysis. In W. W. Powell and P. J. DiMaggio (eds) *The new institutionalism in organizational analysis.* Chicago, IL: University of Chicago Press, pp. 183–203.

Powell, W. W. and DiMaggio, P. J. (eds) (1991) *The new institutionalism in organizational analysis.* Chicago, IL: University of Chicago Press.

Scott, W. R. (1987) The adolescence of institutional theory. *Administrative Science Quarterly,* 32: 493–511.

Scott, W. R. (1995) *Institutions and organizations.* Beverly Hills, CA: Sage.

Scott, W. R. and Meyer, J. W. (1985) The organization of societal sectors. In Meyer and Scott (1985), pp. 129–53.

Tilling, M. V. (2004) Some thoughts on legitimacy theory in social and environmental accounting. *Social and Environmental Accounting Journal,* 24(2): 3–7.

Tolbert, P. S. and Zucker, L. G. (1983) Institutional sources of change in the formal structure of organizations: The diffusion of civil service reform, 1880–1935. *Administrative Science Quarterly*, 28 (March): 22–39.

Wenk, M. S. (2004) EU's eco-management and audit scheme. *Environmental and Quality Management*, 14(1): 59–70.

Williamson, O. E. (1981) The economics of organization: The transaction cost approach. *American Journal of Sociology*, 87: 548–77.

Zucker, L. G. (1977) The role of institutionalization in cultural resistance. *American Sociological Review*, 42(5): 726–43.

Chapter 9

Assurance practice in sustainability reporting

David Owen

INTRODUCTION

Accompanying the growth in sustainability reporting worldwide in recent years has been a discernible increase in the number of reports accompanied by some form of externally prepared assurance statement. The essential purpose of the latter is to enhance the status of sustainability reporting by the inclusion of an independent opinion designed to increase the confidence of report users in the reliability of the reported information. The importance of external assurance in this context is particularly noted in a comprehensive study of sustainability reporting practices worldwide undertaken by the ACCA and CorporateRegister.com (2004) in that it:

> represents the next stage of development in sustainability reporting as approaches become more developed and demands of report users more sophisticated. Organisations which fail to obtain assurance for their reports are likely to face issues of credibility.
>
> (p. 15)

Zadek *et al.* (2004) indicate that there are also additional internal benefits that may accrue to the organization from a sustainability assurance exercise including:

> improved overall management of performance in relation to existing policies and commitments, improved risk management and better understanding of emerging issues.
>
> (p. 16)

The purpose of this chapter is to provide an overview and critical evaluation of current trends in sustainability assurance practice, together with a number of prominent guidelines which have been produced in recent years with a view to informing and standardizing such practice. The critique offered focuses particularly on the contribution current practice makes towards the enhancement of stakeholder accountability.

RECENT TRENDS IN SUSTAINABILITY ASSURANCE PRACTICE

The significant growth in provision of external assurance statements as part of the overall sustainability reporting package on the part of companies across the globe is highlighted in the above-mentioned study by the ACCA and CorporateRegister .com. Drawing on the latter's comprehensive database of significant corporate non-financial reports, covering both hard copy and PDF formats, it is noted that in 2003 nearly 40 per cent included external assurance statements compared with only 17 per cent ten years previously. Later figures appearing in KPMG's (2005) International Survey of Corporate Responsibility Reporting indicate that whilst such practice continues to grow, the rate of growth perhaps appears to be slowing. Utilizing two samples, the top 250 of the Fortune 500 companies (the Global 250) and the top 100 companies from sixteen prominent industrial economies,[1] it is indicated that for the former the number of reports with a formal assurance statement has increased marginally to 30 per cent, as against 29 per cent in 2002, whilst for the latter the increase is from 27 per cent to 33 per cent.

Further analysis of reporting practice contained within the 2005 KPMG survey highlights the somewhat patchy nature of current assurance provision. Significantly, as far as the Global 250 companies are concerned, the majority of statements restrict themselves to assurance on specific information or data sets, with only just over one-fifth covering the full corporate report. There are also clear country and industrial sector differences in assurance provision. For example, in the former context, whilst more than 50 per cent of sustainability reports from the Italian and UK samples contained assurance statements, these were largely conspicuous by their absence in the case of their US counterparts. Additionally, whereas figures from Japan, Canada, Australia, South Africa, France, Spain, Italy and the UK indicate that the prevalence of external assurance is on the increase (fairly dramatically so in the latter European instances), a discernible decline is evident in Scandinavia.[2] As far as sectoral differences in assurance provision are concerned, for both samples utilities, financial services and oil and gas predominate, whilst for all other sectors such practice is very much a minority pursuit. A final point to bear in mind is that assurance provision is overwhelmingly a large company phenomenon. This is clearly evidenced by Salterbaxter and Context's (2005) survey of trends in CSR reporting which suggests that whilst 44 of the top 100 UK companies' reports contained independent assurance statements, the figure for the top 250 only increases to 60.[3]

Turning to the issue of choice of assurance provider, the KPMG (2005) survey reveals that the major accounting firms appear to dominate the market at both global and domestic level. For both the Global 250 and top 100 companies samples, 58 per cent of assurance statements were contributed by accounting firms, with the remainder being largely provided by specialist consultants.[4] Intriguingly, an earlier study carried out for CPA Australia (2004), which drew on a comprehensive data base of 170 assurance statements appearing between 2000 and 2003, predominantly from Australia (33 statements), the United Kingdom (48), mainland Europe (52) and Japan (16), paints a somewhat different picture as regards assurance provision. In this case, whereas accounting firms provide the majority (60 per cent) of assurance statements for mainland Europe, they are notably less prominent in Australia (15 per cent), Japan (37.5 per cent) and the United Kingdom (23 per cent). A further study of sustainability assurance practice by O'Dwyer and Owen (2005), which focused on assurance statements appearing in the reports of 'leading edge' reporters (the sample comprising those appearing in environmental, social and sustainability reports short-listed for the 2002 ACCA and European Sustainability Reporting Awards) provides a possible explanation for the apparent anomalies observed between the KPMG and CPA Australia studies, together with the distinct national differences highlighted in the latter. In the O'Dwyer and Owen study, whilst the overall sample split pretty evenly between accountant and consultant assurance providers, accountants were very much to the fore as regards assuring environmental reports (69 per cent of cases) and correspondingly far less prominent in assuring the more substantial social and sustainability reports (36 per cent). As noted earlier, relatively few comprehensive assurance statements feature in the KPMG survey, whilst for European companies environmental reporting still tends to dominate over social and sustainability reporting.

TOWARDS THE STANDARDIZATION OF ASSURANCE PRACTICE

Early academic studies examining the first wave of assurance practice on corporate environmental reports produced throughout the 1990s (Ball *et al.*, 2000; Kamp-Roelands, 2002) raised fundamental concerns about its rigour and usefulness. Kamp-Roelands pointed to major inconsistencies apparent in terms of subject matter addressed, scope of the exercise carried out, objectives, assurance criteria and procedures applied, level of assurance provided and wording of opinions offered. For their part, Ball *et al.* raised even more fundamental question marks over the key issues of assuror independence and degree of thoroughness with which their work was carried out. They particularly drew attention to evidence of managerial control over the whole assurance process which, together with emphasis being placed by assurance providers on management systems as opposed to performance-based issues, greatly limited the potential of assurance as a vehicle for enhancing corporate transparency and accountability to external stakeholder groups.

170

A major problem facing early assurance providers lay in the absence of any clear standards or guidelines that could be used to govern the approach adopted. This concern has been addressed in recent years by the issuing of sustainability assurance practice guidelines from a number of influential bodies, most notably the Fédération des Experts Comptables Européens (FEE, 2002), the Global Reporting Initiative (GRI, 2002) and the Institute of Social and Ethical Accountability (AccountAbility, 1999, 2003, 2005).

The guidelines issued by the first two of the above bodies have much in common, being largely informed by traditional financial auditing standards and concepts, together with a desire to formalize the structure of assurance statements issued with the aim of avoiding creating any expectation gap 'whereby a user mistakenly assumes that there is more assurance than is actually present' (FEE, 2002, p. 17).

Whilst the FEE and GRI guidelines exhibit minor differences in emphasis,[5] they are in broad agreement concerning the elements that should make up a sustainability assurance statement (see Table 9.1). The GRI guidance does, however, go a little further than FEE in one important respect in that in calling for a brief description of how evidence providing the basis for the conclusion reached is obtained it is noted that this will include a reference to 'the extent to which different categories of stakeholders participated in the planning and execution of the assurance process and indicate any constraints on this process' (GRI, 2002, p. 79).

Whereas the issue of stakeholder engagement at least merits some mention in the GRI guidance, for the AccountAbility series of assurance standards (AccountAbility, 1999, 2003, 2005) it is absolutely central to the assurance process. Underpinning the whole approach to assurance here is a commitment to the overriding principle of 'inclusivity' which acknowledges 'the right of stakeholders to be heard, and the obligation of the organization to account for its actions to these stakeholders in the light of their interests' (AccountAbility, 2005, p. 11). In

Table 9.1 *Suggested elements of a sustainability assurance statement*

A title
An addressee
Name and location of assuror
Scope and objective of the engagement
Delimitation of the respective responsibilities of reporter and assuror
Affirmation of the assuror's independence from the reporting organization
Criteria used to assess evidence and reach a conclusion
Assurance standards used
A clear conclusion/opinion
A statement of any reservations or qualifications
Date of assurance statement

Source: Derived from FEE (2002) and GRI (2002)

operationalizing this principle, the assurance provider is specifically called upon to address within the assurance statement the issues of *materiality*, *completeness* and *responsiveness*. The materiality principle requires a statement to be made as to whether the organization's report contains information about sustainability performance 'required by its stakeholders for them to be able to make informed judgements' (2003, p. 14). Completeness calls for an evaluation of 'the extent to which the reporting organization can identify and understand material aspects of its sustainability performance' (2003, p. 17) which encompasses activities, impacts and stakeholder views. Finally, responsiveness entails an evaluation as to whether the reporting organization 'has responded to stakeholder concerns, policies and relevant standards, and adequately communicated these responses in its report' (2003, p. 18).

A further feature that distinguishes the AA1000 approach towards assurance provision from that of FEE and the GRI lies in the former's stipulation that an assurance statement should carry additional commentary, which, it is suggested, could cover the highlighting of progress in both reporting and assurance since the previous report together with recommendations for improving reporting quality and underlying processes, systems and competencies (AccountAbility, 2003). In sum, a more strategic, 'value added' approach to assurance is advocated which focuses centrally on the usefulness of the report for stakeholders, and is explicitly concerned with driving future performance. The thinking behind this approach is neatly summarized by Jansen-Rogers and Oelschlaegel (2005) who suggest that:

> While the value of assurance to ensure reliable and comparable data for management and certain user groups still remains, today's assurance process needs to go beyond assessment of accuracy to explore the quality of processes such as stakeholder engagement, and organisational learning and innovation, as well as the way in which the organisation aligns strategy with key stakeholder expectations.
>
> (p. 23)

The above discussion clearly indicates that extant guidelines for providing assurance for corporate sustainability reports fall into two distinct categories. Firstly, we have the somewhat cautious 'accountancy'-based approach of FEE and the GRI which is largely concerned with attesting to the accuracy of published data, rather than the relevance of such data for external stakeholder groups. Much emphasis is laid here upon identifying the scope of the work undertaken, in particular highlighting any limitations, and the respective responsibilities of reporter and assuror, whilst clearly stating criteria underpinning the work and any assurance standards employed. This approach has recently been re-enforced by the publication of the International Auditing and Assurance Standards Board's (IAASB) 'International Framework for Assurance Engagements' (IAASB, 2004). The Framework (ISAE, 3000) applies to all assurance engagements other than audits and reviews of historical financial information, and its application became mandatory for all professional accounting bodies from January 2005. ISAE 3000 provides detailed guidance for conducting assurance work right from initial acceptance of the engagement through to issuance of the final statement. Of particular note in terms of the latter is the distinction drawn between 'reasonable assurance engagements' and 'limited review engagements' and the related nature of the conclusions that may be respectively drawn:

> The objective of a reasonable assurance engagement is a reduction in assurance engagement risk to an acceptably low level in the circumstances of the engagement as the basis for a positive form of expression of the practitioner's conclusion. The objective of a limited assurance engagement is a reduction in assurance risk to a level that is acceptable in the circumstances of the engagement, but where that risk is greater than for a reasonable assurance engagement, as the basis for a negative form of expression of the practitioner's conclusion.
>
> (IAASB, 2004, paragraph 2)

Extracts from a fairly typical assurance statement emanating from an engagement conducted in accordance with the principles of ISAE 3000 is provided in Table 9.2. Of particular note here is the cautious tone employed, with responsibility for work undertaken and conclusions reached acknowledged only to the company itself, work being 'planned and performed to obtain all the information and explanations we considered necessary to provide limited assurance' and the negative form of expression provided in the conclusion.[6]

O'Dwyer and Owen's (2005) empirical study of assurance statement practice amongst 'leading edge' UK and mainland Europe reporting organizations draws attention to a similarly limited approach, aimed at providing low assurance levels, generally adopted by accountant assurance providers. One might therefore anticipate that future statements provided by accountants applying ISAE 3000 will predominantly adopt the cautious tone portrayed in Table 9.2. Indeed, it can be argued that this approach is perfectly reasonable given some evidence from a Swedish-based study by Park and Brorson (2005) of fee levels for sustainability assurance work being but a fraction, typically between 4 and 6 per cent, of those for the financial audit, a factor which would certainly preclude the carrying out of the necessary amount of substantive testing to justify a positive form conclusion.

The contrasting approach adopted by assurance providers applying the AA1000 Assurance Standard is partially conveyed in the extracts from the assurance statement included in the Co-operative Financial Services (CFS) 2004 Sustainability Report (see Table 9.3). The bulk of this assurance statement offered detailed commentary on the core issues of completeness, materiality and responsiveness viewed from a stakeholder perspective, some of which is evident in the extracts.

Table 9.2 *Extracts from independent assurance statement in BG's Corporate Responsibility Report, 2004*

Introduction
BG Group plc ('BG Group') engaged us to review the aspects of its 2004 Corporate Responsibility Report ('the Report') relating to the implementation of its Business Principles; the identification, management and reporting of social and environmental risks; and the aggregation of Health, Safety, Security, Environment ('HSSE') and Community data.

This report is made solely for BG Group in accordance with the terms of our engagement. Our work has been undertaken so that we might state to BG Group those matters we have been engaged to state in this report and for no other purpose. To the fullest extent permitted by law, we do not accept or assume responsibility to anyone other than the Company for our review work, for this report, or for the conclusions we have reached.

Work performed
Our work was planned and performed to obtain all the information and explanations we considered necessary to provide limited assurance that the statements made in the Report relating to the processes for the implementation of Business Principles in pages 7 to 9, the processes for identifying, managing and reporting social and environmental risk on pages 9 and 10 and the processes and controls over the aggregation of BG Group corporate data for asset level HSSE and Community, year ended 31 December 2004, are effective.

Conclusions
Based on the above, in our opinion nothing has come to our attention that causes us to believe that BG Group's processes in place for implementing the Business Principles, identifying, managing and reporting social and environmental risk and aggregating corporate data for HSSE and Community are not effective, or that statements made in the Report relating to these Business Principles and related processes are not fairly stated.

Particularly notable in this context was the willingness to offer evaluative comment on issues concerning the reporting organization's systems and processes, together with the highlighting of perceived strengths and weaknesses in both the reporting and performance domains. However, notwithstanding the more strategic stance taken, it is significant to note from Table 9.3 both the assurance provider's express belief that their approach is generally consistent with ISAE 3000 and the 'negative form' opinion offered in their statement. Certainly, the latter is somewhat of a departure from the wording of AA1000-based statements, previously generally given by consultant as opposed to accountant verifiers, which have tended to adopt a positive form in attesting to overall fairness, balance and completeness of reporting (see CPA Australia, 2004; O'Dwyer and Owen, 2005). Again here, the small size of the assurance fee (£48,000), which commendably is plainly disclosed, something which is far from common practice, probably goes a long way towards explaining the approach adopted.

An examination of the full assurance statements referred to in Tables 9.2 and 9.3 reveals much greater robustness and fullness of commentary in the latter

Table 9.3 *Extracts from assurance statement in Co-operative Financial Services'* (CFS) Sustainability Report, 2004

justassurance was commissioned by CFS to provide assurance of its 2004 Sustainability Report. justassurance was paid c. £48,000 for this work. justassurance has no other relationships with CFS that might compromise its independence.

Our approach to assurance is in accordance with the AA1000 Assurance Standard, which requires us to review the completeness, materiality and responsiveness of the Report. We believe our approach is also generally consistent with ISAE 3000.

Completeness
Overall, CFS has a robust process in place for identifying and understanding material aspects of its sustainability performance. It has included in the Report, as far as we have been able to ascertain, all material information on all activities relevant to its Partners.

Accounting systems for environmental performance are exemplary, although there would be benefit in exploring opportunities to streamline data collecting systems for business travel and waste. CIS' Financial Advisers contribute significantly to CFS' carbon footprint. Future reports should describe the boundary between where CFS has control and where it has influence with regard to Financial Advisers, and consider, more fully, targets in this area.

Materiality
The Report addresses, thoroughly, the material impacts of CFS on its stakeholders.

Responsiveness
Responsiveness concerns CFS' reactions to stakeholder issues, including the quality of communication with them.

CFS is making a sustained effort to work with its stakeholders. CIS' customer mandate is a key example. Furthermore, the presentation of this Report is good, and the design and accessibility of print (and website) versions of the Report are of a high standard.

Opinion
On the basis of the work undertaken, nothing came to our attention which suggests that the Report does not properly describe:

■ the completeness of CFS' descriptions of its economic, social and ecological impact on its stakeholders
■ CFS' material impacts on its stakeholders
■ CFS' responses to stakeholder concerns.

statement. The evaluative approach adopted here can certainly be argued to 'add value' from the perspective of external stakeholder groups in terms of imparting a far fuller appreciation of the strengths and weaknesses of the sustainability performance of the reporting organization. However, as O'Dwyer and Owen (2005) argue, there is a danger here, in that combining what is essentially a consultancy function with a separate 'arm's length' assurance exercise may compromise the integrity of the latter. As Gray (2000) points out here, once social accounting and auditing moves away from the focus on 'holding the organisation to account', a fundamental principle of the early pioneers of external social auditing practice (see, for example, Medawar, 1976), it runs the risk of being confined to operating largely as a mere management tool rather than as a mechanism promoting democratic accountability. Particularly problematical here perhaps is the practice of including praise for the organization's achievements within the assurance statement which may well only serve to undermine the perceived independence of the assurance provider (CPA Australia, 2004).

A CRITICAL OVERVIEW OF CURRENT ASSURANCE PRACTICE

Despite the issuing of authoritative guidance for carrying out sustainability assurance engagements in recent years, empirical research focusing on the content of published assurance statements highlights a great deal of ambiguity and variability inherent in current practice. Key issues drawn to attention in this context by the comprehensive CPA Australia (2004) study referred to earlier are the following:

- *variability in the titles of assurance statements*, with, in addition to assurance, the terms audit, validation and verification used fairly extensively (the latter being particularly popular amongst consultants), despite these terms having specific meanings in the professional auditing literature which arguably don't reflect the work undertaken in the sustainability assurance exercise;
- *a tendency not to identify an addressee for the statement*. Indeed, where an addressee is identified, usually by accountants, it tends to be one internal to the organization (generally senior management) despite the fact that the sustainability report itself is usually addressed to external stakeholders;
- *a wide range of apparent objectives for the assignment*, ranging, for example, from attesting to the accuracy and completeness of the whole report to simply focusing on information systems reliability for measuring and recording data, with great variability in the extent of description of the objectives provided;
- *variability in the scope of the assignment*, which is typically decided upon by the organization with no stakeholder input, whilst additionally no indication is generally given of any restrictions in scope that have been imposed by company management;
- *a wide variation in the extent of descriptions offered* concerning the nature, timing and extent of assurance procedures employed, with some providers giving explicit details of, for example, interviews conducted, site visits undertaken and documents reviewed, whilst others gave but scant information;
- *a tendency not to disclose the reporting criteria* (e.g. the GRI or other extant social and environmental reporting guidelines) against which the report has been assessed. This is despite the fact that the FEE, GRI and AA1000 recommendations all stress the importance of suitable criteria being employed in order to

provide some context for the work, and to enable some assessment of completeness of reporting to be made;

■ *a similar reluctance to make any mention of assurance standards used* to govern the work of the assurance provider;

■ *great variability in the wording of the conclusion to the assurance statement*, with a tendency to use terms such as 'balanced', 'fair', 'honest', 'complete', 'reasonable' or 'accurate' whose meaning is far from clear in the context of sustainability reporting. In addition, the majority of statements provided conclusions in the 'positive' form, despite clear evidence of a limited, rather than reasonable, assurance engagement having been conducted.

Somewhat damningly, the study's authors conclude that, on the basis of these findings, report readers would 'often have great uncertainty in understanding how the assurance provider undertook the engagement, what they reviewed and what was the meaning of their conclusion' (p. 67).

O'Dwyer and Owen's (2005) study of assurance statements appearing in a somewhat smaller sample of 'leading edge' reports adopts much the same approach to that of CPA Australia in subjecting their content to rigorous scrutiny. A slightly different angle to the analysis is, however, introduced in that statements are explicitly evaluated against an 'ideal' framework which is derived from the AccountAbility, FEE and GRI guidelines. Whilst a similar variability in assurance practice is highlighted, O'Dwyer and Owen do point to some improvements being made since the earlier study of Ball *et al.* (2000) which employed a closely comparable, albeit longitudinal, sampling method drawing upon reports short-listed for the ACCA (in this case environmental) reporting awards scheme. In particular, it is noted that the extent of work carried out in terms of validating both data systems and data appearing in the report, undertaking site visits and interviewing organizational personnel has noticeably increased, and that the independence of the exercise is more pronounced, in that the intertwining of the roles of assurance provider and performer of consultancy services observed in the earlier study is now very much the exception. In the relatively rare instances in which the assurance provider has performed additional consultancy services it is noticeable that this fact is now clearly acknowledged in the assurance statement. Additionally, a greater degree of focus on the performance dimension, as opposed to confining attention to management systems issues, is discernible, particularly in the case of the slowly growing number of exercises which employ AA1000 methodology.

Notwithstanding the above observed emerging focus on performance issues in assurance statements, O'Dwyer and Owen point to a large degree of management control remaining over the whole process. The simple fact is that assurance providers are appointed by management, who can place any restrictions they wish upon the exercise. Additionally, as was the case with the CPA Australia study, it was found that to the extent that statements are addressed to anyone it is to corporate management, suggesting that any 'value added' by the assurance process accrues to the same constituency.[7] Significantly, whereas interviewing organizational staff members appears to be becoming a standard feature of the assurance process, occurring in 85 per cent of sample cases, interviewing stakeholders is very much the exception, occurring in only 10 per cent of cases. Furthermore, in the relatively few instances (32 per cent) where specific reference was made to materiality it was generally not addressed from a stakeholder perspective. Similarly, completeness was very rarely considered in the context of sufficient information being provided to enable stakeholders to make informed judgements. Finally, in the case of statements (32 per cent) making clear reference to an evaluation having been made of the extent to which the organization had sought to identify stakeholder interests and concerns, a large majority referred to the need for more to be done in this regard.

Taken together, the two detailed empirical studies discussed above suggest that sustainability assurance practice as it stands at the present time is bedevilled by inconsistencies in approach, and certainly offers little in terms of promoting greater levels of corporate accountability to external stakeholders. The advent of ISAE 3000, together with some notable attempts currently being made to develop comprehensive assurance standards that effectively combine the procedural and presentational rigour of the latter with the emphasis on stakeholder responsiveness of AA1000 (see, for example, the KPMG and AccounAbility sponsored study by Iansen-Rogers and Oelschlaegel, 2005), may well succeed in addressing the former problem.[8] Also aiding progress towards this end is likely to be the launch of a professional qualification in sustainability assurance practice under the auspices of AccountAbility and the International Register of Certified Auditors in 2004. For the ambitions of the promoters of such a comprehensive approach to succeed, of course, fees for assurance work would have to be raised considerably in order to support the detailed programme of work that would have to be carried out in the context of such assignments. Difficult as it may be to persuade corporate interests as to the necessity of going down this route, the prospects for injecting some meaning-ful level of stakeholder accountability into sustainability assurance practice are likely to be far harder still to realize.

THE FUTURE DEVELOPMENT OF SUSTAINABILITY ASSURANCE PRACTICE: TOWARDS ENHANCED STAKEHOLDER ACCOUNTABILITY?

As we have already noted, AccountAbility's approach to assurance has, from the start, been avowedly stakeholder centred, an approach which has culminated in the issuing of an exposure draft (AA1000SES) on the specific issue of stakeholder engagement in July 2005. A number of prominent consultancy-based assurance providers, notably CSR Network, Justassurance and Ethics Etc in the UK, have enthusiastically adopted the same perspective in the conduct of assurance engagements. At the same time, many accountant assurance providers have been seemingly reluctant to follow suit. However, signs of change are clearly evident, not only in KPMG's collaboration with AccountAbility, referred to above, but also in FEE's (2004) appeal for assurance standard setters to adopt a more pro-active approach to stakeholder engagement. Significantly, this latter appeal has been taken up by the Dutch-registered accountants body Royal NIVRA in a draft Standard for Assurance Engagements Relating to Sustainability Reports (ED 3410) in December 2004. The draft Standard apparently represents a fundamental shift among accounting standard setters in the direction of addressing stakeholders' concerns. Amongst key provisions are that a prime objective of the assurance engagement is to examine 'whether the information in the sustainability report complies with the requirements that can reasonably be set by the targeted group of stakeholders' (paragraph 11), and that, in addressing the issue of completeness, an assessment should be made as to whether the targeted group represents a 'complete' group of stakeholders (paragraph 20). Furthermore, and perhaps most fundamentally, the draft Standard goes on to recommend that the assurance statement be addressed to the stakeholders of the reporting organization, as this 'makes it clear that their interests are essentially indicative for the planning and performance of the work and the associated reporting' (paragraph 124).

Whilst the apparent emerging consensus on the importance of stakeholders in the assurance process may on the surface seem encouraging, and certainly corporate transparency would be greatly enhanced should the NIVRA initiative be more widely taken up, we still have a long way to go before we could consider stakeholder *accountability* to be meaningfully established. The whole case for stakeholder-centred assurance seems to be based on persuading companies as to its efficacy as a driver of improved (financial) performance. At best, it would seem that stakeholders are being invited to participate in an information-sharing exercise designed to enhance corporate learning and innovation (Zadek *et al.*, 2004). Significantly, no transfer of power whatsoever is being contemplated, whereby stakeholders can hold the organization to account for its activities and actively enforce some degree of responsiveness to their concerns. Adams and Evans (2004) in a detailed analysis of the shortcomings of current assurance practice as a vehicle for enhancing stakeholder accountability go on to suggest concrete ways of transferring some degree of power over the process by, for example, enabling stakeholders to appoint assurance providers and determine the scope of the exercise. However, this still begs the question as to how stakeholders can use the assurance findings in any way that might influence organizational decision-making.

It seems clear that for extending stakeholder accountability, in the sense of meaningfully holding management to account, the whole issue of sustainability assurance has to be looked at in the context of the wider corporate governance system in which it is embedded. Simply addressing assurance statements to stakeholders (or indeed allowing them to appoint the assurance provider and define the assurance scope) achieves very little if the results of the exercise cannot be used in the same way that shareholders may use the results of the financial audit. Simply, there is a need to bring an external stakeholder dimension into CSR internal governance procedures. Admittedly a few companies, notably Camelot and BT, have established Advisory Panels for CSR issues, comprising independent specialists in various areas of stakeholder concern, whose views are channelled to the main company board. However, in these instances the external participants are appointed by corporate management, rather than those they purport to represent. Hence they actually represent no one but themselves, and are therefore directly accountable to no one but themselves. By contrast, forums at which stakeholder groups are directly represented (predominantly employee and local community groups) are confined to consultative committee-type structures completely separated from key strategic decision-making areas.

Essentially, what is missing in the whole debate over the development of sustainability assurance is some intervention by regulatory authorities in the public policy domain, designed to bring about a greater level of corporate accountability to stakeholder groups. In the current voluntaristic climate dominating matters of CSR policy throughout Europe (see Commission of the European Communities, 2002) this seems highly unlikely to happen. It is indeed instructive to note here the specific rejection of introducing a pluralistic approach towards directors' duties, whereby enforceable accountability would be owed to a wider range of stakeholders than merely capital providers, in the long running debate of company law reform in the UK culminating in the 2002 White Paper (see Owen *et al.*, 2001). Quite simply, administrative (reporting) reform being promoted by a growing range of assurance standard setters can achieve little in the absence of accompanying institutional reform providing a forum where such reports may be effectively used (Owen *et al.*, 1997).

Frank (2001) in a vigorous de-bunking of the pretensions of what he terms 'market populism', of which unfortunately the current wave of sustainability reporting and associated assurance exercises is increasingly forming an integral part, stresses that

> What we must have are not more focus groups or a new space where people can express themselves . . . but some countervailing power, some force that resists the imperatives of profit in the name of economic democracy.
>
> (p. xvii)

By effectively side-stepping crucial issues of corporate governance reform in favour of essentially vacuous notions of stakeholder engagement, sustainability assurance practice, as currently conceived in both the reporting and standard setting arenas,

180

fails to introduce the necessary countervailing power to 'hold to account' and thereby fails to enhance stakeholder accountability.

NOTES

1   The countries surveyed are: Australia, Belgium, Canada, Denmark, Finland, France, Germany, Italy, Japan, Netherlands, Norway, South Africa, Spain, Sweden, UK and USA.

2   It is suggested that this may be due to the increasing practice of integrating non-financial information into annual financial reports in these countries. See also Park and Brorson (2005).

3   The discrepancy between the Salterbaxter and Context study and that of KPMG in terms of assurance provision figures for the top 100 companies is probably explained by the fact that the former is based on reports appearing in a slightly earlier period (2003–4).

4   A further minority pursuit amongst reporting organizations is to seek an opinion on aspects of policy and performance from leading figures within the NGO movement. These can essentially be equated with informed journalistic comment and cannot be regarded as examples of assurance statements in any meaningful sense of the term.

5   See O'Dwyer and Owen (2005) for further elaboration of this point.

6   By contrast, a positive form would be of the nature, 'in our opinion BG's processes in place . . . are effective, and that statements made in the Report . . . are fairly stated'.

7   The only exception to management being the addressee, in cases where one was specified, was one statement addressed to its 'readership'.

8   For an interesting account of some practical applications of such a 'hybrid' approach see Boele and Kemp (2005).

REFERENCES

AccountAbility (1999) *AA1000 framework: Standard, guidelines and professional qualification*. London: AccountAbility.

AccountAbility (2003) *AA1000 assurance standard*. London: AccountAbility.

AccounAbility (2005) *AA1000SES AA1000 stakeholder engagement standard exposure draft*. London: AccountAbility.

AccountAbility and the International Register of Certified Auditors (IRCA) (2004) *Certified sustainability assurance practitioner programme: A programme for a certification for sustainability assurance practitioners*. London: AccountAbility and IRCA.

Adams, C. A and Evans, R. (2004) Accountability, completeness, credibility and the audit expectations gap. *Journal of Corporate Citizenship,* 14: 97–115.

Association of Chartered Certified Accountants (ACCA) (2004) *Towards transparency: Progress on global sustainability reporting.* London: ACCA

Ball, A., Owen, D. L. and Gray, R. H. (2000) External transparency or internal capture? The role of third party statements in adding value to corporate environmental reports. *Business Strategy and the Environment,* 9(1): 1–23.

Boele, R. and Kemp, D. (2005) Social auditors: Illegitimate offspring of the audit family? *Journal of Corporate Citizenship,* 17: 109–19.

Commission of the European Communities (COM) (2002) *Corporate social responsibility: A business contribution to sustainable development.* Brussels: COM.

CPA Australia (2004) *Triple bottom line: A study of assurance statements worldwide.* Melbourne: CPA Australia.

Fédération des Experts Comptables Européens (FEE) (2002) *Providing assurance on sustainability reports.* Brussels: FEE.

Fédération des Experts Comptables Européens (FEE) (2004) *FEE call for action: Assurance for sustainability.* Brussels: FEE.

Frank, T. (2001) *One market under God: Extreme capitalism, market populism and the end of economic democracy.* London: Secker and Warburg.

Global Reporting Initiative (GRI) (2002) *Sustainability reporting guidelines on economic, environmental and social performance.* Amsterdam: GRI.

Gray, R. H. (2000) Current developments and trends in social and environmental auditing, reporting and attestation: a review and comment. *International Journal of Auditing,* 4(3): 247–68.

Iansen-Rogers, J. and Oelschlaegel, J. (2005) *Assurance standards briefing: AA1000 assurance standard and ISAE3000.* London: AccountAbility and KPMG.

International Auditing and Assurance Standards Board (IAASB) (2004) *International standard on assurance engagements 3000: Assurance engagements on other than audits or reviews of historical information.* New York: International Federation of Accountants.

Kamp-Roelands, N. (2002) Towards a Framework for Auditing Environmental Reports, unpublished Ph.D. thesis, Tilburg University, The Netherlands.

KPMG (2005) *International survey of corporate responsibility reporting.* Amsterdam: KPMG.

Medawar, C. (1976) The social audit: A political view. *Accounting, Organizations and Society,* 1(4): 389–94.

O'Dwyer, B. and Owen, D. L. (2005) Assurance statement practice in environmental, social and sustainability reporting: A critical evaluation. *British Accounting Review,* 37(2): 205–29.

Owen, D. L., Gray, R. H. and Bebbington, J. (1997) Green accounting: cosmetic irrelevance or radical agenda for change? *Asia-Pacific Journal of Accounting,* 4(2): 175–98.

Owen, D. L., Swift, T. and Hunt, K. (2001) Questioning the role of stakeholder engagement in social and ethical accounting, auditing and reporting. *Accounting Forum*, 25(3): 264–82.

Park, J. and Brorson, T. (2005) Experiences of and views on third-party assurance of corporate environmental and sustainability reports. *Journal of Cleaner Production*, 13: 1095–1106.

Royal NIVRA (2005) *Standard for assurance engagements 3410 exposure draft: Assurance engagements relating to sustainability reports.* Amsterdam: Royal NIVRA.

Salterbaxter and Context (2005) *Trends in CSR reporting 2003–2004.* London: Salterbaxter and Context.

Zadek, S., Raynard, P., Forstater, M. and Oelschlaegel, J. (2004) *The future of sustainability assurance.* London: ACCA.

Chapter 10

Future prospects for corporate sustainability reporting

Markus J. Milne and Rob Gray

INTRODUCTION

This chapter is less about that most risky of enterprises – predicting the future – and more about identifying current trends and evaluating them. It seeks to explore where corporate sustainability reporting appears to be headed and whether or not we should be pleased by this. The first part of the chapter focuses on what *is* being reported, how it is being reported and by whom. It provides an overview of developments in reporting practice since the 1990s, drawing mostly on secondary sources (including the published academic and professional literature, benchmarking analyses and other surveys of reporting practice). We then seek to extrapolate these trends a little. The second part of the chapter takes a more critical look at corporate sustainability reporting. It seeks to assess what corporate sustainability reporting has achieved and what it could possibly achieve. We also seek to explain what we believe it cannot achieve. We will consequently argue that efforts to promote corporate sustainability reporting need to be tempered with a clear understanding of both its existing and its potential limitations. Sustainability is too important to be left to the vagaries of self-reporting and non-critical descriptive study and so there is a constant need to subject all developments in this field to the most robust of criticisms.

We need to state at the outset that there are two fundamental problems of definition with 'corporate sustainability reporting'. These are defining what is (or is not) a 'sustainability' report and, second, what the different parties mean by 'sustainability'. We are, deliberately, not going to get too bogged down in these issues at this point but we do need to introduce this definitional problem briefly.

There are fundamental differences about what corporate reporting for sustainability *means*; what purposes this reporting serves (or might serve), and whose interests are (or might be) served by it. For many organizations, associations and commentators, sustainability reporting is simply seen as an extension and progression of earlier forms of corporate reporting. These began by extending traditional financial reporting to include such things as an organization's *environmental policies* and *impacts* (e.g., resource and energy use, waste flows), and then extended to matters such as an organization's *social policies and impacts* (e.g., health and safety of employees, impacts on local communities, and charitable giving). Such reporting initially tended to appear within the traditional corporate (annual) report. By the late 1980s and early 1990s, however, 'stand-alone' corporate reports were becoming much more common as organizations started to formally address environmental and, later, social issues as they understood them.[1] By the late 1990s, organizations began to produce combined reports that included social, environmental, and financial/economic information as approximations of 'triple bottom line' reporting[2] (Elkington, 1997). These reports are now frequently referred to as 'sustainability reports' – a nomenclature which reflects in part the development of the *Sustainability reporting guidelines* by the Global Reporting Initiative (GRI, 2000, 2002[3]).

Nomenclature thus remains a problem. Reports might be titled as sustainable development reports, corporate social responsibility reports, triple bottom line reports, or even simply annual reports.[4] Nonetheless, as captured in the following quotations, the common basis of such reporting remains concerned with the economic, social and environmental *impacts* of the (mostly for-profit) *organization*, and the (good) *intentions* of its *management*.

Corporate environmental reporting [has become] the 'icebreaker' for a much wider form of corporate responsibility (CR) reporting in the form of sustainability, triple bottom line or corporate social responsibility (CSR) reports. Reporting aimed at communicating with stakeholders, not only on environmental performance, but also in an integrated manner on environmental, social and economic performance, to be transparent and accountable.

(KPMG, 2005, p. 3)

Sustainable Development reporting is the external reporting of the economic, social and environmental performance and impacts of an entity.

(Report of the Taskforce on Sustainable Development Reporting, ICANZ, 2002, p. 1)

Organisations now operate in a world where stakeholders are asking for more transparency and accountability than ever before. Sustainability is the new demand. This is a time of profit with responsibility . . . This interest in the social, environmental and economic sustainability of an organisation's performance is about stakeholders accessing the widest perspective possible, recognising that unless these issues are addressed, there is the potential for them to affect ongoing sustainability and viability. Triple bottom line accounting has a powerful, caring side. But it is very much risk management in action.

(Educational Editorial, KPMG Model Triple Bottom Line Report, 2002b)

Sustainable Development Reporting (SDR) is one tool organisations can use to identify their economic, environmental and social impacts, assess their performance in these areas, make improvements, and identify new opportunities that are consistent with the goals of sustainable development . . . SDR is preferred to TBL, however, because the emphasis on economic, environmental and social in TBL can encourage thinking in 'silos' and conceal other dimensions of sustainable development – such as culture that may not be fully reflected in social dimensions.

(NZBCSD, 2002, p. 8)

These quotations suggest a very particular range of likely purposes and interests to be served by corporate sustainability reporting. As such they may not be entirely gratifying to those who are concerned with issues of broader accountability to society and the sustaining of ecosystems and the natural environment (see below). The potential tensions between shareholders, corporate management and other stakeholder interests appear oversimplified – 'profit with responsibility', for example, is presented as a seemingly uncomplicated matter. Likewise, through risk management, the objective of 'sustainability' reporting (i.e , what it is that is to be sustained) often appears to be the (corporate) *organization*. Before turning to a critique of such reporting, however, in the next sections we outline trends in reporting practice, and attempt to assess where it is headed.

WHO ISSUES CORPORATE SUSTAINABILITY REPORTS? HOW? AND WHAT IS REPORTED?[5]

Since 1990 the number of companies producing social/environmental and/or sustainability reports has risen steadily. ACCA/Corporateregister.com (2004) reports that in 1993 globally less than 100 companies annually produced such information, whereas by 2003 this figure was in excess of 1,500 reports. Over the same period, while early reports were almost exclusively in the form of printed reports, as many as two-thirds of reports were produced electronically (pdf or HTML typically) by 2005.[6] Different surveys report different emphases. Corporate-register.com reports, for the years 2001–3, that Europe accounted for 54 per cent, Asia and Australasia 25 per cent, and the Americas 19 per cent of submitted reports. The Global Reporting Initiative site identifies Japan as the leading country when it comes to reporting in line with GRI guidelines followed by the UK, the US and Spain. The broad pattern of reporting among the largest companies as covered by the KPMG surveys is shown in Table 10.1.

There are four major inferences which are worth drawing from Table 10.1. First, while globalized capitalism may appear to produce homogeneity, countries – even (so-called) developed countries – vary considerably in their involvement in reporting. Second, the numbers appear to be levelling off. After the initial enthusiasm, the number of new reporters is rising more slowly and some reporting organizations are beginning to retreat (recall, that these reports are all *voluntarily* produced). Third, as commentators have frequently noted, the reporting is dominated by the largest companies – while 52 per cent of the very largest companies (the Global 250) report, the proportion of companies reporting falls rapidly as size drops. This means that a table like Table 10.1 almost certainly paints the rosiest of pictures and significantly exaggerates the overall pattern of corporate reporting. Fourth, and finally, it follows from these inferences that we will not be surprised to see that reporting is also a 'developed' country phenomenon – the incidence of reporting is very much lower in countries such as China, Egypt, Bangladesh, Kenya and Chile[7] (see, for example, Kolk, 2003; and Kolk and van Tulder, 2004, for much more on these issues).

While our interest here is with corporate sustainability reporting, it would be improper to overstate the lack of corporate attention to social and environmental matters. Companies in different jurisdictions of the world are required to comply with and report (publicly or to government) upon a range of matters such as employees, health and safety, toxic releases, environmental liabilities, charitable donations and value added. Perhaps most significant of these in the present context

Table 10.1 Trends in reporting by large companies (% of the largest 100 companies producing reports in selected countries)

Country	1996	1999	2002	2005
United States	44	30	36	32
Canada	—	—	19	41
Japan	—	21	72	80
Australia	5	15	14	23
United Kingdom	27	32	49	71
Germany	28	38	32	36
Holland	20	25	26	29
Italy	—	2	12	31
France	4	4	21	40
Denmark	8	29	20	22
Sweden	26	34	26	20
Norway	26	31	30	15
Finland	7	15	32	31
Global 250 % (n)	—	35 (88)	45 (112)	52 (129)
KPMG country average % (n)	17 (220)	24 (267)	23 (440)	33 (525)

Source: Adapted from KPMG (1996, 1999, 2002a, 2005)

is reporting under the European Eco-management and Auditing Standard (EMAS).[8] This provides a mechanism for organizations to develop environmental programmes and management systems and – most notably – the standard requires that companies produce public statements on their performance. There were over 3,000 such EMAS statements issued in 2004 alone. Of these, Germany accounted for 1,700 while Spain, Italy, Austria and Denmark together accounted for over 950 of the statements (Europa, 2005).[9] It may be that reporting on environmental management systems *could* – stress *could* – make development towards sustainability reporting more straightforward but there is no evidence (of which we are aware) on this. It is simply that, to the extent that corporate 'sustainability' reporting proves to be about something almost but not quite entirely unlike 'sustainability', then we would need to spread our gaze wider to talk with authority on 'environmental' or 'social' reporting.

Returning to stand-alone (sometime 'sustainability') reports, research consistently shows that the industrial sector of the organization reporting is highly important (e.g., Hackston and Milne, 1996; Deegan and Gordon, 1996; Gray *et al.*, 1995a; Patten, 1991). Not only is it large companies that report their social and, most commonly, their environmental impacts, but these companies primarily come from the heavy industrial sectors. As shown in Table 10.2, Oil and Gas, Utilities, Chemicals, Mining, and Forest, Pulp and Paper companies have dominated the incidence of reporting statistics since the mid-1990s, but even here, nearly half of the companies in these sectors do *not report*, and the evidence suggests that while such sectors were early into reporting, they have not made continuous gains in the number of companies reporting. The results show even poorer reporting levels for the largest sectors (e.g., Finance, Trade and Retail, Services, Metals, Electronics and Food), although the Finance, Trade and Services sectors have made recent improvements. Recent gains in the number of companies reporting, then, do not appear to be coming from the traditional reporting sectors, but rather from those sectors new to reporting, suggesting the spread of reporting since the 1990s is widening across sectors rather than deepening within them (see Table 10.2).

Finally, before turning to look at assessments of the quality of this reporting (in the next section), a word about verification seems appropriate. The incidence of reports being externally 'verified'[10] has also been growing. In 1993, about 17 per cent of reports overall were externally attested, and by 2003 this figure was about 40 per cent (ACCA/Corporateregister.com, 2004. See also the KPMG surveys). Different regions, however, have different rates of external assurance. Rates of assurance in the US, for example, remain surprisingly low at about 3 per cent or less, and have changed little since the 1990s – *one* of 30, 36 and 32 reports were verified in the US top 100 companies in 1999, 2002 and 2005 respectively (KPMG, 1999, 2002a, 2005). Similarly, the German top 100 has low rates of verification (approx 10 to 14 per cent) that have changed little over the 1999 to 2005 period. In contrast, rates of verification among the UK top 100 have remained constant at

Table 10.2 *% of the largest 100 companies issuing stand-alone reports*[a]

Sector of company (regardless of country of origin)	Number of companies in survey in that sector	1996	1999	2002	2005
Finance, securities and insurance	340	5	8	12	31
Trade and retail	241	11	7	15	22
Other services	144	5	4	6	18
Metals and engineering	141	25[b]	17	24	25
Electronics and computers	131	33	30	24	35
Food and beverage	126	17	22	26	29
Oil and gas	114	43	53	39	52
Automotive	109	—	38	28	32
Construction	108	13	18	17	28
Utilities	101	40	55	50	61
Communication and media	93	7	16	20	29
Transport	68	22	33	37	38
Chemicals and synthetics	67	74	59	45	52
Pharmaceuticals	47	41	50	30	30
Mining	42	25[a]	47	36	52
Forest, pulp and paper	28	56	55	43	50
Total number of companies in survey (top 100 companies from each of 19 countries)	1,900				

Source: Adapted from KPMG (2002a)

Notes: [a] Some degree of caution is required in interpreting this table since the KPMG surveys of 1996, 1999, 2002, and 2005 are based on different numbers of countries' top 100 firms. For example, the 1999 survey is based on 11 countries (and therefore 1,100 companies) while the 2002 survey is based on 19 countries (and 1,900 companies), and the 2005 survey is based on 16 countries (1,600 companies). The industrial makeup of different countries, therefore, may bias results for given sectors
[b] Mining, metals and materials were combined in the 1996 survey, and separated in later surveys

53 per cent over the 1999 to 2005 period (KPMG, 1999, 2002a, 2005). Other countries boast verification rates of 40 per cent (Denmark), 33 per cent (Holland), 16 per cent (Sweden) whilst Japan, for example, has increased the incidence of verification from 5 per cent to 31 per cent and in Italy verification rates have moved from 50 per cent in 1999 to 71 per cent in 2005.

IF THAT IS THE QUANTITY, WHAT IS THE QUALITY?

While increasing rates of verification in some countries hint at the prospect that the quality of reporting is improving, additional evidence is suggested by the UNEP/SustainAbility (1994, 1996, 1997, 2000, 2002, 2004) benchmarking reports, and from more recent trends associated with the Global Reporting Initiative (GRI).

Both of these sources provide guidelines or a template against which to measure report content.[11] At August 2004, for example, 26 organizations reported 'in accordance' with the GRI guidelines, with 503 organizations noted as users of the GRI (ACCA/Corporateregister.com, 2004). At March 2005, the numbers were 51 and 639 (Gray, 2006b), and by November 2005, the 'in accordance' reporters had reached 106, with 732 organizations noted as users of the guidelines. The 2004 UNEP/SustainAbility benchmark survey – *Risk & Opportunity* – also notes that of the 100 reports selected, 92 openly referenced the GRI guidelines (compared to 51 in the 2002 benchmark survey). In that survey, however, average scores by the 12 'In Accordance' GRI reporters were only marginally better (55 per cent of total benchmark score) than the other reporters (48 per cent of total benchmark score) (UNEP/SustainAbility, 2004, p. 41).

The 2004 UNEP/SustainAbility survey also notes that 26 companies were new entrants to the benchmark survey, and that 20 companies exceeded more than 50 per cent of the overall benchmark score, with the top scoring Co-operative Financial Services reaching 71 per cent. The previous 2002 benchmark survey, *Trust Us*, had been far more pessimistic about the state of stand-alone reporting, noting that only 7 companies broke through 50 per cent of the overall benchmark score, that environmental reporting was in decline due to its substitution by social and economic data, that many reports were overloading readers with too much detail and, perhaps most disturbing, that reporting was hitting a plateau with scores virtually unchanged since 2000. It would seem, then, that the GRI has become an important catalyst in re-energizing and lifting the quality of reporting not only among *some* of the largest and leading reporters, but also for *some* newcomers.

Assessing trends in the quality of reporting, however, is difficult and subjective. One reason for this difficulty is that the UNEP/SustainAbility surveys work with the leading 50 or 100 reporters of the day rather than systematically benchmarking the same organizations through time. Nonetheless, the UNEP/SustainAbility surveys do offer insights. The dozen or so reporting leaders have varied over the years, and while 2004 showed an improvement in the overall scores awarded, not all companies have improved. In the 2004 survey, for example, all of the top 50 reporters scored at least 39 per cent of the total benchmark score; in the 1996 survey, 22 of 40 companies scored at least 39 per cent of the total score. However, of the 22 companies listed as scoring at least 39 per cent in the 1996 survey, only 5 of them remain included in the 2004 survey. No doubt some organizations have been subject to takeover, have merged or failed, but clearly some still exist, and have not improved (or perhaps ceased) their reporting (e.g., Body Shop, Monsanto, Dow, IBM, Ontario Hydro, Du Pont, Waste Management, Ciba–Geigy, BASF). And while a careful examination of the benchmark surveys since 1996 shows that companies such as British Telecom, Novo Nordisk, and BP have improved their overall scores by 20 per cent or more, it also shows other organizations have remained static (e.g., Bristol Myers–Squibb, British Airways, General Motors) or slipped backwards (e.g., Baxter).

Additional evidence seems to be a bit thin at the moment. One source is academic studies. Milne *et al.* (2003) and Chapman and Milne (2004), for example, use UNEP/SustainAbility's criteria to analyse a series of New Zealand reports. The conclusions from these studies are that apart from two leading organizations (who are included among UNEP/SustainAbility's 2002 and 2004 top 100) the standard of reporting is very poor. One obvious inference is that for every leading reporter that scores adequately in the UNEP/SustainAbility survey, there are a great many more organizations unable to do so. Thus, Morhardt *et al.* (2002) find that what companies *actually* report falls significantly below the benchmarks provided by guidelines like the GRI and UNEP/SustainAbility. Similarly, Sinclair and Walton (2003) demonstrate that many timber and paper companies do not report on issues significant to their stakeholders.[12]

Confirmatory evidence is also available from the judges' reports from reporting awards schemes designed to reward, comment upon and encourage substantive stand-alone reporting (e.g., ACCA Sustainability Reporting Awards, 2001, 2002, 2003, 2004; European Sustainability Reporting Awards, 2001, 2002, 2003, 2004).

A review of these reports suggests a number of observations on the quality of reports and the reporting process. Particularly noteworthy are references to (1) the failure of organizations to address their core business issues in relation to sustainable development; (2) the failure of organizations to provide a sufficient overview of the organization's activities to provide a context for interpreting the reports; (3) the failure to link the report and organization to the wider political and policy context, with particular reference to lobbying activities; (4) the need to improve the quality of external assurance statements, and how the organization has improved relative to previous recommendations; and (5) the failure to link the organization's reporting to its wider sector through benchmarking. Despite ongoing references to 'sustainability reporting', the 2004 UK Awards judges' report also questions whether corporate social responsibility and sustainability are the same concepts, and questions the manner in which reports concentrate on reporting organizational impacts, while failing to address the state of the ecological environment subject to those impacts – a point we return to shortly.

SO WHERE IS CORPORATE SUSTAINABILITY REPORTING HEADED? SHOULD WE BE PLEASED?

It has taken over a decade to reach this present point in 'sustainability' reporting. And while the inroads made by a purely voluntary approach may seem impressive, the essence of the foregoing data is that to date virtually no progress towards sustainability has been achieved. While it certainly appears to be the case that over the last decade or so there has been a 20-fold increase in the number of annual stand-alone reporters (e.g., 100 to 2,000), this needs to be judged in context.

First, there are approximately 60,000 multinational companies operating worldwide.[13] These come mostly from a selection of 'developed countries' (see Table 10.1). Comparatively, the less than 2,000 reports produced per annum globally is a fairly trivial level of achievement (Gray, 2006a). This suggests that there is a very long way to go, and with trends starting to level off, the prospects for increased levels of reporting do not look terribly good. Second, of the estimated 2,000 reporters, about 600–700 are among the more closely studied reporters in 2005, and of these 600–700 reports, only approximately 30 per cent are externally verified (i.e., 200 reports). Third, a little over 100 reports are 'In Accordance' with the GRI guidelines. Fourth, of the 'leading' reporters, only a very small number (seven in 2,002, and 20 in 2004) get half marks or better on the UNEP/ SustainAbility benchmark score. Based on the standards of the GRI and the UNEP/SustainAbility benchmark criteria, then, perhaps at best 0.2 per cent of multinationals provide credible and reasonable accounts of their vast impacts on society and the environment.

Were the next decade to witness a further 20-fold increase in reporting developments, and the evidence above suggests this is not likely, then we might expect as many as 2,000 companies to be reporting 'In Accordance' with the GRI, and 400 companies doing better than half of the UNEP/SustainAbility benchmark. And while such (unlikely) developments seem impressive, they would barely register a blip on the 60,000 multinationals.

Of course, not all multinationals are equal, either in terms of size (100 account for one-eighth of world output in dollar terms), or in terms of social and environmental impacts. And so if reporting developments occurred among those of the largest, and those with the greatest impacts, there could be more room for optimism, perhaps.[14] The analysis above provides no consistently clear evidence of convincingly improved levels of reporting among the very largest corporations or among those in the more socially and environmentally significant sectors. Although rates of reporting in the Global 250 continue to grow – as does the KPMG average top 100 – rates of reporting in, for example, the US and German top 100s are static. Furthermore rates of reporting in the Oil and Gas, Mining, Forest, Automotive and Chemicals sectors, while relatively high, show little evidence of improvement since the mid-1990s.

Whether or not we should be pleased with the developments in corporate sustainability reporting really depends on what one hopes for from such reporting. On the one hand the overall standard of reports is an improvement on some of the 'green glossies' of the early 1990s. On the other hand, there are few innovations comparable with the early innovations in reporting such as BSO Origin, Danish Steel Works, Body Shop and Traidcraft. Such improvements as we have seen appear to have arisen as a result of: expanding coverage in reports (e.g., to include more social and economic indicators); increasing standardization of report content (following templates like the GRI); increasing interest in engagement with stake-holders; and, to an extent, increases in external verification.

Reporting has not, however, fulfilled the more optimistic expectations of many commentators. Reporting has not, it seems, acted as a catalyst for underlying behavioural changes that could promote substantive attention to sustainable development. Equally, reporting is no nearer fulfilling the demands of accountability (e.g., in the sense of better reflecting social, environmental and sustainability performance). It seems difficult to escape from the gloomy conclusion that reporting developments, and particularly the triple bottom line (see Milne *et al.*, 2005a, 2005b and Gray, 2006a, 2006b), are actually proving to be a hopeless distraction from substantive sustainability or, worse, the very means to frustrate moves towards the changes that sustainability requires. UNEP/SustainAbility's (1994, pp. 67–8) first benchmark survey was seriously optimistic. It predicted that reporting would: expand beyond its core set of reporting elements; embrace full-cost accounting; provide indicators to assess the overall environmental sustainability of industries (through sector reporting) as well as corporate operations; and reduce industry's environmental impacts. The 1994 survey, more tellingly, also saw that the central challenge for reporting was to link up corporate reporting with national sustainable development priorities, targets and reporting systems to enable movement towards a sustainable global economy. The early benchmark survey was clear that corporate environmental performance cannot be separated from the 'wider goals of relieving poverty and promoting improved standards of living in developing countries' (p. 52), and the ultimate aim of sustainable development reporting is 'no net loss of carrying capacity' (p. 18). It also noted (p. 20):

> some products, processes and even entire industries may prove unsustainable – even when run efficiently . . . The data collected and reported by the companies discussed in this report . . . will help establish which products, processes and industries will become building blocks for a more sustainable economy – and which will need to be phased out in the interest of environmental sustainability.

Against these expectations, reporting developments have barely made a mark, and it is noteworthy that either such expectations no longer seem to occupy the pages of the later UNEP/SustainAbility benchmark reports, or if they do, as in the latest 2004 survey, they continue to remain dreams for the future (see, for example, UNEP/SustainAbility, 2004, pp. 43–9). As Jonathon Porritt (2001, p. 3), Chairman of the UK Sustainable Development Commission, argues in the Commission's first annual review, most of us (ministers, companies, local authorities, charities, universities, us!) have failed to place sustainable development at the heart of things, and that remains no less so for corporate reporting.

Social accounting proponents are now having to face up to the possibility that corporate reporting – certainly voluntary corporate reporting – probably could never live up to such expectations because of both the vested corporate interests at play, and the complexities of the reporting task itself. We need to remain open to the prospect that (especially voluntary) reporting, particularly in the name of sustainable development, could do more harm than good – that far from proving emancipatory, it will be fashioned to legitimate ongoing exploitation of people and the environment (see Puxty, 1991; Tinker et al., 1991; Cooper, 1995; Welford, 1997).[15] The essential dilemma associated with such reporting developments has long been noted:

> On the one hand, do we see organisations struggling to define 'environment' in a way which will enable them to avoid morphogenetic change [deep-seated changes in values and behaviour] – a process of definition which is clearly aided by business organizations like ICC, BCSD, CBI etc . . .? On the other hand, do we see environmentalists finding themselves torn between fear that 'environment' is in danger of being captured . . . whilst recognising that these new accounts at least permit a new and long-overdue discourse?
>
> (Gray et al., 1995b, p. 231)

Although research continues to develop, to expose the ways in which corporations might, for example, use reporting to legitimate existing corporate behaviours and/or promote learning and how 'sustainability' reporting continues to open up (potentially) richer discourses between organizations and civil society (see, for example, other chapters in this book), such developments still largely fail to put (ecological) sustainability and social justice at the heart of things, and thereby fail to treat sustainability seriously. We would argue the seriousness of sustainability is avoided in two principal ways. First, virtually all corporate reporters (and, indeed, researchers and commentators) typically ignore both a wider systems conception of sustainability and the growing body of evidence that suggests many aspects of ecology and society are being severely degraded by modern economic activity. Secondly, sustainability is avoided by the very manner in which corporate organizations *do* engage with notions of sustainability and the way in which they translate and define the concept to make it consistent with what many organizations currently do.

Corporate 'sustainability' reports are typically attempts by organizations to provide some sort of a (largely favourable) account for (some of) their impacts on the environment and society. They have tended to be a blend of pictorial, verbal and quantitative description of elements of the enterprise with only occasional direct confrontation of 'externalities' and financial representation of these. There is still very considerable room for (potential) improvement in such reports and, in time, it may be that a 'full-cost accounting' may emerge and prove to be the ultimate form

194

of corporate attempts to develop 'sustainability' reporting.[16] However, it is essential to recognize that reporting about the social and the environmental – in whatever form it is undertaken – remains for us a distinctly different prospect from accounting (or reporting) for sustainability.

Sustainability is a *systems* concept and not an organizational concept (see, for example, Gray, 1992; Milne, 1996a; Gray and Bebbington, 2000; Gray and Milne, 2002, 2004; Milne *et al.*, 2005a, 2005b; Gray, 2006a, 2006b). Sustainability is concerned with equity and justice, and with ecological limits as much as, if not more than, economic efficiency (Gray and Milne, 2004). It is, primarily, a global concept and the question arises whether the concept can have a sensible application at the corporate or even at the regional level. A basic element of this concern is that sustainability emphasizes not just an *efficient* allocation of resources over time, but also a *fair* distribution of resources and opportunities between the current generation and between present and future generations, and a *scale* of economic activity relative to its ecological life support systems.[17] Sustainability suggests broader ecosystem-based approaches that require an understanding of cumulative environmental change, and, most likely, new and alternative decision-making arrangements and institutions. To give effect to sustainability, calls have come for cumulative effects assessments of economic activity, for ecological footprint analyses, for precautionary decision-making principles, and for more just, democratic and participatory decision forums (see, for example, Canter, 1999; O'Riordan and Cameron, 1994; Piper, 2002; Wackernagel and Rees, 1996).

The upshot of viewing sustainability in this way is to seriously question how we could possibly report on an *organization's* sustainability. Our answer, which naturally leads one to question fundamental accounting assumptions like the 'entity' and 'going concern' concepts, is that you cannot, or if you could, it will prove extremely difficult and no (corporate) organization would want to do it. Certainly, no organization is currently doing it.[18] For us (Gray and Milne, 2002, p. 69), sustainability reporting requires:

> a complete and transparent statement about the extent to which the organisation had contributed to – or, more likely, diminished – the sustainability of the planet. For that to occur, however, as we have seen, we need to have a detailed and complex analysis of the organisation's interactions with ecological systems, resources, habitats, and societies, and interpret this in the light of all other organisations' past and present impacts on those same systems. Mission impossible? Most likely, and especially at the level of planetary systems, but one thing is clear: such reporting requires a substantially more complex, involved and testing form of report than a triple bottom line report. Sustainability reporting may be possible, but not until we believe we see a shift in emphasis towards accounting for ecosystems and to accounting for communities.

In part, these are precisely the sorts of developments originally envisaged in the early UNEP/SustainAbility (1994, 1996) reports, and noted earlier. Modern day corporate 'sustainability' reporters, however, seem overly preoccupied with themselves and their own (selected) performance indicators and seem to singularly fail to connect their behaviour to the evidence of wider ecological and social systems failure (Ball and Milne, 2005; Gray, 2006a, 2006b; Gray and Bebbington, 2007; Milne *et al.*, 2005a, 2005b). Attention to global data on climate change, loss of species, biodiversity, water stresses, poverty, etc., and the ever-expanding ecological footprint of humanity (see, for example, Wackernagel and Rees, 1996; UNEP, 1997, 2000; WWF, 2002; Meadows *et al.*, 2004; Millennium Ecosystem Assessment, 2005) is completely absent from corporate reports. Similarly, 'sustainability' reporters steer well clear of reporting their own typically expanding (and hence increasingly unsustainable) ecological footprints and/or their very probable contributions to social injustice. You might, of course, reasonably object that what we are asking (corporate) organizations to do is completely unrealistic and, given our economic systems constraints of ever increasing growth and profitability, beyond the corporate remit. You'd be right. After all, why would any corporation voluntarily wish to admit that it is probably contributing to humanity's exceeding of the ecological carrying capacity of the planet, and in need of being phased out in the interests of environmental sustainability, greater social equity, and the sake of future generations?

Far worse, then, are the existing corporate claims to be *actually* addressing sustainability, and the manner in which organizations do this in their reports. Gray (2006a), Livesey (2002), Livesey and Kearins (2002), Milne *et al.* (2005a, 2006) and Tregidga and Milne (2006) all provide examples of how corporate sustainability reports have managed to (re)present the concept of sustainability as one largely, if not entirely, consistent with *existing* best business practice. For example, Sanford Limited, a public listed New Zealand seafood company, defines sustainable development in these terms:

> Sustainable development has been fully integrated into the Company's operations. The improvement in resource efficiency and competitive market advantages that comes with adopting this philosophy underline the fact that there is strong business case for adopting sustainable development. Reduced shareholder risk is also achieved by being able to:

> ■ Enhance customer loyalty and commitment, and improve prices in the long term.
> ■ Increase supplier commitment.
> ■ Enhance relations with the communities in which we operate.
> ■ Reduce environmental impacts and associated costs.

196

- ■ Strengthen relationships with regulators, banks, insurers and financial markets.
- ■ Attract and retain loyal and committed employees.

By resetting goals year after year we are raising the bar and setting higher standards for ourselves. This continual improvement is central to Sanford becoming a sustainable business. Sustainable development reporting is not just about how we have performed over the past year. It is a balanced way of thinking, acting and driving accountability across Sanford each and every day. If we track how we are doing, we will make progress toward creating a better world for the future. This approach allows us to make decisions that enable all our stakeholders to be sure of the long-term viability of the Company and the communities in which we operate.

(Sanford Limited, Sustainable Development Report, 2003, p. 56)

And similarly British Petroleum suggest:

[sustainability is] . . . the capacity to endure as a group, by renewing assets, creating and delivering better products and service that meet the evolving needs of society, delivering returns to our shareholders, attracting successive generations of employees, contributing to a flourishing environment and retaining the trust and support of our customers and the communities in which we operate.

(Making the right choices: BP Sustainability Report 2004
inside front cover)

Or to put it in a way that completely controverts the original Brundtland definition of sustainable development:

Industry is on a three-stage journey from environmental compliance, through environmental risk management, to long-term sustainable development strategies . . . Business strategies for sustainable development mark the final phase in the journey. The aim is to seek win–win situations which can achieve environmental quality, increase wealth, and enhance competitive advantage . . . For the business enterprise, sustainable development means adopting strategies and activities that meet the needs of the enterprise and its stakeholders today while protecting, sustaining and enhancing the human and natural resources that will be needed in the future.

(International Institute for Sustainable Development, 2004,
quoted in Milne *et al.*, 2006)

197

As Milne *et al.* (2005a, 2005b, 2006) and Gray (2006a) note, such (re)presentations 'succeed in switching our concern away from a business operating with a sustained environment to the sustaining of the business assuming that the planet and society are sound'. Furthermore, as Gray (2006a) goes on to suggest, not only do they implicitly deny evidence of a 'dying planet and increasing social injustice' they open up the door for further ever-increasing 'self-delusional' statements. Statements such as:

> The concept of corporate sustainability has long been very attractive to investors because of its aim to increase long term shareholder value.
>
> (Dow Jones Sustainability Group Indexes Report Quarterly 3/9,
> quoted in Gray, 2006a)

While businesses, their associations, and to a lesser extent supporting professions such as accountancy might be excused for promoting and providing self-interested definitions and discussion of sustainable development, it is of concern that many academics, and particularly social and environmental accounting academics, keen to track and critique corporate developments also seem to be less than careful in opposing the ever-increasing slippage of corporate language concerned with sustainability and sustainable development. Indeed, and perhaps as evidenced by the changing discourse throughout the history of the UNEP/SustainAbility benchmark reports, it seems likely that the concept of sustainability has now become so contaminated with conventional economic and business language that as a basis for reforming corporate behaviour to sustain the earth and our and nature's future, it is now virtually worthless. Until we see some considerable change in the materialistic and economic foundations of Western (and increasingly Eastern) societies, and while corporations remain the most powerful of institutions, corporate 'sustainability' reporting is destined to remain an oxymoron, and with it the means for corporations to continue to exploit the earth and its inhabitants for the benefit of a few. In consequence, and in this respect, one cannot possibly be pleased with corporate sustainability reporting developments.

CONCLUSIONS? THE FUTURE OF SUSTAINABILITY REPORTING?

Despite the overwhelming evidence that successfully predicting the future is a fraught and unreliable process and that any such prediction based on past trends is even more likely to be unreliable, we continue to try to forecast likely futures. Whatever the future of sustainability reporting will actually be, therefore, our best guess must be that it will be unpredictable. Our fears and our hopes about reporting are a different matter, however, and we will spell these out shortly.

What has been achieved with stand-alone reporting and 'sustainability' reporting in particular? On the positive side the biggest achievement has been a complete change in the conversations that organizations and civil society can now hold. Pandora's box has been opened and it is no longer defensible to claim some abstract separation between the economic/financial and the social/environmental – that they are inextricably intertwined is, at last, widely accepted. Thus, it is legitimate to challenge claims about the ineluctable beneficence of the pursuit of economic or financial well-being in a way which has been considered almost heretic for far too long. Students and researchers are now enthusiastic to address corporate social responsibility, accountability and sustainability – a subject for which there was a breathtaking indifference only a few years ago. In addition, the development of practice in sustainability reporting has demonstrated some of the possibilities and difficulties involved in reporting; has offered a few innovative examples of how social, environmental and even sustainable development issues might be addressed and, not insignificantly, has demonstrated that it *is* possible for at least a very few companies to go, voluntarily, some way towards a proper discharge of accountability.

There is, however, also a less optimistic view of developments. Much of the terminology, conceptions and practice have been captured by and used in legitimation by corporations – precisely as Marxian scholars would have predicted (see, for example, Tinker *et al.*, 1991). The reporting fails – quite lavishly – to pass any basic test of quality: you would certainly learn nothing about a corporation's contribution to, or detraction from (ecological and social) sustainability from its sustainability reporting. And while we are celebrating the 2,000 MNCs that are reporting, we need to recall that over 58,000 MNCs are still failing to report on social and environmental issues – and this excludes, for example, all the SMEs and non-profit organizations whose impacts are equally of concern. Finally, and most tellingly, there is no evidence whatsoever that this growth in reporting activity has had anything other than the very slightest impact on the growing desecration and social injustice of planet Earth. Gloomy, isn't it?

What *could* have been achieved by all this activity and, therefore, what might it be possible to achieve in the future? There is no practical (as opposed to political or economic) reason why all organizations could not produce substantive social and environmental reports: the triple bottom line is a perfectly feasible aim. As a first step this seems a significant and worthwhile aim in the interests of accountability if nothing else. Such reporting would not, as we have seen, directly address sustainability, however. There are now practicable ways that allow organizations to begin to approach reporting on their un-sustainability through such things as the production of mass-balances and ecological footprints. Equally, the growing experiments on full(er)-cost accounting offer potentially useful measures of un-sustainability.

Of course, while a pure accountability point of view might suggest that reporting of itself is valuable, could such reporting be more than a patina of respectability attempting to hide the nakedness of international financial capitalism's shameful un-sustainability? The importance of full accountability is that it produces transparency and cuts through the indoctrination and distraction that corporations and inter-national financial capitalism are an unqualified 'good'. It allows the state, civil society and organizations to hold debate with data about the real impacts of material well-being and such matters. This seems to us an essential 'good' in any democratic society. Whether it would lead to any substantial change is a seriously moot point – but it seems the least violent way in which the increasingly urgent and terrifying levels of change might be approached.

So the possibilities and potentialities of sustainability reporting are far from trivial – and might even be life-saving. That's a pretty dramatic aim and certainly a worthwhile ambition. It is our hope – what we anticipate on optimistic days – that substantive legislation will be recognized as essential and that a combination of organizational reporting on un-sustainability, full accountability and a complete change in the focus of power and decision-making to that of the ecosystems in a wider systems conception will empower the demos to take back control over what it is to be human and find a new path towards a 'right living' within a sensible harmony and understanding of ecology. On the bad days we wonder if this is all a waste of time and the sooner our species shuffles off and leaves it to the squirrels and the rest of nature the better. The impenetrable hubris of the human creature – especially the modern western capitalistic, financial, version of that species – in the face of overwhelming evidence suggest, we fear, that humans are just so blindingly stupid that we are profoundly unlikely to ever be challenged by lemmings, dodos or dinosaurs for levels of folly.

The future? In the end it is up to each and every one of us to do what we can. To take choices – about ourselves as individuals, about our networks, families and friends, about our personal and public activities and especially about our contextual, professional, involvements and to try and do what we believe is the right thing to do – not simply what others tell us *can* be done. As John Humphrys (1999, p. 271) puts it, we have to learn to dissent, to argue with things taken for granted or foisted upon us, and just because the odds are against us it doesn't mean we shouldn't try. We are each terribly limited creatures individually but collectively we can achieve enormous amounts. After all, look what we have done to the planet – and that was without even trying!

NOTES

1 This is the 'recent' history of corporate environmental and social reporting. There is a much older history of both research and practice in reporting on corporate environmental, social and employee impacts that dates from the late 1960s and early 1970s. For an overview, see Gray *et al.* (1987) and Gray *et al.* (1996).

2   At its narrowest, the triple bottom line involves measuring and reporting economic, environmental and social performance objectives that are pursued simultaneously. A broader view suggests that the triple bottom line involves assessing an entity's values, strategies and practices and how these can be utilized to achieve economic, environmental and social objectives (SustainAbility, 2003).

3   And see http://www.globalreporting.org/ for more and up-to-date material.

4   ACCA/Corporateregister.com (2004), for example, report on eight types of possible reporting formats: sustainability; corporate responsibility; community; social; social and environmental; environment, health and safety; environment; as well as sections in annual reports with non-financial information. The UNEP/SustainAbility bench-marking reports (1994, 1996, 1997, 2000, 2002, 2004) too show an evolving reference from 'company environmental reporting' (1994, 1996, 1997) through 'company sustainability reporting' (2000, 2002) to 'best practice non-financial reporting' (2004). Similarly, the KPMG International surveys (1993, 1996, 1999, 2002, 2005) refer to 'environmental reporting' (1993, 1996, 1999), 'corporate sustainability reporting' (2002), and 'corporate responsibility reporting' (2005). See also Erusalimsky *et al.* (2006).

5   This section largely draws on ACCA/Corporateregister.com (2004), the KMPG (1996, 1999, 2002, 2005) surveys and the UNEP/SustainAbility benchmarking surveys (1994, 1996, 1997, 2000, 2002, 2004). These sources are the best available but they inevitably cannot provide a complete picture of the state of corporate reporting. It is as well to be aware of the potential limitations in what follows: Corporateregister.com data, for example, is based on the largest depositary of reports, but these are reports either voluntarily supplied to the database or reports Corporateregister.com actively searches for. Corporateregister.com (personal correspondence) currently estimate they feature around 90 per cent of all published corporate non-financial reports, with the exception of HTML only reports and those using only non-latin scripts. The dataset, then, may not be systematically representative of all countries or organizations. Likewise, the KPMG surveys, which are systematic surveys of the global top 250 firms, and the top 100 firms in many countries, only focus on large corporate reporters. The UNEP/SustainAbility surveys, which attempt to measure the quality of reporting rather than systematically survey the extent of reporting, or track trends in it, is limited to data on the 'best' 50 or 100 reports at the time of the survey.

6   The popularity of hard copy/electronic reports, however, appears to be geographically distributed, or perhaps it might reflect that hard copy reports are simply not submitted to the Corporateregister.com database from overseas. In the US and Canada, for example, approximately 250 hard copy reports were filed with the Corporateregister.com database during 2001–3, whereas pdf formats for this period numbered 460. In Europe the numbers equalled about 1,100 hard copy reports and 900 pdf reports, and in Asia and Australasia, the numbers equalled about 480 hard copy reports and 420 pdf reports (ACCA/Corporateregister.com, 2004).

7   These countries are all 'developing' countries and are a haphazard choice although reports about such reporting can be found in *Social and Environmental Accounting Journal* and at www.st-andrews.ac.uk/management/csear.

8   It is probably important to note that adoption of EMAS (as, indeed of ISO 14000; see below) is voluntary.

9   EMAS registrations appear to be tailing off and are certainly less popular than the much less demanding International Standards Organization standard on environmental management systems – ISO14000. ISO 14000 significantly does not require external reporting as a condition of registration. At the time of writing there were 88,000 ISO14000 certifications.

10 There is considerable doubt about the quality of the 'verification', however. See, for example, O'Dwyer and Owen (2005).

11 Reporting 'in accordance' with the GRI guidelines, for example, is a statement about a number of specific things: all the GRI core indicators are reported on (or reasons provided for why not); the eleven reporting principles are followed; a content index is provided for cross-referencing; and a CEO or Board of Directors statement is provided that states that the report is 'in accordance' with the Guidelines (see www.globalreporting.org). The GRI executive does not enforce or validate whether the reporting is consistent with the guidelines, however.

12 A major failing identified by Sinclair and Walton (2003, p. 335) is that companies fail to define the 'corporate profile' (a characteristic, they note, of the GRI), which 'will prevent readers from fully understanding and evaluating the content of a report'.

13 It is extremely difficult to be sure of the exact number of large companies in the world, but various sources including the United Nations Conference on Trade and Development (UNCTAD), the BBC, and the US Department of Justice on Anti-Trust, suggest in excess of 60,000 multinationals, with UNCTAD suggesting such companies are collectively responsible for 11 trillion dollars of output (25 per cent of world output), with the largest 100 companies responsible for half of that (see http://www.ppionline.org/ppi_ci.cfm?knlgAreaID=1088&subsecid=900003&contentid=253303).

14 The importance of reporting – and any optimism related to it – is predicated upon the assumptions that reporting actually reflects social and environmental performance accurately and that it provides the stimulus for improved social/environmental behaviour.

15 While regulated reporting as part of (say) corporate law may well overcome many such problems, that assumes that governments would be willing to legislate for substantive social, environmental and sustainability disclosure. The evidence in many countries is that may well be (currently) a naïve hope.

16 The UNEP/SustainAbility benchmark surveys have remained hopeful that such externalities will be 'fully-costed' and 'internalized' into the cost structures of organizations. Notably, the latest 2004 survey report considers the future of reporting (from 2010 and beyond) to lie in reintegrated single bottom line or 'blended value' reports in which externalities are increasingly internalized. (For other discussions of full cost accounting, see Bebbington et al. (2001) and Howes (2001, 2002), and for a contrary view of corporations internalizing externalities see Bakan (2004). Externalities are defined as costs and benefits that extend to others beyond the decision-making organization without compensation or payment (e.g., waterways polluted by organizations (see, for example, Milne (1996b) and references therein.) Rather than representing a practice of calculating in monetary terms an organization's economic, social and environmental benefits and costs,

however, the term triple *bottom line* has largely proved to date to be used in a metaphorical sense to capture the attempt by organizations to describe, count, and quantify, but rarely monetarise, their external impacts. At its best, the triple bottom line presupposes three (non-integrated) accounts of the financial, the social and the environmental.

17   This conception of sustainability, which most business commentators seem to have overlooked, or conveniently forgotten, has been around for sometime. See, for example, Sadler, 1988; Daly and Cobb, 1989; Daly 1992; Dobson, 1998; and Milne, 1996a, and the references therein.

18   Our point here is that most organizations, and particularly corporations (see Bakan, 2004), do not (and do not wish to) extend their responsibilities beyond their own impacts. Consequently, they are incapable of reporting on systems levels of sustainability. We do acknowledge, however, that some organizations (e.g., Welsh Assembly Government, 2005; Greater London Authority, 2002) have attempted to provide broader systems measures and reports on sustainability by way of, for example, state of the environment reports and ecological footprint analyses (see, for example, www.citylimitslondon.com and www.walesfootprint.org).

REFERENCES

ACCA (2001, 2002, 2003, 2004) *ACCA UK Awards for Sustainability Reporting: Report of the Judges*, ACCA, www.accaglobal.com/sustainability.

ACCA/Corporateregister.com (2004) *Towards transparency: Progress on global sustainability reporting 2004*. London: Certified Accountants Educational Trust.

Bakan, J. (2004) *The corporation: The pathological pursuit of profit and power*. Canada: Constable & Robinson.

Ball, A. and Milne, M. J. (2005) Sustainability and management control. In A. J. Berry, J. Broadbent and D. T. Otley (eds) *Management control: Theory, issues and practices*, 2nd edn. London: Macmillan.

Bebbington, K. J., Gray, R. H., Hibbitt, C. and Kirk, E. (2001) *Full cost accounting: An agenda for action*. London: ACCA.

Canter, L. (1999) Cumulative effects assessment. In J. Petts (ed.) *A handbook of environmental impact assessment*. Oxford: Blackwell, pp. 405–40.

Chapman, R. and Milne, M. J. (2004) The triple bottom line: How New Zealand companies measure up: Corporate environmental strategy. *International Journal for Sustainable Business*, 11(2): 37–50.

Cooper, C. (1995) Ideology, hegemony and accounting discourse: A case study of the National Union of Journalists. *Critical Perspectives on Accounting*, 6: 175–209.

Daly, H. E. (1992) Allocation, distribution and scale: Towards an economics that is efficient, just and sustainable. *Ecological Economics*, 6: 185–94.

Daly, H. and Cobb, J. B. (1989) *For the common good*. Boston: Beacon.

Deegan, C. and Gordon, B. (1996) A study of the environmental disclosure practices of Australian corporations. *Accounting and Business Research*, 26(3): 187–99.

Dobson, A. (1998) *Justice and the environment: Conceptions of environmental sustainability and theories of distributive justice.* Oxford: Oxford University Press.

Elkington, J. (1997) *Cannibals with forks: The triple bottom line of 21st century business.* Oxford: Capstone Publishing.

Erusalimsky, A., Gray, R. and Spence, C. (2006) Towards a more systematic study of standalone corporate social, environmental and sustainability reporting: An exploratory pilot study of UK reporting. *Social and Environmental Accounting Journal*, 26(1): 12–19.

Europa (2005) EU Register of EMAS Organisations, http://europa.eu.it/comm/environment/emas/about/participate/sites_en.htm, accessed 20 November.

European Sustainability Reporting Awards (ESRA) (2001, 2002, 2003, 2004) *Report of the Judges*, www.accaglobal.com/sustainability.

Global Reporting Initiative (GRI) (2000) *Sustainability reporting guidelines on economic, environmental and social performance.* Boston, MA: Global Reporting Initiative, June.

Global Reporting Initiative (GRI) (2002) *Sustainability reporting guidelines.* Amsterdam: Global Reporting Initiative, October.

Gray, R. (1992) Accounting and environmentalism: An exploration of the challenge of gently accounting for accountability, transparency and sustainability. *Accounting, Organisations and Society*, 17(5): 399–426.

Gray, R. (2006a) Does sustainability reporting improve corporate behaviour?, *Accounting and Business Research, Special Issue*, 65–88.

Gray, R. (2006b) Social, environmental, and sustainability reporting and organisational value creation? Whose value? Whose creation? *Accounting, Auditing and Accountability Journal*, 19(6): 793–819.

Gray, R. and Bebbington, J. (2000) Environmental accounting, managerialism and sustainability. *Advances in Environmental Accounting & Management*, 1: 1–44.

Gray, R. and Bebbington, K. J. (2007) Corporate sustainability: Accountability and the pursuit of the impossible dream. In G. S. Atkinson Dietz and E. Neumeyer (eds) *Handbook of Sustainable Development.* London: Edward Elgar.

Gray, R. H. and Milne, M. J. (2002) Sustainability reporting: who's kidding whom? *Chartered Accountants Journal of New Zealand*, July: 66–70.

Gray, R and Milne, M. J. (2004) Towards reporting on the triple bottom line: mirages, methods and myths. In A Henriques and J. Richardson (eds) *The triple bottom line: Does it all add up?* London: Earthscan.

Gray, R., Kouhy, R. and Lavers, S. (1995a) Corporate social and environmental reporting: A review of the literature and a longitudinal study of UK disclosure. *Accounting, Auditing and Accountability Journal*, 8(2): 47–77.

Gray, R. H., Owen, D. L. and Adams, C. (1996) *Accounting and accountability: Changes and challenges in corporate social and environmental reporting*. London: Prentice-Hall.

Gray, R. H., Owen, D. L. and Maunders, K. T. (1987) *Corporate social reporting: Accounting and accountability*. Hemel Hempstead: Prentice-Hall.

Gray, R., Walters, D., Bebbington, J. and Thomson, I. (1995b) The greening of enterprise: An exploration of the (non) role of environmental accounting and environmental accountants in organisational change. *Critical Perspectives on Accounting*, 6: 211–39.

Greater London Authority (GLA) (2002) *CityLimits: A resource flow and ecological footprint analysis of Greater London*. London: Best Foot Forward Ltd, www.citylimitslondon.com.

Hackston, D. and Milne, M. J. (1996) Some determinants of social and environmental disclosures in New Zealand companies. *Accounting, Auditing and Accountability Journal*, 9(1): 77–108.

Howes, R. (2001) Taking nature into account and the evolution of a sustainability accounting framework. In ACCA *Advances in environmental accounting*. London: ACCA, pp. 28–38.

Howes, R. (2002) *Environmental cost accounting: An Introduction and practical guide*. London: CIMA.

Humphrys, J. (1999) *Devil's advocate*. London: Arrow Books, Random House.

Institute of Chartered Accountants of New Zealand (ICANZ) (2002) *Report of the taskforce on sustainable development reporting*. Wellington: ICANZ.

Kolk, A. (2003) Trends in sustainability reporting by the Fortune Global 250. *Business Strategy and the Environment*, 12(5): 279–91.

Kolk, A. and van Tulder, R. (2004) Internationalization and environmental reporting: The green face of the world's multinationals. *Research in Global Strategic Management*, 9: 95–117.

KPMG (1993) *KPMG international survey of environmental reporting 1993*. London: KPMG Environmental Consulting.

KPMG (1996) *KPMG international survey of environmental reporting 1996*. London: KPMG Environmental Consulting.

KPMG (1999) *KPMG international survey of environmental reporting 1999*. London: KPMG Environmental Consulting.

KPMG (2002a) *KPMG international survey of corporate sustainability reporting 2002*. London: KPMG Global Sustainability Services.

KPMG (2002b) *Triple bottom line reporting*, found at: 2002 Model Annual Report, http://kpmgmodels.co.nz/.

KPMG (2005) *KPMG international survey of corporate responsibility reporting 2005*, June, www.wimm.nl.

Livesey, S. (2002) The discourse of the middle ground: Citizen Shell commits to sustainable development. *Management Communication Quarterly*, 15(3): 313–49.

Livesey, S. M. and Kearins, K. (2002) Transparent and caring corporations? A study of sustainability reports by The Body Shop and Royal Dutch/Shell. *Organization & Environment*, 15(3): 233–58.

Meadows, D. H., Randers, J. and Meadows, D. L. (2004) *Limits to growth: The 30 year update*. London: Earthscan.

Millennium Ecosystem Assessment (2005) Living beyond our means: natural assets and human well being, www.millenniumassessment.org/en/Products.BoardStatement.

Milne, M. J. (1996a) On sustainability, the environment and management accounting. *Management Accounting Research*, 7(1): 135–61.

Milne, M. J. (1996b) Capitalising and appropriating society's rights to clean air: A critical commentary on the problem with reporting pollution allowances. *Critical Perspectives on Accounting*, 7(6): 681–95.

Milne, M. J., Tregidga, H. M. and Walton, S. (2003) The triple bottom line: Benchmarking New Zealand's early reporters. *University of Auckland Business Review*, 5(2): 36–50.

Milne, M. J., Tregidga, H. M. and Walton, S. (2005a) Actions not words: Companies 'doing sustainability' in New Zealand? Working paper, University of Otago, www.business.otago.ac.nz/accy/research/working_paper.html.

Milne, M. J., Ball, A. and Gray, R. (2005b) From soothing palliatives and towards ecological literacy: A critique of the triple bottom line. Working paper, University of Otago, www.business.otago.ac.nz/accy/research/working_paper.html.

Milne, M. J., Kearins, K., and Walton, S. (2006) Creating adventures in Wonderland: The journey metaphor and environmental sustainability. *Organization*, 13(6): 801–39.

Morhardt, J. E., Baird, S. and Freeman, K. (2002) Scoring corporate environmental and sustainability reports using GRI 2000, ISO 14031 and other criteria. *Corporate Social Responsibility & Environmental Management*, 9(2): 15–233.

NZBCSD (2002) *Business guide to sustainable development reporting: Making a difference for a sustainable New Zealand*, October.

O'Dwyer, B. and Owen, D. L. (2005) Assurance statement practice in environmental, social and sustainability reporting: A critical evaluation. *British Accounting Review*, 37(2): 205–30.

O'Riordan, T. and Cameron, J. (eds) (1994) *Interpreting the precautionary principle*. London: Earthscan.

Patten, D. M. (1991) Exposure, legitimacy and social disclosure. *Journal of Accounting and Public Policy*, 10: 23–34.

Piper, J. M. (2002) CEA and sustainable development: evidence from UK case studies. *Environmental Impact Assessment Review*, 22: 17–36.

Porritt, J. (2001) Chairman's review in *Sustainable Development Commission's First Annual Review*. London: UK Sustainable Development Commission.

Puxty, A. (1991) Social accountability and universal pragmatics. *Advances in Public Interest Accounting*, 4: 35–45.

Sadler, B. (1988) *Natural capital and borrowed time: The global context of sustainable development.* Victoria, BC, Canada: Institute of the North American West.

Sanford Ltd (2003) *Sustainable development report.* New Zealand: Sanford Ltd.

Sinclair, P. and Walton, J. (2003) Environmental reporting within the forest and paper industry. *Business Strategy and the Environment,* 12: 326–37.

SustainAbility (2003) What is the Triple Bottom Line?, www.sustainability.com/philosophy/triple-bottom/tbl-intro.asp.

Tinker, T, Lehman, C. and Neimark, M. (1991) Falling down the hole in the middle of the road: Political quietism in corporate social reporting. *Accounting, Auditing and Accountability Journal,* 4(2): 28–54.

Tregidga, H. and Milne, M. J. (2006) From sustainable management to sustainable development: A longitudinal analysis of a leading New Zealand environmental reporter. *Business Strategy & the Environment,* 15(4): 219–41.

UNEP/SustainAbility (1994) Company environmental reporting: A measure of the progress business & industry towards sustainable development. London: UNEP/SustainAbility.

UNEP/SustainAbility (1996) *Engaging stakeholders: The benchmark survey.* London: UNEP/SustainAbility.

UNEP/SustainAbility (1997) *The 1997 benchmark survey: The third international progress report on company environmental reporting.* London: UNEP/SustainAbility.

UNEP/SustainAbility (1999) *The social reporting report.* London: UNEP/SustainAbility.

UNEP/SustainAbility (2000) *The global reporters: The 2000 benchmark survey.* London: UNEP/SustainAbility.

UNEP/SustainAbility (2002) *Trust us: The global reporters 2002 survey of corporate sustainability.* London: UNEP/SustainAbility.

UNEP/SustainAbility (2004) *Risk & opportunity: Best practice in non-financial reporting.* London: UNEP/SustainAbility.

United Nations Environment Programme (UNEP) (1997) *Global environmental outlook 1: United Nations environment programme global state of the environment report 1997* (GEO–1), http://www.grida.no/geo1.

United Nations Environment Programme (UNEP) (2000) *Global environment outlook 2000 (GEO–2000).* Norway: UNEP, www.grida.no/geo2000/index.htm.

Wackernagel, M. and Rees, W. (1996) *Our ecological footprint: Reducing human impact on the Earth.* Gabirola Island, BC: New Society Publishers.

Welford, R. (ed.) (1997) *Hijacking environmentalism: Corporate response to sustainable development.* London: Earthscan.

Welsh Assembly Government (WAG) (2005) *Reducing Wales' footprint: A resource accounting tool for sustainable consumption.* Cardiff: Welsh Assembly Government, www.walesfootprint.org

WWF (2002) *Living Planet Report 2002.* Gland, Switzerland: World Wildlife Fund.

Part III

Accounting for sustainable development within organizations

Chapter 11

Full cost accounting

Adam Smith meets Rachel Carson?

Nicolas Antheaume

Rachel Carson is the author of *Silent Spring*, a book in which she denounces the devastating effect of pesticides on the natural environment and the behaviour of firms which sell and use such products. Adam Smith is the author of *The Wealth of Nations*, a founding book for economists. The idea of this improbable meeting is taken from an article published in *The Economist* on 21 April 2005.

INTRODUCTION

In April 2005 *The Economist* devoted its leading article (and its cover) to the idea that market forces could be the environment's 'best friend'. The cover pictured what is most probably a rainforest seen from the sky with a tropical river meandering in the middle. Somewhere on the right-hand side of the picture, part of the river was represented as a giant dollar sign. In particular, the article reported that advances in environmental science are contributing to more accurate valuations of previously taken-for-granted-services such as water filtration and flood prevention. It suggested that if these new values were fed into market mechanisms and included in the cost-benefit analysis of organizations a lot of environmental problems would be addressed through the use of better prices for environmental resources. This chapter explores two questions: (1) should the suggestions contained in this article be a source of inspiration for accountants? And (2) can environmental accounting benefit from advances in environmental science and economics to incorporate better-informed costs and benefits?

The idea of identifying the full costs of an activity is not a new one. As long ago as the 1970s suggestions were put forward, and accounting models proposed, to incorporate a wide range of costs and benefits on top of more traditional information supplied by companies. This idea was pursued and acknowledged by a small but growing number of accounting academics. It gave rise to an area of accounting which Bebbington *et al.* (2001) named 'full cost accounting' (FCA) and defined as 'a system which allows current accounting and economic numbers to incorporate all potential/actual costs and benefits into the equation including environmental (and perhaps) social externalities to get the prices right' (Bebbington *et al.*, 2001). It is argued that this information can help economic agents make better decisions and be used as a base for informing public policy decisions (such as, levying environmental taxes). Thus, by making environmental and social costs more visible and by allowing a comparison with similar benefits, FCA is designed to help organizations make decisions that are more compatible with a sustainable development agenda.

The chapter is organized as follows. The first section will explain the concept of external cost, crucial to the understanding of full cost accounting. A second section will present the tools and methodologies used for full cost accounting. A third section will then review the major attempts at full cost accounting over the last few decades. Finally, a fourth section will outline what insights can be drawn from these experiments and what are the prospects for research in the field of full cost accounting.

THE NOTION OF EXTERNAL COST, A KEY ELEMENT TO FULL COST ACCOUNTING

The concepts of external effect and cost are crucial to understanding the under-pinnings of full cost accounting. They originate from neoclassical economic theory. An external effect can be described as a phenomenon which occurs outside the market system (with which neoclassical economic theory is concerned), or which shows up in the market system but remotely from its source. We speak of an external cost as soon as an external effect has some influence on economic agents in terms of benefit or cost, without any market transaction taking place between those responsible for the damage and those suffering from it. Table 11.1 gives three examples.

Even amongst neoclassical economists, no unanimity exists on the modalities for remedying external effects. Two broad approaches can be identified. The first, in the tradition of Pigou (1920), advocates intervention in the market system (in the form of regulations, taxes, etc.) which would correct its inability to avoid economic agents inflicting damage on each other and to reflect spontaneously the prices of services rendered by ecosystems. Green taxes can be viewed as a solution inspired by the Pigouvian school. The second approach is proposed by Coase (1960). It preaches, whenever transaction costs make it possible, the development of markets where goods and services of an environmental nature would be traded. Emission trading systems draw their inspiration from this school of thought.

In spite of their divergence, the two schools are based on the same concept of

Table 11.1 *Examples of external costs*

An incinerator burns waste from local households and companies. It emits dioxin into the atmosphere. The concentration of this toxin in the milk of cows grazing nearby has reached alarming levels. A major dairy producer and exporter are affected by this situation. So are a number of consumers. The incremental cost of health care due to these emissions shows up in the market system, but no transaction has taken place between those affected by the damage and those responsible for it.

In a developing country, a magnificent set of historical monuments, thousands of years old, is visited by millions of individuals every year. The effects of these hordes of tourists, combined with the nearby development of irrigated fields, are threatening the very existence of this site. Stones, pillars and walls are suffering from the wear and tear of millions of footsteps. Occasional vandals carve or write their names on the walls. The ground is being soaked with water from the neighbouring fields. This water is absorbed by the limestone foundations of the buildings. Seeping humidity has already caused beautiful wall paintings to be lost forever. If nothing is done, entire sections of the building may collapse, leaving future generations with nothing but piles of rubble to admire. Tourists, travel agents, and local farmers derive benefits from the situation above. However, the cost of preventing future damage, or the possible loss of a remarkable site, are being passed on to government, NGOs and future generations without any market transactions taking place.

A portion of highway somewhere in Europe is built alongside a river. There is a waste-treatment system designed to collect rainwater. Whenever it rains, the water washes off the pollutants deposited by passing cars on the asphalt into the river. Just nearby, the treatment plant of a utility draws water from the river, processes it and feeds it into the local water network. Due to increasingly polluted waters the cost of water treatment has soared over the years as the road has become more and more congested. The river's stock of fish has considerably diminished. Some species are not to be seen in the river any more. The incremental cost of water treatment shows up in the market system but once again no transaction has taken place between those affected by the damage and those responsible for it. However, the loss of biodiversity and the loss of the services provided by the river such as a habitat for fauna and flora do not show up in the market system. The incremental cost of water treatment can be identified with some ease as the sole agent concerned is the water-treatment plant. However, accounting for a loss of biodiversity and ecosystem services still poses daunting problems.

external effect and share the need for a monetary evaluation of the services provided by ecosystems (Costanza *et al.*, 1997) and of the damage caused by human activity (European Commission, 1995; Institute of Energy Economics, 1997). Monetary evaluation aims to ensure that the full cost of goods and services (such as gambling at a casino, visiting a historical monument, using raw materials, benefiting from clean air or unpolluted water) is known and that economic agents can take this into account in their calculations. The driving logic is that of an internalization of costs which are, at present, external to the economic calculations of agents.

In the Coasian approach, this monetary valuation is the fruit of the market confrontation between the supply and demand for goods and services. Market prices can then be fed into the calculation of economic agents through such tools as full cost accounting. In the Pigouvian approach, this monetary valuation has to be carried out by scientists and economists so that it can be used as a basis for levying environmental taxes or for full cost accounting purposes.

However, even given these two approaches, entity level full cost accounting still is a valuable activity. Due to a lack of appropriate mechanisms, markets do not yet incorporate all the costs and benefits of goods and services compatible with a sustainable development agenda. As for those economists pursuing a Pigouvian approach, a review of the work of a representative economist such as Smith (1996) will show that the public decision perspective, rather than the entity level one, was privileged.

The body of literature on external cost evaluation methods is extensive. The tools of full cost accounting will be briefly reviewed in the second section of this chapter. However, for a comprehensive overview of the methods devised by mostly, but not exclusively, environmental economists we refer the reader to the work of Smith (1996).

The idea of giving 'non-market' goods and services, and the damage to such services, a monetary value has not met with a consensus. It can be argued that placing a value on such things as life or biodiversity is not morally acceptable as these attributes may have an infinite value. However, pragmatically, safety standards (for buildings, cars, bridges, authorized exposure to hazardous substances) imply a certain value for human life or a willingness to pay to prevent damage to the environment. Using external cost evaluation methods only reveals and makes explicit these values.

It can also be argued that assigning a monetary value to an impact reduces its different irredeemable dimensions (moral, economic, aesthetical, and physical) to only one dimension and forces a ranking of these dimensions upon users of full cost accounting information. A third argument is that the environment should be protected for moral or aesthetic reasons and not economic ones. However, even when all the facets of an impact are not reduced to only one monetary dimension, organizations and individuals do make decisions which de facto imply ranking the dimensions of a problem. External cost evaluation methods, if well implemented, should only reveal existing choices, make these choices more explicit and thereby help to support more informed choices Using external cost evaluation methods assumes that, despite their limitations, using them to experiment with full cost accounting is better than not using them at all.

THE TOOLS OF FULL COST ACCOUNTING

Full cost accounting relies upon a wide variety of methods and tools. They can broadly be classified using two criteria: the type of approach and the type of costs estimated.

Type of approach: bottom up or top down

The type of approach can be defined as bottom up or top down. In a bottom-up approach the emissions and inputs from a given site, service or product are first inventoried using such tools as lifecycle analysis or eco-balances (Bebbington *et al.*, 2001). The lists of inputs and outputs identified in such a way are then translated into a physical damage. The physical damage is given a monetary value using a variety of approaches. If the physical damage concerns human health or damage to crops, market values can be used. If it concerns a loss of ecosystem services, one has to deduce what quantity of that service has been lost and what impact it has had on the welfare of economic agents. In some cases avoidance or abatement costs can also be used as a substitute to the cost of damage. The end result is usually a cost per unit of physical damage or per type of emission. External costs that have been evaluated in such a way are contingent to the site, product, service or technology being evaluated. Their transfer to another context can be problematic.

In a top-down approach, a given external effect, or the value of a given eco-system service, is evaluated at a very global level (a country, a continent or the whole world). For example, the cost of damages due to global warming, or the cost of avoidance of such a phenomenon, can be estimated on a global basis. This cost can then be divided by the total world emissions of greenhouse gasses (weighed according to their global warming potential). The end result is an average cost per unit of emission that is not contingent to any location, site, technology, service or product.

Types of costs

The costs can either be damage costs, avoidance costs or remedial costs and these concepts arc presented in Table 11.2. Each category of costs corresponds to a different choice: avoidance costs assess the cost of avoiding the damage, damage costs focus on the actual damage that has occurred, remediation costs reveal a willingness to pay to repair the damage (which may not correspond to the full value of the damage).

A BRIEF HISTORY OF FULL COST ACCOUNTING

The pioneers of full cost accounting

Early attempts to include social and environmental impacts by converting them into monetary amounts by academics (Estes, 1976) or companies (Abt, 1977) were not successful. This was because putting them into practice was judged either too costly, or too difficult given existing knowledge, or did not entirely meet the

Table 11.2 *Three different types of environmental costs*

	Avoidance cost[a]	Cost of damages cost	Remediation costs
Hypotheses	Compliance with regulatory standards or reduction targets helps achieve an optimal pollution level	The external effects correspond to the damages caused to the receiving environment	Household, state, and local community expenditure represents a collective consent to pay to remedy the external effects of the activity of firms
Calculation	Costs not yet implemented to comply with standards or achieve objectives	Damage caused specifically by the site is quantified and monetised	External costs are charged by relating the emissions of the process to national emissions and applying a weighting to certain emissions because their greater toxicity probably entails greater expenditure
Main limitation	There is no link in the calculation method between the emissions and the damage caused	Hard to find data that reflects the current state of scientific knowledge; in the absence of this, numerous working hypotheses are used	No link between the emissions and the damage caused
Main advantage	Widely used	Link between the emissions and the damage caused	Accessibility of data and reproducibility
Previous use	BSO / Origin, public utilities commissions in the US	Direction Générale-XII, European Commission and US Department of Energy, ExternE project	Antheaume (2004)

Note: [a]Also known as control, reduction, abatement, prevention or shadow costs

desired interest. Table 11.3 provides a short description of some of these early experiments.

Despite the lack of success of early attempts, when environmental threats such as global warming were brought to public attention in the early 1990s, more attempts at full cost accounting (FCA) were pursued. Milne (1992) argued that an attempt should be made to incorporate environmental impacts into accounting-based investment decisions. He reviewed the environmental resource valuation methods used by economists to incorporate environmental considerations into public

Table 11.3 *A description of pioneering proposals for full cost accounting*

Social audit	Abt (1977)	Mandatory and voluntary expenses resulting in improvements in the well-being of employees and of the general public, in safer products and a better protected environment. Presentation as a social statement of income and balance sheet showing the impact of different elements of the firm's socio-economic environment. This approach was put into practice from 1971 through to 1981.
Audit process	Bauer and Fern (1972, 1973)	Accounting model based on a social audit process defined as a commitment to systematically evaluate and communicate any significant activity with a social impact.
		Inventory of a firm's 'social programmes' (control and prevention of pollutions, recruitment of ethnic minorities, sponsorship programmes etc.) and calculation of the 'real' cost of each activity, including overhead and opportunity costs.
Socio-economic statement of operations	Linowes (1972, 1973, 1974)	Statement of a firm's voluntary expenditures, aimed at improving the status of employees, of the general public, of consumers and of the natural environment.
		Linowes recommends that all elements be given a monetary value. Any action by a firm should be analysed in terms of benefits to society and costs to be incurred by the firm.
Statement of social income	Seidler (1976)	Report meant to inventory the costs and benefits for society, linked to the activity of any given entity. The report is presented as a statement of income which includes the following elements: On one side the sum of all benefits to society linked to the entity's activity and for which the company receives no income. On the other side the sum of costs imposed on society for which the entity does not pay any compensation.
Ideal and initial systems	AICPA (1977)	The AICPA proposed an 'ideal' system aimed at taking a firm's social and environmental impacts into account while admitting it was impossible to put it into practice due to: (1) imperfect measurement systems, (2) the high cost of obtaining data, (3) the lack of implementation by some companies and (4) our inadequate understanding of society's complex interactions. An 'initial' system was thus proposed as a compromise, based on a description and discussion of possible actions and indicators in the fields of environmental protection, human resources, suppliers, product safety, customers, local communities.

decision-making. He suggested that accountants might be able to use some of these methods for private decision-making. Although he did not apply any of these methods to a specific case he explicitly linked the idea of full cost accounting to environmental economics and to the concept of external cost

Rubenstein (1992) suggested that the value of environmental impacts linked to the activity of a firm should be subtracted from its added value and that the correction be applied to the profits of a firm. Gray (1992) also put forward the idea of an accounting system which would 'provide calculation of what additional costs must be borne by the organisation if the organisational activities were not to leave the planet worse off' (Gray, 1992, p. 419). These ideas inspired FCA experiments such as the one carried out by BSO/Origin (Huizing and Dekker, 1992) and for Landcare Research New Zealand (Bebbington and Gray, 2001) as well as many others, to which attention now turns.

More recent experiments in FCA

Based on a case study, Rubenstein (1994) and a United Nations (UNCTAD, 1994) report on sustainable forestry management proposed an evaluation method for forests. The first part of the study modelled the additional costs a fictional forest company would have to incur if it pursued one of the two options that were different from its current way of operating and the impact on the return on invest-ment of the organization. The second part contained broad estimates of what external costs a 'business as usual approach' would generate in the future. These costs were then reintegrated in the options studied in the first part and the rate of return on investment was recomputed. It is interesting to note that once these external costs are included in the options the difference in the rate of return on investment between 'business as usual' and one of the more sustainable options narrows to 1 per cent. This suggests that the market does not send the right signals so as to encourage more sustainable options of conducting business. In order to send appropriate signals to equity owners Boone and Rubenstein (1997) suggested that monetized external impacts should be included in an environmental equity account as part of the ownership accounts. Their article reported an experimental approach by a Canadian utility.

Antheaume (2004) carried out an experiment in full cost accounting applied to the case of an industrial process. It aimed at exploring the difficulties of putting full cost accounting into practice. Its specific contribution to the growing body of experiments in full cost accounting was to compare what impacts could be trans-lated into financial information with the impacts that are being left out. The experiment used three different external cost evaluation methods: (1) avoidance cost, (2) ExternE impact pathway and (3) willingness to pay as measured by the environmental expenses of household and government authorities. The most com-prehensive method monetized less than 10 per cent of the flows of the industrial process studied. According to the method used and the assumptions made, external costs vary by a factor of more than 1 to 12,000 per unit of product.

Companies such as Ontario Power Generation (USEPA, 1996), a Canadian utility, BSO/Origin (Huizing and Dekker, 1992), a Dutch consulting firm, Nuclear Electric,[1] a British utility, Volvo (Steen, 1997) a Swedish car manufacturer, Power Gen (Atkinson, 2000), a UK power generator, awg (Anglian Water, 2000; awg, 2001, 2002; Howes, 2000) and Wessex Water (Howes, 2000, Wessex Water, 2000, 2005),[2] British utilities, use or have used FCA methods. FCA has been used as a contribution to capital-budgeting decisions (Ontario Power Generation), as a way of opening up a debate on fiscal environmental policy (BSO/Origin), as a (partisan) means of communication on the benefits of nuclear energy (Nuclear Electric), as a contribution to the ecological design of products (Volvo) or as a way to measure the percentage of profits obtained in an environmentally sensitive manner (awg, formerly Anglian Water and Wessex Water).

In a very thorough review of FCA perspectives, tools and practices Bebbington et al. (2001) also report on experiments undertaken by Landcare Research (pp. 89–98),[3] Forum for the Future and Interface Europe (pp. 98–104),[4] Baxter (p. 104), The Scottish Office (pp. 104–5) and the Centre for Waste Reduction Technology (pp. 105–6).

From environmental full cost accounting to sustainability full cost accounting

Cutting-edge research by Forum for the Future (2003a, 2003b, Bent, 2005, Taplin et al., 2006) and Baxter et al. (2004) has moved beyond strictly environmental accounting to engage wider sustainability issues. We now turn our attention to this research.

Baxter et al. (2004) report on the development and experimentation of a sustainable assessment model (SAM). The SAM uses 22 performance indicators to measure full lifecycle, environmental, economic and resource usage impacts of a project, organization or sector. These impacts are monetized, allowing for comparison, and can be summed into a single measure, the Sustainability Assessment Model Indicator (SAMi) which reflects an overall contribution to sustainable development.

Forum for the Future (FFF), a British non-governmental organization, developed a number of tools and guidelines aimed at promoting the use of sustainable accounting. These tools were experimented in partnership with a number of organizations, included in which were an alcohol producer and a chemical company. Some of these experiments were an input to the development of guidelines and tools in a project guided by the UK department of trade and industry, the Sigma project (Forum for the Future, 2003a, 2003b). Two experiments carried out by FFF will be briefly presented and their contribution to research in the field of FCA outlined.

FFF (Bent, 2005) worked with an alcohol producer to devise a set of accounts which identified the damage imposed to society by that producer (external costs) and the costs to be incurred to discharge its responsibility for this damage (shadow costs). Findings suggest that the costs of closing the gap between current and desired social and sustainable performance is a fraction of the damage actually imposed to society by the consumption of alcohol. This work is interesting as it moves beyond strictly environmental costs to address a wider spectrum of costs.

FFF (Taplin *et al.*, 2006) also worked with a chemical company to develop a framework for sustainable business decision-making. It was applied to a set of refrigerant lubricants in view of comparing external environmental benefits (such as energy savings) and costs. The interest of this work lies in the fact that a proposal is made, at entity level, to quantify and compare the external costs and benefits of a product in a way that is usable by decision-makers.

Policy applications of FCA and impact on FCA at entity level

Advances in environmental sciences and economics are also making more figures available on the value of 'non-marketed' goods and services. Frameworks for policy applications have been developed. On top of informing policy makers, they are progressively giving accountants more tools and data to work with at entity level.[5]

We have chosen to describe the ExternE programme as an example of a major contribution to the development of such frameworks. The ExternE project regroups a vast body of research studies financed by the European Commission. Since 1991 the project has involved more than 50 research teams in over 20 countries and has tackled the monetary evaluation of environmental damages caused by electricity production. The damages assessed include human health (mortality and morbidity), damage to building materials, to crops, to ecosystems, damage caused by global warming and by noise. The methodology developed (Friedrich and Bickel, 2001) is that of the impact pathway approach. Environmental damages are estimated using a bottom-up approach. Emissions from the industrial process are quantified and fed into dispersion models (atmospheric, water and soil pollution are taken into account). The results from the dispersion models can be interpreted in terms of an increase of a given pollutant over a certain geographic zone in a given environment (air, water or soil). These results are then used as variables in dose response functions[6] so as to quantify physically the incremental damage. By incremental damage, we mean the supplementary damages compared to a reference situation in which the industrial process being studied does not take place. Each category of damage is quantified using a combination of market prices, welfare loss, willingness to pay and avoidance cost methods.

One of the first objectives of the project was to provide a comparison of different technologies and fuel cycles for electricity generation over a wide range of locations, fuels and technologies including fossil fuels, nuclear and renewable

Table 11.4 *Policy decisions and legislative proposals which have relied on ExternE know-how to perform economic evaluations*

- Draft directive on non-hazardous waste incineration.
- Large combustion plant directive.
- EU strategy to combat acidification.
- Costs and benefits of the UN–ECE Multi-pollutant, Multi-effect protocol and of proposals under this protocol (e.g. NOx and VOC control).
- Costs and benefits for the emission ceilings directive.
- Air quality limits for PAHs [polycyclic aromatic hydrocarbons].
- Diversion of PVC from incineration to landfill and recycling.
- Benefits of compliance with the EU environmental acquis: quantification of the benefits of air quality improvements.
- Costs and benefits of acidification and ground level ozone (as input to negotiation on the ozone directive 1998).
- Regulatory appraisal of the SO2, NO2 and PM10 air quality objectives for UK Department of the Environment, Transport and the Regions.
- Air quality guidelines on CO and benzene.
- Environmental costs of lorries (a study to incorporate environmental costs in vehicle excise duty rates in UK).
- Second NOx Protocol (for the UN–ECE Task Force on economic aspects of abatement strategies).

Source: www.externe.info, accessed 31 May 2006

energies. The effects of electricity generation are physically, environmentally and socially complex to estimate and involve very large uncertainties. Despite these difficulties the methodology and software developed within this project have been used and applied to support public decisions and has become a well-recognized source for methods and results of externalities estimation. Table 11.4 contains a list of policy decisions which have relied on ExternE know-how. Data has also been made available for use at entity level. For example, accountants can have access to information on the external costs of different sources of electricity generation and could use it to account for external costs at an entity level (see Atkinson, 2000, who does exactly this).

We now turn to the insights drawn from FCA experiments and to perspectives for future research.

INSIGHTS FROM FCA EXPERIMENTS AND PERSPECTIVES FOR FUTURE RESEARCH

The first insight from FCA experiments is that going through the process of FCA helped provide better knowledge of the organization's operations and helped to change several taken-for-granted ways of conducting business.

A second insight, however, is that some of the measures that would move a company towards more sustainable operations are sometimes out of its reach (a company can for example try to minimize transport requirements but will not control the price incentives that would make more sustainable modes of transport attractive).

A third insight is that not all external costs and benefits can be measured. What can be offered, for lack of data and scientific knowledge in some fields, are only incomplete pictures of an entity's external costs and benefits. However, once subtracted from its income, external costs may have a significant impact on an organization's bottom line and turn a profit into a loss, thus suggesting that existing market systems do not send the right price incentives.

Looking forward, FCA has moved from the initial environmental costing attempts to a wider sustainable development perspective. Based on experiments, concepts and frameworks have been developed to better qualify costs and benefits (in terms of timing, type, location and method used). However, more work is needed to better understand how the economic, social and environmental aspects of an entity interact with each other. Ongoing research such as the work on the SAM (Baxter *et al.*, 2004), on extended balanced scorecards (Forum for the Future, 2003b, pp. 30–1) or on new economic indicators[7] should lead to interesting developments in this field. This aspect is being made all the more essential by the fact that FCA enables adding up all the impacts and benefits and trading them off one against the other. As mentioned in a report written by Forum for the Future for the Sigma project (2003b, p. 35) this 'opens up the possibility of comparing £1 worth of climate change damage with £1 of reduced impact from waste or £1 of contribution to the local economy'. This will only be feasible with a good understanding of the context being studied and of the interactions between the economic, social and environmental spheres. It should be a key to improvements in FCA. Then the day when Adam Smith meets Rachel Carson could come very soon.

NOTES

1   Nuclear Electric is a subsidiary of British Energy. See Nuclear Electric's environmental reports for years 1994–5 and 1995–6 and those of British Energy for the following years. See also: British Energy, Changing the Climate of Opinion: Raising the profile of nuclear energy in the sustainable debate, *British Nuclear Industry Forum, MP's symposium*, Royal Academy of Engineers, 6 July 1999.

?   See also http://www.wessexwater.co.uk/strikingthebalance2005/finances/index.aspx?id=1191, accessed 31 May 2006.

3   See also Manaaki Whenua/Landcare Research (2000), *Making a difference for a truly clean green New Zealand: Our report on sustainable development*, Landcare Research.

4   See also Forum for the Future (2000), Annual Report, Forum for the Future, and Howes (2000).

5   See http://www.evri.ec.gc.ca, accessed 31 May 2006. The EVRI is a searchable storehouse of empirical studies on the economic value of environmental benefits and human health effects. See also http://www.externe.info, accessed 31 May 2006. The ExternE project is described in this chapter.

6   For a presentation, in an accounting journal, of what dose response functions are about see Milne (1992).

7   See the work of the New Economics Foundation on new ways of measuring progress: http://www.neweconomics.org/gen/new_ways_top.aspx, accessed 31 May 2006.

REFERENCES

Abt, C. C. (1977) *The social audit for management*. New York: Amacon.

AICPA (1977) *The measurement of corporate social performance*. New York: AICPA.

Anglian Water (2000) *Summary environmental and community report*. Anglian Water.

Antheaume, N. (2004) Valuing external costs – from theory to practice: Implications for full cost environmental accounting. *European Accounting Review*, 13(3): 443–64.

Atkinson, G. (2000) Measuring corporate sustainability. *Journal of Environmental Planning and Management*, 2(43): 325–52.

awg (2001) *Transforming our world: Sustainable development report 2001*. awg.

awg (2002) *The right structure for sustainable growth: awg plc sustainable development report 2002*. awg

Bauer, R. A. and Fern, D. H. (1972) *The corporate social audit*. New York: Russell Sage Foundation.

Bauer, R. A. and Fern, D. H. (1973) What is a corporate social audit? *Harvard Business Review*, 37–48

Baxter, T., Bebbington, J. and Cutteridge, D. (2004) Sustainability assessment model: Modelling economic, resource, environmental and social flows of a project. In A. Henriques and J. Richardson (eds) *The triple bottom line: Does it all add up?* London: Earthscan, pp. 113–20

Bebbington, J. and Gray, R. (2001) An account of sustainability: Failure, success and a reconceptualization. *Critical Perspectives on Accounting*, 12(5): 557–88.

Bebbington, J., Gray, R., Hibbit, C. and Kirk, E. (2001) *Full cost accounting: An agenda for action*. London: ACCA.

Bent, D. (2005) *Towards a monetised triple bottom line for an alcohol producer, using stakeholder dialogue to negotiate a 'licence to operate' by constructing an account of social performance*. London: Forum for the Future.

Boone, C. and Rubenstein, D. B. (1997) Natural solution: Full cost accounting can help companies to integrate environmental considerations into decision making. *CA Magazine*, 130(4): 18–22.

Coase, R. H. (1960) The problem of social cost. *Journal of Law and Economics,* 3: 1–44.

Costanza, R., d'Arge, R., de Groot, R., Farber, S., Grasso, M., Hammon, B., Limburg, K., Naeem, S., O'Neill, R. V., Paruelo, J., Rskin, R. G., Sutton, P. and van den Belt, M. (1997) The value of the world's ecosystem services and natural capital, *Nature,* 387: 253–9.

Estes, R. W. (1976) Socio-economic accounting and external diseconomies. *Accounting Review,* 50(2): 284–90.

European Commission (1995) *ExternE: Externalities of energy,* vol. 1, summary. Brussels–Luxemburg: European Commission.

Forum for the Future (2000) Annual Report. London: Forum for the Future.

Forum for the Future (2003a) *The Sigma guidelines toolkit: Sigma environmental accounting guide.* London: The Sigma Project.

Forum for the Future (2003b) *The Sigma guidelines toolkit: Sustainable accounting guide.* London: The Sigma Project.

Friedrich, R. and Bickel, P. (2001) Estimation of external costs using the impact-pathway approach: Results from the ExternE project series. *TA-Datenbank-Nachrichten,* 10(3): 74–82.

Gray, R. H. (1992) Accounting and environmentalism: An exploration of the challenge of gently accounting for accountability, transparency and sustainability. *Accounting Organisations and Society,* 17(5): 399–425.

Howes, R. (2000) Corporate environmental accounting: accounting for environmentally sustainable profits. In J. Proops and S. Simon (eds) *Greening the accounts.* London: Edward Elgar.

Huizing, A. and Dekker, C. H. (1992) Helping to pull our planet out of the red: An environmental report of BSO/Origin. *Accounting Organisations and Society,* 17(5): 449–58.

Institute of Energy Economics (1997) *ExternE core project, extension of the accounting framework, final report.* Stuttgart: Institute of Energy Economics.

Linowes, D. F. (1972) An approach to socio-economic accounting. *Conference Board Record,* 9(11): 58–61.

Linowes, D. F. (1973) Getting a handle on social audit. *Business and Society Review,* 4: 39–42.

Linowes, D. F. (1974) *The corporate conscience.* New York: Hawthorn Books.

Milne, M. J. (1992) Accounting, environmental resource values, and non-market valuation techniques for environmental resources: A review. *Accounting, Auditing and Accountability Journal,* 4(3): 80–108.

Pigou, A. C. (1920) *The economics of welfare.* London: Macmillan & Co.

Rubenstein, D. B. (1992) Bridging the gap between green accounting and black ink. *Accounting Organizations and Society,* 17(5): 501–8.

Rubenstein, D. B. (1994) *Environmental accounting for the sustainable corporation: Strategies and techniques.* Westport, CT: Quorum Books.

224

Seidler, L. J. (1976) Dollar values in the social income statement. *World, Peat Marwick Mitchell and Co*, pp. 14–23.

Smith, K. V. (1996) *Estimating economic values for nature: Methods for non-market valuation*. Cheltenham, UK, and Brookfield, US: Edward Elgar.

Steen, B. (1997) *The EPS system 1997: A comprehensive presentation*. Göteborg: Chalmers University of Technology.

Taplin, J., Bent, D. and Aeron-Thomas, D. (2006) *Developing a sustainability accounting framework to inform strategic business decisions: A case study from the chemicals industry*. London: Forum for the Future.

UNCTAD (1994) *Accounting for sustainable forestry management: A case study*. New York and Geneva: United Nations.

USEPA (1996) *Environmental accounting case studies: Full cost accounting at Ontario Hydro*. Washington: United States Environmental Protection Agency (USEPA).

Wessex Water (2000) *Report to society*. Bath: Wessex Water.

Wessex Water (2005) *Sustainability indicators*. Bath: Wessex Water.

Chapter 12

Changing organizational attitudes and culture through sustainability accounting

Jan Bebbington

INTRODUCTION

If there is one concept that demands societal change, it is sustainable development (hereafter SD). A desire for SD emerges from the realization that current forms of economic organization create social, environmental and economic effects that, at their most extreme, endanger life on this planet and human life in particular (see, for example, Hawken, 1993; Von Weizsacker *et al.*, 1998; Hawken *et al.*, 1999; Meadows *et al.*, 2004). Regardless, current economic development creates much human and ecological damage, even while falling short of a planetary 'disaster' scenario. The question that this chapter addresses is how, if at all, does social and environmental accounting and reporting (hereafter SEAR) lead to 'change' within organizations such that SD may be pursued. Three aspects are examined to answer that question: (1) what constitutes organizational change, (2) how accounting interventions may be linked to organizational change and (3) the extent to which these interventions may impact upon the broader goal of SD.

THEORIZING ORGANIZATIONAL CHANGE

Two aspects are introduced in this section. First, a conception of what constitutes an organization is developed, paying attention to the role that accounting is thought to play in organizations. Second, a description of organizational change processes is provided. Once these tasks are completed, the terrain within which a discussion of the extent to which sustainability accounting may follow or induce organizational change can be tackled.

Organizations have been variously conceptualized within the management literature, with the 'metaphors of machine and organism' (Smircich, 1983, p. 340) being the most prevalent (see also Morgan, 1986). Under the biological metaphor, organizations are viewed as open systems (Llewellyn, 1994, p. 5) which develop in a dynamic fashion over time in response to disturbances in their environment that puncture organizational boundaries and thereby demand or stimulate some response. Within the membrane of the organization, various elements are assumed to exist. Laughlin (1991, p. 211) synthesizes a variety of conceptualizations of organizations and change processes and identifies three elements within an organization, describing them as:

1   interpretive schemas (including beliefs, values and norms, mission/purpose and metarules);
2   design archetype (including organizational structure, decision processes and communication systems); and
3   sub-systems (which contain the tangible organizational elements).

These elements vary from the relatively intangible to the tangible and each layer presupposes the others. The layers operate together to determine organization activities and as such provide the basis from which we may understand organizations' actions. Accounting could be assumed to fall within the design archetype category whereby accounting techniques permeate decision processes as well as communication systems. In this way, accounting looks in both directions in the above categorization, providing both the articulation of the extent to which organization missions are achieved as well as defining the scope of behaviour for organization participants. Accounting also impacts (as well as being derived from) interpretive schemas and tends to induce a narrow financial focus in some organizations (notably large listed companies). The pivotal role of accounting in boundary maintenance and binding structures is well developed in Llewellyn (1994) and is relevant here because change is thought to arise from cross-boundary pressures.

Laughlin (1991) suggests that organizations are inertial or change resistant and before any possibilities for change exist there needs to be a jolt or disturbance. He does not specify a typology of disturbances, but the empirical material he presents describes the impact of: legal changes leading to a resource problem for the Church of England and the development of a new commercial culture within an organization, which is itself reminiscent of the development of new public management.[1] In a more generic sense, possible disturbances could be seen as including, but not limited to: (1) structural changes in laws or fiscal policies of governments, (2) changes in commercial relationships within an industry/economy, (3) changes in expectations of financial stakeholders and capital markets, (4) changes in technology and/or ways of working within an industry/economy, (5) changes in relationships with stakeholders such as consumers, producers or employees, and (6) changes in societal expectations about certain events/behaviours. These are disturbances which emanate from the external environment. Alternatively and in addition, disturbances could also originate within the organizations, perhaps by appointment of a new chief executive or via the collective actions of employees.

All of these disturbances have been investigated at various times in the accounting literature and all offer different possibilities for changes in particular organizations. The way in which such changes systematically play out in organizational life, however, remains speculative. Indeed, Laughlin (1991, p. 210) notes that 'once disturbed, the argument is that the "track" which the disturbance takes through the organization and the degree of transformation it will generate in the pathway it follows will differ over time and across different organizations. Put generally, there is no single end result for any disturbance, but a number of possibilities.' Drawing from the literature synthesized, however, Laughlin (1991) suggests a number of end states from a jolt and these are summarized in Table 12.1. Implicit in this

Table 12.1 *Summary of Laughlin's (1991) characterization of organization change*[a]

Generic description of change	Sub-category of change mechanism	Description
First order change or morphostatic change (things look different while remaining the same)	Rebuttal	Disturbance deflected so that the organization can return to an inertial state. No permanent change is observed.
	Reorientation	Disturbance results in change (because it cannot be rebutted) but changes are cosmetic and the 'heart' (the interpretive schema) of the organization is not changed.
Second order change or morphogenetic change (the working model of the organization changes fundamentally)	Colonization	Disturbance is significant to the organization and the interpretive schema, design archetype and sub-system (in some combination) change with a new underlying organizational ethos emerging.
	Evolution	There is change to the underlying ethos of the organization. Rather than this change arising directly from a disturbance, the organization itself chooses to change.

Note: [a] See also Gray *et al.* (1995b)

conceptualization is that, regardless of the particular track taken, one may observe a particular end point. Thus disturbances may be linked to outcomes, leaving the particular processes by which the outcomes come about within the 'black box' of the organization.

The extent to which a disturbance leads to one of the behaviours described in Table 12.1 crucially depends on the nature of the organization as well as the nature of the change. In particular, and drawing on Brunsson (1985), two ends of a continuum were identified: organizations with 'weak' '(inconsistent, simple and inclusive) and "strong", (consistent, complex and conclusive) ideologies (aligned to and part of the design archetype and interpretive schemes)' (Laughlin, 1991, p. 222). It is suggested that those with 'strong' ideologies are 'open to adaptive changes, but resistant to fundamental ideological shifts' (p. 222) whereas those with 'weak' ideologies are 'more open to manipulation and fundamental change' (p. 222). As a result, it would appear that in order to understand change/non-change in organizations in response to environmental/social/SD disturbances an appreciation of the nature of the disturbances as well as the nature of the particular organization is required. Organization change, one may infer, is a contingency theory-type problem with change being contingent on disturbances and how they interact with the interpretative schema, design archetype and subsystems of the organization in question and contingent on the environment within which such events take place. To say that organizational change is under-specified and under-theorized is, therefore, self-evident. Change is difficult to describe due to the complexity of the underlying phenomena, the difficulty of gathering research data on organizational change, and conceptual limitations. Despite this, there have been some attempts to make sense of this change process within SEAR.

LINKING ACCOUNTING TO ORGANIZATIONAL CHANGE

Four aspects are developed in this section. The first instance, the accountability framework, is briefly described as it is the usual (although often implicit) framework of SEAR. Organizational change, therefore, should be considered in the context of this framework. Second, the nature of disturbances which have been investigated in the literature are outlined and discussed. Third, a discussion of what changes have been observed and those that remain elusive are described. Finally, broad conclusions are provided.

An expectation that organizations would change in response to disturbances (which themselves arise from the realization that organizations are part of a system which is destroying both the natural environment and people's lives) can be predicted from an accountability perspective. Briefly (but see Gray *et al.*, 1996 for an in-depth exposition), an accountability framework explains the nature of the relationship between two parties where one (the principal) passes instructions to the other (the agent) concerning expectations about actions. The agent then both undertakes actions as instructed and provides an account of those actions.

Where instructions change (perhaps to forbear from environmentally damaging activities) or where the context within which the relationship is played out changes (for example, when laws regarding what is acceptable behaviour change) then one would expect to see different accountabilities being created. In the same manner, the accounts of actions one is responsible for would also change in such a situation. It is these expectations that lead to a focus in SEAR on: (1) the context within which behaviour takes place (for example, consideration of ethical investment, changing legal requirements, development of industry codes of conduct); (2) the actions of organizations in response to changes in context (for example, development of new forms of performance appraisal, project evaluation or budgeting systems); and (3) how reporting of performance reflects alterations in instructions and actions. Indeed, the focus on reporting in order to impute changes in actions or the relative impact of disturbances can be explained in such a framework. It does, however, beg the question as to what constitutes a disturbance that will demand an organizational response.

Disturbances that are likely to result in change are not systematically addressed in the SEAR literature beyond a broadly shared assumption that various social and environmental crises should constitute a disturbance. It is possible, however, to infer from the literature those things that researchers have assumed are disturbances of note and Table 12.2 reviews a sample of these.

As is apparent from Table 12.2, various writers have identified a number of types of disturbances which they believe would be significant enough to change the terms of the relationship between principal and agent in an accountability relationship. A tentative typography of disturbances can, therefore, be inferred. One could suggest that change could be triggered by: (1) changes in legislation, (2) events which challenge the legitimacy of an industry or organization, (3) expectations of environmental performance emerging from the media, (4) generalized expectations that entities should be environmentally responsible and (5) the development and use of particular tools or techniques for managing the natural and social environment within which organizations operate.

In addition, Larrinaga-González and Bebbington (2001) also suggest that there may be assemblages of disturbances which interact together and impact upon organizations. Disturbances, therefore, may well be multiple and may manifest themselves one by one in organizations or may come in groupings (with resulting different potential force and possibilities for change). The question then becomes: how powerful are these various categories of disturbances, as it is the strength of disturbance which dictates the likelihood of change? In many ways it is too early (in any event there is a lack of empirical data) to hypothesize what disturbances are likely to be most powerful. It could be plausible to suggest that legal requirements are the most powerful because they are the most formalized. It may be, however,

Table 12.2 *Disturbances which are assumed to lead to change*

Study	Assumed disturbance and change relationship
Brown and Deegan (1998)	Media attention focused on particular community issues results in increased voluntary disclosure.
Buhr (1998)	Changing government regulations for sulphur dioxide emission abatement lead to both reduced levels of pollution and reporting of the technological actions leading to that reduction in pollution.
Buhr (2001)	North American Free Trade Agreement would alter the terms of corporate activity and lead to reporting disclosures.
Buhr (2002)	Pressure arising from a legitimacy crisis with regard to the environmental performance of the pulp and paper industry will lead to reporting.
Deegan and Rankin (1996)	Successful prosecutions for environmental crimes would lead to accounts of those prosecutions.
Gray *et al.* (1995b)	Generalized greening pressures would change organizational routines and this would be reflected in accounts of performance.
Gray *et al.* (1998)	Changes in the environmental agenda and environmental law would require significant/material actions and hence the financial ramifications of change would be reflected in financial statements.
Gray *et al.* (1997)	Development of a social bookkeeping system and social report would alter the way in which an organization views itself and accounts for itself.
Larrinaga-González and Bebbington (2001)	Development of tools for environmental management would result in use of those tools and hence a different way of operating.
Larrinaga-González *et al.* (2002)	Passage of legislation requiring environmental reporting would result in a change in the accounts of activities provided by organizations in line with the legislative requirement.
O'Dwyer (2005)	Undertaking a social audit would lead to questioning of organizational activities.
Unerman and Bennett (2004)	Shell's internet-based stakeholder dialogue approach creates possibilities for communication (informed by Habermas' ideal speech situation). It is implied that if 'good' communication is achieved then change will happen in the organization–stakeholder relationship.

that in certain circumstances public/media pressures are more powerful (and here one thinks of the Brent Spar).[2] At the same time, observing an absence of change despite a powerful disturbance would also be instructive. All this, however, begs the question of what change should entail.

In the same way as disturbances have been variously conceptualized, so too have the nature of the changes expected. While it is not always clear what change is being sought, it can be inferred that change ranges from changes in organizational social and environmental impacts; to change in corporate rationales, routines and practices; and alterations in the beliefs/attitudes of organization participants. Evidence for changes of these sorts is mixed.

There is some evidence that SEAR interventions have led to reduced relative environmental impacts (see, for example, Bebbington *et al.*, 2001, who note that both Interface Carpets and BSO/Orgin achieved reductions in relative environmental impact by using full cost accounting). Likewise, initiating social and environmental reporting (see, for example, Bebbington and Gray, 2001) has led to reduced environmental impact because tracking impact has led to better control being exercised over impacts. These changes, however, are relatively minor and tend to be in relative impacts not absolute impacts. In the case of BSO/Origin, for example, increases in absolute environmental impact still arose even with relative efficiency improvements.

There is also evidence (see, for example, Bennett and James, 1998a, 1998b; Schaltegger and Burritt, 2000; Gray and Bebbington, 2001) that organizations have made changes to their internal routines, including associated accounting routines, in response to social and environmental disturbances. One change which is much talked about is the emergence of stakeholder dialogue processes whereby those who were previously external to the organization have some ability to interact (and maybe affect) the actions and/or rationales of the organization (for a cautionary view of its effectiveness, see Owen *et al.*, 2000, 2001).

One area where change is also evident is in the area of reporting on social and environmental impacts: both within the annual report and accounts package (for an example of a longitudinal study, see Gray *et al.*, 1995a) and within stand-alone reporting (see SustainAbility/United Nations Environment Programme, 2000, 2002, 2004). The potential significance of organizations producing new forms of accounts is twofold. First, such accounts could be seen as evidence that something within the organization has changed, albeit that researchers do not directly observe those changes. What can be seen, however, are corporate assertions that they have (in many instances, new) committees, audits, targets and objectives with regard to social and environmental performance. As Neu *et al.* (1998) suggest, reporting thus provides a window into organizational life and enables us to 'read between the lines' to understand management mindsets (Neimark, 1992). The second reason why new forms of accounts potentially signal change is through an accountability lens. If accounts are the outcome of accountability relationships, new forms of account may signal that new forms of responsibility and accountability also exist. It is much less clear that reporting reflects a process by which organizations have self-consciously taken on broader responsibilities (see, for example, Adams, 2004, who identifies that reporting does not necessarily reflect organizational performance). The possibility that this may be the case or that society may seek to hold organizations to account on the basis of these new forms of disclosure does, however, exist. An accountability-informed exploration of accounting, however, is challenged by legitimacy theory. This conception of why organizations produce these accounts also has implications for the topic of organizational change.

Legitimacy theory (see Deegan, 2002, for an overview and Dowling and Pfeffer, 1975, and Lindblom, 1994 for the basis of the theory) proposes that in response to legitimacy pressures (or disturbances in Laughlin's terms) organizations most usually either: (1) change their behaviour (and may then use reporting to communicate that change in behaviour), (2) without any change in underlying behaviour/impact, change perceptions of performance among influential stake-holders (and use reporting to effect a change in perception), (3) manipulate perceptions by deflecting attention (by use of reporting) or (4) change expectations of duties (again via reporting). One of the limitations of legitimacy theory is that it may not always be clear which strategy is being pursued (for example, evidence of pressure and reporting does not tell you if organizational change has taken place, but see Buhr, 1998, who studies pressure, behaviour *and* reporting). In addition, given a number of the above strategies are effected via reporting, presence of reporting can be difficult to interpret. Further, it is often acknowledged (see Deegan, 2002, pp. 290–1) that organizations could have multiple reasons for reporting and a relative dearth of direct inquiry into rationales (but see O'Dwyer, 2002) means that legitimacy theory explanations dominate the literature. In any event, in the context of this chapter legitimacy theory provides a framework that suggests that reporting may or may not reflect underlying organizational changes. Legitimacy theory-informed investigations, however, tend to assume that organizations use social and environmental reporting to ensure that change does not happen.

The last category of change that may be sought is change in the underlying rationale of organizational activity. Alternative ways of thinking about the world, that are motivated by ensuring that people and the ecology are not destroyed, are evident in the literature (see, for example, Maunders and Burritt, 1991; Cooper, 1992; Birkin, 1996). These and other authors suggest that in order for 'disaster' to be averted some underlying change in individual, company and societal rationales have to take place (such reasoning is also at the root of early critiques of SEAR found in Puxty, 1991, and Tinker et al., 1991). As far as one can ascertain such things, it would appear that underlying attitudinal change is not happening, or at least if it is happening researchers have yet to uncover it. Rather, an eco-modernization discourse appears to be the norm (see Newton and Harte, 1997; O'Dwyer, 2002, 2003, and in a slightly different form Everett and Neu, 2000). One may also suggest, however, that to expect such changes may be hopelessly naïve and optimistic (a point I return to later).

In summary, the literature in this area contains several themes which inform the question as to whether disturbances of sufficient force arise from the social/ environmental agenda to change organizations. First, there is evidence that there are changes in aspects of organizations' operations in response to disturbances. The disturbances, however, are not of the size and nature to generate highly visible or fast changes. Rather the timeframe within which disturbances require action is such that organizations can gradually change rather than be pressed into rapid change (see Gray *et al.*, 1998; Buhr, 1998). Evidence for change can be found in terms of different routines being undertaken, the use of various tools and techniques for managing impacts and different forms of account of those impacts. If one were looking, however, for fundamental change in attitudes and rationales of organizations, or a questioning as to whether or not the capitalistic form of enterprise is possible or desirable within the context of the social and environmental agenda, then one would be disappointed. Change of this nature does not appear to be taking place and, as a result, it would appear at the current moment that organizational change for SD is not evident in the research undertaken, or at least what change there is falls short of researchers' hopes and expectations.

CHANGE FOR SD

To date the focus has been on the SEAR literature rather than specifically on accounting for SD. This focus was adopted for two reasons. First, there is relatively little literature that takes SD as its starting point (but see Bebbington and Thomson, 1996; Milne, 1996; Bebbington, 2001; Gray and Milne, 2002, 2004; Baxter *et al.*, 2004; Birkin *et al.*, 2005). Second, the scale of changes that may be required to be relatively socially and environmentally responsible pale into insignificance when one considers the challenge of SD. Organizational change for SD is a stepwise change in scale of challenge. In this context, several additional points should be made.

The scale at which change should sensibly be thought of in terms of pursuing SD may not necessarily be at the micro/organizational level and hence a focus on organizations may not be productive. It makes more sense to talk of the SD profile of a country, region or ecosystem because SD tends to describe properties of a physical system in some physical space. In short, SD is normally a spatial concept (see also Gray and Milne, 2004, p. 78). In contrast, accounts are produced for organizations which, unless they are single location, are not likely to operate within one region/ecosystem or country. The SD profile of an organization, therefore, would be very difficult to create. Despite this, there may be some ability to specify some aspects of impact that are in scale with demands of SD. For example, an ecological footprint[3] or mass balance of an organization's activities could be linked to the ecological-carrying capacity of the area within which it operates: this would be more obviously suitable for forestry, fishing and agriculture based organizations.

In a similar vein, a full social audit could provide some idea of the impact of the organization on social sustainability aspects of a region.

Further, SD is an emergent property of the system under consideration. That is, SD patterns arise from the interaction of all activities within a system. Accounting, with its focus on entities, tends to be more atomistic in its focus and as a result the impacts that arise from the combined activities of a business community, for example, are not usually accounted for. It may, however, be the case that in seeking to account for SD that we end up with different entities to account for. It is plausible, for example, to examine a political region like Scotland (which has calculated its own ecological footprint as have many countries) and trace the elements of that footprint which arise from particular industries. Providing accounts of groups of organizations would be a new activity for accounting academics.

Finally, the timeframe over which SD may meaningfully be pursued may not be in years but in decades. It may be that the effects of other levers for change beyond accounting (such as consumer preferences, legal/regulatory frameworks or in response to political movements) are the most important levers in the pursuit of SD. Changes in these arenas may feed into organizational change over a timeframe that does not generate immediately visible change and as a result examining changes in accounting/reporting activities may be mis-specified. For example, if an organization predicts/creates/responds to changes in consumer demand for more energy-efficient products then their financial performance, and accounts of such, may not differ from previous accounts (that is, a focus on external measures of performance will not capture this change). Likewise, the gradual implementation of laws with regard to employment relations would affect the social profile of an organization (and hence its impact on the social aspects of SD) but may not result in visible change processes. It could be that change is happening but a narrow and time-limited focus would not detect this.

This section briefly sought to highlight particular challenges of seeing organizational change with respect to accounting for SD. It is worth noting that accounting and SD specifically (rather than SEAR research) is in its infancy. Accounting for SD raises more challenges than merely accounting for a 'triple bottom line' and some of these challenges were alluded to above. These issues are far from resolved or empirically explored, but are areas where future research is likely to focus.

CONCLUDING COMMENTS

This chapter has reviewed the SEAR literature using the lens of organizational change. Organizations, the nature of disturbances and what change entails were all discussed within the chapter with significant uncertainties in terms of conceptualization arising at each juncture. Evaluating whether or not accounting interventions lead to change is, therefore, difficult. It would appear that there is evidence of change in organizational routines and responsibilities; in use of accounting tools and techniques; and in the types of accounts that organizations produce of their performance. Change in underlying attitudes and rationales of organizations, however, does not appear to be forthcoming. Further, if such a question is placed in the context of the more challenging framework of change to achieve SD then the extent to which organizations appear to have changed to embrace that agenda is minimal. Likewise, the power of accounting and reporting to induce and reflect such changes may also be minimal. This does not, however, mean that change is not possible: albeit the timeframe within which change may emerge is likely to be considerable (those who do not believe we have time to play with in this matter will find such a conclusion frustrating). Attention, therefore, turns to what the future may hold in this context.

The literature reviewed in this chapter seems to suggest that organizations and individuals within organizations are change resistant to even relatively minor alterations in activities or changes to mindsets. Yet at the same time an expectation that change should be emerging in response to the SD agenda exists. This sets up a tension that the literature appears not to have fully investigated. Thus failure to detect change may arise from: (1) the SD agenda not enacting itself on organizations in a timeframe or in a way that would lead to change being evident, (2) research methods used to attempt to identify change not being of sufficient quality to observe changes, (3) change may be taking place but is not observed by researchers yet, (4) changes are taking place but are not strongly patterned and as such coherent explanations have yet to emerge from empirical work or (5) some other explanation that we currently cannot identify.

One observation that can be drawn from the above is that there is a relative dearth of studies of change that focus on particular organization settings (but see Gray *et al.*, 1997; Buhr, 1998, 2002; Bebbington and Gray, 2001; Larrinaga-González and Bebbington, 2001). The most likely way in which we would be more informed on organizational change is via in-depth case studies of change moments in organizations. Inferring change from reporting patterns (observed on a longitudinal or cross-sectional basis) provides one lens into the organization, but not one best suited to uncovering less obvious changes or failed change initiatives. Further, longitudinal cases are likely to yield better insights into organizational change. Given the relatively recent history of accounting/reporting for SD, it is too early to see 5- to 10-year case studies of organizational change, yet it is this type of study that is required.

Many of the studies referenced above examine whether or not change follows some sort of 'event' or trend and in very few instances is the researcher an active party in initiating change. The literature thus begs the question of how one may engage with organizations in order to generate some form of organizational change and if it is desirable to do so. There are conflicting views on how best engagements could be done from: working with, confronting, working through organizations and/or viewing organization change as some sort of dialogical process (see Thomson and Bebbington, 2005). The impact of engagement on organization change, therefore, may be a productive way in which to pursue this line of inquiry.

The final point that is worth considering is whether or not as a research community we have developed sufficiently robust frames of reference to research organizational change. Organizations are complex entities and change is a complex and dynamic process. Theorizing using accountability, legitimacy or stakeholder theory may, therefore, be insufficient for the task at hand. As a result, before this field can develop it may be that more work is needed exploring the value of institutional theory, different political economy lenses (for example, a neo-Gramsci lens – see Levy and Egan, 2003), structuration theory (see Buhr, 2002) and other theories that we currently are not familiar with in SEAR. Such explanations, coupled with more in-depth and sustained empirical investigations, would help shed light on this complex but vital area where we have so much to learn.

NOTES

1   New public management is a term used to describe an array of initiatives unleashed on the public sector in recent years including: creation of quasi-markets, public–private sector partnerships and quangos to control public sector provision. These initiatives are viewed to have been accompanied by an ideological agenda that introduces rationales and approaches that are at odds with a traditional public sector ethos.

2   In brief, in June 1995 Shell and Greenpeace were involved in a dispute over whether or not the Brent Spar (an oil storage platform) should be sunk in the North Sea. Despite the British Government giving approval to disposal at sea, the Greenpeace occupation of the Brent Spar, the media attention which followed the occupation and a consumer boycott of Shell led to the organization reversing its disposal decision. This high profile confrontation is often used as an illustration of how legally mandated courses of action (the dumping) may be reversed as a result of media pressure and exposure.

3   The ecological footprint approach seeks to determine the impact of a person, city or country in terms of how much land would be required to support consumption activities. Energy used, food consumed and waste assimilation capacity required to support human activity can all be equated with an amount of land that would be/is used. Land is used as a common metric because it is a visually powerful way to communicate impact to individuals (the pedagogic value of the ecological footprint is noted by Constanza, 2000). It is also a powerful common currency because land is a finite resource (although land quality is not) and measuring lifestyles in this manner brings inequalities in land appropriation into sharp contrast and also highlights the extent to which the current ecological capacity of the planet is being exhausted (see Loh, 2000, who calculates that the ecological footprint of the world's population was at least 30 per cent larger than the total

biologically productive land available). See also Wackernagel and Rees (1996) and Rees (2000).

REFERENCES

Adams, C. (2004) The ethical, social and environmental reporting-performance gap. *Accounting, Auditing and Accountability Journal*, 17(5): 731–57.

Baxter, T., Bebbington, J. and Cutteridge, D. (2004) Sustainability assessment model: Modelling economic, resource, environmental and social flows of a project. In A. Henriques and J. Richardson (eds) *The triple bottom line: Does it all add up?* London: Earthscan, pp. 113–20.

Bebbington, J. (2001) Sustainable development: A review of the international development, business and accounting literature. *Accounting Forum*, 25(2): 128–57.

Bebbington, J. and Gray, R. (2001) An account of sustainability: Failure, success and reconceptualisation. *Critical Perspectives on Accounting*, 12(5): 557–605.

Bebbington, J. and Thomson, I. (1996) *Business conceptions of sustainable development and the implications for accountancy*. London: ACCA Research Report.

Bebbington, J., Gray, R., Hibbit, C. and Kirk, E. (2001) *Full cost accounting: An agenda for action*. London: Association of Chartered Certified Accountants.

Bennett, M. and James, P. (1998a) *Environment under the spotlight: Current practice and future trends in environment-related performance measurement for business*. London: Association of Chartered Certified Accountants.

Bennett, M. and James, P. (1998b) *The green bottom line: Environmental accounting for management*. Sheffield: Greenleaf.

Birkin, F. (1996) The ecological accountant: From the cogito to thinking like a mountain. *Critical Perspectives on Accounting*, 7(3): 231–57.

Birkin, F., Edwards, P. and Woodward, D. (2005) Accounting's contribution to a conscious cultural evolution: An end to sustainable development. *Critical Perspectives on Accounting*, 16(3): 185–208.

Brown, N. and Deegan, C. (1998) The public disclosure of environmental performance information: A dual test of media agenda setting theory and legitimacy theory. *Accounting and Business Research*, 29(1): 21–42.

Brunsson, N. (1985) *The irrational organisation: Irrationality as a basis for organisational action and change*. London: Wiley.

Buhr, N. (1998) Environmental performance, legislation and annual report disclosure: The case of acid rain and Falconbridge. *Accounting, Auditing and Accountability Journal*, 11(2): 163–90.

Buhr, N. (2001) Corporate silence: Environmental disclosure and the North American Free Trade Agreement. *Critical Perspectives on Accounting*, 12(4): 405–21.

Buhr, N. (2002) A structuration view on the initiation of environmental reports. *Critical Perspectives on Accounting,* 13(1): 17–38.

Constanza, R. (2000) The dynamics of the ecological footprint project. *Ecological Economics,* 32: 341–5.

Cooper, C. (1992) The non and norm of accounting for (m)other nature. *Accounting, Auditing and Accountability Journal,* 5(3): 179–86.

Cooper, C., Taylor, P., Smith, N. and Catchpowle, L. (2005) A discussion of the political potential of social accounting. *Critical Perspectives on Accounting,* 16(7): 951–74.

Cooper, D. and Hopper, T. (eds) (1990) *Critical accounts: Reorientating accounting research.* London: Macmillan.

Deegan, C. (2002) Introduction: The legitimising effect of social and environmental disclosures – a theoretical foundation. *Accounting, Auditing and Accountability Journal,* 15(3): 282–311.

Deegan, C. and Rankin, M. (1996) Do Australian companies report environmental news objectively?: An analysis of environmental disclosures by firms prosecuted successfully by the Environmental Protection Authority. *Accounting, Auditing and Accountability Journal,* 9(2): 50–67.

Dowling, J. and Pfeffer, J. (1975) Organisational legitimacy: Social values and organisational behaviour. *Pacific Sociological Review,* January: 122–36.

Everett, J. and Neu, D. (2000) Ecological modernization and the limits of environmental accounting? *Accounting Forum,* 24(1): 5–29.

Gray, R. and Bebbington, J. (2001) *Accounting for the Environment,* 2nd edn. London: Sage.

Gray, R. and Milne, M. (2002) Sustainability reporting: Who's kidding whom? *Chartered Accountants Journal of New Zealand,* 81(6): 66–70.

Gray, R. and Milne, M. (2004) Towards reporting on the triple bottom line: Mirages, methods and myths. In A. Henriques and J. Richardson (eds) *The triple bottom Line: Does it all add up?* London: Earthscan, pp. 70–80.

Gray, R., Kouhy, R. and Lavers, S. (1995a) Corporate social and environmental reporting: A review of the literature and a longitudinal study of UK disclosure. *Accounting, Auditing and Accountability Journal,* 8(2): 47–77.

Gray, Rob, Owen, Dave and Adams, Carol (1996) *Accounting and accountability.* Hemel Hempstead: Prentice-Hall.

Gray, R., Walters, D., Bebbington, J. and Thomson, I. (1995b) The greening of enterprise: An exploration of the (non) role of environmental accounting and environmental accountants in organizational change. *Critical Perspectives on Accounting,* 6(3): 211–29.

Gray, R., Dey, C., Owen, D., Evans, R. and Zadek, S. (1997) Struggling with the praxis of social accounting: Stakeholders, accountability, audits and procedures. *Accounting, Auditing and Accountability Journal,* 10(3): 325–64.

Gray, R., Bebbington, J., Collison, D., Kouhy, R., Lyon, B., Reid, C., Russell, A. and Stevenson, L. (1998) *The valuation of assets and liabilities: Environmental law and the impact of the environmental agenda for business*. Edinburgh: Institute of Chartered Accountants of Scotland.

Harte, G. and Owen, D. (1987) Fighting de-industrialisation: The role of local government social audits. *Accounting, Organizations and Society*, 12(2): 123–41.

Hawken, P. (1993) *The ecology of commerce: A declaration of sustainability*. New York: Harper Business.

Hawken, P., Lovins, A. and Lovins, H. (1999) *Natural capitalism: The next industrial revolution*. London: Earthscan.

Larrinaga-González, C. and Bebbington, J. (2001) Accounting change or institutional appropriation? A case study on the implementation of environmental accounting. *Critical Perspectives on Accounting*, 12(3): 269–92.

Larrinaga-González, C., Carrasco, F., Caro, F. J., Correa, C. and Paez, J. M. (2001) The role of environmental accounting in organizational change: An exploration of Spanish companies. *Accounting, Auditing and Accountability Journal*, 14(2): 213–39.

Larrinaga-González, C., Carrasco, F., Correa, C., Llena, F. and Moneva, J. M. (2002) Accountability and accounting regulation: The case of the Spanish environmental disclosure standard. *European Accounting Review*, 11(4): 723–40.

Laughlin, R. (1991) Environmental disturbances and organization transitions and transformations: Some alternative models. *Organizational Studies*, 12(2): 209–32.

Lehman, G. (1999) Disclosing new worlds: A role for social and environmental accounting and auditing. *Accounting, Organizations and Society*, 24(3): 251–66.

Levy, D. and Egan, D. (2003) A neo-Gramscian approach to corporate political strategy: Conflict and accommodation in the climate change negotiations. *Journal of Management Studies*, 40(4): 803–29.

Lindblom, C. (1994) The implications of organizational legitimacy for corporate social performance and disclosure. Paper presented at the Critical Perspectives on Accounting Conference, New York.

Llewellyn, S. (1994) Managing the boundary: How accounting is implicated in maintaining the organisation. *Accounting, Auditing and Accountability Journal*, 7(4): 4–23.

Loh, J. (2000) *Living planet report 2000*. Switzerland: World Wildlife Fund.

Maunders, K. and Burritt, R. (1991) Accounting and ecological crisis. *Accounting, Auditing and Accountability Journal*, 14(3): 9–26.

Meadows, D., Randers, J. and Meadows, D. (2004) *The limits to growth: The 30 year update*. London: Earthscan.

Milne, M. (1996) On sustainability, the environment and management accounting. *Management Accounting Research*, 7(1): 135–61.

Morgan, G. (1986) *Images of organization*. Beverly Hills, CA: Sage.

Neimark, M. (1992) *The hidden dimensions of annual reports: Sixty years of social conflict at General Motors*. New York: Markus Wiener Publishing.

Neu, D., Warsame, H. and Pedwell, K. (1998) Managing public impressions: Environmental disclosures in annual reports. *Accounting Organizations and Society*, 23(3): 265–82.

Newton, T. and Harte, G. (1997) Green business: Technist kitsch? *Journal of Management Studies*, 34(1): 75–98.

O'Dwyer, B. (2002) Managerial perceptions of corporate social disclosure. *Accounting, Auditing and Accountability Journal*, 15(3): 106–36.

O'Dwyer, B. (2003) Conceptions of corporate social responsibility: The nature of managerial capture. *Accounting, Auditing and Accountability Journal*, 16(4): 523–57.

O'Dwyer, B. (2005) The construction of a social account: A case study in an overseas aid agency. *Accounting, Organizations and Society*, 30(10): 279–96.

Owen, D., Swift, T. and Hunt, K. (2001) Questioning the role of stakeholder engagement in social and ethical accounting, auditing and reporting. *Accounting Forum*, 25(3): 264–82.

Owen, D., Swift, T., Humphrey, C. and Bowerman, M. (2000) The new social audits: Managerial capture or the agenda of social champions. *European Accounting Review*, 9(1): 81–98.

Patton, D. (1992) Intra-industry environmental disclosures in response to the Alaskan oil spill: A note on legitimacy theory. *Accounting, Organizations and Society*, 17(5): 471–5.

Puxty, A. G. (1991) Social accountability and universal pragmatics. *Advances in Public Interest Accounting*, 4: 35–46.

Rees, W. (2000) Eco-footprint analysis: Merits and brickbats. *Ecological Economics*, 32: 121–30.

Schaltegger, S. and Burritt, R. (2000) *Contemporary environmental accounting: Issues, concepts and practice*. Sheffield: Greenleaf.

Smircich, L. (1983) Concepts of culture and organisational analyses. *Administrative Science Quarterly*, 28: 339–58.

SustainAbility and United Nations Environment Programme (2000) *The global reporters*. London: SustainAbility and United Nations Environment Programme.

SustainAbility and United Nations Environment Programme (2002) *Trust us: The global reporters 2002 survey of corporate sustainability reporting*. London: SustainAbility and United Nations Environment Programme.

SustainAbility and United Nations Environment Programme (2004) *Risk and opportunity: Best practice in non-financial reporting*. London: SustainAbility and United Nations Environment Programme.

Thomson, I. and Bebbington, J. (2005) Social and environmental reporting in the UK: A pedagogic evaluation. *Critical Perspectives on Accounting*, 16(5): 507–33.

Tinker, A. M., Lehman, C. and Neimark, M. (1991) Falling down the hole in the middle of the road: Political quietism in corporate social reporting. *Accounting, Auditing and Accountability Journal*, 4(2): 28–54.

Unerman, J. and Bennett, M. (2004) Increased stakeholder dialogue and the internet: Towards greater corporate accountability or reinforcing capitalist hegemony? *Accounting, Organizations and Society*, 29(7): 685–707.

Von Weizsäcker, Ernst, Lovins, Amory and Lovins, Hunter (1998) *Factor four: Doubling wealth, halving resource use*. London: Earthscan.

Wackernagel, M. and Rees, W. (1996) *Our ecological footprint: Reducing human impact on the Earth*. Philadelphia: New Society Publishers.

Chapter 13

Sustainability accounting and accountability in the public sector

Amanda Ball and Suzana Grubnic

INTRODUCTION

The agenda for research and practice in sustainability accounting and accountability has been played out in an almost exclusively for-profit, corporate setting. In comparison, the huge potential of the public sector for advancing the agenda is often overlooked. We see a need to rectify this situation, and hope that this chapter will stimulate enthusiasm among practitioners, students and researchers for sustainability accounting and accountability in public sector organizations (PSOs).

So, what is it about the public sector that deserves our attention? Size, for one thing. Internationally, the public sector accounts for some 40 per cent of all economic activity. Its huge operational impacts on the environment, society and economy *alone* suggest that it is time to find out how sustainability accounting and accountability in the public sector might help move things forward. As an example, in the New Zealand public sector,

> The combined central and local government sectors consume approximately one fifth of GDP. Collectively, central government is the country's biggest employer, largest landowner, and consumes significant proportions of resources. It has been estimated . . . that central government (including the police, defence force, health, universities, etc.) and local government consume some 2.6 billion KWh of energy per annum and release 0.6 million tonnes of $CO2$ equivalents per annum.[1]

This chapter will emphasize more than just the scale of the public sector, however. It will argue that there are fundamental differences between public and private sector[2] organizations. PSOs exist to deliver on public policy, and have a social value base and purpose. These underlying reasons for existing lead to PSOs assuming far greater responsibilities for sustainable development (hereafter SD) than the corporate sector has ever been expected to take on. What is needed, therefore, is a distinctive agenda for sustainability accounting and accountability in the public sector. By which we mean one which properly reflects the potential of PSOs as policy bodies in translating the heroic demands of the environmental agenda into tangible policies and programmes, and thus giving substance to the idea of living sustainably on the planet.

To set the context for the chapter we first explain: what forms of organization can be considered PSOs; what responsibilities for SD fall to PSOs; and what accounting and accountability mechanisms are employed or desirable in relation to these responsibilities. We then turn to some developments in practice (note that we tend to focus on UK public sector initiatives because this is where we have done most of our research). This allows us to think about the possible impact of practice and to evaluate its merits relative to what might be desirable. Our objective is to highlight some problems, opportunities and future prospects for sustainability accounting and accountability research and practice in relation to the array of organizations which make up this complex but compelling sector.

WHAT DO WE MEAN BY THE PUBLIC SECTOR?

In order to consider what the concepts of sustainability accounting and accountability mean for PSOs, we first need to explain what kinds of organizations make up the public sector, and what they do. The following attempt by two leading public sector accounting researchers to delineate the public sector is a good start:

> The public sector is that part of a nation's economic activity which is traditionally owned and controlled by government . . . the public sector is composed of those public organizations which provide utilities and services to the community and which have traditionally been seen as essential to the fabric of our society.
>
> (Broadbent and Guthrie, 1992, p. 3)

Following the emphasis in this definition on *government ownership and control*, the public sector includes:

- National government ministries, departments and executive agencies;
- Regional government authorities;
- Local government authorities, health care providers and emergency service organizations;
- Public corporations and trading funds; and
- An array of other research and educational institutions and foundations.

Still maintaining an emphasis on *government ownership and control*, a practical approach is to define the public sector as those organizations included in Whole of Government Accounts (WGA – these use Generally Accepted Accounting Principles to produce a single set of consolidated accounts for the public sector as if it were a single entity).[3] Table 13.1 shows PSOs which fall within UK WGA.

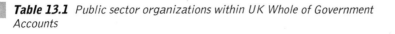

Table 13.1 *Public sector organizations within UK Whole of Government Accounts*

Central government
Comprises:

- 58 Departments
- 197 Non-departmental public bodies (NDPBs)[a]
- 51 Government central funds

Departments are legally part of the crown, receive funding from Parliament, and exist to implement policy and advise ministers. Examples: Department of Health, Ministry of Defence, Office of the Deputy Prime Minister.

NDPBs are not legally part of a government department, but are funded principally through grants from sponsoring a government department. They exist to carry out set functions within a government framework, or to act in an advisory capacity. Examples: Arts Council of England, the Environment Agency, Basic Skills Agency, Economic and Social Research Council, and the Tate Gallery.

Government central funds (sub-classified into trusts and pension schemes). Examples: Consolidated Fund, and Armed Forces Pension Scheme.

Central government in the UK encompasses devolved administrations in Scotland (the Scottish Parliament), Wales (the National Assembly for Wales) and Northern Ireland (the Northern Ireland Assembly).

Local government
The local government organizations listed in UK WGA are statutorily separate bodies, funded through a combination of local taxes, government grants and charges for services, and are responsible for the provision of services in a defined geographical area. Primary local government services are education, social services, housing, local planning, local highways, environmental health, and refuse collection and disposal. The following are listed:

| | Geographical area | | | |
	England	Scotland	Wales	N. Ireland
Unitary	47	33	22	
District	238			26
County	34			
Metropolitan	36			
London Borough	33			
Greater London Authority & Functional	5			
Police	37	6	4	
Fire	30	6	3	
Waste Disposal	6			
Passenger Transport	6	1	1	
Parks Authority	9	2	3	

continued on p. 246

Table 13.1 – Continued

National Health Service
Health care trusts are legally separate bodies, derive income mainly from primary care trusts, and provide health services to the population:

	Geographical area		
	England	Wales	N. Ireland
Non-Foundation Trust	279		
Foundation Trust	25	14	19

The UK WGA lists National Health Service trusts in England, Wales and Northern Ireland, but not for Scotland. There are no NHS trusts with statutory powers in Scotland following the NHS Reform (Scotland) Bill passed on 6 May 2004. The bill provides a legislative framework to proposals set out in the White Paper, *Partnerships for Care*, published in February 2003. The bill places a duty on Ministers and Health Boards to promote health improvement. The NHS in Scotland is organized into 15 Health Boards, 6 Special Health Boards and the Mental Welfare Commission. Health Boards are responsible for allocating funds, developing local health plans and taking part in regional and national planning. Health Boards have been involved in establishing Community Health Partnerships in an attempt to integrate primary care and specialist services with social care. The 'Scottish Health Statistics' publishes *Scottish Health Service Costs* (*Cost Book*) and reveals numbers of secondary care organizations and some primary care organizations. For the year April 2004 to March 2005, 89 hospitals excluding long-stay hospitals and 200 long-stay hospitals are listed. As at 1 October 2005, 1,050 GP practice addresses are listed and gives an indication of the level of primary care. Numbers of dentists, opticians and pharmacists are not given. The NHS also includes community services such as those provided by district nurses, health visitors and midwives.

Public corporations and trading funds
Legally separate bodies that derive at least 50% of income from the sale of goods and services to the general public. Seventy are listed in UK WGA. Examples: British Broadcasting Corporation, Meteorological Office, and Companies House.

Source: UK Whole of Government Accounts website, see www.wga.gov.uk, CPIDFA.v2pdfdocument, accessed 17 March 2006.
Note: [a] We note that not all NDPBs are included in UK WGA. In fact, there are over 1,000 NDPBs listed on the Cabinet Office website, see http//www.direct.gov.uk/Gtgll/GuideToGovernment/fs/en, accessed 13 June 2006

Whilst Table 13.1 demonstrates something of the great diversity of the public sector and PSO activities, in order to progress our discussion we also need to understand more about what makes PSOs *distinctive*. This question is hugely important, and has driven academic debate over many years. The central concern has been about whether there is any real difference between the nature of the tasks performed by public and private sector organizations. Broadbent and Guthrie's (1992) definition of the public sector makes reference to this distinction through its emphasis on 'services to the *community*' which are 'essential to the *fabric of our society*' (emphasis added).

Boston *et al.* (1996) provide an illustration of the controversies which set the context for the sector. Their example centres on the possibility of 'contracting out' prison management (under contracting out public sector authorities retain responsibility for providing and funding services and maintaining standards, but delivery is undertaken by another, sometimes commercial, organization):

> Advocates of contracting out argue that public ownership and control tends to be wasteful and inefficient – characterised by rigid work practices, excessive staffing levels, and provider capture. They contend that exposing prison management to the rigours of competition will yield significant gains in productive efficiency, as well as more innovative and humane penal management practices. Critics . . . point to the problems of specifying desired outcomes, establishing appropriate performance targets, monitoring subsequent performance, and enforcing the relevant contractual obligations . . . they . . . note the potential risks of opportunistic behaviour on the part of commercially orientated prison managers . . . critics . . . also argue that, as a matter of principle, the imposition of punishment on behalf of the community should be undertaken by institutions of a wholly public nature. Only in this way . . . can the community signify, directly and unequivocally, its abhorrence of actions that violate commonly accepted norms.
>
> (Boston *et al.*, 1996, p. 8)

The prison service is a 'social ordering' (Pollitt, 2003) or 'guardianship' (Le Grand, 2003) function. In most countries governments take on these tasks, which include law and order, defence, education, health care, housing, and social care. These tasks can also be thought of as keeping the population safe from threats of discord, violence or, more broadly, *freedom from fear*. When Aneurin Bevan spoke of freedom of fear as justification for the establishment of the National Health Service in the UK in 1948, he was referring to the fear of illness by the working class and the fear of not having the means to pay for care (Pollock, 2004; Lessing, 1998; and see Quirk, 2005).

Some public sector tasks, then, result from political decisions, influenced by what society perceives as needs and also doing the right thing. This means that some PSO functions (like the prison service) have a high degree of political salience, because it falls to some PSOs to bring to fruition the 'heroic aspirations' (Pollitt, 2003, p. 12) of politicians to take action on public concerns. In the UK, the responsibilities of the prison service, for example, encompass the challenges of looking after convicted prisoners 'with humanity' and helping them 'lead law-abiding and useful lives'.[4] It is for these sorts of reasons that Boston *et al.* point to the view that some tasks like providing a prison service fall to public agencies *as a matter of principle*.

Alternatively, some services are argued to be too risky and/or unprofitable for private competitors to supply. Boston *et al.* raise the spectre of self-interested, 'commercial' behaviour on the part of prison managers. For example, private sector

247

involvement in the prison service might lead to a perverse motive to keep prisons full. Under contracting out arrangements, it is in the interest of the private sector to receive payments – whereas it is in the public interest to keep crime numbers low. Some services are also characterized by 'consequentiality' – that is, whether or not services can afford to make mistakes (Pollitt, 2003). Certainly, in the UK, the company Securicor became a household name following a string of breakouts by convicted prisoners from the hands of guards in Securicor's prisoner-escort service.

From an economist's perspective, the prison service is explained as a 'public good'. The basic idea here is that the prison service (as an example) would be undersupplied if left to competitive markets because it is difficult to exclude individuals from using the protective benefits the service offers.[5] The economist's argument is that without general taxation, less than scrupulous citizens would 'free ride' since they would benefit from the service whether or not they paid towards it. The result is under-supply.

Finally, public sector work is sometimes 'thankless and often unpleasant' (Pollitt, 2003, p. 10) or seemingly mundane, a situation compounded by a lack of resources; and so the work simply falls to the public sector because no one else is prepared to do it (Ball and Seal, 2005). So a further underlying issue is whether people working in PSOs with social purposes such as prisons have more ethical motivations in comparison to people employed in the private sector. Ethically motivated reasons for working in PSOs (a public sector ethos) have been reported in research studies (including Brewis, 1999; Boyne, 2002), whereas private sector managers are more strongly motivated by personal economic prosperity (Boyne, 2002).

These issues of difference between the public and private sector tasks are not simply a matter of academic debate. Crucially, a belief that there is little underlying difference between the sectors and their activities (except that the public sector is less efficient) has influenced drastic changes that have taken place in the public sector internationally since the 1980s (Boston et al., 1996; Broadbent and Guthrie, 1992; Olsen et al., 1998; Pollitt, 2003; Guthrie et al., 2005). This belief has combined with a number of factors to undermine the traditional model encapsulated in Broadbent and Guthrie's (1992) definition of the public sector. Perhaps most notable is an entrenched public scepticism towards 'big government' – as reflected in sentiments about 'rigid work practices, excessive staffing levels, and provider capture' in the 'contracting out' side of the argument in Boston et al.'s prison service example. The reforms, often referred to as New Public Management (hereafter NPM, see Hood, 1991, 1995), have included the privatization of many publicly owned industries (selling off the organization's assets on the stock exchange to create for-profit companies); contracting-out services; and the creation of 'public–private partnerships' (where public objectives are pursued by partnerships of public and commercial organizations, see Pollitt, 2003).

These changes are continuing to evolve and provide an important context within which we must evaluate PSO sustainability accounting and accountability. The authors maintain, however, that public service tasks must still be understood in terms of a social value base and a public service ethos; and that PSOs still play a crucial role as policy bodies in social welfare.

PSOs AND SD

What, then, are the responsibilities of the public sector for SD? Answering this question is key to establishing what sustainability accounting and accountability might mean in the public sector. At a first level, in common with any private sector organization, PSOs arguably have responsibilities for implementing sound 'housekeeping' measures – that is, taking measures for the sound management of operational impacts on the economy, environment and society. Even at this first level, however, we argue that there is widespread acceptance that there are higher expectations of *public* (as opposed to private) organizations to set high standards (Pollitt, 2003, p. 10) in respect of good housekeeping:

> Public agencies . . . have a *civic responsibility* to properly manage public goods, resources, and/or facilities in a way that promotes sustainable development objectives and promotes the public interest . . . Given their size and influence, public agencies are expected to *lead by example* in reporting publicly and transparently on their activities to promote sustainability.
>
> (Global Reporting Initiative, *Sector Supplement for Public Agencies*, 2005, pp. 7–8, emphasis added)

> Government will *lead by example*. The UK Government buys £13 billion worth of goods and services each year. For the wider public sector this figure is £125 billion. We want to ensure that we spend your money sustainably, starting with a commitment to buy cleaner cars and by our new offsetting scheme to reduce the carbon impacts of air travel.
>
> (Prime Minister Tony Blair's foreword to UK national SD strategy [HM Government, 2005, p. 3], emphasis added)

This chapter has argued, however, that it is the nature of the tasks performed, a social value base and a role in public policy, that sets the public sector apart from the private sector. The basic reasons why the public sector exists explored in the chapter so far also set the context for the responsibilities PSOs take on for SD. These responsibilities extend much further than good/green housekeeping.

Commitments made at major international conferences (including the 1992 United Nations Conference on Environment and Development in Rio, and the 2002 United Nations World Summit on Sustainable Development in Johannesburg), and in international treaties on climate change, ozone protection, marine pollution, hazardous waste, world heritage (and so on), have influenced many governments in producing national strategies for SD – such as the recent UK strategic framework, *Securing the future: Delivering UK sustainable development strategy* (HM Government, 2005). Of course, the SD agenda is not driven solely by government. But government's role in framing the broad political discourse, in developing legislative frameworks to embed responsible wealth creation (Porritt, 2004) and in re-defining broad public policy objectives through the lens of SD are crucial if we are to learn to live sustainably.

Thinking back to our earlier discussion, there is probably no better illustration of *heroic aspirations* for the outcomes of public policy than the SD agenda; or of *freedom from fear* of the consequences of having grown our economic system beyond the capacity of the surrounding ecosystem to sustain it:

> Make the wrong choices now and future generations will live with changed climate, depleted resources and without the green space and biodiversity that contribute both to our standard of living and our quality of life. Each of us needs to make the right choices to secure a future that is fairer, where we can all live within our environmental limits. That means sustainable development.
>
> (HM Government, 2005, p. 3)

As this chapter has argued, the promises and commitments made by governments have a significant impact on PSOs. The UK national strategy, for example, is intended to act as a catalyst to improving the overall response to SD in the public sector. The global and national agenda leads to a cascade effect, whereby PSOs take on responsibilities for SD of *whole orders* of importance over the demands placed on the private sector.

Even a cursory review of the UK government's Sustainable Development Unit (SDU) website[6] amply illustrates this point. Primary government departments have been asked to identify 'high level contributions' to delivering the national strategy; whilst all central government departments were required to produce a Sustainable Development Action Plan by the end of 2005. Departments are likely to delegate these responsibilities to other PSOs (CIPFA, 2005). Table 13.2 shows the contributions identified by the National Health Service. Importantly, though, the government's SDU website acknowledges that SD 'cannot be achieved by Government alone' and seems to us to illustrate the dependence of government on the involvement in SD of more or less the *whole gamut* of PSOs identified in Table 13.1.

For example, amongst *Non-Departmental Public Bodies (NDPBs)*, the government's SDU singles out the Environment Agency, English Nature and the Sustainable Development Commission as 'essential to the monitoring and delivery' of SD. Twenty-five other NDPBs are listed and identified as 'involved with the delivery of

Table 13.2 NHS high level commitments to SD

1. The National Health Service (NHS) as a Corporate Citizen. This has been identified as one of the NHS Chief Executive's five new priorities for the next ten years. As part of that work we will fund the Sustainable Development Commission Healthy Futures programme to develop the capacity of NHS organizations to act as good corporate citizens.

2. Food and Health Action Plan. We will work with the farming and food industries to coordinate action, including action to take forward policies in this Strategy, through a Food and Health Action Plan to be published in early 2005 fulfilling the commitment to such a plan in our Strategy for Sustainable Farming and Food. This will be backed up with wider action in the Food Standards Agency Strategic Plan.

3. Transport and Health. Following evaluation, we will build on the Sustainable Travel Towns pilots to develop guidance for local authorities, Primary Care Trusts (PCTs) and others on whole-town approaches to shifting travel from cars to walking, cycling and public transport.

4. Healthy Sustainable Communities. We will extend the current healthy communities initiative to more deprived communities from 2006, and we will use collaborative techniques to support action through local partnerships. We are also giving PCTs the means to tackle health inequalities and improve health.

5. Health Impact. Department of Health representatives located in the regions will lead the work with regional and local government and the NHS to ensure that regional partner policies and activities take account of their health impact, e.g. housing, transport, planning, employment, education and skills, environment, rural affairs, crime and community safety.

Source: UK Government Sustainable Development Unit website, see http://www.sustainable-development.gov.uk/government/department/index.htm, accessed 27 March 2006

sustainable development' – including the Commission for Racial Equality, the National Forest Company, and the Scottish Environment Protection Agency.

Links are provided to the *devolved administrations* for Scotland, Wales and Northern Ireland. Although their roles in SD are not explained, it is pertinent to note that the Welsh Assembly is required *by statute* to promote SD in the exercise of its functions. Specifically, the Assembly is required under section 121 of the Government of Wales Act 1998 to prepare a scheme for how actions will enable further progress on SD. The latest scheme published in 2004 is entitled 'Starting to Live Differently' and supersedes the first Sustainable Development Scheme adopted in 2000.[7] We argue that these schemes constitute – potentially – a very powerful framing device for that Government, and should cascade into departmental initiatives.

There is also reference to the role of *regional government* in SD, including the Regional Development Agencies set up by government to 'be the strategic drivers of sustainable economic development'.

In referring to *local government authorities*, the website stresses the importance placed in the national SD strategy on partnership working with local government. More generally, many local authorities have been pursuing SD for a number of years, developing initiatives which can be tracked back to Rio, 1992, and which have culminated in an agenda for sustainable communities (Ball, 2002, 2005a; CIPFA,

2005). As Christie (2000, p. 18) summarizes, '[i]f one examines Agenda 21, as developed at the Rio Summit of 1992, approximately half the actions essential to putting us on a path towards sustainable development within this century must be taken . . . by local government'.

To summarize, it falls to many PSOs as policy bodies to assume responsibilities for moving the SD agenda forward. Notably, this brief review of those responsibilities suggests a different way of dividing up the public sector from the approach taken so far in the chapter (in Table 13.1, for example, with divisions for government departments, NDPBs etc.). Alternatively, the public sector can be divided up between PSOs with missions with a substantial environmental or SD component; and PSOs who must re-define core responsibilities and tasks (such as health, education and justice) through an SD lens. For PSOs in the latter category, we see this initial responsibility as hugely important in a society which is itself a long way from understanding the implications of SD – except, perhaps, 'that it must be about how we progress from the current non-sustainable state, to some future, more sustainable existence' (O'Riordan, 1998, p. 102). Accordingly, government departments like the NHS, for example, are taking their first, seemingly tentative, steps towards understanding high-level commitments to SD.

More optimistically, we see an affinity between a public service ethos and the notions of community and fair resource distribution inherent in SD. In contrast, corporate priorities lie with the providers of share capital rather than the well-being of the community or surrounding ecosystems; and it is simply inappropriate to 'ask corporations to take . . . decisions that affect our futures' (Gray and Bebbington, 2001, p. 316; and cf. Matten et al., 2003, and O'Dwyer, 2003).

ACCOUNTING AND ACCOUNTABILITY FOR SD IN PSOs

We now turn to the question of what accounting and accountability mechanisms are desirable in relation to PSO responsibilities for SD. We see the development of sustainability accounting in the public sector as desirable if it *enables progress* on SD. In this context, we see sustainability accounting as useful if it can be used to define what is an organizationally or institutionally significant contribution (cf. Hopwood, 1978, p. 57); as a vehicle for envisaging how policies and programmes translate well-intentioned, but vague political objectives for SD into action and change; and as a frame of reference for developing a basic understanding of how natural systems work and developing a precautionary approach to undertaking core tasks and activities.

Linked to our argument that it has fallen to many PSOs to take the lead on the SD agenda, we see disclosures about how the organization's primary policies, programmes and services are linked to SD as the key to developing a PSO sustainability accounting and accountability agenda. The critical lesson from ongoing assessment of corporate sustainability disclosures (UNEP/SustainAbility, 1994, 1996, 1997, 2000, 2002, 2004) has been an unwillingness to question underlying business models and engage with the essential issues of sustainability impacts:

> Usually, the critical issues are linked directly to the company's core business, yet they are often ignored. A biotechnology-based company fails to refer to genetic engineering, for example, or an auto or oil industry [report] chooses to ignore the global warming agenda. The banks are also a prime example of this problem: they are happy to discuss green housekeeping measures, but most provide little or no information on the social and environmental issues associated with their mainstream financial activities.
>
> (UNEP/SustainAbility, 1997, p. 28)

Analogously, in the public sector the 'essential issues' are to do with identifying 'high level commitments' (as government has put it) and re-defining policy objectives through the lens of SD. Thus we envisage sustainability accounting which encompasses an account not only of the importance of good 'housekeeping' (better management of estate; green procurement; efficiencies in waste, energy, transport and so on); but of policy and programmes for action on SD.

Following its development, we see sustainability accounting in PSOs as providing the basis of structured information about what the organization is contributing. One potential benefit is that people in organizations use the account of the actions on SD as the basis of further action, which will in turn allow greater possibility for development of sustainability accounting (Ball et al., forthcoming). And ultimately this information could provide the basis of external evaluation – i.e. accountability, or 'being held to account for . . . actions' (Stewart, 1995, p. 26) on SD in the wider society and culture.

Whilst we argue that sustainability disclosures by PSOs are generally desirable, a key factor in the uptake of sustainability accounting and accountability will be the development of tangible measures to guide, encourage and legitimize practice. These emerging measures, in turn, will be important in influencing the nature of disclosures, and therefore deserve the attention of researchers and students. Accordingly, we now briefly consider some key developments in the UK PSO context.

There are at present no mandatory or voluntary standards agreed by governments in the UK to encourage sustainability accounting and accountability across the wider public sector (NAO, 2005; Ball, 2005b).[8] In the context of government departments, however, a 'Framework for Sustainable Development on the Government Estate' developed by the Department for Environment, Food and Rural Affairs has recently been used to coordinate a whole government report on SD 'housekeeping' issues, including waste, energy use and procurement (see

CIPFA, 2005; NAO, 2005). Importantly, the National Audit Office (NAO, 2005, p. 16) note the insistence of government that this framework and cross-government reporting is not a substitute for individual departmental accountability for SD performance. In short, it seems that government are encouraging, if not insisting on, departments reporting on their commitments to SD.

There is a rather longer history of initiatives to encourage sustainability accounting and accountability in local government. Lewis (2000) explains how guidance from Friends of the Earth, the Local Government Management Board (LGMB) and the Local Government Association issued between 1989 to 1991 encouraged two environmental audit approaches in local government: the State of the Environment Report (SOE) (which assesses the local environment in terms of waste, air and water quality, conservation and transport etc.) and the Policy Impact Assessment (which assesses operational impact on the environment). In the mid-1990s the Audit Commission and the LGMB were encouraging uptake of environmental management systems in local government, which would (broadly) assess the environmental impact of authorities as service providers. And since about 2000, the main thrust of guidance to local authorities encourages the use of 'quality of life indicators', which are intended to track broad SD trends in a local area (see Audit Commission, 2005; Ball, 2005b; HM Government, 2005). Quality of life indicators build on a long process of development by national and local governments, going back to the World SD Summit in Rio in 1992. They are used by a large number of local authorities (some for over ten years) to track and understand local sustainability issues (Audit Commission, 2005; Ball, 2005a, 2005b; Bennet and van der Lugt, 2004).

There is a welcome, if very recent, trend towards the key institutions of public sector accountancy responding to the SD accounting and accountability agenda. The National Audit Office has indicated its willingness to be involved in 'any government initiative to help develop and promote good sustainable development reporting' (NAO, 2005, p 3).

A more prominent development is the involvement of the Chartered Institute of Public Finance and Accountancy (CIPFA) – the predominant body for public sector accounting and finance in the UK – in issuing a discussion paper on how to advance sustainability reporting in PSOs (Ball, 2005; Ball and Soare, 2005). Building on this, at the time of writing CIPFA published a framework for PSO sustainability reporting, produced in partnership with Forum for the Future, a leading UK SD charity (CIPFA, 2005). We see this development as potentially very influential in practice.

Finally, we anticipate that the Global Reporting Initiative (GRI) 'GRI Sector Supplement for Public Agencies' (GRI, 2004) will be of some influence in the UK public sector, based on the GRI's claims to provide the basis of worldwide standardized, comparable, reporting on sustainability (GRI, 2002). For example, the Supplement forms the substantive basis of a review by the National Audit Office of government departments' attempts at accounting for their high-level responses to SD. Advancing the triple bottom line concept developed for use in the private sector, the GRI (2004) advocate sustainability reporting as a vehicle to assess operational economic, environmental and social impacts of government agencies. We argue, however, that the Supplement gives inadequate attention to the central issue of policy responsibilities and impacts. Pertinently, the NAO similarly argue that the Supplement would need 'further adaptation' (NAO, 2005, p. 9) because of its focus on disclosure on 'housekeeping operations, with less attention to the disclosure of policy impacts and outcomes' (NAO, 2005, p. 7).

On the plus side, the GRI Supplement arguably emphasizes disclosures on inclusiveness in policy making, placing particular emphasis on stakeholder engagement. Such disclosures in public sector SD reports represent a key accountability mechanism because of the fundamental need for democratic involvement in the direction and governance of public institutions (Broadbent, 1999), and in the evaluation of policy outcomes. For PSO organizations which are grappling with the implications of SD, there is arguably no substitute for the involvement of individual citizens and groups who bring their knowledge and insights to test and stimulate engagement with SD (cf. Medawar, 1978). In this context, we note that PSOs are already adept at developing stakeholder relations, providing the opportunity of 'voice' through a number of mechanisms ranging from user group consultations to individual satisfaction questionnaires. A series of papers by Hill *et al.* (1997, 1998, 2001) on the implementation of a social audit within general practice in southern Scotland is a notable contribution in this context, with social audit conceived of as 'an open participatory process of dialogue which assesses and reports on the social relationships and performance of the health centre'(1998, p. 1481).

To summarize, efforts are now being made by a number of important institutions of government and accountancy to bring some pressure to bear on PSOs in disclosing performance on SD. These are important in highlighting what might be desirable – for example, the need for attention to policy outcomes (rather than just housekeeping) and attention to inclusiveness in policy-making. At this critical stage when PSOs are being encouraged to make disclosures, we see a need for researchers and students to provide more by way of a theoretical background to inform the development of emerging frameworks for sustainability accounting and accountability. In an overview chapter such as this there is not really scope for a conceptual contribution, but we are mindful here of the work of Burritt and Welch (1997a) in drawing attention to emphasizing stakeholder accountability and the imperative of living within the limits of natural systems.

Key factors in whether the idea of sustainability accounting and accountability will travel and be taken up more widely include sustained effort and resource on the part of those institutions who want to do the promoting (Ball and Soare, 2005; Hopwood, 1978). This means there is also an important role for researchers in engaging directly with the powerful institutions of accounting and government who will lend legitimacy to emerging frameworks (Ball and Soare, 2005). There is also the question of the extent to which PSOs are able or willing to respond to demands for accounting and disclosure. And it is to these questions that we now turn.

ASSESSMENT OF PSO SUSTAINABILITY ACCOUNTING AND ACCOUNTABILITY

Many PSOs are already adept at reporting on their social roles in communities, and we argue that this *should* provide something of a basis for accounting and accountability on SD. PSOs must meet corporate, for-profit standards of accountability (i.e. demonstrating proper financial stewardship), but also have '*an additional dimension of accountability in respect of their not-for-profit objectives*' (Perrin, 1985, p. 22, emphasis in original). There is currently intense interest in understanding and measuring the *outcomes* (effectiveness) of policies, for example social inclusion, child safety, and student performance in schools. Whilst this is much more elusive than measuring input or output factors – for example, places or spending in schools (Sanderson, 2001) – nevertheless, it has *in part* been demonstrated through non-financial measures and narratives. A key question, therefore, is whether existing commitments to *social accountability* provide any basis for *sustainability accounting and accountability*.

Drawing on our discussion so far, however, we see two key factors as limiting the ability of PSOs to work towards sustainability accounting and accountability. First, in the context of materially affluent, capitalistic societies like the UK, SD is a radical political concept. It challenges deeply held beliefs about what constitutes human progress (economic growth, inalienable rights to high levels of personal consumption, and so on), and requires a basic understanding of ecological thresholds and how to live within the limits of natural systems. In this context, it is significant that the current UK government framework for SD for the first time removed economic growth *per se* as an objective, preferring to seek to ensure a just society where needs are met and an ecologically secure environment as the base for meeting those needs. The implications of the Framework and wider SD agenda for PSO sustainability accounting and accountability are profound; and we argue that a guiding principle must be that PSOs ultimately respond with an account of action which is proportionate to the order of challenge which SD poses.

In this context, a recent and thoughtful review of Westminster government department reporting on SD by the National Audit Office (NAO) is important in providing not only insights into how well departments are doing in terms of discharging accountability for performance, but also for its insights into how departments have responded to taking on responsibilities for SD *per se* (NAO, 2005). These two matters are inextricably linked.

For example, the NAO found that departments with a substantial environmental

256

component to their tasks seem more adept at reporting than others without this component. And across all reporters, SD is more often treated as an environmental (as opposed to social justice or economic) issue. And departments generally were reporting on operational or 'housekeeping' issues, but far fewer reports made links between key policies issues and the government's SD framework (even though, as we noted earlier, major departments have been asked to identify their high-level commitments to the SD framework).

We see all of these findings as reflecting the order of challenge many departments may face in re-framing an array of guardianship tasks (health, education, justice and so on) through the lens of SD. More specific findings are also instructive here. For example, the NAO (2005) cite the Department of Trade and Industry report as disclosing the aim of 'prosperity for all' (p. 13) (another heroic aspiration!), which indicates a broad vision or direction of travel; whereas the Department for Education and Skills had not linked its strategic aims to an SD framework. Similarly, few departments had conceived of defined SD outcomes (p. 26). An example of the latter is the Department of Work and Pension's vision of 'end[ing] child poverty by 2010' (p. 13). For this department, at least, it seems that sustainability accounting is serving a role in defining what is organizationally significant.

More generally, the NAO findings seem to us to hint at how, if left unsupported, PSOs could simply be confounded by the sustainability accounting/accountability agenda because the underlying need to un-bundle the implications of SD is simply too difficult to deal with. For example, in the education and health sectors there is a long-standing liberal-democratic tradition of social justice, which has to do with equality of opportunity and access so that life chances depend on motivation and aptitude and not on such factors as class, gender or ethnicity. And, intuitively, health care and education organizations would seem to have a key role in at least one of the five key principles in the national SD strategy (HM Government, 2005) – i.e. 'ensuring a strong, healthy and just society'. It seems to us that what is being asked of public sector education and health sector organizations is the question of how traditions of social justice (doing the right thing as a matter of principle in Boston et al.'s terms) are linked with a sustainability agenda. But this question actually represents an extraordinarily complex political and moral agenda, which has so far eluded most governments and, indeed, the environmental movement itself (Foley et al., 2005).

What comes out of all this is a need for researchers and students to make contributions of a fundamental nature, which help in understanding the nature of SD accounting and accountability in PSOs whose core tasks have to do with social welfare and justice. As an indication of what is required, for example, we see a need to ask fundamental questions about the forms of service provision (location, scale, processes of delivery etc.) that better protect and enhance the life of citizens.

The second factor which we see as important in PSOs' ability to respond to the

257

sustainability accounting and accountability agenda is the tremendous influence of the NPM, linked to such intellectual drivers as the 're-invention of government' (Osborne and Plastrik, 1997) and the widely held belief that PSOs offer low standards and poor VFM (Taylor Gooby, 2005) In the UK public sector the 'Gershon Report' (Gershon, 2004) is the most recent example of this continuing 'reforming' influence on Government policy, identifying auditable and transparent efficiency gains of over £20 billion in 2007–08 across the public sector.

The danger here is that, under intense political pressure to find savings, public sector managers will at best be 'incentivized' to look for 'controllable, efficiency-based environmental measures . . . such as recycling, energy efficiency, and waste management . . . [which] are easier to manage . . . than environmental matters which challenge basic values and assumptions' (Burritt and Welch, 1997b, pp. 6–7). Indeed, Burritt and Welch (1997b) examined the environmental disclosures of Commonwealth (national government) entities in Australia, and found that under the commercial orientation of the reforms, there is a tendency for a dampening effect on environmental disclosures *per se*, and a concentration on 'easier to manage' environmental issues.

Similarly, a programme of work by Ball (Ball, 2002, 2005a, 2005b, forthcoming; Ball and Soare, 2005; Ball and Seal, 2005) examines how NPM policies for 'modernization' affect local government authorities' capacity to respond to the sustainability accounting agenda. This work indicates the need for research that engages with questions of how the regulatory frameworks under which PSOs operate can be changed – so that sustainability accounting/accountability is integrated into existing, mainstream systems for accounting and accountability. On a positive note, Ball *et al.* (forthcoming) point to the potential for public authorities to demand sustainability reporting as a condition of the contracting process in public–private partnerships (PPPs) in environmentally sensitive services such as waste management. In this context, PPPs are highlighted as a fascinating focus for researchers to explore the relative commitments of public and private sector players to the SD agenda, and in relation to reconciling the interests of different stakeholders. More generally, however, there is a dearth of work which has sought to understand the extent of sustainability disclosures in the wider public sector and the capacity of PSOs to respond to demands for sustainability accounting and accountability.

The GRI (2004) presents a good attempt to overview developments internationally, providing for example insights into work in Eastern countries such as Japan, and also countries such as Mexico. Ball (2005b) overviews developments from a UK perspective and (on a positive note) indicates some significant innovations that have come from the public sector. For example, for the devolved governments of both Wales and Scotland, there are reports that provide an ecological footprint analysis.[9] These footprints are being developed by an increasing number of public sector organizations (Audit Commission, 2005) to capture resource use and environmental impacts as a result of community consumption, and are supplemented with information on resource flows and narratives. As an example of a narrative, scenario reporting enables an understanding of what a sustainable Wales might look like. Using the state of the environment reports, the ecological footprint and quality of life indicators, public sector sustainability accounting has done a great deal to demonstrate the potential of moving away from the concept of the organization as the accounting entity. These approaches account and report at higher levels of aggregation (for example, looking at the cumulative effects of economic activity in a locality); and represent a huge advance in developing multi-level/multi-agency thinking on SD (Ball, 2005b; Bennet and van der Lugt, 2004). An important question for future research and practice is whether and how private sector sustainability reporting might be generated and combined with accounts produced in the public sector, so that it is also meaningful at larger scales (Bennet and van der Lugt, 2004).

There are very few qualitative studies of sustainability accounting in PSOs, but the available findings are instructive in thinking about public sector managers' values and the transformative potential of sustainability accounting. Adams *et al.* (2005) use their study of an Australian water authority's experience to highlight public sector managers' motivations and behaviour. In contrast to prior research with private sector managers (O'Dwyer, 2003), the managers here were committed to developing sustainability reporting, leading to an integration of sustainability issues into the organization's strategic planning process. These findings echo those from Ball's case studies in English and Canadian local authorities, where managers demonstrated commitment to the SD agenda and progressing sustainability accounting (Ball, 2005a, 2005b).

To summarize, simply in order to understand the extent of developments, we see a need for work on international comparison, work in different areas of the public sector to those already studied, and studies of different approaches to accounting and accountability. We are particularly concerned, however, to seeing more questioning of achievements (or otherwise) of PSOs which have experimented with sustainability accounting and accountability. We also see a role for researchers in helping those who are making these advances possible to stay engaged, to retain their organizational legitimacy, and to feel supported in a context where sustainability accounting and accountability may be viewed as too radical a concept, or not widely accepted.

CLOSING THOUGHTS

In this chapter we have sought to provide a flavour of what amounts to a very diverse and complex, but also distinctive and compelling, sector of the economy. We have highlighted the need for a distinctive agenda for sustainability accounting and accountability research and practice in the public sector, and indicated where researchers have already made contributions to understanding the outworking and transformative potential of sustainability accounting and accountability in PSOs. We have indicated numerous opportunities for opening up what amounts to a hugely important future agenda for research and practice, and so we will not repeat them all here. However, we wish to underline the importance of research which makes contributions of a fundamental nature to the development of principles and practice in PSO sustainability accounting and accountability. Following Pallot (1991) we see sustainability accounting and accountability as an opportunity to achieve a better accounting framework for PSOs in a post-NPM world. By which we mean a framework in which community perspectives can help in accounting for the tasks of PSOs, and PSO relationships and contributions in communities which live within the limits of ecological systems.

Our motivation for writing this chapter is our fundamental belief, as members of the larger society and culture, in the benefits PSOs might bring in moving the SD agenda forward, and in helping set new terms by which the next generations might live. As Medawar has argued 'it is . . . clear that the main reason why ordinary people have very little idea about what goes on in government, business and other major centres of power is not that they are not interested, but that they are not told' (Medawar, 1978, p. 36). Whilst it would be naïve to over-state the potential of sustainability accounting and accountability in transforming PSOs, we see sustainability disclosures as a key mechanism for engaging more people in the working of the public sector and in understanding its contribution to SD. We hope that we have conveyed some of our enthusiasm for work in this area – and persuaded others that it may be worthwhile.

NOTES

1   Source: Energy Efficiency and Conservation Authority Internal report to Government Energy Efficiency Leadership Programme (2000) cited in New Zealand Ministry for the Environment report on *Triple Bottom Line Reporting in the Public Sector* (2002, p. 21): see http://www.mfe.govt.nz/publications/ser/triple-bottom-line-summary-1-dec02.pdf, accessed 13 June 2006.

2   In this chapter we use the term 'private sector' to denote the for-profit corporate sector. The private sector, existing primarily for profit purposes, seeks to earn capital gains for owners, with social gains being inimical to this objective. We acknowledge, however, that many countries have significant 'third' or 'voluntary' sectors made up of *private* organizations, including charities, clubs, trade unions and so on. In this sense they are part of the private sector – but most of them do not exist to make a profit. As Perrin (1985) explains, some 'public' services can be provided from different organizational and financial frameworks that can be philanthropic in nature. For example, in the UK, most schools are publicly owned and financed by local government, but can be owned by charities or religious organizations.

3   We put Table 13.1 together to show that the public sector encompasses a wide range of organizations and activities, many of which have no connection with each other, even though they are consolidated in a single financial statement. We recognize that the use of commercial-style accounting (GAAP) may not be appropriate in the public sector; and that the use of GAAP in the public sector has been linked with government policies internationally for transferring services to the private sector or disposing of public assets (see, for example, Carlin, 2005; Newberry, 2003).

4   See   http://www.hmprisonservice.gov.uk/abouttheservice/statementofpurpose/, accessed 22 March 2006.

5   The idea that there are public goods/services for which it is impossible to sustain a competitive market is widely accepted in economic theory. The theory of public goods is generally credited to the economist Paul Samuelson (1954). For a discussion in the context of public sector accounting see Barton (1999).

6   See   http://www.sustainable-development.gov.uk/government/index.htm,   accessed 30 March 2006.

7   National Assembly for Wales (2004), *Starting to Live Differently: The Sustainable Development Scheme of the National Assembly for Wales*, National Assembly for Wales, Wales.   http://wales.gov.uk/themessustainabledev/content/review/revised-scheme-e.htm, accessed 27 March 2006.

8   We note however that there are measures in place in some states of Australia requiring the preparation of state of the environment reports, and a directive in Hong Kong approved in 1999 requiring public agencies to produce an annual environmental performance report (GRI, 2004).

9   See   http://www.scotlands-footprint.com,   and   http://www.walesfootprint.org. Documents of interest include: Best Foot Forward (BBF) (2004), *Scotland's Footprint: A Resource Flow and Ecological Footprint Analysis of Scotland*, BBF, Oxford, http://www.scotlands-footprint.com/downloads/full%20Report.pdf., and also World Wildlife Fund (WWF) and Stockholm Environment Institute (2005), *Reducing Wales' Ecological Footprint: A Resource Accounting Tool for Sustainable Consumption*, WWF, Cardiff, http://walesfootprint.org/pdf/20048WWWFAIIWaleEng.pdf, both accessed 1 March 2006.

REFERENCES

Adams, C., McNicholas, P. and Zutshi, A. (2005) Making a difference: Journeying with an organisation towards social and environmental accountability. Paper presented at the 3rd Australasian CSEAR Conference, Deakin University, 30 March–1 April.

Audit Commission (2005) *Local quality of life indicators: Supporting local communities to become sustainable*. London: Audit Commission, August.

Ball, A. (2002) *Sustainability accounting in UK local government: An agenda for research*. London: Association of Chartered Certified Accountants (ACCA) Research Report no. 78.

Ball, A. (2005a) Environmental accounting and change in UK local government. *Accounting, Auditing and Accountability Journal*, 18(3): 346–73.

Ball, A. (2005b) *Advancing sustainability reporting for public service organisations: A discussion paper*. London. Chartered Institute of Public Finance and Accountancy.

Ball, A. (forthcoming) Environmental accounting as workplace activism. *Critical Perspectives on Accounting*.

Ball, A. and Seal, W. (2005) Social justice in a cold climate: Could social accounting make a difference? *Accounting Forum*, 29(4): 455–73.

Ball, A. and Soare, V. (2005) Advancing sustainability reporting in public service organisations: Reflecting on a strategy of institutional engagement. Paper presented at the New Public Sector Workshop, University of Edinburgh Management School, 27–28 October.

Ball, A., Broadbent, J. and Jarvis, T. (forthcoming) On waste management, the challenges of the PFI, and 'sustainability accounting' as a tool to aid in implementation. *Business Strategy and the Environment*.

Barton, A. (1999) Public and private sector accounting: The non-identical twins. *Australian Accounting Review*, 9(2): 22–31.

Bennet, N. and van der Lugt, C. (2004) Tracking global governance and sustainability: Is the system working? In A. Henriques and J. Richardson (eds) *The triple bottom line: Does it all add up? Assessing the sustainability of business and CSR*. London: Earthscan, pp. 45–58.

Boston, J., Martin, J., Pallot, J. and Walsh, P. (1996) *Public management: The New Zealand model*. Auckland: Oxford University Press.

Boyne, G. A. (2002) Public and private management: What's the difference? *Journal of Management Studies*, 39(1): 97–122.

Brewis, J. (1999) On the front line: Experiences of managing the new public services. Paper presented at the 3rd International Research Conference of the Knowledge, Organizations and Society Research Unit, University of Staffordshire, April.

Broadbent, J. (1999) The state of public sector accounting research: The APIRA conference and some personal reflections. *Accounting, Auditing and Accountability Journal*, 12(1): 52–7.

Broadbent, J. and Guthrie, J. (1992) Changes in the public sector: A review of recent 'alternative' accounting research. *Accounting, Auditing and Accountability Journal*, 5(2): 3–31.

Burritt, R. L. and Welch, S. (1997a) Accountability for environmental performance of the Australian Commonwealth public sector. *Accounting, Auditing and Accountability Journal*, 10(4): 532–61.

Burritt, R. L. and Welch, S. (1997b) Australian Commonwealth entities: An analysis of their environmental disclosures. *Abacus*, 33(1): 1–19.

Carlin, T. M. (2005) Debating the impact of accrual accounting and reporting in the public sector. *Financial Accountability and Management*, 21(3): 309–36.

Chartered Institute of Public Finance and Accountancy/Forum for the Future (2005) *Sustainability reporting framework for the public services*. London: CIPFA.

Christie, I. (2000) Sustainability and modernisation: Resolving tensions by providing complementarity. Paper presented at the World Wildlife Fund UK (WWF–UK) Conference, RSA London, 15 February.

Foley, J., Grayling, T. and Dixon, M. (2005) Sustainability and social justice. In N. D. Pearce and W. Paxon (eds) *Social justice: Building a fairer Britain*. London: Politico's Publishing, pp. 178–98.

Gershon, P. (2004) Releasing resources to the front line: Independent review of public sector efficiency. London: HM Treasury, available at http://www.hm-treasury.gov.uk/media//879E2/efficiency_review120704.pdf, accessed 9 September.

Global Reporting Initiative (2002) *Sustainability reporting guidelines*. Amsterdam: GRI.

Global Reporting Initiative (2005) *Sector supplement for public agencies*, March. Amsterdam: Global Reporting Initiative.

Gray, R. and Bebbington, J. (2001) *Accounting for the environment*. London: Paul Chapman/Association of Chartered Certified Accountants, London.

GRI (2004) *Public agency sustainability reporting: A GRI resource document in support of the public agency sector supplement*. London: GRI.

Guthrie, J., Humphrey, C., Jones, L. R. and Olson, O. (eds) (2005) *International public management reform: Progress, contradictions and challenges*. Greenwich, CT: Information Age Publishing.

Hawken, P., Lovins, A. B. and Lovins, L. H. (2002) *Natural capitalism: The next industrial revolution*. London: Earthscan.

Hill, W. J., Cotton, P. and Fraser, I. (1997) Piloting the social audit in primary health care. *Social and Environmental Accounting*, 17(2): 7–10.

Hill, W. J., Fraser, I and Cotton, P. (1998) Patients' voices, rights and responsibilities: On implementing social audit in primary health care. *Journal of Business Ethics*, 17(13): 1481–97.

Hill, W. J., Fraser, I. and Cotton, P. (2001) On patients' interests and accountability: Reflecting on some dilemmas in social audit in primary health care. *Critical Perspectives on Accounting*, 12(4): 453–69.

HM Government (2005) *Securing the future: Delivering UK sustainable development strategy*, CM6467. London: The Stationery Office.

Hood, C. (1991) A public management for all seasons? *Public Administration*, 69(1): 3–19.

Hood, C. (1995) The 'new public management' in the 1980's: variations on a theme. *Accounting, Organizations and Society*, 20(2/3): 93–109.

Hopwood, A. (1978) Social accounting: the way ahead? Paper presented at a seminar on social accounting organised by the Chartered Institute of Public Finance and Accountancy, London, January.

263

Le Grand, J. (2003) *Motivations, agency, and public policy: Of knights & knaves, pawns & queens.* Oxford: Oxford University Press.

Lessing, D. (1998) *Walking in the shade: Volume two of my autobiography, 1949–1962.* London: Flamingo/HarperCollins.

Lewis, L. (2000) Environmental audits in local government: A useful means to progress in sustainable development. *Accounting Forum,* 24(3): 296–318.

Matten, D., Crane, A. and Chapple, W. (2003) Behind the mask: Revealing the true face of corporate citizenship. *Journal of Business Ethics,* 45(1–2): 109–20.

Medawar, C. (1978) Ways of measuring organisational performance. Paper presented at a seminar on social accounting organised by the Chartered Institute of Public Finance and Accountancy, London, January.

Ministry for the Environment (2002) *Triple bottom line reporting in the public sector: Summary of pilot group findings.* Wellington: Ministry for the Environment.

National Audit Office (2005) *Sustainable development reporting by government departments.* London: National Audit Office.

Newberry, S. (2003) 'Sector neutrality' and NPM 'incentives': Their use in eroding the public sector. *Australian Accounting Review,* 13(2): 28–34.

O'Dwyer, B. (2003) Conceptions of corporate social responsibility: The nature of managerial capture. *Accounting, Auditing and Accountability,* 16(4): 523–57.

O'Riordan, T. (1998) Civic science and the sustainability transition. In D. Warburton (ed) *Community and sustainable development participation for the future.* London: Earthscan, pp. 98–116.

Olsen, O., Guthrie, J. and Humphreys, C. (eds) (1998) *Global warning! Debating international developments in new public financial management.* Oslo: Cappelen Akademisk Forlag.

Osborne, D. and Plastrik, P. (1997) *Banishing bureaucracy: The five strategies for reinventing government.* Reading, MA: Addison Wesley.

Pallot, J. (1991) The legitimate concern with fairness: A comment. *Accounting, Organizations and Society,* 16(2): 201–8.

Perrin, J. R. (1985) Differentiating financial accountability and management in governments, public services and charities. *Financial Accountability and Management,* 1(1): 11–32.

Pollitt, C. (2003) *The essential public manager.* Maidenhead: Open University Press.

Pollock, A. (2004) *NHS plc: The privatisation of our health care.* London: Verso.

Porritt, J. (2004) Locating the government's bottom line. In A. Henriques and J. Richardson (eds) *The triple bottom line: Does it all add up? Assessing the sustainability of business and CSR.* London: Earthscan, pp. 59–69.

Quirk, B. (2005) For the greater good. *Public Finance,* October: 14–20.

Samuelson, P. (1954) The pure theory of public expenditure. *Review of Economics and Statistics,* 36(4): 387–9.

Sanderson, I. (2001) Performance management, evaluation and learning in 'modern' local government. *Public Administration,* 79(2): 297–313.

Stewart, J. (1984) The role of information in public accountability. In A. Hopwood and C. Tomkins (eds) *Issues in public sector accounting.* Oxford: Philip Allan, pp. 14–15.

Stewart, J. (1995) Appointed boards and local government. *Parliamentary Affairs,* 48(2): 26–241.

Taylor-Gooby, P. (2005) Attitudes to social justice. In N. D. Pearce and W. Paxon (eds) *Social justice: Building a fairer Britain.* London: Politico's Publishing, pp. 106–32.

UNEP/SustainAbility (1994) *Company environmental reporting: A measure of the progress of business & industry towards sustainable development.* London: UNEP/SustainAbility.

UNEP/SustainAbility (1996) *Engaging stakeholders: The benchmark survey.* London: UNEP/SustainAbility.

UNEP/SustainAbility (1997) *The 1997 benchmark survey: The third international progress report on company environmental reporting.* London: UNEP/SustainAbility.

UNEP/SustainAbility (2000) *The global reporters: The 2000 benchmark survey.* London: UNEP/SustainAbility.

UNEP/SustainAbility (2002) *Trust us: The global reporters 2002 survey of corporate sustainability.* London: UNEP/SustainAbility.

UNEP/SustainAbility (2004) *Risk & opportunity: Best practice in non-financial reporting.* London: UNEP/SustainAbility.

Chapter 14

Environmental and social assessment in sustainable finance

Andrea B. Coulson

INTRODUCTION

It is hard to raise finance today without some form of environmental or social assessment. As will be discussed, the motives for such 'sustainability' considerations in financial investment decisions are mixed and consequences of, on the one hand, mainstream financial institutions increasingly recognizing environmental and social risks to profitability. For example, many commercial loans now routinely contain an environmental credit risk assessment and investment portfolios contain some form of environmental and social risk consideration (Pearce and Ganzi, 2003; Coulson, 2002). On the other hand, niche products have been developed to reflect an ethical preference for how money is invested and the consequences that investment has on the environment and society. For example, premium loan rates and conditions are offered on mortgages for environmentally sensitive home improvements and investors are offered a range of specialist socially responsible investment fund opportunities (Sparkes, 2002).

As the product market in sustainable finance has developed, the margins between the mainstream and niche products have become blurred. How to evaluate the impact of social and environmental performance on profitability remains a problem for product providers and their market constituents (Stichele, 2004; Lou and Ganzi, 2002). Thus, a debate on the degree to which profit may be sacrificed for ethics is questionable, as is how to 'value' the impact of so called ethical concerns.

The purpose of this chapter is to highlight the nature of environmental and social criteria included in financial decisions and the range of approaches used by financiers to evaluate corporate environmental and social performance. While important, a debate on trading profit and ethics is set aside. In evaluating financial investment decisions it is important to note that the focus of the chapter will be on the provision of business finance. Personal finance is outside the scope of the analysis.

This chapter will address in turn the issues arising when corporate investment is financed by debt and equity, highlighting how the nature of the financial product affects environmental and social considerations. Particular attention is paid to investors' understanding of the term 'sustainability accounting and reporting', including reference to their own disclosure practice and the practical steps that have been taken to standardize decision processes and develop indices on which to benchmark the performance of their investments.

DEBT

Loan finance

It is well documented that as environmental legislation has increased bank lenders have developed risk-assessment procedures to offset potential liability for environmental damage caused by their borrowers.[1] Lenders have been particularly concerned that they may be directly liable for contaminated land taken as security for a debt, a traditional method of credit risk mitigation, or that they face the indirect environmental risk of credit default if a borrower's environmental costs adversely impact their ability to repay a loan (Smith, 1994). In addition, there is evidence that the increased scale and frequency of pollution incidents and natural disasters has provoked lenders to adopt environmental and social credit policies (Coulson, 2002, 2001; Ulph et al., 1999). It is unclear whether in such instances lenders are accepting some form of social responsibility or seeking to limit risk to their reputation through association with a polluter or a combination of both. From an ethical perspective it has been argued that a lender financing corporate activity should take some responsibility for the social and environmental impact of their transactions as a form of good corporate governance.

In response to liability debates in particular, lenders have argued that it is not their role to police corporate activities (BBA, 1993). However, in addition to environmental assessments, social concerns are increasingly becoming an addition to many high street banks' credit assessment procedures with 'sustainability' concerns governed by a combination of a bank's corporate responsibility and risk agendas. Taking up the challenge of social investment issues, a number of banks such as Deutsche Bank have launched dedicated micro-credit funds to encourage sustainability at home and in developing countries. Less common are ethical policies such as the one promoted by the UK's Cooperative Bank under which loans for activities that are perceived to damage the environment and society are rejected from the outset. The Cooperative Bank will not lend to any company associated with arms or tobacco trading or manufacture and is famous for its extensive consultation with depositors and other stakeholders as a means of determining current ethical policy concerns (Corporation of London, 2002).

In terms of the nature of environmental and social criteria included in financial decisions, the primary consideration (whether ethical or risk based) is the sector of business activity in which the potential borrower is involved. For those interested in looking beyond the main business activity to subsidiary and related business trans-actions a detailed review of the financial accounts of a business may be necessary. An example of the potential scope of such analysis was demonstrated by Friends of the Earth (FoE) in a study of the pulp and paper industry (Matthew and van Gelder, 2001). In the study, FoE used the financial statements and notes to accounts of Asia Pulp and Paper (APP) and its related holdings to identify how the APP Group was financed and, in particular, which banks had provided it with debt finance to support its activities. While criticized by the bank industry for failing to acknowledge the timing of bank investments and related credit policy development the study illustrates the extent to which NGOs may attempt to hold banks accountable and the potential role that traditional financial information related to shareholders and investments can play in decision-making.

There is certainly evidence that fears of environmental liability have led lenders to focus their analysis on the borrower's main business activity as well as past and present land use of business premises. In terms of direct liability, the value of asset impairment due to environmental effects is examined first through the financial statements. Traditional criticisms levied at financial reporting by lenders are that financial statements are historic and untimely. While sustainability reports try to avoid at least one of these criticisms (with a forward-looking view) they remain largely annual events and require supplementary timely updates from other sources. Given lenders' interest in risk and business viability they use accounts as a source of primary financial indicators but supplement this information with sustainability accounts and reports, private management accounts of financial and business positions, and projections[2] (Holland, 1998). In the case of environmental risk assessment, evidence may additionally be drawn from environmental impact assess-ments and independent property valuations conducted by the borrowers or, in the absence of information, under a special commission by the bank (Coulson, 2001). This gives some indication that traditional financial statements and in some cases sustainability accounts and reports are considered inadequate for liability assessment.

Studies of credit risk assessment have revealed that further considerations vary between banks and range from a borrower's geographical location to the implica-tions of climate change issues such as flooding or other weather-related risks. In terms of social assessment, issues include, for example, human rights concerns for employee welfare, child labour policies, operations in areas of conflict and war. In some cases potential borrowers may voluntarily make such information public depending on their formal sustainability accounting and reporting practice (Cooper, 2002; Coulson, 2002). Lenders have revealed that if it is publicly unavailable such information would be part of the 'private' information requested by them and could extend to inspection of pollution consents and permits. Sustainability accounting and reporting is often viewed as the provision of additional information within the financial statements and annual report and accounts or a stand-alone report or web-based account of social and/or environmental issues. Interestingly, lenders' views are somewhat broader than this and include more informal sources of management information available to them within a business at any point in time. It is noteworthy that lenders' requests for information are far from uniform and are contingent on the lending situation and relationship between lender and borrower. The implications for a standard form of sustainability accounting and reporting are thus limited but lenders recognize investment in sustainability accounting and reporting as an example of good management.

In terms of their own sustainability accounting and reporting practice, banks such as the Cooperative, who publicly promote ethical screening of loans, report on the number of loans rejected on the basis of their ethical policy as part of their own sustainability accounting and reporting procedures. Alternatively, most commercial lenders in the UK do not carry out such screening. They argue that few loans are rejected purely on environmental or social grounds (normally the business is a poor financial performer and has other issues), thus to try and capture such information would arguably be misleading and distort performance results (Scott and John, 2002).

Given banks' acknowledgement that on average certain industrial sectors pose higher credit risks, the provision of information on the banks' portfolio exposure to different sectors could provide an insight into their environmental credit exposure. This brings us back to a traditional issue of bank reporting and the problem that banks either do not disclose their loan book separately or do not report sufficient detail for such analysis. In addition, it may be argued that the level of sector investment is not necessarily an indication that they are not managing social and environmental factors within their portfolio. The most common view of lenders[3] is that they will work with a borrower to try to reduce harm. In their defence, they pose the challenge that if finance is not available to dirty companies, who will then pay for clean up activities? On this basis lenders reveal credit policies that encourage dirty companies to improve their position for the common good and their combined long-term profitability. Given banks' concern for lender liability, it is certainly in their commercial interest to manage such risk. Much comes down to bank transparency on the credit policy and procedures they apply and their impact (Stichele, 2004). Thus, while increased disclosure is favoured, consensus on a standardized reporting format on credit provision has not been reached. Further, technical difficulties distinguishing environmental and social performance from financial performance mean that establishing the impact of credit risk assessment on financial provision is very difficult, both in a borrower's accounts and the accounts of their lenders

The next section will address in more detail the definition, interpretation and use of 'sustainability accounting and reporting' by a bank lender. Taking the specific example of Barclays,[4] particular reference is made to environmental and social assessment for project finance and issues surrounding how lenders report such assessment.

Project finance

The credit risk considerations noted above equally apply to environmental and social considerations in project finance as well as loan finance. In contrast to loan finance, an increased motive for environmental and social assessment in project finance appears to be the need to manage a bank's risk to reputation as opposed to liability management (Bullied, 2005; Watchman, 2005). In this instance banks are concerned not only for their public (customer and shareholder) reputation but increasingly their reputation within the bank community itself. This is important in the case of project finance because many transactions are carried out as part of a syndication exercise and one weak link could jeopardize the whole transaction. Further, the scale of financial provision and international nature of finance is a reflection of power and potential influence of the lender(s) concerned. Banks involved in project finance have come under particular pressure from NGOs (such as BankTrack[5]) to recognize the importance of their decisions for high-profile projects such as the Baku–Tbilisi–Ceyhan (BTC) pipeline (Freshfields,[6] 2005; BankTrack, 2004).

Such pressures have led a coalition of banks to develop and adopt the 'Equator principles'.[7] The aim of the Equator principles is to establish a global framework for the assessment of environmental and social issues within project finance. The benchmark is based on the International Finance Corporation minimum environmental and social criteria for the projects that it provides financial support to. Since the principles' launch in June 2003, over 30 financial institutions have adopted the Equator principles. Implicitly they categorize projects with a total cost of finance of $50 million or more as A high, B medium, or C low, in environmental and social risks as a precondition of financial consideration. In turn, for category A and B projects borrowers must conduct an environmental assessment and prepare an environmental management plan.

Barclays and Equator

For some banks Equator adoption has marked the start of social and environmental considerations in project finance while for others it is recognition of established practice. In the case of Barclays, social and environmental lending consideration in both commercial lending and project finance has been on the agenda since the early 1990s, the primary driver being risk management. Today, sustainability issues are driven through to practice by two board standards. One is on corporate responsibility, the other is on credit risk. The board standards are supported at an operational level by detailed lending guidelines on risk assessment covering 32 business sectors. This is not to say that Barclays is beyond repute. It has been the subject of many high profile NGO campaigns (see, for example, FoE, 2005, 2004; IRN and FoE, 2004). Addressing its critics Barclays publish information on environmental and social risk assessment in lending including details on Equator adoption as an integral part of their formal annual Corporate Responsibility Reporting process supplemented by more detailed and current disclosure on their website.[8] For example, Figure 14.1 and Table 14.1 are extracts from Barclays' website outlining the nature and scope of Barclays Environmental and Social Impact Assessment (ESIA) Policy.

While detailed accounts of the ESIA process are evident, how sustainability accounting and reporting is used in the analysis of project finance is not directly addressed and there appears to be a lack of information regarding specific sources of information that form the basis of assessment. In the absence of such information, the lender's own definition of sustainability accounting and reporting provides a valuable insight into the potential use that sustainability accounting and reporting can serve.

During a personal interview in summer 2005, Chris Bray (Head of Environmental Risk Policy Management, Barclays plc) was asked to define Sustainability Accounting and Reporting. He replied 'to me accounting is intended to be a consistent description of something that is going on – figures on the web or in a report represent a fairly blunt means of trying to identify what is going on. For example, figures such as number of referrals to the Environmental and Social Risk Policy Team represent a tiny proportion of how we approach these sorts of things. Environmental and social risk management is far more qualitative than quantitative.' Chris went on during the interview to note 'that is why it is often more useful to respond to specific requests for information'.

Such a critique of quantitative assessment equally applies when looking at the industry as a whole. For example, any bank comparison or collective industry representation of the volumes of deals against which Equator is applied requires agreement and application of a common benchmark on the stage at which transactions are passed or declined. It is commonly quoted that Equator adoptors account for about 80 per cent of cross-border project finance. What does this mean? The remaining 20 per cent of project finance could represent a huge number of smaller but damaging projects. Are the non-adoptors more or less active in project finance? It is important to look at what the number represents and some sort of qualitative label needs to be attached to them because quoting absolutes can be misleading.

NGOs have called for banks to disclose the number of deals declined on the basis of the Equator principles. However, this is arguably easier for those new to the risk arenas, who are adopting a compliance-driven approach, to validate implementation

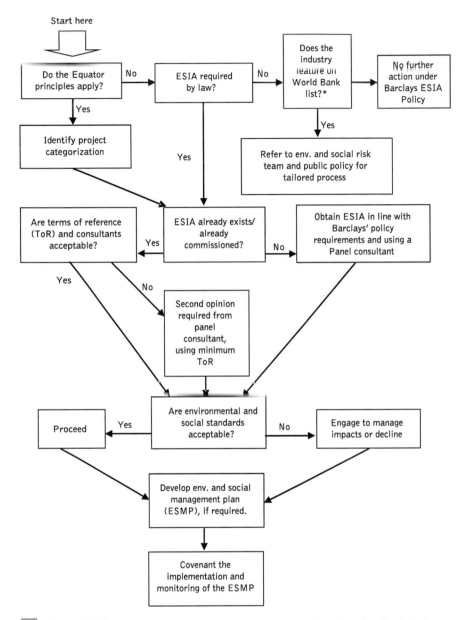

Figure 14.1 Barclays' ESIA Policy Process (extract from Barclays' website)

Note: * A list of environmentally sensitive industries taken from the *World Bank Operational Manual: Operational Policies,* OP 4.01, January 1991.

and count the results. During the interview detailed above, Chris Bray noted the problem 'if a bank has a well briefed, competent, and confident business line familiar with Equator and with the parameters of Equator then lenders won't chase the deals that are no hopers. What is the point of creating *work in progress* if you

Table 14.1 *'Barclays' minimum requirements for an ESIA' (extract from Barclays' website)*

- An assessment of the project impacts and related project categorization in line with the Equator Principles.
- An assessment of the project against:
  - IFC Policies
  - World Bank Guidelines
  - Currently and reasonably anticipated legislation (both national and international)
  - Current and reasonably foreseeable sector-specific policies, e.g. forestry, water infrastructure, which are proposed/supported by internationally recognized non-governmental organizations
  - Voluntary Principles on Security and Human Rights (where appropriate)
  - Industry best practice.
- The ESIA scope takes into consideration:
  - Physical resources – landscape, topography, soils, air quality and climate (including global warming/Kyoto Protocol), surface water, ground water, geology/seismology,
  - Ecological resources – flora, fauna, habitats and species, fisheries, aquatic biology, wildlife, forests, rare/endangered species, wilderness or protected areas,
  - Marine issues – bathymetry, currents, waves, tides, sediment transfer, sea level rise, marine water quality, sediment quality, marine archaeology,
  - Human and economic development – including, but not necessarily limited to, population and communities (numbers, locations, compositions, resource dependency, employment); industries; infrastructural facilities (including water supply, sewage, flood control, drainage); transportation (roads, harbours, airports, navigation) and traffic (particularly during construction); land use planning (including dedicated area uses); power sources and transmission; agricultural development; mineral development; tourism resources,
  - Quality of life values – including, but not necessarily limited to, socio-economic values; public health; noise disturbance; recreational resources and development; aesthetic values, archaeological or historical treasures; cultural values,
  - The level and adequacy of public consultation. This should include details of: public meetings/hearings and attendance; press releases a list of questions asked and the project responses to these; notifications/consultation with the principal community/interest groups, timing of consultation and whether it would constitute prior, informed consultation,
  - A review of material relating to the assessment of alternatives (including project approaches and locations which could achieve the same or the equivalent results, as well as the 'Do-Nothing' option) made by the project sponsor. This should consider, from a broad prospective, whether there are alternative approaches or locations which require more detailed consideration and how that may be undertaken,
  - Identification of the extent to which the proposed project would irreversibly and irretrievably commit resources or curtail the potential uses to the environment. For example, highways that cut through wetlands or natural estuary can result in irretrievable damage to those sensitive ecosystems.

know that it is going to be declined?' If banks provide an informal pre-screen of opportunities, finance may never be formally declined against Equator criteria because analysis would not reach that stage and as such the level of declines would appear low and could lead to the criticism that Equator is not being applied.

To adopt 'the spirit of Equator' a bank essentially needs to justify why they are progressing a transaction and be able to justify that the overall benefit outweighs any technical shortfall or numeric threshold. Attesting to Barclays' Equator adoption Chris Bray points to a quote by external training consultants Sustainable Finance Ltd following a Barclays workshop on due diligence October 2004. The quote, as detailed on Barclays' website, reads – 'The [Barclays] group had a well-developed existing set of policies and procedures, sustainability business line interface already in place that worked, ensuring a very high level of rigour in the practical application of social and environmental issues in project due diligence.'

From Barclays' point of view the impact of Equator adoption has been to raise and level the playing field in terms of social and environmental assessment. A critical mass of Equator adoptors has broken down borrower resistance to assessment. In addition, it means that external advisers around the project finance world have to be cognisant with Equator. For example, Chris Bray noted 'consultants and lawyers are now thinking Equator and are often involved in a project long before a bank is' meaning that 'Equator is engineered in at the outset'.

The future of the Equator project remains uncertain. IFC is currently reviewing and amending its standardization process and there are increased calls for Equator adoptors to move towards some formal association with an ombudsman and some means of auditing performance. In some ways Equator adoptors and other project financiers are already policed as their projects are typically high profile and operating in the spotlight of civil society interest groups at a local and global level. Such risk to reputation may in fact be one reason for banks not to adopt Equator and open their bank to scrutiny. This may be a more appropriate means of policing that ensures that there is no advantage or disadvantage to Equator adoptors. However, for policing in its current form to be effective there is a need to recognize the problems faced by those engaged in sustainability accounting and reporting. Namely, recognizing the need to balance the demand for performance measures against engagement and balance evidence of pure compliance against details of more substantive procedures.

This challenge increases in importance if set within the context of concerns that NGOs in addition to borrowers could become victims of corporate capture by lenders. Arguably, if engagement between NGOs and banks on Equator performance remains behind closed doors policing by such civil interest groups may be deemed insufficient. Thus, it is important that NGOs as well as lenders are held accountable for their activities and encouraged to maintain a transparent approach.

The next part of this chapter provides a critical investigation of how sustainability accounting and reporting can be, and is, used by equity investors and highlights some common themes on developing sustainability accounting and reporting to those noted above.

EQUITY

Socially responsible investment

Today socially responsible investment (SRI) is wide ranging and is the domain of both specialist SRI funds and mainstream investors, such as Schroders, who employ dedicated sustainability analysts within their financial analyst team. Two types of screening are said to characterize SRI decisions, 'negative' and 'positive' screening. Negative screening, for example, involves avoidance of investment in companies perceived to have a 'negative' impact on the environment and society such as those involved in the manufacture or processing of weapons, nuclear power and tobacco. Companies of this type are normally screened out of a portfolio on a sectoral basis according to their core business activity. In a method similar to that used by lenders, company accounts may be subject to scrutiny to establish subsidiaries or related business activities. Investment decisions in such cases may rest on issues of governance and transparency of such commercial relationships through reference to disclosures made by the constituent.

A positive screen involves actively seeking investment in companies with a 'positive' impact on the environment such as those involved in renewable energy generation or recycling. For example, Jupiter Ecology Fund (launched in 1988) was one of the first investment funds responding positively with a focus on sustainability. In such cases it is likely that the company's reports and accounts (both financial and otherwise) will be subject to close scrutiny by the investor (Corporation of London, 2002; Kreander, 2001). Financial institutions adopting positive screening methods often actively encourage sustainability accounting and reporting as an indicator of good management practice. For example, in 2001 Morley Fund Management became the first fund manager to require large UK companies to publish environmental reports as part of its voting policy. If a FTSE 100 company does not publish an environmental report, Morley will vote against the adoption of the company's report and accounts at the AGM. Further, identification of investor views on what sustainability accounting and reporting should constitute involves a more detailed investigation of their investment objectives and assessment methods and this area is less transparent. When it comes to establishing the SRI investment rationale the dominant subject of debate has been whether or not SRI investors sacrifice profits (Lou and Ganzi, 2002) and/or influence behaviour. This debate is ongoing.

Since the end of the 1990s SRIs have also promoted the use of 'engagement' as an investment tool. The general strategy behind engagement is that an investor will develop a relationship with members of the companies in whom they invest and use this relationship to try and persuade them of the need to change their behaviour, highlighting the need for their constituents to be accountable for their activities and try to evoke 'positive' change and increased social responsibility. To maintain insider trading regulations, information provided during the engagement process must be publicly available. Three strategic approaches to engagement are common: an issues basis (e.g. corporate governance), a company focus (e.g. pension disclosures) or a combination of the two. In turn, engagement methods are wide ranging including: informal 'dialogue'; shareholder action in terms of voting shares; shareholder resolutions and buying shares; public campaigns and collaborative action by a group of investors. Each of these engagement methods could arguably lead to dialogue although a divestment appears to be closing down potential dialogue (Green, 2003; Hummel and Timmer, 2003; Dresner, 2002).

Engagement is viewed by some as providing an opportunity to move SRI away from debates about the trade-off between investment ethics and returns and to encourage dialogue and debate on issues such as sustainability accounting; however, it is not without its critics. There have been claims that engagement risks information asymmetry and corporate capture. This claim equally applies to engagement between equity investors and their constituents and debt providers and their borrowers (Roberts *et al.*, 2003; Tomkins, 2001; Elsas and Krahnen, 1998; Baskin, 1988). Further, it may be argued that engagement is deterring the disclosure of information through the formal production of accounts. The power of the investor is an important issue when evaluating such a claim and it is important to remember that insider trading rules serve to maintain engagement at an appropriate level ensuring that everything discussed as part of the equity engagement process is in the public domain. Accounting and reporting can play an important part in this accountability process by ensuring that the process is transparent. A formal process of public reporting ensures 'equity' between investors and helps mitigate the risk of information asymmetry. Alternatively, a positive quality of engagement as a research method is that it can allow for an aesthetic assessment of sustainability including judgements as to the management ability of the business and physical assets quality in a similar way to that recognized by debt investors. When considering the nature of sustainability accounting and reporting it is proposed that the regulation of reporting and market regulation should be considered together.

Given the potential range of SRI strategies and assessment methods, there is clearly a tension between establishing credible benchmarks for engagement and recognizing the diversity of SRI approaches to engagement and indeed means of investor feedback. In order to evaluate the success of such engagement ambitions it is necessary to establish some indicators on company engagement as a basis for evaluating performance as part of their own sustainability accounting and reporting practice. In November 2003 European Sustainable and Responsible Investment Forum (Eurosif) launched 'The Corporate Sustainability and Responsibility Research Quality Standard' as a set of voluntary (signatories) quality and integrity principles that ask signatories to commit to using independent sources to assess companies; being transparent on the methodology they use; and being independent of outside influence (Eurosif, 2004; Howard-Boyd, 2003).

Having recognized the need for such an approach, a number of sustainability indices have been developed to support financial investment decisions. FTSE4Good and Dow Jones Sustainability Indexes[9] are prime examples of independent sources that offer benchmarking tools designed for financial analysts (involved in both equity and debt finance) to evaluate corporate sustainability performance. Launched in 1999 and 2001 respectively, the Dow Jones Sustainability Indexes and FTSE4Good have earned prominence and credibility for their basis on established global equity index series. As an example of their success FTSE4Good reports on use of the index by the financial sector: 'CIS UK FTSE4Good Tracker Trust, the Direct Line FTSE4Good UK Tracker Fund, Normura Global SRI fund in Japan and Legal and General's FTSE4Good Global and UK Tracker funds. A number of banks have also purchased licenses to offer structured products based on the FTSE4Good indices, including UBS, Credit Suisse First Boston and Nordea Bank' (FTSE, 2005, p. 12).

Both indexes involve the assessment of general and specific sustainability criteria that are selected through extensive stakeholder consultation and updated to account for current issues. As in the case of screening by SRI themselves, exclusions in the indexes typically include non-nuclear weapons, nuclear power, nuclear weapons systems, tobacco producers, and extractors/processors of uranium. Examples of companies excluded by FTSE4Good also include companies alleged to have breached WHO [World Health Organization] Code on the marketing criteria for breast milk substitutes. In this instance new marketing criteria have been developed in extensive engagement with the industry concerned. Any changes in criteria are introduced in phased stages allowing constituents negotiated deadlines for meeting requirements (FTSE, 2005, 2003). It is apparent from a review of the methods of assessment applied by the indexes that sustainability accounting and reporting is viewed as only one means of telling an organization's story of sustainability. As such, it is considered as a 'reporting mechanism' on indicators of good corporate management alongside considerations of policy making and management system.

The indexes solve the problems of rights to information and risks of information asymmetry by providing an independent service to investors and also help to standardize information provision and encourage equity in decision-making through benchmarking. It may be argued that there remains a question of the appropriateness of criteria established given the potential power of the indexes. However, both indexes extensively report on their internal decision-making procedures and democratic efforts to identify appropriate criteria.

SUMMARY

As noted at the start of this chapter, it is hard to raise debt and equity finance today without some form of environmental or social assessment. Thus, the practice of sustainability accounting and reporting and its development plays an important role in financial provision. Traditional sustainability accounting and reporting is seen as a sign of good management but is not necessarily an adequate basis to meet the variety of information demanded for financial assessment. A review of the contribution of sustainability accounting and reporting to finance decisions reveals that both borrowers and their financiers face problems establishing meaningful indicators for environmental and social performance and evaluating their impact on financial performance. As a result, it is perceived that there is a lack of transparency among those trying to raise finance. The solution for lenders and investors is to engage with business to achieve clarification and debt financiers have the advantage of access to private information.

Lack of transparency among the financial sector regarding their decision criteria and methods of assessment makes it difficult to determine their definition of sustainability accounting and reporting and the role that it plays in the decision process. This is further complicated by competitive differences and requirements to maintain confidentiality.

It is evident from research that in terms of debt finance, adequacy of asset and liability valuation and disclosure is an important issue. Lenders' access to private information means that they have access to timely, current information. Evidence from lenders reveals that they are looking to accounting 'to tell a story' and the context within which information is provided is critical to their evaluation. This is equally true for evaluation of their investments and when reporting their own performance. In the case of equity investment, comparability of their potential constituents is an important issue. For both types of finance, issues of information asymmetry and corporate capture dominate debates on the value of the engagement process as a means of developing sustainability accounting and reporting solutions leading to the proposal that development in sustainability accounting and reporting needs to be considered as part of debates on market regulation. There are also implications for reliance by civil interest groups on sustainability accounting and reporting to police corporate activities. It is proposed that there needs to be a greater appreciation of problems faced by those seeking to develop sustainability accounting and reporting to ensure that policing targets are more than compliance testing and recognize substantive achievements in environmental and social assessment taking place in the financial sector and among their borrowers. An important source of information is the development of indexes such as FTSE4Good and Dow Jones Sustainability Index that provide an independent and equitable benchmarking of corporate environmental and social performance including the financial sector.

278

NOTES

1 The US case of Fleet Factors is the most common point of reference for developing legislation across Europe and the rest of the world.

2 In the case of debt finance investors have potential access to both public and private information provided by the borrower whereas equity investors only have access to public information (Holland, 1998). The reason for this is to maintain insider trading controls in the market and distinguish owners and managers of a business.

3 With the exception of banks such as the Cooperative Bank.

4 Research for the case study included a series of interviews with Chris Bray, Head of Environmental Risk Policy Management, Barclays plc, conducted during August 2005.

5 BankTrack highlights commitment to the Collevecchio declaration which calls on financial institutions to adopt a precautionary principle and decline investment on the basis of social and environmental criteria. The declaration launched in 2003 has been signed by more than 100 NGOs.

6 The risk of lender liability in the context of project finance was recently raised by a review of current practice by Freshfields (legal advisers).

7 See http://www.equator-principles.com.

8 See http://www.barclays.co.uk.

9 See websites http://www.ftse.com/ftse4good and http://www.sustainability-indexes.com.

REFERENCES

BankTrack (2004) *Principles, profits or just PR – triple P investments under the Equator principles: An anniversary assessment.* June. Amsterdam: BankTrack.

Baskin, J. B. (1988) The development of corporate financial markets in Britain and the US 1600–1914: Overcoming asymmetric information. *Business History Review.* summer: 197–237.

BBA (1993) *Position statement: Banks and the environment.* September. London: British Bankers' Association.

Bullied, Roz (2005) Legal risk from Equator principles? *Environmental Finance,* April: 4.

Cooper, Graham (2002) 'Room for improvement' on banks' green risks. *Environmental Finance,* October: 7.

Corporation of London (2002) *Financing the future: The London principles – the role of UK financial services in sustainable development.* London: Corporation of London.

Coulson, A. B. (2001) Corporate environmental assessment by a bank lender: The reality? In J. J. Bouma, M. Jeucken and L. Klinkers (eds) *Sustainable banking: The greening of finance.* Sheffield: Greenleaf Publishing, published in association with Deloitte & Touche, pp. 300–11.

Coulson, A. B. (2002) *Benchmarking study: Environmental credit risk factors in the pan-European banking sector.* October. London: ISIS Asset Management plc (now F. & C. Asset Management).

Coulson, A. B. and Monks, V. (1999) Corporate environmental performance considerations within bank lending decisions. *Eco-Management and Auditing,* 6(1): 1–10.

Dresner, Sarah (2002) *Assessing engagement: A survey of UK practice on socially responsible investment.* Report produced in collaboration with Just Pensions, February. London: Just Pensions.

Elsas, R. and Krahnen, J. P. (1998) Is relationship lending special? Evidence from credit-file data in Germany. *Journal of Banking and Finance,* 22: 1283–1316.

Eurosif (2004) *Eurosif transparency guidelines for the retail SRI fund sector.* Paris: Eurosif.

FoE (2004) Indian and Thai activists pressure Barclays. Press release, 9 December. London: FoE.

FoE (2005) *Barclays and the financing of the Narmada dams.* Briefing, London: FoE.

Freshfields (2005) *Banking on responsibility. Part 1 of Freshfields Bruckhaus Deringer Equator principles survey 2005: The banks.* July. London: Freshfields Bruckhaus Deringer.

FTSE (2003) *FTSE4Good Index Series: Inclusion criteria.* London: FTSE.

FTSE (2005) *FTSE4Good Index Series: Impact of new criteria and future directions. 2004–2005 Report.* London: FTSE.

Green, Duncan (2003) *Do UK charities invest responsibly?: A survey of current practice.* Co-published by EIRiS, Just Pensions and the UK Social Investment Forum. London: Just Pensions, May.

Holland, J. (1998) Private voluntary disclosure, financial intermediation and market efficiency. *Journal of Business Finance and Accounting,* 25(1): 29–68.

Howard-Boyd, Emma (2003) Closing the gap. *Environmental Finance,* February: 24.

Hummel, H. and Timmer, D. (2003) *Money and morals: The development of socially responsible investing among Dutch pension funds.* Produced in collaboration with the Dutch Association of Investment Analysts (VBA). Universiteit Nyenrode (the Netherlands Business School): Breukelen.

IRN and FoE (2004) *Barclays and the Karahnjukar project.* Briefing, International Rivers Network and Friends of the Earth. January. London: FoE.

Kreander, N. (2001). *An analysis of European ethical funds.* Occasional Research Paper no. 33, Association of Chartered Certified Accountants. Glasgow: University of Glasgow, Centre for Social and Environmental Accounting Research.

Lou, C. and Ganzi, J. (2002) *2001 performance review: Profit-driven sustainability funds*. North Carolina: Environment and Finance Enterprise, August.

Matthew, Ed. and Willem van Gelder, Jan (2001) *Paper tiger, hidden dragons*. May. London: FoE.

Pearce, B. and Ganzi, J. (2003) *Engaging the mainstream with sustainability: A survey of investor engagement on corporate social, environmental and ethical performance*. Sponsored by Royal & SunAlliance. London: Forum for the Future.

Roberts, J., Sanderson, P., Barker, R. and Hendry, J. (2003) *In the mirror of the market: The disciplinary effects of company/fund managers meetings*. IPA Conference paper. Madrid, 13–16 July.

Scott, Paul and John, Steve (2002) Banks look to indirect impacts. *Environmental Finance*, November: 22–3.

Smith, D. R. (1994) *Environmental risk: Credit approaches and opportunities, an interim report*. Prepared for UNEP Roundtable on Commercial Banks and the Environment, 26–7 September. Geneva: UNEP.

Sparkes, Russell (2002) *Socially responsible investment: A global revolution*. London: Wiley.

Stichele, Myriam Vander (2004) *Critical issues on the financial industry: Somo financial sector report*. Amsterdam: Somo.

Tomkins, C. (2001) Interdependencies, trust and information in relationships, alliances and networks. *Accounting Organizations and Society*, 26: 161–91.

Ulph, A., McKenzie, G., Jewell, T., Steele, J. and Wolfe, S. (1999) *The financial implications of environmental legislation*. ESRC End of Award Report (L320253226).

Watchman, Paul (2005) Beyond Equator. *Environmental Finance*, June: 16–17.

Part IV

Other issues

Chapter 15

The nature of NGO accountability

Motives, mechanisms and practice

Brendan O'Dwyer

> One doesn't scrutinize magic too closely, otherwise it loses its charm.
>
> (Clark, 1991, p. 53)

INTRODUCTION

Until the early 1990s, non-governmental organizations (NGOs) were not subjected to intense scrutiny regarding their accountability, governance, legitimacy or wider societal impacts (Edwards and Fowler, 2003; Lloyd, 2005; Najam, 1996; Unerman and O'Dwyer, 2006a). Najam (1996, p. 339) claims that 'most NGO scholars also happen[ed] to be NGO believers' who had implicit faith in NGOs' work, be it as advocates of specific causes such as human rights and social justice, providers of relief and humanitarian assistance, or as facilitators of development. This enabled the emergence of a myth of NGO infallibility and a concomitant reluctance to closely scrutinize the presumed 'magic' of NGOs' work (Lloyd, 2005; Najam, 1996). However, NGO numbers have since grown exponentially and their influence in arenas such as international business and governance has escalated (Doh and Teegen, 2002).[1] The increasing popularity of non-state actors with various donors (Fisher, 1997) and increasing dissatisfaction with conventional politics has meant that NGOs have moved from being 'ladles in the global soup kitchen to a force for transformation in global politics and economics' (Edwards and Fowler, 2003, p. 1; Doh and Teegen, 2002; Salamon, 1994). Commenting in the early 1990s, one analyst suggested that this 'quiet revolution' in the role and influence of NGOs could 'prove to be as significant to the latter twentieth century as the rise of the nation state was to the latter nineteenth century' (Salamon, 1994, p. 109, cited in Fisher, 1997, p. 440). Hence, NGOs, in whatever form, have now become subject to much more critical scrutiny, especially regarding their accountability, both internally and externally. In response to some of these pressures, a group of five international NGOs, Amnesty International, Oxfam, Save the Children, Greenpeace and CARE International, launched an accountability charter – a collectively developed code of conduct – in June 2006 (INGO, 2006; Russell, 2006). This chapter examines the nature of this recent emergence of interest in NGO accountability. It focuses particularly, albeit not exclusively, on the nature and practice of NGO accountability for their impacts on social sustainability.

Sustainability is concerned with both the sustenance of the natural ecology (eco-efficiency) and the justice and equity with which the fruits of that ecology are employed (eco-justice) (Bebbington, 2001; Bebbington and Gray, 2001). By focusing on issues of social sustainability, this chapter concentrates upon eco-justice which deals primarily with the social- and equity-related concerns arising from development (that is the distribution of the costs and benefits of development). This 'social' element of sustainability or 'social justice' is a central concern for NGOs who advocate on issues surrounding human welfare, rights and development. It involves ensuring equity of access to key services, equity between generations, equity within generations, the widespread participation of citizens in all areas of political activity, and a system of cultural relations in which the positive aspects of disparate cultures are valued and protected (Bebbington, 2001; Hawke Research Institute for Sustainable Societies, 2005).

The chapter is structured as follows. Firstly, I consider the nature of NGOs and specify broadly the type of NGOs addressed. I then briefly consider the motives for, and the complexity surrounding, NGO accountability. Prevailing mechanisms of NGO accountability are subsequently scrutinized with particular reference to emerging accountability mechanisms drawing on key elements of social accounting processes. Examples of these approaches are discussed and succeeded with a brief review of recent evaluations of NGO accountability practice. This highlights low levels of accounting and reporting by many NGOs.[2]

WHAT IS AN NGO?

There is little consensus on how to define and classify NGOs (Doh and Teegen, 2002; Fisher, 1997; Martens, 2002; Vakil, 1997). The term 'NGO' embraces a huge range of institutions with little in common beyond the label 'NGO' (Gray et al., 2006). These can encompass voluntary associations, credit unions, farmers' co-operatives, consumer groups, religious organizations, and trade unions (Hudson, 1999, p. 1). In their various forms, NGOs have multiplied since the 1990s, taken on new functions, and established innovative and exceptionally complex and wide-ranging formal and informal linkages with one another, with government agencies, with social movements, with international development agencies and with transnational issue networks (Fisher, 1997). This sheer range eludes definition, hence complicating simple specifications of their accountability (Gray et al., 2006). Vakil

(1997) does, however, suggest that NGOs can be broadly distinguished by their essential organizational attributes comprising their *orientation* – the types of activities they engage in – and their *level of operation* – at international, national or local community level. He identifies six orientation categories: welfare, development, development education, networking, research, and advocacy. I primarily consider international and national advocacy-oriented NGOs who have significant potential, particularly when working together, to influence public policy making. My focus, however, also encompasses NGOs who mix significant advocacy activities with a separate core orientation such as development education or welfare.[3] Examples of international and national NGOs which would fall into this categorization are Amnesty International, Greenpeace, World Wildlife Fund (WWF), Friends of the Earth, Christian Aid, and Oxfam International.

MOTIVES FOR NGO ACCOUNTABILITY

The aforementioned calls for more explicit demonstrations of NGO accountability have derived from perceptions of their increasing power and presence in a variety of fields. They have grown rapidly in numbers (Ebrahim, 2005, 2003a; Edwards and Fowler, 2003; Fisher, 1997; Salamon *et al.*, 1999), received increased levels of funding[4] (Edwards and Fowler, 2003; SustainAbility, 2003) and enhanced their development profile (Ebrahim, 2005, 2003a, 2003b; Vakil, 1997; Zadek, 2003). This has enabled them to increase their influence on governments and businesses (Bendell, 2000; Doh and Teegen, 2002; Edwards and Hulme, 1992; Fisher, 1997; Kamat, 2003; Keck and Sikkink, 1998; Naidoo, 2004; Onishi, 2002; Spar and Mure, 1997). Furthermore, some NGOs' involvement in widely publicized scandals[5] (Gibelman and Gelman, 2001; Jepson, 2005; Kearns, 1994) has further accentuated the calls for improved accountability.

International NGOs have been particularly influential in shaping and driving corporate responsibility and sustainability agendas (SustainAbility, 2003; Unerman and O'Dwyer, 2004, 2006a, 2006b). This has led to questions being asked of their own performance in these areas (Lloyd, 2005). Central to many of these concerns are questions of NGO legitimacy and representativeness in their actions and in their statements. For example, with respect to NGOs advocating particular development policies in developing countries, queries about their accountability tend to focus on whether they speak *as* the poor, *with* the poor, *for* the poor, or *about* the poor (Slim, 2002).

Many of the calls for greater NGO accountability emanate from bodies, often supported by the business sector, who fear exposure or threat from specific NGOs (Gray *et al.*, 2006; Maitland, 2003; Upadhyay, 2003). This has raised suspicions that these sources are motivated by a desire to suppress NGOs who might challenge particular agendas (Gray *et al.*, 2006). Wherever these demands emanate from, they do reflect many NGOs' growing success in advocacy. Some NGOs, however, resent the *extent* of these accountability demands, especially when promoted by business interests (see O'Dwyer *et al.*, 2005):

> It appears that NGOs are being singled out in contrast to businesses (and even many governments) that are even less accountable than they are.
>
> (Edwards, 2000, pp. 22–3)

Until recently, discussions of NGO accountability tended to focus primarily on their stewardship or proper use of the financial resources provided to them (Dixon *et al.*, 2006; Ebrahim, 2005, 2003a; Goddard and Assad, 2006; Lewis and Madon, 2004). Accountability for impacts on 'clients' such as host communities or other societal groups which NGOs purport to serve has been downplayed (Lloyd, 2005; Najam, 1996). Broader conceptions of and motives for accountability have, however, emerged from within NGOs. For example, the UK-based consultancy SustainAbility (2003, p. 17) identifies four internal drivers of NGO accountability comprising: morality (accountability is right in principle); performance (accountability improves effectiveness); political space (accountability increases credibility and thus political space); and wider democratization (accountability of NGOs strengthens democracy in the general political environment). These internal drivers exude a sense of moral obligation which sees accountability as crucial to the achievement of an NGO's mission and to the maintenance of its integrity (Ebrahim, 2003a). Demonstrating accountability for wider societal impacts is central to these motives.

THE COMPLEXITY OF NGO ACCOUNTABILITY

While most organizations encounter the oft-competing demands of multiple constituencies, many NGOs face these demands more acutely and regularly than do private firms (Dixon *et al.*, 2006; Ebrahim, 2005, 2003b). NGOs' multiple constituencies include *patrons* – usually comprising donors, foundations, governments, and other partner NGOs (Edwards and Hulme, 1996b; Najam, 1996) – to whom they may be upwardly accountable (Fowler, 1996; Lloyd, 2005; Najam, 1996) and *clients/beneficiaries* – groups to whom NGOs provide services to or advocate on behalf of, including communities or regions *indirectly* impacted by NGO activities (Ebrahim, 2003b; Lloyd, 2005; Najam, 1996) – to whom they may be downwardly accountable (Edwards and Hulme, 1996b; Fowler, 1996; Najam, 1996). They are also potentially accountable to staff, supporters/members, coalition partners, their peers and to their mission (Brown and Moore, 2001; Ebrahim, 2003b; Lloyd, 2005; Najam, 1996). The extent of the, often permanent, tensions between many of these constituencies can lead to widely conflicting perspectives on how NGOs should operate and account for their broader impacts on these groups and on society generally (Fowler, 1996).

In practice, these conflicts can lead to the most influential stakeholders gaining prominence. This potentially subverts NGOs' achievement of their key longer-term missions given powerful stakeholders such as donors are often impatient for results (Lloyd, 2005; Najam, 1996; Unerman and O'Dwyer, 2006a). For example, there are many cases of NGO accountability to and performance on behalf of beneficiaries being sacrificed in order to accord with donor stakeholder requirements[6] (Dixon et al., 2006; Ebrahim, 2005, 2003a, 2003b; Edwards and Hulme, 1996a; Hudson, 2000; Lloyd, 2005; Najam, 1996; O'Dwyer, 2005a). Some NGOs have even altered their missions to accord with donors' desires to secure their survival (Dillon, 2004; Najam, 1996). This threatens the adoption of 'strategic accountability' – accounting for medium- to long-term impacts on other organizations and the wider societal environment – in favour of 'functional accountability' – accounting for short-term impacts and resource use (Najam, 1996).

NGO accountability is further complicated as NGOs belong to organizational forms with no simple, widely agreed measure of organizational performance, unlike governments and businesses who may be evaluated respectively in terms of political support or financial returns (Fowler, 1996). For example, it is difficult for an NGO like Amnesty International to definitively demonstrate its influence on changing a country specific human rights policy that may have helped empower a certain segment of society (see, O'Dwyer et al., 2005). Many second and third order effects from NGO actions exist (O'Dwyer et al., 2005; Uphoff, 1995). If 'positive' effects from NGO actions evolve such as, for example, 'a sustainable change in agricultural production . . . [or] the development of a strong grassroots federation' (Edwards and Fowler, 2003, p. 106) or a change in government policy on the death sentence, this is often due to a number of forces and actors coming together rather than from one NGO advocating in isolation. It is therefore perhaps unsurprising that some NGOs are reluctant to take credit (or account) for these collective efforts (O'Dwyer et al., 2005).

The complexities surrounding NGOs' oft-competing constituencies and the lack of definitive 'measurement' bases outlined above have fuelled resistance among certain NGOs to demands for enhanced accountability. Various arguments employed include: the potential for enhanced accountability to be used by vested interests to punish NGOs if they are seen to be subversive in some way, especially by host governments in regions which are politically more vulnerable (Edwards and Hulme, 1996a; O'Dwyer et al., 2005; SustainAbility, 2003); the threat to the diversity, innovation and speed of response in the 'sector' in favour of politicization and patronage (Edwards and Fowler, 2003; SustainAbility, 2003); and the lack of available resources for many NGOs to implement systematic systems of accountability (Ebrahim, 2003a; Fowler, 1996; Jepson, 2005; SustainAbility, 2003). Much of this resistance is driven by concerns surrounding the impact enhanced accountability may have on NGOs' power to contribute to social sustainability. The following quote from a recent World Social Forum workshop on 'civil society accountability' illustrates this concern:

> Does engaging with our own accountability give us [civil society/NGOs] more power or render us powerless? . . . [A]ccountability should not lead to powerful stakeholders, such as donors . . . influenc[ing] the vision and mission of the organisations they support [but should] communicate the ways in which they are contributing to social change.
>
> (Litovsky, 2005a, pp. 5–6)

Further resistance may be passive mainly due to the fact that many NGO leaders do not seem to know what to do about the issue of accountability. For example, six environmental NGO (ENGO) chief executives (CEOs) recently reflected on issues of NGO accountability and governance in a UK lecture series.[7] Responses to an audience questionnaire indicated that a substantial proportion of those attending were unconvinced that the CEOs' recognition of accountability as an NGO issue was being translated into actions within their organizations. As Jepson (2005) elaborates:

> There was a sense that the issue is enormously complex and that ENGO leaders are struggling to know what to do.
>
> (p. 517)

Whatever the concerns of NGOs generally and the apparent struggles of some NGO CEOs, a plethora of accountability mechanisms have evolved from the NGO 'sector' since the 1990s. The following section reviews some of these while placing a special emphasis on emerging mechanisms drawing on key elements of social accounting processes.

MECHANISMS OF NGO ACCOUNTABILITY

Ebrahim (2003b) outlines five broad accountability mechanisms used by NGOs.[8] These include: reports and disclosure statements; performance assessments and evaluations; forms of participation; self-regulation; and social audits (accounts) (Ebrahim, 2003b, p. 825). Table 15.1 indicates a number of characteristics of these mechanisms including: who the mechanisms provide accountability to; why they are used; and whether they focus on short-term functional or longer-term strategic issues. Ebrahim (2003b), however, claims that most of the mechanisms are deficient in offering broad-based accountability addressing impacts on social sustainability:

> Most mechanisms . . . undervalue long-term and qualitative assessments
> that are essential for understanding the *real impacts* of . . . [NGO] activity.
>
> (p. 826, emphasis added)

Despite his rather pessimistic prognosis, Ebrahim (2003b) suggests that one of these
mechanisms, social auditing (or accounting), integrates many of the characteristics
of the other four accountability mechanisms into a process which can both improve
on and enhance the reporting of NGOs' impacts on key groups in society. Social
accounting is underpinned by forms of stakeholder dialogue which Edwards and
Fowler (2003) argue are needed to address the problem of accounting for broader
societal impacts and/or performance:

> [NGO accountability] . . . must [involve] a process of negotiation between
> stakeholders rather than the imposition of one definition or interpretation
> of 'effectiveness' [or impact] over another.
>
> (p. 196)

Through its explicit encouragement of engagement with stakeholders, social
accounting facilitates downward accountability to beneficiaries *and* upward
accountability to donors (where relevant). It also encourages the development of
social information systems (Dawson, 1998; Dey, 2004; Gray *et al.*, 1997) and can
operate as a valuable means of organizational learning if stakeholder perspectives are
fed back into, and allowed to influence, organizational decision-making processes.
Indeed, in the 1990s, when discussing the difficulties and dilemmas surrounding
NGO performance and accountability, Fowler (1996) recommended the adoption
of a continuous process of multiple stakeholder involvement akin to social accounting in order to expose and embrace competing stakeholder demands (see also
Thomson and Bebbington, 2005). It has subsequently influenced NGO accounting
and reporting with varying degrees of success (see Dey, 2004; Dawson, 1998;
Keystone, 2005; O'Dwyer, 2005a; Pearce, 1996; Volunteer Vancouver, 1999). A
key example of a project attempting to promote and advance these types of
mechanisms is the Global Accountability Project (GAP) of the UK charity One
World Trust (Blagescu *et al.*, 2005).[9]

The Global Accountability Project (GAP) is part of a programme of work by
One World Trust aimed at enhancing the accountability of the decision-making
processes of international NGOs to the individuals, communities and societies they
affect. The GAP framework unpacks NGO accountability into four dimensions:
transparency, participation, evaluation, and complaint and response mechanisms,
all of which are central to stakeholder-focused accountability processes (see
ActionAid International, 2004a, 2004b; Dey, 2004; Gray *et al.*, 1997; O'Dwyer,
2005a) (see Table 15.2). To demonstrate accountability, GAP argues that NGOs
need to integrate all four of the above dimensions into its policies, procedures and

Table 15.1 *Characteristics of NGO accountability mechanisms*

Accountability mechanism	Accountability to whom? (upward, downward, or to self)	Inducement (internal/external)	Organizational response (strategic/ functional)
Disclosures/ reports	Upward to funders and oversight agencies Downward (to a lesser extent to clients or members who read the reports)	Legal requirement Tax status Funding requirement (external threat of loss of funding or tax status)	Primarily functional, with a focus on short-term results
Performance assessment and evaluation	Upward to funders Significant potential for downward accountability from NGOs to communities	Funding requirement (external) Potential to become a learning tool (internal)	Primarily functional at present, with possibilities for longer-term strategic assessments
Participation	Downward from NGOs to clients and communities Internally to NGOs themselves	Organizational values (internal) Funding requirement (external)	Primarily functional if participation is limited to consultation and implementation Strategic if it involves increasing bargaining power of clients vis-à-vis funders
Self-regulation	To NGOs themselves, as a sector Potentially to clients and donors	Erosion of public confidence due to scandals and exaggeration of accomplishments (external loss of funds; internal loss of reputation)	Strategic in that it concerns long-term change involving codes of conduct
Social auditing (accounting)	To NGOs themselves (by linking values to strategy and performance) Downward and upward to various stakeholders	Erosion of public confidence (external) Evaluation of social, ethical, environmental, and ethical performance on a par with economic performance (internal)	Functional to the extent it affects the behaviour of a single organization Strategic to the extent it affects NGO–stakeholder interaction, promotes longer-term planning and becomes adopted sector-wide

Source: Adapted from Ebrahim (2003b, p. 825)

Table 15.2 *The four dimensions of international NGO accountability: the GAP framework*

- *Transparency*: The provision of accessible and timely information to stakeholders and the opening up of organizational procedures, structures and processes to their assessment.
- *Participation*: The process through which an organization enables key stakeholders to play an active role in the decision-making processes and activities which affect them.
- *Evaluation*: The process through which an organization monitors and reviews its progress and results against goals and objectives; feeds learning from this back into the organization on an ongoing basis; and reports on the results of the process.
- *Complaint and response mechanisms*: Mechanisms through which an organization enables stakeholders to address complaints against its decisions and actions, and ensures that these are properly reviewed and acted upon.

Source: Adapted from Blagescu *et al.* (2005, p. 4)

practice at all stages of decision-making and implementation in relation to its key stakeholders. While the framework does not indicate the need for formal reports, it does suggest various means of information dissemination including the worldwide web and public meetings. It specifically proposes an appeals procedure for stakeholders where they feel their information requests have been denied, along with a detailed, accountable process for considering complaints against an NGO. This framework, especially the latter aspect involving complaint and appeals mechanisms, seems to go well beyond much of the stakeholder engagement/dialogue practices of most of the corporate sector (see O'Dwyer, 2005b; Rasche and Esser, 2006; Thomson and Bebbington, 2005).

Another initiative embracing many of the social accounting dimensions above has emerged from an organization linked to the UK Institute of Social and Ethical Accountability (ISEA), called Keystone. Keystone initially sought to develop a set of reporting guidelines for non-profit organizations under the umbrella term ACCESS (Bonbright, 2004; Zadek, 2003) aimed at seeking social and environmental (as well as financial) 'returns' (Bonbright, 2004, p. 5). Keystone has now developed a method focused on developing the practice of accountability among organizations dedicated to social change. Again, key elements of the approach have much in common with social accounting (audit) approaches such as the GAP framework where organizations reflect on their mission, theory of change and immediate objectives through stakeholder engagement.

Keystone require that NGOs report publicly, openly and accurately what stakeholders say about their work. Their method claims to enable organizations to develop reporting models that are specific to their unique contexts (Litovsky, 2005b). They view accountability positively as a potential driver of social activity and change rather than a constraint upon NGOs:

> Public reports that are inclusive of all stakeholder views allow for trans-
> parent and interactive stakeholder commentary – creating the conditions
> for collective accountability for social change.
>
> (Keystone, 2005)

More broadly, many practitioners and academics have brought together current
evidence of NGO accountability mechanisms in order to provide an accountability
roadmap for NGOs. For example, Cronin and O'Regan (2002) outline a Framework of Accountability Mechanisms and Tools (FAIT) in order to both analyse and,
more importantly, enable development aid NGOs to plan for enhanced accountability in a more demanding environment. They argue against using off-the-shelf
models in order to implement NGO accountability and, as with the GAP and
Keystone initiatives, they call for stakeholder-defined measures of performance in
reports. Like the GAP framework, they insist that reporting must be accompanied
by an assessment and an assurance that stakeholders can demand reports and
information, are *able* to appraise reports and information, *and* have the ability to
operate sanctions based on their appraisals. Within the specific context of development NGOs, Cronin and O'Regan (2002) suggest using unique reporting mechanisms such as participatory videos, story telling, drama, and proverbs in order to
listen carefully to and report on the voices of participants. They also emphasize the
importance of feeding any information going upward to donors – such as strategies,
appraisals and budgets – downwards to potential beneficiaries or their
representatives.

EXPERIENCES AND EVALUATIONS OF NGO ACCOUNTABILITY

Key elements of the social accounting mechanisms referred to above emerged from
the UK NGO 'sector'. For example, in the early 1990s, the UK NGO, New
Economics Foundation (NEF), in conjunction with Traidcraft plc,[10] pioneered a
form of social accounting that was voluntary in nature and rooted in stakeholder engagement. This aimed to assist organizations, both commercial and
otherwise, in understanding and improving their societal impact. The method was
developed primarily to enable an account of performance to be reported which
extended beyond the information presented within the structures of the financial
statements (see Dey, 2004; Gray *et al.*, 1997). In 1996, Traidcraft plc's sister charity
Traidcraft Exchange began producing social accounts. Since 2000, the social
accounts of the two organizations have been combined and published on the
internet.[11, 12]

The focus on stakeholder engagement in the emerging frameworks for NGO
accountability seeks to give voice to those in the wider society most impacted

by NGO advocacy and activity. It also aims to counter the aforementioned concerns surrounding performance measurement by allowing stakeholder groups to determine what they want accounted for. In practice, however, many NGOs have struggled with how to include diverse stakeholders in a more equal and participatory way in their accountability processes (Dey, 2004; O'Dwyer, 2005a; Raynard, 1998). In some instances, processes of engagement, often undertaken under the umbrella term 'participation', have been shambolic (Dillon, 2004; Ebrahim, 2003b; Najam, 1996; O'Dwyer, 2005a) given they have often ignored pervasive power and resource differentials and failed to become embedded in organizational decision-making processes (Dey, 2004; Dillon, 2004; O'Dwyer, 2005a). Lessons learned from less successful cases of stakeholder engagement (see Dey, 2004; O'Dwyer, 2005a) have led to the cautious adoption of social accounting by some high-profile NGOs. For example, while reflecting on the communication/disclosure of social impact information implied by the adoption of stakeholder-focused social accounting mechanisms, Dawson (1998) expressed concern that NGOs such as Oxfam could suffer from information being used out of context resulting in reduced public support. She also feared that exposure of failed programmes or adverse impacts could work against large NGOs like Oxfam. Problems surrounding the selection of stakeholder voices to include in external reports given their competing views, diverse nature and the possibility of raising unrealistic expectations were also raised.

There have, however, been some successes where NGOs have prioritized less powerful stakeholder voices as part of accountability processes. ActionAid International, a development agency focused on fighting poverty, developed the ALPs (Accountability, Learning and Planning) system (ActionAid International, 2000, 2004a, 2004b) which, despite involving huge organizational stress and change (Scott-Villiers, 2002), focused successfully on determining its impact on key beneficiary stakeholders such as poor and marginalized groups and on including these groups in decision-making affecting them (see Table 15.3). While the process has not been without its problems (see ActionAid International, 2004b, pp. 45–8) management commitment to accountability and assessment of impacts on poor and marginalized members of society has been central to its continuing influence as a key broad-based internal accountability mechanism.

There is also evidence of emerging institutional mechanisms supporting more holistic accountability among NGOs. In Hong Kong, a high-profile working group set up to examine how to improve the public (as opposed to donor) accountability of NGOs recommended the adoption of stakeholder-focused social accounting/ auditing processes to be implemented on a voluntary basis through a combination of self-regulations within the NGO sector and the installation of an external accreditation system. The group recommended a staged process towards the eventual widespread adoption of social accounting (Centre for Civil Society and Governance, 2005).

295

Table 15.3 *ActionAid International's accountability to 'weaker' stakeholders as part of the ALPS system*

Accountability to the poor and our partners

Our commitment to poor and marginalized people holds us accountable to them for the quality of our work, and that of our partners.

In ActionAid we have multiple accountabilities – to donors, other staff, partners, governments, communities and the poor and marginalized people within them. However, accountability – to poor people, especially women and girls – is central to the spirit of *Fighting poverty together*.

ALPS seeks to put this spirit into practice. It means that the priorities and perspectives of poor people should inform the decisions we make at all levels in ActionAid, and the decisions made by our partners. It means that we must be transparent in sharing full information about the outcomes of meetings, plans, budgets and expenditures with partners, communities and poor people.

This is a real challenge as we increasingly expect staff and partners to make sure that:

■ Poor and marginalized groups, especially women and girls, take part in programme-level planning. This will include such groups developing their own indicators of progress.
■ They invite poor and marginalized members of the community in particular to be involved in monitoring, reviewing and evaluating what progress has been made within programmes.
■ Where possible, poor and marginalized members of the community and partners are directly involved in recruiting and appraising members of front-line staff, of both partners and ActionAid.

Source: ActionAid International (2000, p. 5)

Current institutional arrangements such as the GRI guidelines may also facilitate improved sustainability reporting by NGOs. For example, two NGOs, the Center for Human Rights and Environment (CEDHA) and the International Institute for Sustainable Development (IISD), reflected on their use of the GRI guidelines for sustainability reporting to publicly account for their environmental and social performance (IISD, 2005). They highlighted how the guidance enhanced their attempts to promote 'continual dialogue with investors, customers, advocates, suppliers and employees' and to 'build, sustain, and continually refine stakeholder engagement' (p. 4). While outlining some problems with the GRI guidance they concluded that if NGOs are flexible, holistic in their thinking, and willing to adapt the guidelines to best meet their needs, then they can prove beneficial. They recommended that a specific NGO sector supplement be produced by the GRI for NGOs wishing to engage in some form of so-called sustainability reporting. The development of such a supplement is now on the GRI's agenda.

EVALUATIONS OF NGO ACCOUNTABILITY

Despite the initiatives outlined in the last section, formal reporting by NGOs on their social and environmental impacts is rather scarce. According to the UK-based consultancy SustainAbility (2003, pp. 22–4), only a handful of large NGOs are producing sophisticated so-called 'sustainability' reports and these mainly address their environmental management and performance. For example, WWF (UK) now produces its own environmental report, while others like Amnesty International have come under pressure from members to initiate reporting in this vein (SustainAbility, 2003).

SustainAbility (2003, p. 24) used an amended version of their ranking scheme for assessing corporate sustainability reporting quality to scrutinize a number of social/environmental reports produced by a broad collection of NGOs, including Oxfam GB, WWF (UK) and Friends of the Earth (UK). The NGOs analysed varied widely in size and available resources but the top score achieved (out of 100) was 45 with an average score of 29. According to this ranking scheme, these NGOs lagged considerably behind their corporate partners in both the quality and coverage of their reporting.

As part of the GAP process, One World Trust assessed and compared the accountability of a number of international NGOs,[13] transnational companies and inter-governmental organizations. This limited review focused in detail on two 'core organizational dimensions [deemed] crucial to fostering greater accountability . . . member control and access to [online] information' (Kovach et al., 2003, p. iv). The survey found that international NGOs were the worst performers when it came to providing access to online information. The authors also expressed surprise at the extent of the absence of information regarding the way NGOs' money was spent and how well they were achieving their aims. Access to information about decision-making procedures was also limited. However, international NGOs tended to have mechanisms in place to avoid minority member dominance. Given the limited dimensions of accountability used and the small number of NGOs assessed, these results should be interpreted cautiously.[14]

A recent study by Unerman and O'Dwyer (2004) questions the willingness of some international NGOs to apply the same standards of accountability to themselves that they demand of others. The Corporate Responsibility Coalition (or CORE) is a group of NGOs who campaigned to introduce legislation in the UK parliament which would require all but the smallest UK-based businesses to comply with certain minimum corporate social responsibility (CSR) and social and environmental accountability (SEA) requirements.[15] The CORE Coalition's literature stated that the reason it was necessary to have mandatory CSR/SEA requirements was that with a voluntary approach to CSR/SEA, many corporations had simply ignored the negative impact their activities have on many people:

297

> in a globalised world, decisions and actions can have unforeseen con-
> sequences in many different locations . . . corporations must ensure that,
> as a minimum, their business activities do not have an adverse impact on
> the various 'stakeholders' they affect.
>
> (CORE, 2003, p. 1)

Equally, Unerman and O'Dwyer (2004) argued that many unforeseen consequences could flow from the actions and decisions of (large) NGOs (see also Unerman and O'Dwyer, 2006b). The CORE coalition promulgated a number of minimum CSR and SEA standards encompassing, among other issues, the publication of sustainability reports and the enactment of substantive stakeholder engagement exercises. To ascertain the extent to which members of this NGO coalition in the UK were complying with these standards of responsibility and accountability, Unerman and O'Dwyer (2004) conducted an in-depth content analysis of the entire websites of the coalition's founder members[16] for evidence of their implementation of the CSR/SEA requirements they proposed. Overall, they found relatively minimal CSR/SEA-related disclosures by most of the CORE coalition founders. Given that they defined these CSR/SEA disclosures in accordance with the CORE coalition's own requirements for CSR/SEA in commercial organizations, and that most of these definitions were equally applicable to the impact of NGO activities as they were to the impact of corporate activities, the authors found these low levels of NGO disclosure to be surprising.

CONCLUDING COMMENTS

This chapter provides a flavour of emerging developments in NGO accountability, a field that is rapidly growing in prominence and importance. Given the vast expanse of NGOs, this review is limited to those NGOs who are primarily involved in advocacy which either directly or indirectly seeks to enable some form of progress towards social sustainability. There are, however, many advocacy NGOs who have no such objectives and seek to advocate for policies that threaten this goal. For example, many powerful NGOs advocate (covertly and overtly) for free trade and economic policies that run counter to concerns to promote social sustainability (Gray *et al.*, 2006). Other NGOs, while claiming to exhibit concern for social sustainability, actually operate to capture or dilute the reformist/radical characteristics central to social sustainability. There are also NGOs actively targeting and seeking to discredit NGOs promoting social sustainability as part of their advocacy work. More in-depth examinations of these organizations' accountability are essential if the social sustainability cause is to be sustained. This makes it crucial for NGOs seeking to contribute to social sustainability to embrace enhanced accountability on their terms in order to pressure those with less virtuous aims into demonstrating their own accountability.

298

Under pressure NGO leaders seeking guidance on accountability do, however, need to be careful about imposing accountability regimes from the business or private sector. The way a sector defines its accountability influences its distinctive identity and role in society (Jepson, 2005). The NGO 'sector' addressed here is characterized by a distinctive accountability regime with different subjects and mechanisms of accountability (Goodin, 2003). Consequently, these NGOs 'must develop their own tools, processes and systems and then convince others of their efficacy and merit' (Jepson, 2005, p. 518). I agree with Jepson (2005) who argues that the NGO accountability debate needs to pause in order to provide the time and space to develop and test concepts and tools that together might create an accountability suited to NGOs and avoid rushing to accept externally imposed and often inappropriate short-term mechanisms.

NOTES

1 For example, at the public policy level, NGOs have a good record in influencing EU-level policies generally and specifically on trade in GM foods, global warming and the pricing of anti-viral pharmaceuticals in developing countries (Doh and Guay, 2006). The NGO Working Group on the United Nations' Security Council has also, in a relatively short time, become an influential forum at the United Nations. The Working Group meets regularly with ambassadors of virtually all Council-member delegations, thereby enjoying access to and influence over the highest levels of United Nations decision-makers (Unerman and O'Dwyer, 2006b).

2 A crucial caveat needs to be outlined at this early stage in the chapter. While recent research critiquing some NGO accounting and reporting practices is reviewed, this apparent lack of accounting reporting is not used here to imply that these NGOs are unaccountable. It merely implies that they are possibly not affording accountability enough consideration (although see INGO, 2006, and Russell, 2006) given their often powerful role in influencing public policy, particularly in Europe. There is a danger that the limited analyses outlined later in the chapter may be latched upon for purely political reasons by those who would seek to destroy the influence many NGOs wish to make to the cause of social sustainability.

3 Hudson (2002, pp. 404–5) notes that advocacy is a growth area for all types of NGOs and can form part of a package of objectives for some NGOs. In this chapter, I consider those NGOs whose primary purpose is to advocate for certain public policies or decision-making around their key issue(s) of concern.

4 According to Salamon et al. (1999, p. 8) the global non-profit sector is a $1.1 trillion industry that employs close to 19 million full-time equivalent paid workers. These figures do, however, need to be interpreted with caution. Firstly, the definition of a non-profit entity in Salamon et al.'s (1999) study is very wide, encompassing cultural, arts and sports groups, trade and professional associations, traditional charitable organizations, organizations involved in religious worship (although these were not included in the figures quoted above), non-governmental organizations

(NGOs) engaged in development work, grassroots development organizations, lower and higher education institutions, hospitals, organized social movements and social services groups among others (Salamon *et al.*, 1999, pp. 466–8). This implies that the NGO 'sector' examined in this chapter is considerably smaller than this. Secondly, this data, which has been widely cited in some recent NGO accountability studies (see SustainAbility (2003, p. 2)), relates to 1995 (Salamon *et al.*, 1999, p. 7).

5 For example, the disastrous response of diverse and competing human rights NGOs to the crisis in Rwanda led to a coalition of NGOs to initiate their own code of conduct, humanitarian charter and ombudsman under the umbrella of the Humanitarian Accountability Project (HAP) (see Callamard, 2004).

6 It is often claimed that too much research and NGO attention is focused on this upward, external accountability to patron stakeholders at the expense of downward accountability to the 'clients' NGOs are supposed to serve (Najam, 1996).

7 This was the 'green power: green responsibility' lecture series convened by Linacre College and the Environmental Change Institute of the University of Oxford during February and March 2004. The ENGO CEOs came from Friends of the Earth (FoE), SustainAbility, Royal Society for the Protection of Birds (RSPB), Campaign to Protect Rural England (CPRE), World Wildlife Fund (WWF) (UK) and the Wildlife Conservation Society, New York (WCS) (see Jepson, 2005).

8 For a comprehensive list of current NGO accountability mechanisms, see One World Trust (2005).

9 The AA1000 standard developed by the Institute of Social and Ethical Accountability in the UK in 1999 is another example of a 'social accounting (audit)' framework to enable NGO accountability. For more details, see Chapter 4 by Adams and Narayanan.

10 Traidcraft plc is not an NGO *per se* but much of its experimentation with social accounting took place in its sister organization Traidcraft Exchange, a small charitable company limited by guarantee which was partially involved in advocating for fair trade. NEF's key aim is to improve the quality of life by promoting innovative solutions that challenge mainstream thinking on economic, environment and social issues.

11 These can be viewed at www.traidcraft.co.uk.

12 The NEF/Traidcraft approach was very influential in the development of the AA1000 methodology of the Institute for Social and Ethical Accountability outlined by Adams and Narayanan in Chapter 4 of this text.

13 These comprised Amnesty International, CARE International, International Chamber of Commerce, International Confederation of Free Trade Unions, International Federation of Red Cross and Red Crescent Societies, Oxfam International and World Wildlife Fund (WWF).

14 WWF (UK) was one of the NGOs that agreed to be evaluated by GAP as it felt that it might offer guidance on what WWF (UK) might do regarding its accountability as well as alerting the wider WWF-network to the accountability issue. Its chief executive indicated that WWF (UK)'s relatively poor ranking in the GAP evaluation

proved a wake-up call and a spur for action for the organization in relation to its accountability (see Jepson, 2005, p. 522).

15 The founding members of the CORE coalition were Amnesty International UK, Christian Aid, Friends of the Earth (FoE), New Economics Foundation (NEF) and Traidcraft.

16 With the exception of Friends of the Earth.

REFERENCES

AccountAbility (1999) *AA1000 framework: Standard, guidelines and professional qualification*. London: AccountAbility.

ActionAid International (2000) *ALPS (Accountability, Planning and Learning System)*, ActionAid International, url: http://www.actionaid.org/wps/content/documents/alps_1832005_114916.pdf, accessed 4 September 2006.

ActionAid International (2004a) Taking stock II: Summary of ALPS review 2004. ActionAid International, url: http://www.actionaid.org.uk/1417/global_review.html, accessed 4 September 2006.

ActionAid International (2004b) ActionAid International: Taking stock II – synthesis report 2004, http://www.actionaid.org/wps/content/documents/synthesis_report_1832005_131515.pdf, accessed 4 September 2006.

Bebbington, J. (2001) Sustainable development: A review of the international development, business and accounting literature. *Accounting Forum*, 25(2): 128–57.

Bebbington, J. and Gray, R. (2001) An account of sustainability: Failure, success and a reconceptualisation. *Critical Perspectives on Accounting*, 12(5): 557–605.

Bendell, J. (ed.) (2000) *Terms for endearment: Business, NGOs and sustainable development*. Sheffield: Greenleaf.

Blagescu, M., De Las Casas, L. and Lloyd, R. (2005) *Pathways to accountability: A short guide to the GAP framework*. London: One World Trust.

Bonbright, D. (2004) NGO accountability and performance: Introducing ACCESS. *AccountAbility Forum*, 1(2): 2–6.

Brown, D. and Moore, M. (2001) Accountability, strategy and international NGOs. *Nonprofit and Voluntary Sector Quarterly*, 30(3): 586–7.

Brown, D., Moore, M. and Honan, J. (2004) Building strategic accountability systems for International NGOs. *AccountAbility Forum*, 2: 31–43.

Burall, S., Neligan, C. and Kovach, H. (2003) *Power without accountability: The global accountability report*. London: One World Trust.

Callamard, A. (2004) HAP international: A new decisive step towards accountability. *AccountAbility Forum*, 1(2): 44–57.

Centre for Civil Society and Governance (2005) *A report of the task force on NGO statistics and social auditing*. University of Hong Kong, 30 May, http://web.hku.hk/~ccsg/APPCReport-TaskForce-Final.doc (pdf file), accessed 4 September 2006.

Clark, J. (1991) *Democratizing development: The role of volunteer organizations*. London: Earthscan.

CORE (2003) With rights come responsibilities. London: Corporate Responsibility Coalition, 7 August.

Cronin, D. and O'Regan, J. (2002) *Accountability in development aid: Meeting responsibilities, measuring performance*. A Research Report for Comhlamh. Dublin: Comhlamh Aid Issues Group.

Dawson, E. (1998) The relevance of social audit for Oxfam GB. *Journal of Business Ethics*, 17(13): 1457–69.

Dey, C. (2004) Social accounting at Traidcraft plc: An ethnographic study of a struggle for the meaning of fair trade. Paper presented at the APIRA conference Singapore, 4–6 July.

Dillon, E. (2004) Accountabilities and power in development relationships. *Trocaire Development Review 2003/4*. Dublin: Trocaire, pp. 105–17.

Dixon, R., Ritchie, J. and Siwale, J. (2006) Microfinance: Accountability from the grass-roots. *Accounting, Auditing and Accountability Journal*, 19(3): 405–27.

Doh, J. P. and Guay, T. R. (2006) Corporate social responsibility, public policy, and NGO activism in Europe and the United States: An institutional stakeholder perspective. *Journal of Management Studies*, 43(1): 47–73.

Doh, J. P. and Teegen, H. (2002) Nongovernmental organizations as institutional actors in international business: Theory and implications. *International Business Review*, 11: 665–84.

Ebrahim, A. (2003a) Making sense of accountability: Conceptual perspectives for Northern and Southern Nonprofits. *Nonprofit Management and Leadership*, 14(2): 191–212.

Ebrahim, A. (2003b) Accountability in practice: Mechanisms for NGO's. *World Development*, 31: 813–29.

Ebrahim, A. (2005) Accountability myopia: Losing sight of organizational learning. *Nonprofit and Voluntary Sector Quarterly*, 34(1): 56–87.

Edwards, M. (1993) Does the doormat influence the boot?: Critical thoughts on UK NGOs and international advocacy. *Development in Practice*, 3: 163–75.

Edwards (2000) *NGO Rights and Responsibilities: A New Deal for Global Governance*. London: Foreign Policy Centre.

Edwards, M. and Fowler, A. (2002) Introduction: Changing challenges for NGDO management. In M. Edwards and A. Fowler (eds) *NGO management*. London: Earthscan.

Edwards, M. and Fowler, A. (eds) (2003) *NGO management*. London: Earthscan.

Edwards, M. and Hulme, D. (1992) Scaling-up the developmental impact of NGOs: Concepts and experiences. In M. Edwards and D. Hulme (eds) *Making a difference: NGOs and development in a changing world*. London: Earthscan, pp. 13–27.

Edwards, M. and Hulme, D. (1996a) Too close for comfort? The impact of official aid on non-governmental organisations. *World Development*, 24(6): 961–73.

Edwards, M. and Hulme, D. (1996b) *NGO performance and accountability: Beyond the magic bullet*. West Hartford, CT: Kumarian Press.

Fisher, W. F. (1997) Doing good? The politics and antipolitics of NGO practices. *Annual Review of Anthropology*, 26: 439–64.

Fowler, A. F. (1996) Assessing NGO performance: Difficulty, dilemmas, and a way ahead. In M. Edwards and D. Hulme (eds) *Beyond the magic bullet: NGO performance and accountability in the post-Cold War world*. West Hartford, CT: Kumarian Press.

Gibelman, M. and Gelman, S. R. (2001) Very public scandals: Nongovernmental organisations in trouble. *Voluntas: International Journal of Voluntary and Non-profit Organisations*, 12(1): 49–66.

Goddard, A., and Assad, M. J. (2006) Accounting and navigating legitimacy in Tanzanian NGOs. *Accounting, Auditing and Accountability Journal*, 19(3): 377–404.

Goetz, A. M. and Jenkins, R. (2002) Voice, accountability and development: The emergence of a new agenda. *Human development report 2002*. New York: UNDP.

Goodin, R. E. (2003) Democratic accountability: The third sector and all. Working Paper no. 19, Hauser Center for Nonprofit Organisations.

Gray, R., Bebbington, J. and Collison, D. (2006) NGOs, civil society and accountability: Making the people accountable to capital. *Accounting, Auditing and Accountability Journal*, 19(3): 319–48.

Gray, R. H., Dey, C., Owen, D. L., Evans, R. and Zadek, S. (1997) Struggling with the praxis of social accounting: Stakeholders, accountability, audits and procedures. *Accounting, Auditing and Accountability Journal*, 10(3): 325–64.

Hawke Research Institute for Sustainable Societies (2005) Position paper: Redefining social sustainability, http://www.unisa.edu.au/hawkeinstitute/research/eco-position.asp, accessed 4 September 2006.

Hudson, A. (1999) Organizing NGOs' international advocacy: Organizational structures and organizational effectiveness. Paper presented at the NGOs in a Global Future conference, University of Birmingham, 11–13 January.

Hudson, A. (2000) Making the connection: Legitimacy claims, legitimacy chains and northern NGOs' international advocacy. In D. Lewis and T. Wallace (eds) *After the 'new policy agenda'? Non-governmental organisations and the search for development alternatives*. West Hartford, CT: Kumarian Press.

Hudson, A. (2002) Advocacy by UK-based development NGOs. *Nonprofit and Voluntary Sector Quarterly*, 31(3): 402–18.

IISD (2005) *Model International Agreement on Investment for Sustainable Development*. Winnipeg, Manitoba: International Institute for Sustainable Development.

303

International Non-Governmental Organisations Accountability Charter (INGO) (2006) http://www.worldywca.info/index.php/ywca/content/download/2174/23424/file/account_charter.pdf, accessed 13 June.

Jepson, P. (2005) Governance and accountability of environmental NGOs. *Environmental Science and Policy*, 8: 515–24.

Kaldor, M. (2002) Civil society and accountability. *Human Development Report Office Occasional Paper*. Geneva: United Nations Development Programme.

Kamat, S. (2003) NGO's and the new democracy. *Harvard International Review*, 25: 65–70.

Kearns, K. P. (1994) The strategic management of accountability in nonprofit organisations: An analytical framework. *Public Administration Review*, 54(2): 185–92.

Keck, M. E. and Sikkink, K. (1998) *Activists beyond borders: Advocacy networks in international politics*. Ithaca: Cornell University Press.

Keystone (2005) *Core Propositions and Methodology*, http://www.keystonereporting.org/model/methodology, accessed 4 September 2006.

Lewis, D. and Madon, S. (2004) Information systems and nongovernmental development organisations: Advocacy, organisational learning, and accountability. *The Information Society*, 20: 117–26.

Litovsky, A. (2005a) *The future of civil society*, Workshop Report from the World Social Forum, 30 January, Keystone (c/o AccountAbility), London, http://www.keystonereporting.org/files/WSF%202005%20Workshop%20Report%20Keystone.pdf, accessed 1 September 2006.

Litovsky, A. (2005b) Stakeholder engagement and NGO accountability: The new frontier for innovation. *Accountability Forum*, 2(6): 25–35.

Lloyd, R. (2005) *The role of NGO self regulation in increasing stakeholder accountability*. London: One World Trust.

Loft, A., Humphrey, C. and Turley, S. (2006) In pursuit of global regulation: Changing governance and accountability structures at the International Federation of Accountants (IFAC). *Accounting, Auditing and Accountability Journal*, 19(3): 428–51.

Maitland, A. (2003) Accountability 'vital' if NGOs are to retain trust. *Financial Times*, London 26 June, p. 6.

Martens, K. (2002) Mission Impossible? Defining nongovernmental organisations. *Voluntas: International Journal of Voluntary and Nonprofit Organisations*, 13(3): 271–85.

Naidoo, K. (2004) The end of blind faith? Civil society and the challenges of accountability, transparency and legitimacy. *AccountAbility Forum*, 1(2): 14–25.

Najam, A. (1996) NGO accountability: A conceptual framework. *Development Policy Review*, 14: 339–53.

O'Dwyer, B. (2005a) The construction of a social account: A case study in an overseas aid agency. *Accounting, Organizations and Society*, 30(3): 279–96.

O'Dwyer, B. (2005b) Stakeholder democracy: Challenges and contributions from social accounting. *Business Ethics: A European Review,* 14(1): 28–41.

O'Dwyer, B., Unerman, J. and Brocklebank, C. (2005) Non-government organisational accountability: The case of Amnesty Ireland. Paper presented at the 17th International Congress on Social and Environmental Accounting Research, St Andrews University.

One World Trust (2005) *NGO Accountability Initiatives,* http://www.oneworldtrust.org/?display=ngoinitiatives, accessed 4 September 2006.

Onishi, N. (2002) Nongovernmental organisations show their growing power. *The New York Times,* 22 March, p. A10.

Pearce, J. (1996) *Measuring social wealth: A study of social audit practice for community and cooperative enterprises.* London: New Economics Foundation.

Rasche, A. and Esser, D. E. (2006) From stakeholder management to stakeholder accountability: Applying Habermasian discourse ethics to accountability research. *Journal of Business Ethics,* 65(3): 251–67.

Raynard, P. (1998) Coming together: A review of contemporary approaches to social accounting, auditing and reporting in nonprofit organizations. *Journal of Business Ethics,* 17: 1471–9.

Russell, J. (2006) NGO accountability: A charter for success. *Ethical Corporation Magazine* online (5 June), http://www.ethicalcorp.com/, accessed 14 June 2006.

Salamon, L. M. (1994) The rise of the nonprofit sector: A global 'Associational Revolution'. *Foreign Affairs,* 73(4): 109–22.

Salamon, L. M., Anheier, H. K., List, R., Toepler, S. and Sokolowski, S. W. (eds) (1999) *Global civil society: Dimensions of the nonprofit sector.* Baltimore: Johns Hopkins University.

Scott-Villiers, P. (2002) The struggle for organisational change: How the ActionAid accountability, learning and planning system emerged. *Development in Practice,* 12(3–4): 424–35.

Slim, H. (2002) *By what authority? The legitimacy and accountability of non-governmental organisations.* The International Council on Human Rights Policy. International Meetings on Global Trends and Human Rights – Before and After September 11, Geneva 2002, online at http://www.ichrp.org/paper_files/119_w_02.doc, accessed 4 September 2006.

Spar, D. L. and Mure, L. T. (1997) The power of activism: Assessing the impact of NGOs on global business. *California Management Review,* 45(3): 78–101.

SustainAbility (2003) *The 21st century NGO: In the market for change.* Executive Summary. London: SustainAbility.

Thomson, I. and Bebbington, J. (2005) Social and environmental accounting in the UK: A pedagogic evaluation. *Critical Perspectives on Accounting,* 16(5): 507–33.

Unerman, J. and O'Dwyer, B. (2004) NGO accountability and the CORE coalition. Paper presented at the University of Sydney Accounting and Business Law Seminar series.

Unerman, J. and O'Dwyer, B. (2006a) On James Bond and the importance of NGO accountability. *Accounting, Auditing and Accountability Journal,* 19(3): 305–18.

Unerman, J. and O'Dwyer, B. (2006b) Theorising accountability for NGO advocacy. *Accounting, Auditing and Accountability Journal*, 19(3): 349–76.

Upadhyay, A. (2003) NGOs: Do the watchdogs need watching?, http://www.globalpolicy.org/ngos/credib/2003/0613panel.htm, accessed 4 September 2006.

Uphoff, N. (1995) Why NGOs are not a third sector: A sectorial analysis with some thoughts on accountability, sustainability and evaluation. In M. Edwards and D. Hulme (eds) *Beyond the magic bullet: NGO performance and accountability in the post-Cold War world*. West Hartford, CT: Kumarian Press.

Vakil, A. C. (1997) Confronting the classification problem: A taxonomy of NGOs. *World Development*, 25(12): 2057–70.

Volunteer Vancouver (1999) *What social auditing can do for voluntary organizations*. Vancouver: Volunteer Vancouver.

Yakel, E. (2001) The social construction of accountability: Radiologists and their record keeping practices. *The Information Society*, 17(4): 233–45.

Zadek, S. (2003) *In defence of non-profit accountability*. London: Ethical Corporation, 19 September.

Chapter 16

Developing silent and shadow accounts

Colin Dey

INTRODUCTION

The quantity of voluntary, unregulated social, environmental and sustainability reporting (SER hereafter) in the UK and elsewhere has risen substantially in recent years, particularly amongst multinational corporations. Yet such disclosures still fail to satisfy some critics who argue that they are selective and unreliable (see, for example, Adams, 2004; O'Dwyer and Owen, 2005). Contrary to the rhetorical claims which usually accompany modern SER, such disclosures may not augment organizational accountability, and may instead be viewed as managerialist attempts to resist meaningful organizational change and to control and manipulate stakeholder sentiment (see, for example, Owen *et al.*, 2000). Whilst industry itself may promote 'self-policing' voluntary regimes (see, for example, BITC, 2003), some critics argue that much more direct intervention, in the form of mandatory regulation of corporate disclosure (and/or governance) processes, is necessary to improve the quality of modern SER (CORE Coalition, 2003). However, tangible progress in this area has been slow, and the last-ditch abandonment of the government's (already weakened) measures in 2005 has ended any immediate prospect of improvements in mandatory SER in the UK at least.

In the absence of complete and reliable 'official' SER, and given the apparent level of institutional resistance towards this, it seems legitimate to consider whether alternative sources of 'unofficial' corporate accountability information may be used. Such a suggestion is not new; indeed, there is a long history of various forms of what is generally referred to as external social reporting (for detailed reviews, see Gray *et al.*, 1996; Gallhofer and Haslam, 2003). In general terms, the use of such external social reports may be advocated on the grounds that:

> first, [they] act as a 'balancing view' in the face of the considerable resources that organisations have at their disposal to put their own point of

view and to offer their own emphasis on their activities. Secondly, [they] can be motivated by the realisation that if organisations will not discharge their own duty of accountability then it is possible for other bodies to do it on their behalf.

(Gibson *et al.*, 2001)

Against the backdrop of a rapid increase in what are arguably flawed corporate SER disclosures, a renewed interest in forms of external social reporting as a counter-balance (or 'counter accounting')[1] to current practice seems worth pursuing. More-over, at the same time as concerns have risen over the quality of modern SER, recent advances in information technology and global communications, and the emergence of various 'new social movements' in civil society have greatly increased the availability of 'unofficial' accountability information and in turn improved the scope for practical development of external social reporting.

This chapter focuses on the potential of two relatively recent and emerging forms of external social reports, which, drawing on the work of Gray (1997) and Gibson *et al.* (2001), may be referred to as 'shadow' and 'silent' accounts. The starting point for silent and shadow accounting lies in the differences which exist between what is usually promised by SER and what is generally delivered. Such differences, if studied more closely, may reveal certain 'gaps' in disclosure, and it is the identification of these gaps, by exploiting the vast increase in public availability of, and access to, wider sources of information about corporate behaviour, that forms the basis of an argument for alternative forms of silent and shadow dis-closures. By comparison to the 'official' social and environmental accountability information contained in SER reports currently being disclosed by the organization, one may define these disclosures as:

1   the corresponding 'unofficial' or *silent* account of corporate SER, compiled from 'nuggets' of relevant information obtained via all other formal corporate disclosure channels, including company annual reports, press releases, market-ing campaigns etc.; and
2   a *shadow* account consisting of other relevant accountability information that is readily available in the public domain, produced independently of the subject organization, and published externally from it.

As a possible avenue of empirical development, this chapter explores the potential of silent and shadow accounts and reviews the extent to which both academics and other interested groups have already begun to explore it. The chapter concludes by tentatively outlining the ways such reports might be usefully developed further on a practical level. Before doing so, however, the next section of the chapter establishes in more detail the background to, and basis for, silent and shadow accounts.

308

MINDING THE GAPS: A BASIS FOR SILENT AND SHADOW ACCOUNTS

Samples of published SER disclosures have been empirically reviewed in the accounting literature to examine the quality of reporting. Evaluating disclosures is a subjective task that may use a wide range of criteria, but the basic principles of the AA1000 reporting process guidelines (ISEA, 1999), so often used by disclosers to legitimize their reports, represent an obvious quality benchmark. Yet even when judged in detail against these guidelines, and similar frameworks such as GRI (Global Reporting Initiative, 2002), disclosures still appear to suffer from significant deficiencies (see, for example, Owen *et al.*, 2001; Stittle, 2002; Belal, 2002; Unerman and Bennett, 2004; O'Dwyer and Owen, 2005). Indeed, the criticism of modern CSR extends further, by questioning the underlying purpose of these 'cutting-edge' voluntary reporting standards and guidelines, in terms of their implicit managerialism (Owen *et al.*, 2000). Together, such concerns point to the existence of a 'gap' between what is demanded and what is delivered by current 'best practice' disclosure regimes (Adams and Evans, 2004). This 'gap' has been described variously as: a 'reporting–performance portrayal gap' (Adams, 2004); an 'assurance expectations gap' (Swift and Dando, 2002); a 'legitimacy gap' (Moerman and Van der Laan, 2005); and as a 'credibility gap' (Dando and Swift, 2003; O'Dwyer and Owen, 2005). The existence of a 'gap' has also been identified by industry-sponsored surveys (see, for example, ECC Kohtes Klewes and Fishburn Hedges, 2003) as well as by leading NGOs (see, for example, Christian Aid, 2003).

It seems that there may be different possible definitions of this gap. In fact, it may be measured in (at least) three different ways. Firstly and most straightforwardly, it may be viewed as the difference between the *lack of completeness* of reporting and the comprehensive picture of overall social performance initially promised by corporate rhetoric and in voluntary reporting standards. Recent studies, including both samples of several high-profile disclosers (Belal, 2002) as well as more detailed examinations of individual companies (Gray, 1997; Gibson *et al.*, 2001; Adams, 2004), have demonstrated in compelling ways that current forms of SER, despite claims to the contrary, continue to be highly selective in what is measured and communicated to the reader. We will review the evidence presented in these studies in more detail later in this chapter.

Secondly, if SER disclosers are exhibiting undesirable tendencies towards selective reporting, then the role of external assurance in the process becomes especially important. However, once again critics contend that there are significant shortcomings in this part of the SER process. In their review of a sample of assurance statements, O'Dwyer and Owen (2005) questioned both the independence of the assurance process as well as the extent to which management exerted control over the exercise. Such managerialism drew the authors to the conclusion that assurance statements are 'merely more "value added" for management as they manage key risks imposed by various stakeholder groups who need to be controlled' (p. 209). The 'gap' identified above may also therefore be seen as the difference between the *poor reliability* of given assurances and the credibility promised in disclosure.

Finally, the gap between what is demanded and what is delivered by current SER practice can also be construed as the difference between the *controls and restrictions* placed on dialogue processes and the freedoms and rights of participants promised by dialogue organizers (Owen *et al.*, 2001; Unerman and Bennett, 2004). 'Stakeholder dialogue' appears attractive by implying some kind of 'genuine' consensus-based space for dialogue in which companies will listen and respond to the voices of stakeholders. However, it may instead function as a carefully controlled marketing instrument in which stakeholders, lured in by the illusion of influence, simply 'teach' companies about themselves, enabling companies to 'learn' to identify the most troublesome and/or powerful groups and how to control them more effectively (Thomson and Bebbington, 2005).

The existence of such gaps in modern SER is a matter of fundamental concern because issues of completeness and reliability of SER are central to notions of stakeholder *accountability* (Gray *et al.*, 1996) while confidence in, and integrity of, stakeholder dialogues is essential to satisfying notions of stakeholder *democracy* (O'Dwyer, 2005). Following the basic assumptions of accountability theory, the development of an effective counterpoint to current practice, which seeks to evidence the gaps identified above, becomes desirable since an increase in the quantity and quality of information (via silent and shadow accounts) may yield a corresponding increase in accountability (Gray *et al.*, 1996). Having established a motivation for silent and shadow accounts, the next section briefly outlines the history of experimentation with external social reporting and reviews the main academic research undertaken in recent years.

EXPERIMENTS TO DATE IN SILENT AND SHADOW ACCOUNTING

Whilst the broad idea of using externally produced 'counter-disclosures' as a remedy against perceived deficiencies in the accountability of corporations is well established, practical experimentation with this idea has been somewhat patchy. Since the 1970s external social reporting has manifested itself in different guises without ever fully establishing itself, while its development has been supported and sustained by more familiar and long-standing cultural traditions, including investigative journalism (Pilger, 2004), as well as (perhaps more significantly) the grassroots activism of various social movements and campaigning pressure groups (Lubbers, 2003). In recent years, such traditions have been supported by the internet as a medium for the dissemination of 'counter-information' (Gallhofer *et al.*, 2006). The significance of such wider cultural phenomena for the development of new forms of 'counter-accounting' is worth emphasizing. In fact, current experiments with counter-accounting and counter-information are perhaps more likely to owe their existence to civil society and the work of various campaigning NGOs than to the efforts of accounting academics.

The work of organizations such as Social Audit Ltd[2] and Counter Information Services (CIS) in the 1970s is perhaps the most celebrated of the antecedents of modern SER (and counter-SER) practice (see Medawar, 1976; Geddes, 1991; Gray *et al.*, 1996; Gallhofer and Haslam, 2003). The name 'social audit' is perhaps especially eye-catching, and although strictly the intellectual property of the company of the same name (and ultimately misleading – the term *social account* would have been more accurate) it has endured and persisted in general usage. In essence, both organizations were established to publish 'counter-information' as a response to the (then) perceived absence of, and demand for, accountability disclosures. The output of Social Audit Ltd and CIS was substantial, but it had declined by the mid-1980s, and this continued until the emergence in the late 1980s of the popular phrase 'greenwash'[3] (Greer and Bruno, 1996), which reflected growing social and media awareness of possible corporate manipulation of environmental issues (mass awareness of which had been invigorated by headlines about global warming). By the early 1990s, this had turned into a backlash against the early pioneers of ethical consumerism; Body Shop's claims of social and environmental responsibility were especially subject to criticism and even an external 'social audit' (Entine, 2003). In the accounting literature, some research was undertaken to review the impact of pressure groups on published SER (Tilt, 1994), while calls were also made for improved independent 'monitoring' of the activities of multinational corporations (Bailey *et al.*, 1994), which potentially involved some form of regulated external accountability reporting (Bailey *et al.*, 2000).

By the mid-1990s, the first experiments in modern SER practice were beginning to emerge. As this grew into a rapidly rising groundswell of corporate, governmental and media enthusiasm for voluntary social and environmental reporting, the use of counter-information techniques waned. Although the quantity of emerging SER practice was recognized to be relatively low, a sense of optimism drove forward attempts to improve 'best practice'. In academia and beyond, efforts were increasingly directed pragmatically at trying to encourage corporations and assist in the development of the theory and practice of modern SER (see, for example, Zadek *et al.*, 1997).

In an effort to boost the relatively low volume of disclosure at that time, and prompt more critical reflection on the state of SER, Gray (1997) mooted the idea of reviving forms of external social reporting. However, rather than simply reproducing the approach pioneered in the 1970s by Social Audit Ltd and Counter Information Services, Gray devised a new and intriguingly different form of corporate 'silent' accounting. To illustrate the concept, Gray produced a silent account based on the 1994 annual report of the large pharmaceutical company Glaxo plc.

The simple premise of this idea was to identify relevant information from Glaxo's annual report (referred to as 'silent' because such information, although published, was not 'officially' labelled or recognized as SER) and to effectively 'create' a new piece of SER by collating this relevant information in a new document. Silent accounts could be seen not only as a cheap and quick way of increasing disclosures, but also as 'greater than the sum of their parts' by (re)creating a picture of organizational accountability based on 'broad' areas of activity concerning four 'key' stakeholders: employees, community, customers and environment; as well as a further category covering corporate mission and governance issues. These categories were chosen partly on the grounds that they typically featured in corporate annual reports. Clearly, as Gray himself acknowledged, they were by no means a complete list, but in the absence of more complete and inclusive corporate disclosures, a wider picture of stakeholder accountability could not be easily generated. Indeed, to overcome this problem, Gray appears to have envisaged his experiment as an initial test of the feasibility of a more complete and coherent form of organization-centred SER (see especially Gray et al., 1997).

By the late 1990s, concerns about the pervasive absence of corporate SER began to gradually diminish, while a new set of concerns grew over the quality of emerging corporate disclosures. To find new ground upon which a critical evaluation of SER might be developed, a number of accounting academics started various separate research projects which sought to develop new forms of external social reporting.[4]

Gray's initial experimentation with silent accounting was radically revised by a group of researchers including the same author to incorporate a form of external social reporting which was termed 'shadow accounts'. Shadow accounting represented a more familiar rediscovery of the external social reports of the 1970s. Crucially, however, in seeking to illuminate further the shortcomings of corporate accountability disclosures, it recognized the increasing quantities of, and access to, counter-information in the public domain. Such information could be relatively easily gathered by academic researchers and published, not simply as a separate document, but in parallel with 'unofficial' silent accounts (or, if they were available, 'official' SER), using the same categories and subject headings.

To this end, Gibson et al. (2001) produced a series of combined reports on the activities of well-known UK companies, from different industry sectors, which had yet to produce their own dedicated social or environmental reports. These pioneering silent and shadow accounts presented the reader with a (hitherto unavailable) picture of corporate accountability which directly juxtaposed corporate and non-corporate sources of information. The accounts were deliberately presented to the reader without much additional editorializing or analysis and relied on the information-gathering exercise alone for their impact. A second, and perhaps less justifiable, characteristic of these reports was their relatively uncritical use of shadow information sources, which in the Gibson et al. accounts relied mainly on (potentially inaccurate) broadsheet newspaper articles. The shadow account did not independently establish the veracity or, for that matter, qualify the content of some material as allegations rather than accepted fact. Such an approach could in a strict sense be construed as potentially libellous, but more importantly it risked implying a double-standard whereby shadow sources did not need to be subjected to the same scrutiny as corporate sources. Nevertheless, despite its possible shortcomings, putting combined silent and shadow reports together in this way served as a compelling basis for revealing significant gaps in the completeness of corporate (non)-disclosure, as well as the extent to which easily available shadow information could be used, both to illuminate the gaps in knowledge of aspects of corporate behaviour missing from disclosures as well as to challenge the (mis)representation of events portrayed in corporate reports.

Around the same time as the notions of silent and shadow accounting were being developed by Gray and others in the mid to late 1990s, a separate project on external social reporting was undertaken by Adams (2004) to explore what she termed the 'reporting–performance portrayal gap'. Adams' case study, in contrast to the 'silent' study of a 'non-reporting' corporation by Gray (1997), examined a corporation (known only by the pseudonym 'Alpha') that had already been producing SER for some years. Using the accountability framework set out in the established social and environmental reporting standards of AA1000, Adams analysed Alpha's published SER (for the years 1993 and 1999) by contrasting it against what the author was able to research and uncover about the chosen company from a wide range of (carefully verified) 'shadow' external information sources for the same time periods. In a broadly similar fashion to the experiments of Gibson et al. (2001), Adams used (and identified in some detail) a wide range of sources of 'shadow' information to illuminate the shortcomings of completeness present in SER disclosures. Like the Gibson et al. research, these shortcomings included situations where (1) shadow information was found to conflict in some way with the comparable corporate account, or (2) where shadow information cast light on something material to stakeholders which was not included in the SER report.

Perhaps more than any other recent experiments in external social reporting, Adams' research evidenced clear deficiencies in completeness in the company's voluntary SER. Although the rhetoric of Alpha's later (and supposedly 'improved') 1999 corporate SER report examined by Adams seemed to imply a narrowing of the 'gap', her study found little evidence of this, and she concluded that, despite several years of development, the disclosure produced by the company under examination still suffered from substantial completeness deficiencies, as well as significant audit and credibility flaws. By comparison, Adams' work is more analytical and drew its own conclusions in a more 'editorialized' style than the Gibson et al. accounts. However, at the same time, for a number of entirely justifiable reasons (both legal and intellectual), the identity of Adams' chosen company was concealed in the paper, whilst the Gibson et al. reports left the company identities (and arguably some of the wider value of the work to a non-academic audience) preserved.

Table 16.1 below attempts to summarize the main characteristics of each of the three experiments reviewed earlier. The basic format of these experiments is compared, as well as the extent to which each uses an explicit framework. The table also attempts to summarize the coverage of each experiment in examining 'gaps' in completeness, dialogue and assurance. While all three experiments have a clear and understandable focus on exploring notions of completeness, the approach of Adams (2004) is perhaps the most comprehensive because of the way it combines the basis of a recognized framework (i.e. AA1000 and GRI reporting standards) with a relatively wider range of shadow information sources and a more explicitly analytical approach to the exploration of completeness 'gaps'. Adams' work is also commendable in that it acknowledges the importance of other gaps in assurance and dialogue processes (although it does not review these issues in as much depth).

In fairness to the Gray and Gibson *et al.* experiments, it is important to emphasize that Adams' use of shadow information as an analytical tool is perhaps made easier by the fact that she was comparing shadow information against the weight of a stand-alone SER report (within which explicit dialogue and assurance processes are supposed to happen) than against a more slight and intangible notion of 'unofficial' silent accounts (in which such organizational accountability mechanisms may not exist).

COUNTER-INFORMATION, NEW SOCIAL MOVEMENTS AND CIVIL SOCIETY

Before further drawing together the strands of 'silent' and 'shadow' accounting research reviewed so far, it is important to first develop the point raised earlier in this chapter concerning the significant and ongoing contribution of other parts of civil society to forms of external social reporting. As the previous section of the chapter noted, it can be argued that much of what academic accountants have done to evidence gaps in existing SER has in fact relied on wider sources of counter-information available in the public domain. The general theme of corporate abuse of power has become increasingly prominent (see, for example, Klein, 2000; Monbiot, 2000; Hertz, 2001), as has popular interest in the issue in specific settings such as the fast food or supermarket industries (see, for example, Schlosser, 2002; Blythman, 2004). In addition, though, this rising mass disapproval towards corporate (mis)behaviour has roots in more politically active parts of civil society. Public discontent with the social and environmental impacts of modern capitalism has been expressed through the activities of what may be termed 'new social movements'. Such social movements include the activities of a range of campaigning pressure groups and other non-governmental organizations (NGOs). The work of

Table 16.1 Recent academic experiments in external social reporting

	Silent account of Glaxo plc (Gray, 1997)	Silent/shadow accounts of Tesco and HSBC (Gibson et al., 2001)	The ethical, social and environmental reporting-performance portrayal gap at 'Alpha' (Adams, 2004)
Basic format	Silent account	Separate silent and shadow accounts – both with same structure	Comparison of stand-alone SER with shadow information for years 1993 and 1999
Section headings	Corporate mission/governance and four 'key' stakeholders	Corporate mission/governance and four 'key' stakeholders	(1) Subject headings cover range of four broad environmental issues (2) Overall coverage of key AA1000 and GRI principles
Sources used (corporate and shadow)	Company Annual Report (1994)	Company Annual Report (2000) UK Broadsheet Newspapers (WWW and CD-ROMs) Limited additional sources from wider media	Corporate SER Reports (1993 and 1999) Many wider sources from the WWW: business related, anti-corporate NGOs, consumer groups, business and trade journals, newspaper CD-ROMs, etc.
Source material presentation	Quoted excerpts from company annual report	Quoted excerpts from company annual report and shadow sources	Editorialized summaries and selective comparisons of SER and shadow information

continued on p. 316

Table 16.1 – Continued

	Silent account of Glaxo plc (Gray, 1997)	Silent/shadow accounts of Tesco and HSBC (Gibson et al., 2001)	The ethical, social and environmental reporting-performance portrayal gap at 'Alpha' (Adams, 2004)
Analytical framework used	Implicit notion of stakeholder accountability	Stakeholder accountability	AA1000/GRI key principles
Coverage of silent/shadow accounting (in)completeness	No direct evidence, some accompanying discussion on incompleteness	Presentation of silent and shadow information in parallel, no follow-up analysis	Detailed comparison between and analysis of SER and shadow information (but only where shadow information was available)
Coverage of corporate SER credibility/assurance	None (not applicable)	Not covered	Brief outline of quality of audit procedures
Treatment of shadow accounting completeness and reliability	Not applicable	Shadow sources not qualified or independently verified	All shadow sources independently verified
Coverage of embeddedness/stakeholder dialogue	None (not applicable)	Not covered	Brief coverage of (lack of) evidence of dialogue
Treatment of corporate identity	Corporate identity not concealed	Corporate identities not concealed	Corporate identity concealed

campaigning NGOs in influencing the behaviour of corporations has for many years received relatively little attention in the accounting literature (although see, especially, Tilt, 1994).

Such work is clearly a potentially vast source of information for shadow accounts, and indeed the role of campaigning NGOs in mobilizing corporate counter-information via the internet has now received more attention from some accounting academics (Gallhofer et al., 2006). These movements seek to raise global awareness of social and environmental issues and to hold organizations more accountable by mobilizing grassroots action against corporations and governments (Crossley, 2003). Globalization, the emergence and spread of internet technology and the growth of organized, grassroots social networks have all conspired to create the widespread public demand for counter-information about institutional accountability practices (Lubbers, 2003). Anti-corporate websites allow disgruntled individuals the chance to air their views to a global audience and to involve themselves and share information with diffuse networks of like-minded people (Kahn and Kellner, 2005). 'Anti-corporate' campaigning groups such as *Corporate Watch*[5] run websites that act as 'portals' to a range of electronic information sources, allowing easy access to a huge amount of information.

The significance of 'grievances' against modern capitalism and globalization within 'new social movements', and their focus on perceived moral deficiencies of corporate behaviour (Crossley, 2003), resonates strongly with the work of the critical accounting community (see, for example, Cooper et al., 2003; Everett, 2003). Indeed, NGOs that have chosen to produce their own 'shadow' or 'counter' disclosures of specific corporate targets usually choose corporations that already provide high levels of voluntary SER. By arguably failing to close the 'gap' required to reassure or convince stakeholders, SER is interpreted and labelled by external stakeholder representatives as more 'greenwash', and thus may actually serve to mobilize action. One strategy that seems to be increasingly adopted by some NGOs to tackle such corporate 'propaganda' is to publish their own counter-information[6] in ways which *directly* confront existing corporate-controlled SER.

Like the academic studies discussed in the previous section, these external 'shadow' reports seek to collect and present wider external sources of information about the social and environmental impacts of the chosen corporation. To this author's knowledge, the most active NGO in this area (in terms of publishing specific corporate 'shadow' reports) is Friends of the Earth (FoE). To date FoE (in collaboration with other more specific issues-based activist groups) has published a number of external social reports such as *Failing the challenge: The other Shell report 2002* (FoE, 2003a) and the *Amec counter report 2002* (FoE, 2003b). Shell, of course, is a particularly high-profile discloser of SER and its publications have frequently been held up as an example of both 'best practice' and 'bad practice'. The FoE document was ostensibly a retrospective review of Shell's 2002 social report, which, had it done so, would have reflected the general approach taken in the academic accounting domain by Adams (2004) and to some extent by Gibson *et al.* (2001). However, an examination of the content of the report reveals a series of short narrative 'case-studies' of various communities directly affected by Shell's multi-national operations. The scope and structure for these narratives was not explicitly pre-defined. Some evidence was based on current data, while other information appeared to relate to events that took place much earlier than 2002; some views were supported by quotes from community members, others were not; and there was no overall 'mapping' of Shell's worldwide operations. Only two pages out of the 28-page report dealt with claims made by Shell in its own disclosures, and while the document explicitly acknowledged the existence of wider sources of third-party evidence on Shell's behaviour, it does not make use of most of this evidence.

Rather than using their report to simply state the difference between what Shell itself 'says' and what other stakeholders 'know about' Shell, FoE's approach is heavily editorialized, in that FoE's objective is really to (in Shell's own words) 'tell Shell' what it thinks of Shell's behaviour. This may of course be an entirely justifiable objective in itself: the notion of an explicit 'counter-accounting' that is intentionally partial and political is well established, as this chapter has acknowledged. Consequently, and in sharp contrast to the work of Adams (2004), the FoE report does not evaluate Shell's own SER in a systematic way using the principles of disclosure standards such as AA1000. It also fails to address some novel aspects of Shell's SER practices, such as its web-based dialogue (but see Unerman and Bennett, 2004). Whilst FoE are in many ways right to draw attention to the selective bias and unreliability of the Shell report, they counter this with what is arguably an even more selective and unreliable report of their own. The report is therefore perhaps better viewed as an interesting piece of 'investigative journalism' or even 'counter-propaganda' that is intentionally provocative, generates media coverage, and creates a platform for the 'voices' of marginalized stakeholders to be heard.

Whilst FoE's work falls short as a piece of systematic 'shadow' accounting, other examples of NGO-based reporting appear to exhibit characteristics which more closely resemble the academic experiments discussed earlier. At the same time as British American Tobacco (BAT) was publishing its first social report (BAT, 2002), the anti-smoking pressure group Action on Smoking and Health (ASH) produced *British American Tobacco: The other report to society* (ASH, 2002a). In line with most modern SER, BAT claimed that their report was constructed using both the AA1000 accounting and audit standard and the GRI disclosure guidelines. It included considerable efforts to engage directly with stakeholders through dialogue processes, and was also 'verified' by an external consultant. In response, the ASH document closely shadowed these processes and attempted to evidence in detail areas of disclosure where the BAT report fell short of the AA1000 guidelines. The ASH report criticized the scope of the social report, arguing that BAT had failed to identify its most important stakeholders. It also questioned the credibility and transparency of the report, concluding that BAT had failed to provide reliable information to stakeholders. ASH also criticized the management of the company's 'stakeholder dialogue' process (a dialogue to which it had been invited to but chose to ignore) on the grounds that there were 'virtually no areas where BAT and ASH can find common cause – we characterise BAT's relationship with public health as a zero-sum game' (ASH, 2002b).

In addition to the reports published by ASH, BAT's SER disclosures have also attracted the attention of accounting academics. Moerman and Van Der Laan (2005) echo the work of ASH in critically reviewing BAT's 2002 social report, while the assurance gap in BAT's reporting has also been criticized elsewhere (O'Dwyer and Owen, 2005). Like ASH, Moerman and Van der Laan also use AA1000 and GRI frameworks as a benchmark, and their critique of the 'smoke and mirrors' of BAT's disclosures shares much in common with the conclusions offered by ASH. However (crucially, from the perspective of this chapter), they do not set out to explicitly compare BAT's report with external 'shadow' reports. Their work focuses more on discussing the significance of the existence of gaps in BAT's reporting rather than filling in those gaps with shadow information.

Table 16.2 below follows the broad format of Table 16.1 earlier in seeking to distil the basic characteristics of the NGO-based shadow reports reviewed here. As one might expect, NGO-based reporting appears to be more adversarial in its use of shadow information as 'ammunition' against its corporate target. This stance appears to be taken at the expense of a relative weakness in the reports to systematically analyse completeness, assurance and dialogue gaps in SER using a clear accountability framework. Nevertheless, the ASH report is potentially interesting in its specific focus on social reporting and the standards and frameworks used to construct the BAT report. ASH also demonstrate an awareness of the importance of dialogue and assurance processes. In these respects the ASH report is much more closely aligned with the experimentation in the accounting literature reviewed earlier.

The next section of the chapter attempts to identify the limitations and difficulties that are likely to be faced by NGOs, academics and others who might seek to produce such reports. Taking this into account, a tentative structure for future experimentation with shadow and silent accounting is then presented.

TOWARDS A FRAMEWORK FOR SILENT AND SHADOW ACCOUNTS

A review of experiments to date with forms of silent and shadow accounting suggests that academics and NGOs appear to share a common interest in illuminating the shortcomings of current SER, with a focus on evidencing (at least some) gaps in the completeness of published disclosures. By comparison, however, there

Table 16.2 Recent NGO experiments in external social reporting

	Failing the Challenge: The Other Shell Report (FoE, 2003a)	British American Tobacco: The Other Report to Society (ASH, 2002a)
Basic format	Glossy 28-page 'mimic' of Shell SER publication	Simple 46-page text
Section headings	Emphasis on 'real-life' accounts based on a selective coverage of Shell's impact in specific locations No stakeholder or issues-based section headings	(1) Issues-based headings (2) Impact in specific locations (3) Sub-headings covering implications for BAT's social accounting process
Additional sources	Not explicitly defined in scope, but all referenced. A range of media and counter-information sources	Not explicitly defined in scope, but wide range of referenced sources covering tobacco industry including government and scientific evidence, trade, medical and marketing journals, anti-tobacco campaign groups etc.
Analytical framework	Selective comparisons	AA1000 principles
Coverage of corporate SER (in)completeness	Many comparisons between shadow information and SER but no systematic coverage	Draws on shadow and 'silent' evidence to demonstrate shortcomings in completeness with reference to AA1000 principles
Coverage of corporate credibility/assurance process	None	No detailed review – limited to short recommendations
Coverage of corporate stakeholder dialogue processes	None	Partial review focusing on direct experience of shortcomings in dialogue process; reasons for rejecting participation explained
Treatment of shadow accounting reliability	Sources are referenced but not verified	Sources are referenced but not verified

are some interesting differences. The experiments of academics such as Gibson *et al.* (2001) and more especially Adams (2004) appear to offer more rigour and systematic coverage; they are more solidly grounded and promising theoretically, in contrast to the emerging 'counter-accounting' reports of NGOs like FoE and ASH which appear to be (quite deliberately) partisan and adversarial. This raises important questions (which are beyond the scope of this chapter) about the nature and objectives of external social reporting, including whether such reports should subscribe to the types of standards of completeness and reliability used to measure the quality of (corporate) SER, or instead abandon such benchmarks and restrict external social reporting to the deliberately selective presentation of 'counter-information'. Indeed, in the context of some recent initiatives by high-profile campaigning NGOs to move away from adversarial tactics and seek to develop more collaborative relationships with corporations, the development of more consistent, complete and reliable forms of external social reporting could be viewed as a useful platform for constructive dialogue.

Putting such theoretical questions to one side, it is clear that NGO-based reports, despite their possible differences in motive, style and substance, will continue to provide a valuable resource for collating more systematic shadow accounts, particularly in circumstances where they are produced by organizations (such as FoE) which are directly active in campaigning for improvements in corporate accountability, and which conduct their own primary research. The *ex post* experiments of Gibson *et al.* (2001) and Adams (2004) could therefore be revisited and developed further by using new empirical subjects. However, academic involvement in silent and shadow accounting could also extend more directly towards civil society by encouraging and offering guidance to NGOs to produce more consistent and complete shadow accounts. In the same way that academics have sought to develop organization-centred SER by experimenting with organizations, there is some pragmatic justification for this idea. Publishing shadow accounts through NGOs may also help to protect academics from the possible risks surrounding the use of counter-information and the threat of libel action (although the onus would still be on researchers to either qualify or verify any allegations being reprinted); while the outputs from such experiments could also be disseminated more widely to a non-academic audience. Of course, how these reports should be put together, and how they are used within an overall political strategy by NGOs, are clearly important issues, especially as there appears to be a lack of consistency amongst the NGO reports reviewed in this chapter. On these particular questions, it may be that some academic guidance on the development and practical application of silent and shadow accounts would be useful.[7]

Drawing on the discussion so far, what lessons may be learnt in terms of the practical guidelines that silent and shadow accounting should follow? In some ways the most straightforward answer to this question (and following closely from methods employed by Adams, 2004) is to apply to silent and shadow accounts the relevant principles that are currently used to guide organization-centred SER. These include the current AA1000 and GRI guidelines and standards, which, whilst perhaps not 'perfect', are nevertheless used to good effect by academics to critique current SER. In doing so, it seems fair to acknowledge that both silent and shadow accounting share the need for clear and explicit frameworks which seek to

construct, in as complete and transparent a way as is possible, a picture of organizational accountability based on the limits of the available information. Managing the
potentially vast range of available information sources from a diverse range of
accountability mechanisms requires additional careful thought. In putting to one
side readily available corporate SER disclosures, the challenge is to identify (within
defined boundaries of scope) and scour (within defined boundaries of availability
and verifiability) relevant accountability mechanisms and other information sources
for 'nuggets' of useful and material information, and at the same time one might
also seek to highlight those places where such nuggets do *not* exist. For silent
accounts, this is much more restrictive in focusing on the reconstruction of organizational (non)disclosure, but in general terms, one may perhaps conceive of a series
of 'layers' which silent and shadow accounts might consist of. These layers may
include the following:

1   statement of objectives (including engagement/follow-up strategy with
    corporation);
2   identification of stakeholders (and basis of including/ignoring them);
3   organizational accountability mechanisms examined;
4   wider shadow information sources used (or rejected?), including clear qualifica-
    tion of sources where they are allegations rather than verifiable fact;
5   assessment of completeness of corporate (and shadow) accounts, possibly
    including 'maps' of information sources and availability of sources;
6   assessment of formal stakeholder dialogue processes and outcomes, including
    (where available) additional primary evidence from stakeholders;
7   assessment of level of assurance offered by corporate (and shadow?) account-
    ability mechanisms;
8   formal invitation to (or evidence of) feedback to the exercise offered to com-
    pany management and stakeholders.

The development of this tentative structure in practice is certainly challenging,
especially in mapping the potentially large quantity of shadow information sources,
and of interpreting and applying the criteria of completeness and reliability. At
the same time, though, the availability of relevant information, and the potential
for useful collaboration with NGOs and other external social reporting agencies,
present many interesting opportunities for future research.

NOTES

1   While a more explicitly political or emancipatory objective for external
    social reporting (whereby such disclosures become tools to educate and empower

stakeholders, and challenge existing hegemonic social forces) might be thought of as 'counter accounting' (Gallhofer *et al.*, 2006), detailed discussion of this concept is beyond the scope of this chapter. Nevertheless, it is clearly an important avenue of research which merits development in its own right (see also Gallhofer and Haslam, 2004; Thomson and Bebbington, 2005). Instead, this chapter focuses solely on what might be regarded as more 'conventionally recognizable' and systematic methods of silent and shadow accounting, that seek to address information gaps by producing accounts based on criteria including completeness and verifiability.

2 Despite ceasing publication of its external social reports in 1976, Social Audit Ltd continues to operate, although it now focuses more exclusively on the pharmaceutical industry. For more information, see http://www.socialaudit.org.uk.

3 'Greenwash' is now the subject of its own 'awards' and was defined at the *2002 Greenwash Academy Awards* as 'the phenomenon of socially and environmentally destructive corporations attempting to preserve and expand their markets by posing as friends of the environment and leaders in the struggle to eradicate poverty'.

4 See also the 'critical financial analysis' developed and applied to the privatized utilities in the UK by Shaoul (1998).

5 See www.corporatewatch.org.uk.

6 NGOs involved in activism and advocacy will typically use a number of different strategies to engage with corporations (Bliss, 2002).

7 It is even possible to envisage wider efforts to improve the legitimacy of shadow reporting, for example through the invitation to submit shadow reports to existing corporate SER reporting awards schemes, or the establishment of expert-reviewed 'shadow reporting awards'.

REFERENCES

Action on Smoking and Health (2002a) *British American Tobacco: The other report to society*. ASH.

Action on Smoking and Health (2002b) *BAT social report revisited: ASH comes to BAT*. ASH.

Adams, C. (2004) The ethical, social and environmental reporting performance portrayal gap. *Accounting, Auditing and Accountability Journal*, 17(5): 731–57.

Adams, C. and Evans, R. (2004) Accountability, completeness, credibility and the audit expectations gap. *Journal of Corporate Citizenship*, 14: 97–115.

Bailey, D., Harte, G. and Sugden, R. (1994) *Making transnationals accountable*. Routledge.

Bailey, D., Harte, G. and Sugden, R. (2000) Corporate disclosure and the deregulation of international investment. *Accounting, Auditing and Accountability Journal*, 13(2): 197–218.

Belal, A. (2002) Stakeholder accountability or stakeholder management? A review of UK firms' social and ethical accounting, auditing and reporting practices. *Corporate Social Responsibility and Environmental Management*, 9(1): 8–25.

Bliss, T. (2002) Corporate advocacy groups. Friend or foe? In J. Andriof *et al.* (eds) *Unfolding stakeholder thinking*. Greenleaf, pp. 251–67.

Blythman, J. (2004) *Shopped: The shocking power of British supermarkets*. Fourth Estate.

British American Tobacco (2002) *Report to society*. BAT.

Business in the Community (2003) *Indicators that count: Social and environmental indicators – a model for reporting impact*. BITC.

Christian Aid (2003) *Behind the mask: The real face of corporate social responsibility*. Christian Aid report.

Cooper, C., Neu, D. and Lehman, G. (2003) Globalization and its discontents: A concern about growth and globalization. *Accounting Forum*, 27(4): 359–64.

CORE Coalition (2003) *With rights come responsibilities*, online at http://www.amnesty.org.uk/business/campaigns/core/index.shtml.

Crossley, N. (2003) Even newer social movements? Anti-corporate protests, capitalist crises and the remoralization of society. *Organization*, 10(2): 287–307.

Dando, N. and Swift, T. (2003) Transparency and assurance: Minding the credibility gap. *Journal of Business Ethics*, 44(2): 195–200.

ECC Kohtes Klewes and Fishburn Hedges (2003) *Global stakeholder report 2003*.

Entine, J. (2003) *A social and environmental audit of Body Shop: Anita Roddick and the question of character*, online at http://www.entine.com.

Everett, J. (2003) Globalization and its new spaces for (alternative) accounting research. *Accounting Forum*, 27(4): 400–24.

Friends of the Earth (2003a) *Failing the challenge: The other Shell report 2002*. FoE.

Friends of the Earth (2003b) *Amec counter report 2002*. FoE.

Gallhofer, S. and Haslam, J. (2003) *Accounting and emancipation: Some critical interventions*. Routledge.

Gallhofer, S. and Haslam, J. (2004) Accounting and liberation theology: Some insights for the project of emancipatory accounting. *Accounting, Auditing and Accountability Journal*, 17(3): 382–407.

Gallhofer, S., Haslam, J., Roberts, C. and Monk, E. (2006) The emancipatory potential of online reporting: The case of counter accounting. *Accounting, Auditing and Accountability Journal*, 19(5): 681–718.

Geddes, M. (1991) The social audit movement. In D. L. Owen (ed.) *Green reporting*. Chapman-Hall, pp. 215–41.

Gibson, K., Gray, R. H., Laing, Y. and Dey, C. R. (2001) The silent accounts project: Draft silent and shadow accounts 1999–2000 (separate publications for Tesco plc and HSBC Holdings plc), online at http://www.st-andrews.ac.uk/~csearweb/aptopractice/silentacc.html.

Global Reporting Initiative (2002) *Sustainability reporting guidelines.* GRI.

Gray, R. H. (1997) The silent practice of social accounting and corporate social reporting in companies. In S. Zadek *et al.* (eds) *Building corporate accountAbility: Emerging practices in social and ethical accounting, auditing and reporting.* Earthscan.

Gray, R., Owen, D. and Adams, C. (1996) *Accounting and accountability.* Chapman-Hall.

Gray, R. H., Dey, C. R., Owen, D., Evans, R. and Zadek, S. (1997) Struggling with the praxis of social accounting: Stakeholders, accountability, audits and procedures. *Accounting, Auditing and Accountability Journal,* 10(3): 325–64.

Greer, J. and Bruno, K. (1996) *Greenwash: The reality behind corporate environmentalism.* Third World Network.

Hertz, N. (2001) *The silent takeover: Global capitalism and the death of democracy.* Heinemann.

ISEA (1999) *AccountAbility 1000: A foundation standard in social and ethical accounting, auditing and reporting.* ISEA.

Kahn, R. and Kellner, D. (2005) Oppositional politics and the internet: A critical/reconstructive approach. *Cultural Politics,* 1(1): 75–100.

Klein, N. (2000) *No logo.* Flamingo.

Lubbers, E. (ed.) (2003) *Battling big business.* Common Courage Press.

Medawar, C. (1976) The social audit: A political view. *Accounting, Organizations and Society,* 1(4): 389–94.

Moerman, L. and Van Der Laan, S. (2005) Social reporting in the tobacco industry: All smoke and mirrors? *Accounting, Auditing and Accountability Journal,* 18(3): 374–89.

Monbiot, G. (2000) *Captive state: The corporate takeover of Britain.* Macmillan.

O'Dwyer, B. (2005) Stakeholder democracy: Challenges and contributions from accountancy. *Business Ethics: A European Review,* 14(1): 28–41.

O'Dwyer, B. and Owen, D. L. (2005) Assurance statement quality in environmental social and sustainability reporting: A critical examination. *British Accounting Review,* 37(2): 205–30.

Owen, D. L., Swift, T. A., Humphrey, C. and Bowerman, M. (2000) The new social audits: Accountability, managerial capture or the agenda of social champions? *European Accounting Review,* 9(1): 81–98.

Owen, D. L., Swift, T. A. and Hunt, K. (2001) Questioning the role of stakeholder engagement in social and ethical accounting. *Accounting Forum,* 25(3): 264–82.

Pilger, J. (2004) *Tell me no lies: Investigative journalism and its triumphs.* Jonathan Cape.

Schlosser, E. (2002) *Fast food nation.* Penguin.

Shaoul, J. (1998) Critical financial analysis and accounting for stakeholders. *Critical Perspectives on Accounting,* 9: 235–49.

Stittle, J. (2002) UK corporate ethical reporting: A failure to inform – some evidence from company annual reports. *Business and Society Review,* 107(3): 349–70.

325

Swift, T. and Dando, N. (2002) From methods to ideologies: Closing the assurance expectations gap in social and ethical accounting, auditing and reporting. *Journal of Corporate Citizenship*, 8: 81–90.

Thomson, I. and Bebbington, J. (2005) Social and environmental reporting in the UK: A pedagogic evaluation. *Critical Perspectives on Accounting*, 16(5): 507–33.

Tilt, C. A. (1994) The influence of external pressure groups on corporate social disclosure: Some empirical evidence. *Accounting, Auditing and Accountability Journal*, 7(4): 47–72.

Unerman, J. and Bennett, M. (2004) Increased stakeholder dialogue and the internet: Towards greater corporate accountability or reinforcing capitalist hegemony? *Accounting, Organizations and Society*, 29(7): 685–707.

Zadek, S., Evans, R. and Pruzan, P. (1997) *Building corporate accountability: Emerging practice in social and ethical accounting and auditing*. Earthscan.

Chapter 17

Sustainability accounting and education

David Collison, John Ferguson and Lorna Stevenson

Technology and markets typically serve the most powerful segments of society. If the primary goal is growth, they produce growth as long as they can. If the primary goals were equity and sustainability they could also serve those goals.

Once the population and economy have overshot physical limits of the Earth there are only two ways back: involuntary collapse caused by escalating shortages and crises, or controlled reduction of the ecological footprint by deliberate social choice.

(*Limits to growth: The 30-year update*, Meadows *et al.*, 2005, p. 234)

education is the most vital of all resources . . . education, which fails to clarify our central convictions, is mere training or indulgence. For it is our central convictions that are in disorder, and, as long as the present anti-metaphysical temper persists, the disorder will grow worse. Education, far from ranking as man's greatest resource, will then be an agent of destruction.

(*Small is beautiful*, Schumacher, 1973, pp. 64 and 83)

INTRODUCTION

For the purposes of this chapter the term 'sustainability accounting' will be taken to equate to the range of topics normally included within social and environmental accounting (SEA). To some extent, the terms will be used interchangeably in this chapter though we acknowledge that much of what constitutes SEA stops seriously short of engaging with the notion of sustainability. Within the SEA canon we could include technical eco-efficiency issues including environmental management accounting, implications for and critiques of conventional accounting and reporting, and critiques and prescriptions of innovative forms of reporting: 'sustainability accounting' draws on all these areas but, ideally, also explicitly recognizes the limitations of the biosphere and its profound implications for peaceful human co-existence.

In this chapter we address: the socializing effects of education itself; the values implicit in accounting and business education and whether the changes – which we believe to be necessary – can be achieved through more learning or are impossible without 'unlearning' (see Ghoshal, 2005 and also Schumacher, 1973); the development of social and environmental accounting education in universities; as well as professional perspectives and developments. Outside the study of accounting and its related disciplines, sustainability education initiatives have led to eponymous cross-disciplinary degrees, and UK government rhetoric purports to be embedding sustainability in the curriculum at all levels. Indeed the time of writing coincides with the inception of the United Nations Decade of Education for Sustainable Development (2005–14). While these developments go beyond the scope of this chapter, they are acknowledged as part of the wider context, to which the first sections of this chapter are readily applicable.

The need for wider societal acceptance of the requirement for fundamental change in values and aspirations, and the reflexive relationship of this acceptance with political will and leadership, as attenuated by the hegemonic power of vested interests, bestride all discussions of this issue. The education of those, in particular, who will exercise leadership and offer expertise in matters of economic and business decisions, is no trivial matter in this wider context.

Before considering sustainability accounting education per se it seems necessary first to consider the nature of education itself. The truly awesome challenges presented by expanding an already unsustainable, ecological footprint in our fragile world require a fundamental shift in societal values. This need prompts us to consider central aspects of the nature and role of education.

THE SOCIALIZING EFFECTS OF EDUCATION

Functionalist perspectives on education, in particular, those which adhere to the Parsonian view of the education system as being a meritocracy which serves as the 'engine of democracy', have been repeatedly challenged in the sociology literature since the early 1960s (Apple, 1995, p. 9). A 'resurgence' of various forms of Marxist, phenomenological, and interactionist perspectives began to emerge which recognized the significance of conflict and ideology in education. Whilst there are serious disagreements within this literature in terms of how education contributes to existing power asymmetries, prominent figures within this field, such as Althusser, Apple, Bernstein, Bourdieu, Gramsci, and Illich, all acknowledge the importance of examining the role of education in reproducing and sustaining relations of power (Karabel and Halsey, 1977, p. 4; see also Apple, 1995).

One aspect of the education process, the curriculum (or more precisely, the selection and organization of knowledge), has received considerable attention in terms of the role it plays in the 'creation and recreation of ideological hegemony' (Apple, 1995, p. 17).[1] As Apple and Christian-Smith (1991) point out, it is naïve to consider the curriculum to be a 'neutral' collection of knowledge. On the contrary, what is considered to be 'legitimate' or 'official' knowledge is the result of complex power relations which 'signal more profound political, economic and cultural relations and histories' (Apple and Christian-Smith, 1991, p. 3). In describing what he calls the 'selective tradition', and which could equally describe the selective processes in education curricula, Raymond Williams (1989) states:

> From a whole possible area of past and present, in a particular culture, certain meanings and practices are selected for emphasis and certain other meanings and practices are neglected or excluded. Yet within a particular hegemony, and as one of its decisive processes, this selection is presented and usually successfully passed off as 'the tradition', 'the significant past'. What has then to be said about any tradition is that it is in this sense an aspect of contemporary social and cultural organization, in the interest of the dominance of a specific class.

Therefore, the knowledge and culture of powerful groups is defined and passed on as not only the most 'legitimate', but as common sense (Apple, 1995).

In the case of the accounting curriculum, the official curriculum is developed, both directly and indirectly, through complex power relations between a range of constituents including: professional accounting bodies (through the development of accounting standards and accreditation requirements for university programmes), corporate law (which sets the way in which companies must report), lobbyists (who play a significant role in influencing company law and accounting standards), universities, lecturers and students. In addition, each of these constituents will be 'structured by the class, gender, sexual and race inequalities' that organize society (Apple, 2004, p. 189).

Whilst the structuring effects of class, gender, sex and race may not be formally included on the 'overt' curriculum, the norms and values which they embody will underpin it to the extent that they will still inform students' sense of what is right and wrong. This is referred to by Illich as the 'hidden curriculum' (see also Apple, 1995; Bebbington and Thomson, 2001). In business and accounting education, the knowledge and values produced and distributed to students tend to implicitly privilege a particular group of people – corporate shareholders (this argument will be further developed in the following section). Furthermore, this privileging is taken as common sense, as natural. According to Bebbington and Thomson (2001),

329

it is the prevalence of these hidden assumptions which explain why 'bolt-on' courses on CSR or business ethics ultimately fail – because they do not sufficiently challenge the underlying commonsense assumptions which help maintain and reproduce current social arrangements.

This can be further explained by reference to one aspect of the hegemonic process. In order to maintain its own legitimacy, the ruling power must integrate many interests, 'even opposing groups under its banner' (Apple, 1995, p. 27). One way of integrating oppositional cultures (in the context of the curriculum) is to pay them lip-service; to allow them to be mentioned, or in the case of CSR, to be included as an addition or an option, but to never integrate them to the extent that they modify the core values which the curriculum embodies.[2] Thus it is important to realize that whilst the selection of knowledge is never a neutral activity, it is neither, nor need it be, a *complete* 'mirror reflection of ruling class ideas' (Luke, 1988, p. 24; see also McIntosh, 2002).

Values implicit in accounting education

The relationship between accounting theory and the values implicit in neoclassical economic theory have long been acknowledged in the accounting literature (Cooper, 1980; Cooper and Sherer, 1984; Tinker, 1980). For example, Tinker (1980, p. 149) points out that neoclassical economic theory has 'probably contributed more than any other [theory] to the practice of accounting'. Drawing primarily on positivist philosophy, both neo-classical economics and (hence) accounting theory assume (and assert) a 'value-neutral' posture which claims to be liberated from any particular political view of the world. However, such posturing conceals the 'value-impregnated' ontological and epistemological underpinnings of this perspective, which can be considered ideological in the sense that it is 'imbued with certain beliefs' which help maintain relations of domination (Frankfurter and McGoun, 1999, p. 161; see also Thompson, 1990).

In particular, neoclassical economics assumes individuals are free to act in their own (economic) self-interest and that, by doing so, economic growth ensues, which in turn should maximize the welfare of society. For a succinct and robust critique of these assumptions see Gray *et al.* (1996): this critique demonstrates that even in a society that is not remotely close to exceeding its sustainable ecological footprint, this model is not only flawed, but deeply dishonest. In our unsustainable world it is not only unjust, but also a threat to our existence. The influence of this perspective is especially apparent in Anglo-American capitalist economies[3] where private sectional interests are enshrined in legal structures and socio-economic norms. These inherently divisive values (see Birkin *et al.*, 2005) generally assume that the only participants in the wealth-creating process that should have their interests maximized are shareholders. In treating the economic rights of capital owners as innately superior, negative impacts from corporate activity, such as environmental degradation, are treated as externalities: the inherently divisive nature of such socio-economic arrangements gives incentives to powerful vested interests to use their hegemonic influence, through, inter alia, lobbying and propaganda (see, for example, Beder, 1997; Stauber and Rampton, 1995) to resist any internalizing of the externalities borne by wider society. Social and environmental concerns are therefore only of relevance to corporations insofar as they impact upon their 'bottom line': they are 'externalising machines'[4] (Bakan, 2004).

It is the 'ideology of shareholder capitalism' which gets taught on accounting courses, the fundamental moral underpinnings of which are 'buried by scientific-sounding abstractions' (Wolfe, 1993, p. 2). This guise of 'technical rationality' conceals a hegemonic discourse which not only sustains relations of power but imbues students with the notion that wider society and the natural environment should be treated as 'externalities' (McPhail and Gray, 1996). Speaking of business education in general, Ghoshal states: 'By propagating ideologically inspired amoral theories, business schools have actively freed their students from any sense of moral responsibility' (Ghoshal, 2005, p. 76).

Whilst some business schools and accounting departments offer courses in business ethics or social and environmental accounting they are considered by many to be merely 'a drop in the river of the heavy mental conditioning for capitalism' (Wolfe, 1993, p. 2). As Ghoshal (2005, p. 88) points out:

> If deans really intend to infuse a concern for ethics and for responsible management in the research and teaching that are carried out at their institutions, they have to acknowledge that the tokenism of adding a course on ethics will not achieve their goals. As long as all the other courses continue as they are, a single, stand-alone course on corporate social responsibility will not change the situation in any way.

In other words, the first real step towards engendering social and environmental awareness amongst accounting students, to paraphrase Ghoshal, is not to create new courses but to stop teaching some old ones. It is against this challenging background that those who wish to change the nature of accounting education have to operate. Since they typically lack the means to stop the teaching of certain ideas – indeed such a stark statement of that aspiration even has, perhaps regrettably, an uncomfortable ring to it, redolent of book burning – there seems little choice but to challenge them where and how one can, but with a recognition of the magnitude of the task.

DEVELOPMENTS AND CHALLENGES IN SEA EDUCATION

There has been a steady examination of SEA education in the literature – including what it might comprise, what it might achieve, how it should be addressed, and why students do and do not choose to study SEA – though this body of work is not enormous. Discussion of social issues in the context of teaching accounting appears to have first been highlighted in the mid-1970s (Mathews, 2001). However, it was not until the late 1980s that more widespread academic interest was paid to the area of SEA education. This interest has grown throughout the 1990s to date, focusing for the bulk of this period mainly on environmental issues, but more recently on social dimensions once again (Parker, 2004; Mangion, 2005).

In the context of discussing the goals SEA teaching might have, Mathews (2001) suggested that SEA issues can be used to develop the moral thought processes we might expect of those charged with managing social and environmental resources to meet society's needs and in line with the public interest credentials of their profession. However, though not dissenting from his aims, Bebbington and Thomson (2001) showed how Mathews' failure to consider potential resistance on several levels may well result in his well-meaning suggestions failing to achieve their aim. In seeking to address the challenge of the wider hegemonic discourse described above, Bebbington and Thomson have drawn on key figures in the radical educational literature (see also Thomson and Bebbington, 2004). Key to their argument is Illich's (1971) idea of the hidden curriculum, and Freire's (1996) approaches to education. Bebbington and Thomson (2001) stated that:

> The hidden curriculum forms the bedrock of most people's assumptions of right/wrong and possible/impossible and this knowledge set is never explicitly taught but is implicit in the other material taught. As a result, the 'hidden curriculum' is never critically examined as to its 'reasonableness'.
>
> (p. 354)

Freire's 'Banking' education was characterized as 'teaching where "motionless, static, compartmentalized and predictable" knowledge is conveyed to students who are assumed to be "passive, patient, listening receptacles" ' (p. 354) and which thus continues to hide the curriculum. This was contrasted with Freire's 'Dialogic' or 'Problem Posing' education which Bebbington and Thomson claimed 'allow[s] the potential for identifying and transcending the hidden curriculum' (p. 354). They concluded:

> there is no such thing as a neutral education process. Education either functions as an instrument that is used to facilitate the integration of the younger generation into the logic of the present system and to bring

conformity with it, or it becomes a practice of freedom, the means by which men and women deal critically and creatively with reality and discover how to participate in the transformation of their world (Freire, 1996, p. 16).

(p. 355)[5]

There have been a wide variety of interpretations of how to implement SEA education. One end of the spectrum, for example, restricts the definition of SEA to a narrow environmental accounting and grafts environmental disclosures on to the standard Anglo-American financial reporting model (Sefcik *et al.*, 1997). An alternative understanding of the possibilities of SEA education is highlighted by Bebbington and Thomson (2001, p. 354):

> SEA is not merely an interesting extension of the accounting knowledge set, but questions the way in which we understand and organise our individual lives and social institutions . . . The problem of low levels of SEA education can be linked to the failure of conventional accounting to make its own assumptions explicit (or its success in keeping them hidden!).

This highlights nicely the potential role of accounting education in either: making sustainability more difficult by failing to equip those who study accounting (and go on to practise the accounting art) with the knowledge and ability to question the status quo and founding principles of their discipline; or in advancing sustainability by enabling those educated in accounting to respond to new needs and public interest obligations in a conceptually coherent and fundamental way.

Mangion (2005) examined the literature on how SEA can be incorporated into higher education curricula, and identified the following options:

- embed SEA into existing financial-based accounting teaching;
- teach SEA as a stand-alone course – usually after the undisputed essentials of an accounting degree have been addressed;
- create (unusually) a specialized stream in SEA issues;
- include SEA in a general 'accounting theory' course.

Such a grafting of SEA ideas into a regime, which at heart is inimical to its spirit may be better than nothing: Gordon (1998) described how a compulsory accounting theory course itself engendered greater awareness of, and changed reactions to, SEA issues in final-year undergraduate accounting students. However, it has been suggested (Owen *et al.*, 1994; Lewis *et al.*, 1992; Humphrey *et al.*, 1996; Gibson, 1997) that piecemeal solutions such as those listed above, as opposed to funda-mental reappraisal of the content and process of accounting degrees, are unlikely to equip the next generation of accounting professionals with sufficient social, ethical and environmental awareness for their public interest role.

Owen *et al.* (1994) performed the first survey of the provision, form and context of SEA in British universities in 1992/3. This work was replicated and updated in the UK by Stevenson (2002) for 1997/8, and in Australia by Mangion (2005) for 2004/5. The aim of Owen *et al.*'s original (1994) survey of British universities' SEA teaching was to:

> identify the degree to which students are exposed to [SEA] material in their undergraduate degree studies and to explore more qualitative issues concerning, amongst other things, the aims of such teaching, the nature of the material being covered or, alternatively, reasons for neglecting the subject area.
>
> (Executive Summary, p. 1)

Key findings of the research included:

- peripheral (at best) coverage of SEA in many undergraduate accounting degree programmes;
- SEA coverage present often as a final year (with low numbers) option;
- SEA not seen as 'generally accepted "core" accounting degree material';
- individual 'champions' playing a key role in establishing and maintaining SEA teaching – these individuals often having a research record in the discipline;
- dominance of 'environmental' over 'social' issues, reflecting the influence of the professional accounting and general media;
- student expectations and perceptions of professional accreditation requirements appearing to strongly influence academics' ideas of the acceptability of SEA material.

In the context of this last point, a potentially vicious circle is highlighted by Blundell and Booth's (1988) suggestion that a major obstacle to student acceptance of social accounting material is their perception of its lack of relevance to accounting practice (see also Collison *et al.*, 2000). Some recent evidence of how these issues are perceived within the profession is presented later in the chapter.

The picture of the state of SEA education some four years after the Owen *et al.* (1994) research (Stevenson, 2002) was little different. In particular, environmental accounting was still the most popular teaching topic, and the importance of environmental issues on national and international agendas was identified as a primary facilitator for what SEA did exist. However, though the most important reason for teaching SEA – creating student awareness of the wider obligations of corporate behaviour – was unchanged, fewer 'part' and more 'full' SEA courses were reported (respectively 47 per cent and 24 per cent of respondents in 1998 compared with 57 per cent and 11 per cent in 1994). Nonetheless, overall little appeared to have changed despite a steady growth in the attention given to SEA in the academic accounting literature (Mathews, 1997; Stevenson, 2002).

In 2005 in Australia Mangion surveyed all accounting academic staff in all 38 Australian universities to examine the extent of SEA education provided in them. She reported that SEA is taught in the majority of Australian institutions' accounting degree programmes, mainly within other mainstream courses (73 per cent of respondents reported a part course, 10 per cent a full SEA course). Potentially significantly, the number of full courses is expected to increase in the next two years – 24 per cent of survey respondents said that they expected their higher education institution to offer a full stand-alone SEA course within the next two years. In contrast with Owen *et al.*'s (1994) and Stevenson's (2002) findings of the popularity of environmental accounting in SEA curricula, social accountability was identified by Mangion's (2005) population as the most widely studied topic.

We might interpret the popular delivery of SEA within existing financial-based accounting education as reflecting a compromise in the light of curriculum space constraints, or alternatively as providing a means of contextualizing and highlighting accounting's fundamental tenets (as suggested by Bebbington and Thomson, 2001), or indeed as a stage of curriculum acceptance and integration some way between cursory comment and a full SEA module. Further exploratory work would be needed for more informed comment on the applicability of any of these potential interpretations.

Despite an apparent lack of consensus as to what should be taught in SEA education, Mangion (2005) states that there are 12 topics currently comprising SEA in university teaching: environmental accountability – external reporting; environmental accountability – management; social accountability; theoretical framework for SEA; sustainable development; social audit; financial social reporting; non-financial reporting; social/ethical reporting; human asset accounting; SEA history; and comparative and international SEA/reporting.

To begin to explore the characteristics that might help explain why academics choose to teach or not to teach SEA, Stevenson (2000) described SEA educators in British universities in 1998. Age, gender and type of institution[6] appeared not to influence whether a full SEA course was offered, though such courses did seem to be taught by those with a stated interest[7] in SEA and a higher degree in accounting or education. Those staff involved in part SEA courses were more likely to be male respondents with a noted interest in SEA, whilst academics reporting no SEA teaching at their institution were more likely to be male with a first degree and/or PhD in economics. This perhaps highlights a progression from Humphrey *et al.*'s (1996) report that:

> A number of interviewees complained of the way much accounting teach-
> ing had been allowed to continue in isolation of findings emerging from

contemporary research. The sense of frustration on the part of some SEA researchers was nicely captured in an observation by one interviewee that she had 'become increasingly fed up with doing research on the one hand and teaching on the other and the two never linking up .

(p. 86)

However, this appears not to be a worry confined to SEA; the issue was highlighted in a wider context in the previous decade by Lee (1989) when he described the practice-education loop in accounting that, in the main, excluded research. (See also AECC, 1990; Davis and Sherman, 1996; Macve and Carey, 1992; Sterling; 1973.)

The accounting profession clearly plays a key role in influencing university-level accounting education, while also being open to influence, at least at the margin, by educational and research initiatives within academe. In addition, professional education itself as well as post-qualification education are of central importance to an informed professional response to the challenge of sustainability.

EDUCATION AND THE ACCOUNTING PROFESSION

A wide-ranging study of the implications of the developing environmental and sustainability agenda for the education of professional accountants (Gray *et al.*, 2001; and see also Gray and Collison, 2002) serves as an appropriate point of departure for this section of the chapter. That study included interviews with a range of leading members of the profession and other 'opinion formers'; questionnaire surveys of academics and undergraduate students; and interviews with, and a questionnaire survey of, recruiters. An overview of some central concerns raised in that study is provided by Table 17.1. It presents what Gray *et al.* acknowledge to be two extremes of concern across relevant dimensions. The element of caricature implicit in the way these views are imputed to academic/practitioner perspectives is made very clear in the original, but nonetheless the framework does serve as a useful analysis of the spectrum of possible views across complementary dimensions.

Table 17.1 *Two extremes of concern across relevant dimensions*

Academic, principles-driven point of view		The issues		Practitioner, client-driven point of view
Sustainability	⟵	The environment	⟶	Marginal issues
Public interest	⟵	The profession	⟶	Client serving
Transcendence	⟵	Education and training	⟶	Technical
Central	⟵	Relevant degrees	⟶	Not important

Source: Adapted from Gray *et al.* (2001, p. 4)

Central to the issues summarized in Table 17.1 is the reflexive relationship between the posture that the profession takes in regard to sustainability issues and the educational process, which is largely driven by that posture, but which in the long term has the potential to change it. Bebbington (1997, p. 373) has stated that education in 'environmental accounting' (EA) which she interprets broadly to include accounting for sustainable development,

> offers a significant opportunity to enable the next generation of account-
> ants to understand better the biases and limitations of conventional
> accounting, as well as to develop an appreciation of the possibilities intro-
> duced by EA.

This potential is, of course, attenuated by the optional, and even sporadic, nature of EA education and its apparent lack of appeal to many – a point acknowledged by Bebbington, and many others as discussed above. A majority of accounting students base their optional courses on perceived career relevance (Collison *et al.*, 2000; Gray *et al.*, 2001) and of course their core courses may be largely driven by accreditation constraints. Thus the scope for the inertia of the status quo to marginalize and impede educational influence by restraining participation rates must be acknowledged; but it does not mean that there are no grounds for hope: 'Despite this reservation, the enabling potential of EA for those who undertake it as a part of their course of study remains potent' (Bebbington, 1997, p. 373).

Notwithstanding the challenges of the hidden curriculum, identified above, a key recommendation – or at least aspiration – offered by Gray *et al.* (2001) related to relevant degrees and was offered as a way of attempting to break the vicious circle just described. In the context of a wide-ranging discussion of how to change the education (not the training) of professional accountants, the role of the university was emphasized:

> If there is one key to this whole area it must be, in our view, an increase in
> the use of relevant graduates *but with a major change in how relevant degrees
> are taught*.
>
> (Gray *et al.*, 2001, p. 163, emphasis in original)

To the extent that the profession itself is perhaps the only source of influence which can quickly make a systemic shift in the way that its future leaders are educated, much depends on whether and how it can review its role and priorities. Central to this must be a genuine re-avowal of the primacy of the wider public interest over the commercial interests of its members or their clients. Steps that can be taken by the professional bodies include raising awareness of members through CPD courses and through changes to their core syllabuses. While such steps may be of limited value in themselves, in terms of the deeper reappraisal needed to change outlooks –

they *may* contribute to a change in the climate in which accounting and business is presented and discussed in practice and in academe, as well as *possibly* leading to real changes in the curriculum.[8]

Perspectives of professional bodies: some recent evidence

In this section we present hitherto unpublished results of a survey of European professional accountancy bodies, which sought views of the importance attached to SEA in the training of accountants as well as information on the extent of its coverage in the professional syllabus of each body. This was a small-scale survey, conducted in 2002/3, and was restricted to those professional bodies represented on the Sustainability Working Party of the European Federation of Accountants (FEE). Since the bodies surveyed are likely to represent those (in Europe) which are most proactive in these matters, the results may well be somewhat unrepresentative of the overall picture but are unlikely to overstate the profession's engagement with social, environmental and sustainability issues. The survey was explicitly addressed to the education departments of the professional bodies.

Questions regarding importance of SEA issues employed a 'Likert' 1–5 scale in which strong disagreement or strong agreement with a statement was indicated by '1' and '5' respectively. Most emphatic agreement was with the following two statements: 'These issues are important for the profession' (4.3 mean score) and 'Many accountants/auditors underestimate their importance' (4.4). Almost as strong agreement (4.2) was with the suggestion that these issues need more emphasis in education and training. Weaker, but still fairly clear, support (3.9) was given to the need to include these issues in the education of all professional accountants and auditors. The likelihood of strong demand for courses that include such topics (assuming they were given appropriate publicity) showed the lowest level of support but nonetheless the balance of opinion was in agreement (3.3). These perceptions underline the need for leadership by the professional bodies in raising awareness of, and acting to address, the importance of these issues. To the extent that professional bodies do not do this, and merely act as conduits for the provision of services to help members meet client needs, they will be failing in their duty to serve the wider public interest.

Respondents were also asked to indicate, for a range of subject areas, the emphasis currently given to social/environmental/sustainability issues in the syllabuses of their professional bodies' courses by indicating a score from 1 to 5 corresponding to 'none' and 'significant' respectively. In considering the results it should be borne in mind that 7 of the 14 bodies replying to the questionnaire indicated that social/environmental/sustainability issues were not mentioned in any of their courses.

All scores were decidedly towards the 'no emphasis' end of the spectrum with the lowest score (1.2) being achieved for Financial Management/Finance/Investing.

The next lowest score (1.4) was for Management Accounting. Both of these low scores are in spite of the fact that in each of these areas the profile of sustainability-related[9] issues is growing fast. An ongoing UN initiative to raise awareness of the benefits and techniques of environmental management accounting is perhaps testimony to the sluggish response of many accounting bodies to exploit even this area where environmental responsibility and profit-based measures of success can, to some extent at least, be pursued simultaneously. (See Adams, 2002, for further discussion of the tardy response of the profession to the challenges of sustainability.) Respondents to the questionnaire showed slightly higher measures of emphasis for the subject area of Financial/Corporate Reporting (1.6) while the greatest attention (or least inattention) is paid to 'Professional/Ethical issues' and 'Auditing/ Assurance Services' (both 1.7).

While inclusion in students' professional syllabuses is necessary to ultimately ensure a common level of awareness for all accountants – as well as being important to help make a difference to the content of accredited degree courses – there is also an important role for post-qualification education in these areas. Of the 14 respondents to the questionnaire only 4 provided or sponsored any post-qualification courses in the area of SEA.

A separate (global) survey of engagement by the profession with the sustainability agenda appeared in a very wide-ranging ACCA/UNEP report (Adams, 2002) produced for the 2002 World Summit on Sustainable Development in Johannesburg. It included a report on a questionnaire survey that was sent to all the professional accountancy bodies that are members of the International Federation of Accountants. This survey covered a range of sustainability-related issues but two questions were about education. The results showed that, out of 60 respondents, 15 have 'begun the process of integrating social, environmental or sustainable development principles into the academic syllabus' though it was noted that there was a shortage of details to back up such claims. Respondents who were including the issues in post-qualification courses (CPD) numbered 12.

While these glimpses of professional awareness and activity show some acknowledgement of the importance of these issues for their members' education, they hardly inspire strong grounds for hope, let alone optimism, that the profession will act as a significant agent of change in the foreseeable future.

CONCLUSIONS

There is ample evidence of why humanity's relationship to its environment must change, and of why this implies fundamental changes in relationships within the human family. This means that accounting must change to render the powerful more accountable and to reflect and serve wider interests than those of a narrow section of society. In *Limits to growth*, Meadows *et al.* (2005) include, in their vision for a sustainable society, more 'understanding of whole systems as an essential part of each person's education'. Whole systems in the context of accounting and economic organization include the social and environmental 'externalities' which sectional interests impose on others, as well as the long-term impacts of a short-sighted focus on conventionally measured economic growth. Accounting's continued complicity in privileging certain short-term interests lies at the heart of a web of interactions which provides incentives to, and which helps to, legitimize the fundamentally unsustainable. Radicalized changes in humanity's outlook on sustainability will of course come – possibly in a matter of a few decades. The question is whether these changes will come quickly enough to avoid environmental and social catastrophe: for an enlightened and relatively gradual adaptation to take place, education – for accountants and many others – must be at least a necessary, if not a sufficient, condition.

NOTES

1   We acknowledge that both 'ideology' and 'hegemony' are contested terms within the social sciences. Within the context of this chapter, ideology is taken to refer to a set of ideas or beliefs which serve to legitimate the 'power of a dominant social group or class' (Eagleton, 1991, p. 5; see also Thompson, 1990). 'Hegemony' is being applied in the Gramscian sense, to describe social scenarios whereby the powerful do not have to impose power on subordinate groups because less powerful groups accept prevailing conditions and constraints as *natural* or as *common sense* (see Boggs, 1976; Eagleton, 1991). Gramsci distinguished hegemony from more coercive forms of power, such as direct physical coercion (for example, by the police or armed forces) (Boggs, 1976).

2   In the context of textbooks, Apple and Christian-Smith (1991, p. 11) explain that whilst progressive items may be mentioned, they will not be developed in depth, and it is through this 'mentioning' that dominant cultures maintain an ideological hegemony. Drawing on Bernstein's concept of recontextualization, Thomas (2003) describes how discourse can be acquired and appropriated by different fields to suit their own context or agenda. This is described by Apple and Christian-Smith (1991, p. 10) as 'reaching into [other] cultures' and shuffling those cultures on to their own ideological 'terrain'.

3   Values which are being spread as shareholder capitalism (or globalization) displace social market forms of capitalism (see, for example, Coates, 2000; Collison, 2003; Dore, 2000; Hutton, 1995).

4   Indeed Ray Anderson, founder and chairman of Interface Inc., the world's largest commercial carpet manufacturer, describes the corporation as a 'present day instrument of destruction' because of its compulsion to 'externalise any cost that its unwary or uncaring public will allow it to externalise' (Bakan, 2004, p. 71).

5   Thomson and Bebbington (2005) also apply Freire's ideas to social and environmental reporting itself, arguing that the provision of accounts by organizations can

340

be viewed as a process of education in relation to the users (both internal and external) of such reports.

6   Former polytechnics in the UK which were permitted to call themselves 'university' after changes to the law in 1992 are often referred to in the UK as 'new' universities; they are distinguished from 'old' or 'traditional' universities which were called 'university' pre-1992. See Dyson (1995) for a fuller discussion of this. It is widely believed that these two types of university differ in aims and culture.

7   These interests are stated in the *British Accounting Review Research Register*, a bi-annual publication which lists academic accounting staff, with their teaching and research interests, in higher education institutions in the British Isles.

8   Gray *et al.* (2001) include a detailed set of proposals for developing, at both university and professional levels, environmental, social and public interest issues within accounting education and training.

9   Of course the term sustainability, as used, for example, in the phrase 'sustainability report', need not and often does not imply any recognition of the fundamental challenges posed by a genuine attempt to be sustainable (for a rather pithy and arresting comment on this example of obfuscation through the 'capture' of language see Gray, 2002).

REFERENCES

Accounting Education Change Commission (1990) AECC urges priority for teaching in higher education. *Issues in Accounting Education*, 5(2): 330–31.

Adams, Roger (2002) *Industry as a partner for sustainable development: Accounting*. London: Association of Chartered Certified Accountants and United Nations Environment Programme.

Apple, M. (1995) *Education and power*. London: Routledge.

Apple, M. (2004) Cultural politics and the text. In S. Ball, *The RoutledgeFalmer reader in sociology of education*. London: RoutledgeFalmer.

Apple, M. and Christian-Smith, L. (eds) (1991) *The politics of the textbook*. London: Routledge.

Bakan, J. (2004) *The corporation: The pathological pursuit of profit*. London: Constable and Robinson.

Bebbington, J. (1997) Engagement, education and sustainability: A review essay on environmental accounting. *Accounting, Auditing and Accountability Journal*, 10(3): 365–81.

Bebbington, J. and Thomson, I. (2001) Commentary on: Some thoughts on social and environmental accounting education. *Accounting Education: An International Journal*, 10(4): 353–5.

Beder, S. (1997) *Global spin: The corporate assault on environmentalism*. Totnes: Green Books.

Birkin, F., Edwards, P. and Woodward, D. (2005) Accounting's contribution to a conscious cultural evolution: An end to sustainable development. *Critical Perspectives on Accounting*, 16: 185–208.

Blundell, L. and Booth, P. (1988) Teaching Innovative accounting topics. Student reaction to a course in social accounting. *Accounting and Finance*, May: 75–85.

Boggs, C. (1976) *Gramsci's Marxism*. London: Pluto Press.

Coates, D. (2000) *Models of capitalism: Growth and stagnation in the modern era*. Cambridge: Polity Press.

Collison, D. J. (2003) Corporate propaganda: Its implications for accounting and accountability. *Accounting, Auditing and Accountability Journal*, 16(5): 853–86.

Collison, D. J., Gray, R. H., Owen, D. L., Sinclair, C. D. and Stevenson, L. (2000) Social and environmental accounting and student choice: An exploratory research note. *Accounting Forum*, 24(2): 170–86.

Cooper, D. J. (1980) Discussions of towards a political economy of accounting. *Accounting, Organizations and Society*, 5: 161–6.

Cooper, D. J. and Sherer, M. J. (1984) The value of corporate accounting reports: Arguments for a political economy of accounting. *Accounting, Organizations and Society*, 9: 207–32.

Davis, S. W. and Sherman, W. R. (1996) The Accounting Education Change Commission: A critical perspective. *Critical Perspectives on Accounting*, 7: 159–89.

Dore, R. (2000) *Stock market capitalism: Welfare capitalism*. Oxford: Oxford University Press.

Dyson, J. R. (1995) Accounting research and teaching in Scotland. *Accounting Education: An International Journal*, 4(2): 137–51.

Eagleton, T. (1991) *Ideology: An introduction*. London: Verso.

Frankfurter, G. M. and McGoun, E. G. (1999) Ideology and the theory of financial economics. *Journal of Economic Behaviour and Organization*, 39: 159–77.

Freire, P. (1996) *Pedagogy of the oppressed*. London: Penguin. In J. Bebbington and I. Thomson (2001) Commentary on: Some thoughts on social and environmental accounting education. *Accounting Education: An International Journal*, 10(4): 353–5.

Ghoshal, S. (2005) Bad management theories are destroying good management practices. *Academy of Management Learning and Education*, 4(1): 75–91.

Gibson, K. (1997) Courses on environmental accounting. *Accounting, Auditing and Accountability Journal*, 10(4): 584–93.

Gordon, I. M. (1990) Enhancing students' knowledge of social responsibility accounting. *Issues in Accounting Education*, 13(1): 31–46.

Gray, R. H. (2002) The cloak of sustainability: A modern fable. *Social and Environmental Accounting Journal*, 22(2): 10.

Gray, R. and Collison, D. (2002) Can't see the wood for the trees, can't see the trees for the numbers? Accounting education, sustainability and the public interest. *Critical Perspectives on Accounting*, 13: 797–836.

Gray, R. H., Owen, D. L. and Adams, C. (1996) *Accounting and accountability: Changes and challenges in corporate social and environmental reporting*. London: Prentice-Hall.

Gray, R., Collison, D., French, J., McPhail, K. and Stevenson, L. (2001) *The professional accountancy bodies and the provision of education and training in relation to environmental issues*. Edinburgh: Institute of Chartered Accountants of Scotland.

Humphrey, C., Lewis, L. and Owen, D. (1996) Still too distant voices? Conversations and reflections on the social relevance of accounting education. *Critical Perspectives on Accounting*, 7: 77–99.

Hutton, W. (1995) *The state we're in*. London: Jonathan Cape.

Illich, I. D. (1971) *Deschooling society*. London: Calder & Boyars. In J. Bebbington and I. Thomson (2001) Commentary on: Some thoughts on social and environmental accounting education. *Accounting Education: An International Journal*, 10(4): 353–5.

Karabel, J. and Halsey, A. H. (1977) *Power and ideology in education*. New York: Oxford University Press.

Kuasirikun, N. (2005) Attitudes to the development and implementation of social and environmental accounting in Thailand. *Critical Perspectives on Accounting*, 16: 1035–57.

Lee, T. (1989) Education, practice and research in accounting: Gaps, closed loops, bridges and magic accounting. *Accounting and Business Research*, 19(75): 237–53.

Lewis, L., Humphrey, C. and Owen, D. (1992) Accounting and the social: A pedagogic perspective. *British Accounting Review*, 24(3): 219–33.

Luke, A. (1988) *Literacy, textbooks and ideology: Postwar literacy instruction and the mythology of Dick and Jane*. London: Falmer Press.

McIntosh, N. B. (2002) *Accounting, accountants and accountability: Poststructuralist positions*. London: Routledge.

McPhail, K. J. and Gray, R. H. (1996) Not developing ethical maturity in accounting education: Hegemony, dissonance and homogeneity in accounting students' world views. Dundee University Discussion Paper (ACC/9605).

Macve, R. and Carey, A. (eds) (1992) *Business, accountancy and the environment: A policy and research agenda*. London: Institute of Chartered Accountants in England and Wales.

Mangion, D. (2005) An examination of social and environmental accounting education in Australian universities. British Accounting Association Accounting Education Special Interest Group Annual Conference, 25–7 May.

Mathews, M. R. (1997) Twenty-five years of social and environmental accounting research: Is there a silver jubilee to celebrate? *Accounting, Auditing and Accountability Journal*, 10(4): 481–531.

Mathews, M. R. (2001) Some thoughts on social and environmental accounting education. *Accounting Education: An International Journal*, 10(4): 335–52.

Meadows, D. H., Jorgen Randers, J., Dennis, L. and Meadows, D. L. (2005) *Limits to growth: The 30-year update*. London: Earthscan.

Owen, D., Humphrey, C. and Lewis, L. (1994) *Social and environmental accounting education in British universities*. London: ACCA–The Certified Accountants Educational Trust.

Parker, L. (2004) Social and environmental accountability research: A view from the commentary box. *Plenary Presentation & Forum: Published Research in Social and Environmental Accounting*, 3rd Australasian Conference on Social and Environmental Accounting Research (CSEAR). In D. Mangion (2005) An examination of social and environmental accounting education in Australian universities. British Accounting Association Accounting Education Special Interest Group Annual Conference, 25–7 May.

Schumacher, E. F. (1973) *Small is beautiful*. London: Abacus.

Sefcik, S. E., Soderstrom, N. S. and Stinson, C. H. (1997) Accounting through green-colored glasses: Teaching environmental accounting. *Issues in Accounting Education*, 12(1): 129–40.

Stauber, J. and Rampton, S. (1995) *Toxic sludge is good for you*. Maine: Common Courage Press.

Sterling, R. (1973) Accounting research, education and practice. *Journal of Accountancy*, September: 44–52.

Stevenson, L. (2000) A description of social and environmental accounting educators in UK universities in 1990. *Social and Environmental Accounting Journal*, 20(2): 12–15.

Stevenson, L. (2002) Social and environmental accounting teaching in UK and Irish universities: A research note on changes between 1993 and 1998. *Accounting Education: An International Journal*, 11(4): 331–46.

Thomas, P. (2003) The recontextualization of management: A discourse-based approach to analysing the development of management thinking. *Journal of Management Studies*, 40(4): 775–801.

Thomson, I. and Bebbington, J. (2004) It doesn't matter what you teach? *Critical Perspectives on Accounting*, 15: 609–28.

Thomson, I. and Bebbington, J. (2005) Social and environmental reporting in the UK: A pedagogic evaluation. *Critical Perspectives on Accounting*, 16: 507–33.

Thompson, J. B. (1990) *Ideology and modern culture: Critical social theory in the era of mass communication*. Cambridge: Polity Press.

Tinker, T. (1980) Towards a political economy of accounting: An empirical illustration of the Cambridge controversies. *Accounting Organizations and Society*, 5: 147–60.

Williams, R. (1989) Hegemony and the selective tradition. In S. de Castell, A. Luke and C. Luke (eds) *Language, authority and criticism: Readings on the school textbook*. London: Falmer Press.

Wolfe, A. (1993) We've had enough business ethics. *Business Horizons*, May–June: 1–3.

Chapter 18

Postscript and conclusions

Jan Bebbington, Brendan O'Dwyer and
Jeffrey Unerman

It is not possible to summarize in a few short pages all the themes that could be drawn from the various chapters of this book. Nor is such a task appropriate, because the chapters largely stand by themselves. What we wish to draw out, however, in this final chapter is a sense of the most important implications that face accounting practitioners and researchers who seek to develop a form of accounting that is sufficiently responsive to the demands of sustainable development (hereafter SD). There are two themes that we will develop to assist with this task. First we will suggest the ways in which accounting (because of the nature of the discipline itself) will find the concept of SD problematic. Then we will propose some theoretical and practical developments that would be required in order for the discipline of accountancy to embrace the SD agenda and thereby to become a more effective and useful tool in any moves towards SD.

SD INTO ACCOUNTING: PROBLEMATIC IDEAS

It will have been evident from several of the chapters of this book that accounting for SD is not considered to be a simple case of expanding conventional accounting (which one could argue focuses on economic aspects of performance) to include accounts of both social and environmental aspects of performance. Although SD is often considered to be a 'three legged stool', or conceptualized in business terms as the 'triple bottom line', various chapter contributors suggest that SD is not a simple sum or balancing of three accounts. Rather, sustainability has two distinct aspects that require further elaboration when considering the possibilities of the discipline of accounting fully articulating SD concerns. These characteristics are, firstly, a focus on *ecological space and carrying capacity of ecosystems* and, secondly, *a commitment to equity* (on both an intra- and inter-generational basis). Both of these aspects make SD a radical and challenging concept, help explain why there is much resistance to this concept (albeit that such resistance is less trenchantly expressed) and underlie problems in easily linking accounting and SD.

SD, in essence, is a spatial concept. That is, SD concerns itself with the impact of human activities in particular spatial scales. Most commonly the scale used in the international development literature concerns itself with the combined impact of the world's population on the planet. At this level of resolution it is apparent that the ecological diversity and resilience of the planet is under threat from too great a burden being placed on it by humanity (both in terms of excess utilization of resources such as water and productive capacity of soils, as well as the pollution impact arising from activities; most notably increasing concentrations of greenhouse gases). Linking this ecosystem-based consideration of the ecological element of SD to the operations of corporate entities is extremely difficult.

While an entity may provide a robust and complete account of its ecological impact this will rarely be sufficient information to ascertain if the organization is operating in accordance with the demands of ecological sustainability. Additional information is required, namely knowledge of the total carrying capacity of the ecosystem – which further needs to be allocated in some manner to entities that share that ecosystem. The idea that all humans in the world should have an equal entitlement to emit a set amount of carbon (adjusted for differences in temperature, for example) is an example of such a rationing mechanism. Of course, there are no such agreements for the planet as a whole and only in some ecosystems, and only for some resources and ecosystem services, has this formal allocation been achieved. Such allocations are usually effected via legal and/or regulatory means of some sort. Permits to extract resources or allowances to pollute are examples of such devices.

As a result, if one wished to know if an entity was ecologically sustainable then several conditions would have to be met: (1) the regulatory regime in which the entity operated would have to have been developed so as to satisfy the criteria of ecological sustainability, (2) the rights of various individuals and entities within that ecosystem to undertake certain activities and create certain impacts would have had to have been allocated in some manner, and (3) then an account of the extent to which the organization had met its obligations to act in defined (sustainable) ways would have to be provided. At that stage, and only at that stage, would it be possible to use corporate accounts of ecological impacts to evaluate the ecological sustainability of that organization. It should be apparent from a cursory examination of the current environmental regulatory structures that such a regime is not in place (and especially not in place with respect to the major environmental concern of our time, greenhouse gas emissions). This is without even considering the complexity that would be required to understand the accounts of a multi-ecosystem entity (which would encompass the majority of trans- and multi-national corporations and the vast majority of national-level corporations as well). As a result, while careful environmental reporting may be laudable in and of itself, it most usually falls short of being an account of ecological sustainability.

The second area where the principles of SD become problematic for entity-level assessment is how a commitment to inter- and intra-generational equity can be expressed. SD has emerged from debates about global inequalities, and contains a commitment to ensuring equity between all those alive today and also between current and future generations. While the commitment to such equity is easily morally justifiable, translating such concerns into entity-level assessments using the tools of social accounting is not easy. Social accounting, incorporating some form of stakeholder analysis, falls short of expressing inter- and intra-generational equity on several grounds. First, social accounting as it presently stands has no mechanism for considering needs of future generations or how current activities impact on these needs. While it is hard to imagine how such an account could be produced or how entities could respond to such an account, it remains the case that our collective imaginations have yet to consider such an account. This failure negates social accounting providing a full SD account.

Within the parameters of intra-generational equity, social accounting also falls short. The provision of information about how certain stakeholders have been affected by the behaviour of an entity does not amount to a full account of SD impacts. In particular, it is usually the relatively powerful stakeholders in direct relationship with an organization who feature in any account (most usually employees, local communities and to a lesser extent customers). Powerless stakeholders such as those living in impoverished communities near heavily polluting production facilities operated by multinationals but located in developing nations, and who are adversely impacted by entity behaviour, usually have little or no ability or opportunity to give effective voice to their concerns in stakeholder dialogues. In any event, for both powerful and powerless stakeholders, a sense of what is fair, just and cognate with principles of a sustainable society has never been articulated in social accounts to the best of our knowledge – even assuming that the stakeholders upon whom an entity's operations impact have the requisite knowledge, skills and resources to articulate these issues. Once again, the best that seems to be possible is to provide an account of how wages, for example, compare to a minimum legally required wage level for a particular job. Unless such mandated wages levels reflect a societal preference for SD, an account of such compliance with mandated standards cannot be equated with SD.

In summary, the provision of an economic, social and environmental account of entity-level interactions falls short of constituting a full account of SD. In part the failure of accounting to achieve this end is due to structural impediments within society. If society cannot specify what constitutes social or ecological sustainability, any accounting system that draws its mandate from societal rules will also fall short of a SD account. The best that could emerge from accounting would be a partial picture of the ecological and social impacts of an entity. This data would provide a starting point for an evaluation of SD impacts, but is not in itself sufficient for such an account.

THEORY AND EVIDENCE

The final points that we wish to develop look forward in time, and relate to how accounting for SD may evolve in the future. Two aspects need to be developed to bring about a maturation of this field. First, there needs to be more empirically driven investigations that focus upon exploring attempts at accounting for SD. Presently (and as evident from Ian Thomson's Chapter 1) research is narrowly focused around a sub-set of issues that are connected to accounting for SD, but not directly focused on it. As a result, the evidential background that could be used to understand and further develop accounting for SD does not exist. In particular, exploring the themes of how to link spatial and inter/intra-generational imperatives in SD to entity-level accounts would be a crucial task of such investigations. Such a task is likely to involve the use of a number of different, but complementary, in-depth research methods.

The second gap in the area of accounting for SD relates to the need to develop more useful and sophisticated theoretical lenses in order to help us better understand the practices that we observe being undertaken in the name of SD. While legitimacy theory has been a widely used tool for consideration of the motives driving social and environmental reporting, it is less clear how it could be applied in accounting *for* SD. Rather, theories are needed to explain, inter alia: the linkages between the public policy agenda for SD and how such an agenda becomes embedded (or not) in the workings of the private, public and third sector; the way in which SD becomes part of organizational discourses, and the impact of adoption of SD by organizations; and how managerial action in the name of SD is initiated and sustained over time, and the impacts of such actions. Institutional theory is likely to play a role in such debates, but other lenses will also have to be discovered, developed, refined and applied to this area in order to help develop and structure our understanding

CLOSING POINTS

As has been argued within this book, the SD agenda poses crucial and urgent questions and problems for the future of humanity. By focusing on the economic and largely ignoring the social and environmental impacts of entities, accounting as it is currently structured operates in a manner which at best hides, and at worst reinforces and furthers, the unsustainability of business, public sector and non-governmental organizations.

Addressing the questions and resolving the problems posed by SD is very far from easy. Accounting can play a number of potentially important roles in helping to address and resolve these urgent issues, and thus could help to make the world (or the manner in which humans through organizational operations impact on the world) less unsustainable. But to be effective, this would require a fundamental shift in a number of accounting practices and in the assumptions upon which a number of these practices are based.

We sincerely hope that this book reaches out not just to accounting students, but also to anyone else interested in developing a broader role for accounting in society in this manner. If the book is successful in helping to change perceptions regarding the impact on sustainability of current accounting practices, and/or regarding the potential of accounting to help move us towards a more sustainable future, it will have been a very worthwhile endeavour. We live in hope that societal commitments to SD will develop sufficiently quickly and deeply to avoid environmental catastrophe, and hope that the material presented and discussed in this book will contribute towards much more socially and environmentally just and sustainable business, public sector and third sector (NGO) practices.

Index

Note: *italic* page number denote references to figures/tables.

359